Fodor's 2003

Costa Rica

The Guide
for All Budgets

Completely
Updated

Where to Stay,
Eat, and Explore

On and Off
the Beaten Path

When to Go,
What to Pack

Maps, Travel Tips,
and Web Sites

Fodor's Travel Publications • New York, Toronto, London, Sydney, Auckland
www.fodors.com

Fodor's Costa Rica 2003

EDITOR: Melisse J. Gelula

Editorial Contributors: Gregory Benchwick, Dorothy MacKinnon, George Soriano, Jeffrey Van Fleet, Carol Weir

Maps: Bob Blake and Rebecca Baer, *map editors*

Design: Fabrizio La Rocca, *creative director*; Guido Caroti, *art director*; Jolie Novak, *senior picture editor*; Melanie Marin, *photo editor*

Cover Design: Pentagram

Production/Manufacturing: Colleen Ziemba

Cover Photo (Bird-watcher at Monteverde Cloud Forest Biological Reserve): Steve Dunwell/The Image Bank

Copyright

ISBN 1-4000-1030-6

ISSN 1522–6131

Important Tip

Although all prices, opening times, and other details in this book are based on information supplied to us at press time, changes occur all the time in the travel world, and Fodors cannot accept responsibility for facts that become outdated or for inadvertent errors or omissions. So **always confirm information when it matters,** especially if you're making a detour to visit a specific place.

Special Sales

Fodor's Travel Publications are available at special discounts for bulk purchases for sales promotions or premiums. Special editions, including personalized covers, excerpts of existing guides, and corporate imprints, can be created in large quantities for special needs. For more information contact your local bookseller or write to Special Markets, Fodor's Travel Publications, 280 Park Avenue, New York, NY 10017. Inquiries from Canada should be directed to your local Canadian bookseller or sent to Random House of Canada, Ltd., Marketing Department, 2775 Matheson Boulevard East, Mississauga, Ontario L4W 4P7. Inquiries from the United Kingdom should be sent to Fodor's Travel Publications, 20 Vauxhall Bridge Road, London, England SW1V 2SA.

PRINTED IN THE UNITED STATES OF AMERICA

10 9 8 7 6 5 4 3 2 1

CONTENTS

Maps

ON THE ROAD WITH FODOR'S

A **TRIP TAKES YOU OUT OF YOURSELF.** Concerns of life at home completely disappear, driven away by more immediate thoughts—about, say, what marvels will beguile the next day, or where you'll have dinner. That's where Fodor's comes in. We make sure that you know all your options, so that you don't miss something that's around the next bend just because you didn't know it was there. Mindful that the best memories of your trip might have nothing to do with what you came to Costa Rica to see, we guide you to sights large and small all over the country. You might set out to relax on the beaches at Manuel Antonio, but back at home you find yourself unable to forget spotting your first blue morpho as it flitted past your screened-in cabana and hiking the perimeter of Volcán Arenal. With Fodor's at your side, serendipitous discoveries are never far away.

About Our Writers

Our success in showing you every corner of Costa Rica is a credit to our extraordinary writers. Although there's no substitute for travel advice from a good friend who knows your style, our contributors are the next best thing—the kind of people you would poll for travel advice if you knew them.

Nostalgic about a three-day slog through Corcovado National Park (with water up to his knees the entire way) accomplished on his previous visit to Costa Rica, **Gregory Benchwick,** a travel writer on South and Central America, dropped everything to update the Pacific Coast chapters of this book. Gregory was the editor and writer for Bolivia's only English newspaper, *The Bolivian Times* and he recently contributed to *Fodor's Belize and Guatemala* and *Fodor's Chile.*

Melisse Gelula loves Central America. She has cave-tubed in Belize, white-water rafted in Guatemala, joined a patron saint parade in Nicaragua, traversed the rainforest tree tops on a Costa Rican canopy tour, and driven a rental car across El Salvador. She has contributed to many Fodor's guides as an editor and travel writer including *Fodor's Belize and Guatemala* and *UpClose Central America,* respectively.

Seasoned traveler and prolific journalist **Dorothy MacKinnon** took up a post in San José, from which to contribute to the *Tico Times* on travel, restaurants, and nonprofit development stories—and to update the Nicoya Peninsula chapter of this guide. She has written on travel and other topics for several North American newspapers, including the *Toronto Star* and *The Washington Post.*

George Soriano began exploring Costa Rica four years ago and hasn't stopped yet. Based in San José, he is has worked as an editor at the English-language *Tico Times* and has written for several publications on Central America and Mexico. In addition to researching and updating the San José and Central Valley chapters, he works as a naturalist guide.

San José–based freelance writer **Jeffrey Van Fleet** has spent the better part of the last decade enjoying Costa Rica's long rainy seasons and Wisconsin's winters. (Most people would try to do it the other way around.) He saw his first resplendent quetzal, that bird-watcher's Holy Grail, while researching this guide. Jeff is a regular contributor to Costa Rica's English-language *Tico Times* and has written for Fodor's guides to Chile and Central and South America.

Carol Weir is a journalist who splits her time between Costa Rica and the United States. She is regular contributor to *Fodor's Costa Rica,* and this year updated the Essential Information and Destination chapters. When in the States she has worked as a reporter covering the Hispanic community for two daily newspapers in her home state of South Carolina.

You can rest assured that you're in good hands—and that no property mentioned in the book has paid to be included. Each has been selected strictly on its merits, as the best of its type in its price range.

How to Use This Book

Up front is Smart Travel Tips A to Z, arranged alphabetically by topic and loaded with tips, Web sites, and contact information. Destination: Costa Rica helps get you in the mood for your trip. Subsequent chapters in *Fodor's Costa Rica 2003* are arranged regionally. All city chapters begin with exploring information, with a section for each neighborhood (each recommending a good tour and listing sights alphabetically). All regional chapters are divided geographically; within each area, towns are covered in logical geographical order, and attractive stretches of road between them are indicated by the designation En Route. To help you decide what you'll have time to visit, all chapters begin with our writers' favorite itineraries. (Mix itineraries from several chapters, and you can put together a really exceptional trip.) The A to Z section that ends every chapter lists additional resources. Portraits, essays about Costa Rica's incredible biodiversity, are followed by a wildlife glossary and a Spanish vocabulary. The Books and Movies section suggests enriching reading and viewing.

Icons and Symbols

★   Our special recommendations
✕   Restaurant
🏠   Lodging establishment
✕🏠   Lodging establishment whose restaurant warrants a special trip
⚑   Campgrounds
🍼   Good for kids (rubber duck)
☞   Sends you to another section of the guide for more information
✉   Address
☎   Telephone number
🕐   Opening and closing times
💰   Admission prices (those we give apply to adults; substantially reduced fees are almost always available for children, students, and senior citizens)

Numbers in white and black circles ③ ❸ that appear on the maps, in the margins, and within the tours correspond to one another.

For hotels, you can assume that all rooms have private baths, phones, TVs, and air-conditioning unless otherwise noted and that all hotels operate on the European Plan (with no meals) if we don't specify another meal plan. We always list a property's facilities but not whether you'll be charged extra to use them, so when pricing accommodations, do ask what's included. For restaurants, it's always a good idea to book ahead; we mention reservations only when they're essential or are not accepted. All restaurants we list are open daily for lunch and dinner unless stated otherwise; dress is mentioned only when men are required to wear a jacket or a jacket and tie. Look for an overview of local dining-out habits in Smart Travel Tips A to Z and in the Pleasures and Pastimes section that follows each chapter introduction.

Don't Forget to Write

Your experiences—positive and negative—matter to us. If we have missed or misstated something, we want to hear about it. We follow up on all suggestions. Contact the Costa Rica editor at editors@fodors.com or c/o Fodor's at 280 Park Avenue, New York, NY 10017. And have a fabulous trip!

Karen Cure
Karen Cure
Editorial Director

Costa Rica

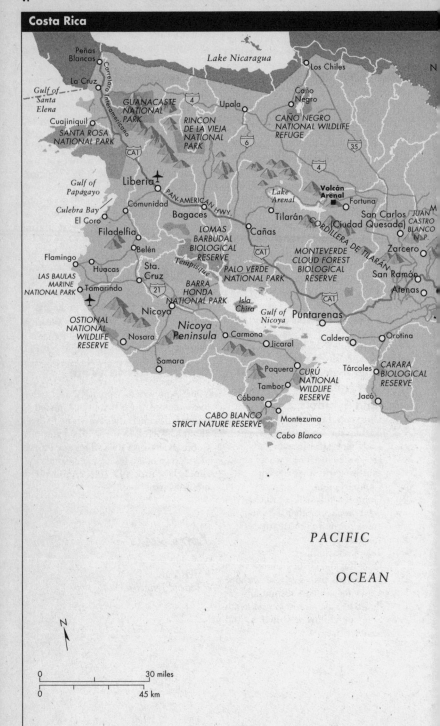

Peñas Blancas
La Cruz
Gulf of Santa Elena
Cuajiniquil
SANTA ROSA NATIONAL PARK
Carretera Interamericana
GUANACASTE NATIONAL PARK
RINCON DE LA VIEJA NATIONAL PARK
Lake Nicaragua
Los Chiles
Upala
Caño Negro
CAÑO NEGRO NATIONAL WILDLIFE REFUGE
N
4
6
35
4
CA1
Gulf of Papagayo
Liberia
Comunidad
Bagaces
PAN. AMERICAN HWY.
Lake Arenal
Volcán Arenal
Fortuna
San Carlos (Ciudad Quesada)
JUAN CASTRO BLANCO N.S.P.
M
Culebra Bay
El Coro
Filadelfia
Belén
Tilarán
Cañas
LOMAS BARBUDAL BIOLOGICAL RESERVE
CA1
CORDILLERA DE TILARÁN
MONTEVERDE CLOUD FOREST BIOLOGICAL RESERVE
Zarcero
San Ramón
Atenas
Flamingo
Huacas
LAS BAULAS MARINE NATIONAL PARK
Tamarindo
Sta. Cruz
Tempisque
21
BARRA HONDA NATIONAL PARK
PALO VERDE NATIONAL PARK
Isla Chira
Gulf of Nicoya
Puntarenas
CA1
Nicoya
OSTIONAL NATIONAL WILDLIFE RESERVE
Nosara
Samara
Nicoya Peninsula
Carmona
Jicaral
Caldera
Orotina
Paquera
Tambor
Cóbano
CURÚ NATIONAL WILDLIFE RESERVE
Tárcoles
CARARA BIOLOGICAL RESERVE
Jacó
CABO BLANCO STRICT NATURE RESERVE
Montezuma
Cabo Blanco

PACIFIC

OCEAN

N

| 0 | | 30 miles |
| 0 | | 45 km |

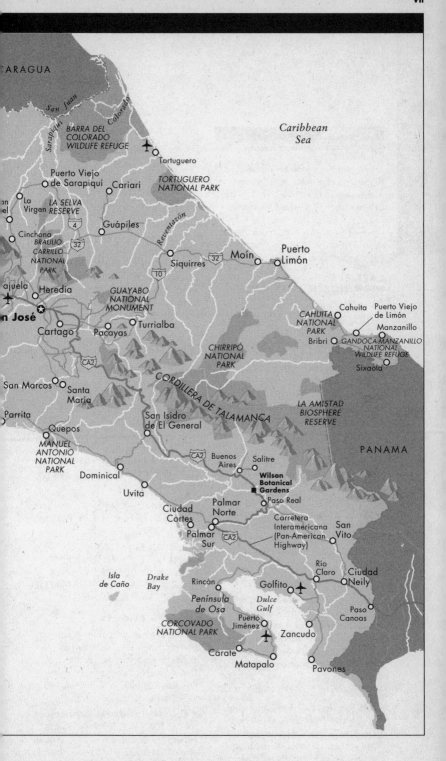

ESSENTIAL INFORMATION

AIR TRAVEL

BOOKING

When you book **look for nonstop flights** and **remember that "direct" flights stop at least once.** Try to avoid connecting flights, which require a change of plane. For more booking tips and to check prices and make online flight reservations, log on to www.fodors.com.

CARRIERS FROM NORTH AMERICA

Costa Rica's main tourist season—corresponding roughly with the dry season, from mid-December to April—coincides with Christmas and Easter, so book your airline tickets well ahead of time. During this time, weekly charter flights serve Costa Rica from half a dozen American and Canadian cities, most landing in Liberia, Guanacaste. Ask a travel agent about charter options.

➤ MAJOR AIRLINES: **American** (☎ 800/433–7300). **Continental** (☎ 800/231–0856). **Delta** (☎ 800/221–1212). **United** (☎ 800/241–6522). **US Airways** (☎ 800/428–4322).

➤ SMALLER AIRLINES: **Copa** (☎ 506/222–6640). **Grupo TACA** (☎ 800/535–8780). **Lacsa** (☎ 800/225–2272). **Mexicana** (☎ 800/531–7921).

CARRIERS WITHIN CENTRAL AMERICA

Given Central America's often difficult driving conditions—distances that appear short on a map can represent hours of driving on dirt roads pocked with craters—**consider domestic flights.** Because car-rental rates are so steep, flying can often be actually cheaper than driving as well.

Costa Rica has two domestic airlines, SANSA and Travelair. SANSA flies from Juan Santamaría International Airport, near Alajuela, to the following Costa Rican destinations: Barra del Colorado, Coto 47, Golfito, Liberia, Nosara, Palmar Sur, Puerto Jiménez, Punta Islita, Quepos, Samara, Tamarindo, Tambor, and Tortuguero. SANSA also flies between Quepos and Palmar Sur. One-way fares range from $44 to $66.

Travelair has daily flights from Tobias Bolaños Airport, in the San José suburb of Pavas, to Barra del Colorado, Carrillo, Drake Bay, Golfito, Puerto Jiménez, Liberia, Nosara, Palmar Sur, Punta Islita, Quepos, Tamarindo, Tambor, and Tortuguero. More than a dozen flights also run between those destinations, saving you the trouble of returning to San José. Prices range from $44 for a one-way hop between San José and Quepos to $75 for a one-way trip to Liberia.

Note that domestic flights on both SANSA and Travelair technically impose a luggage weight limit of 11.3 kg (25 pounds)—*including* carry-ons—on their domestic flights, as the planes are tiny. Excess weight, if safety permits, is charged by the pound.

Copa, Lacsa, and Grupo Taca airlines have flights to Panama City, Panama, and Managua, Nicaragua.

➤ AIRLINES: **Copa** (☎ 506/223–7033). **Grupo Taca** (☎ 506/296–0909). **Lacsa** (☎ 506/296–0909). **SANSA** (☎ 506/221–9414 or 506/441–8035). **Travelair** (☎ 506/220–3054).

CHARTER FLIGHTS

Several charter companies in San José, Travelair included, offer charter flights to places not served by scheduled flights. Helicopteros Turisticos Tropical and Helinorte provide helicopter service.

➤ CHARTER COMPANIES: **Aero Costa Sol** (☎ 506/440–1444). **Aerolineas Turisticas** (☎ 506/232–1125). **Aeronaves** (☎ 506/282–4033 in San José; ☎ 506/775–0278 in Golfito). **Heli-**

copteros Turisticos Tropical (☎ 506/
220–3940). **Helinorte** (☎ 506/232–
7534).

CARRIERS FROM THE U.K.

American Airlines flies from
Heathrow to Miami, and Virgin
Atlantic flies from Gatwick to Miami,
where you can connect with flights to
San José. British Airways flies weekly
from Gatwick to San José via Puerto
Rico. You can also fly from London
to San José on Iberia, but you have to
change planes in Madrid and Miami.
United Airlines flies from Heathrow
to Washington, D.C., where another
flight serves Costa Rica via Mexico.

➤ AIRLINES: **American Airlines**
(☎ 0345/789–789). **British Airways**
(☎ 0345/222–111). **Iberia** (☎ 0171/
830–0011). **United Airlines** (☎ 0845/
844–4777). **Virgin Atlantic**
(☎ 01293/747–747).

CHECK-IN AND BOARDING

Always **ask your carrier about its
check-in policy.** Plan to arrive at the
airport about 2½ to 3 hours before
international flights. If you arrive less
than an hour before your flight is
scheduled to leave, you may not be
allowed to board. Allow at least a
half hour for domestic flights within
Costa Rica. Note that when you fly
out of Costa Rica, you'll have to pay
a $17 airport departure tax at Juan
Santamaría Airport. At press time,
there was some debate about raising
departure tax to $21.

Assuming that not everyone with a
ticket will show up, airlines routinely
overbook planes. When everyone
does, airlines ask for volunteers to
give up their seats. In return, these
volunteers usually get a certificate for
a free flight and are rebooked on the
next flight out. If there are not
enough volunteers, the airline must
choose who will be denied boarding.
The first to get bumped are passengers who checked in late and those
flying on discounted tickets, so **get to
the gate and check in as early as
possible,** especially during peak
periods.

Always **bring a government-issued
photo ID to the airport;** even when it's
not required, a passport is best.

CUTTING COSTS

The least expensive airfares to Costa
Rica must usually be purchased in
advance and are nonrefundable. It's
smart to **call a number of airlines, and
when you are quoted a good price,
book it on the spot**—the same fare
may not be available the next day.
Always **check different routings** and
look into using different airports.
Travel agents, especially low-fare
specialists (☞ Discounts and Deals,
below), are helpful.

Consolidators are another good
source. They buy tickets for scheduled
international flights at reduced rates
from the airlines, then sell them at
prices that beat the best fare available
directly from the airlines, usually
without restrictions. Sometimes you
can even get your money back if you
need to return the ticket. Carefully
read the fine print detailing penalties
for changes and cancellations, and
**confirm your consolidator reservation
with the airline.**

➤ CONSOLIDATORS: **Cheap Tickets**
(☎ 800/377–1000).**Discount Airline
Ticket Service** (☎ 800/576–1600).
Pino Welcome Travel (800/247–
6578). **Unitravel** (☎ 800/325–2222,
WEB www.unitravel.com).**Up & Away
Travel** (☎ 212/889–2345, WEB www.
upandaway.com). **World Travel
Network** (☎ 800/409–6753).

ENJOYING THE FLIGHT

State your seat preference when
purchasing your ticket, and then
repeat it when you confirm and when
you check in. For more legroom, you
can request one of the few emergency-
aisle seats at check-in, if you are
capable of lifting at least 50 pounds—
a Federal Aviation Administration
requirement of passengers in these
seats. Seats behind a bulkhead also
offer more legroom, but they don't
have under-seat storage. Don't sit in
the row in front of the emergency
aisle or in front of a bulkhead, where
seats may not recline.

Ask the airline whether a snack or
meal is served on the flight. If you
have dietary concerns, **request special
meals when booking.** These can be
vegetarian, low-cholesterol, or kosher,
for example. It's a good idea to pack

some healthy snacks and a small (plastic) bottle of water in your carry-on bag. On long flights, try to maintain a normal routine, to help fight jet lag. At night, **get some sleep.** By day, **eat light meals, drink water** (not alcohol), and **move around the cabin** to stretch your legs. For additional jet-lag tips consult *Fodor's FYI: Travel Fit & Healthy* (available at bookstores everywhere).

FLYING TIMES

From New York, flights to San José last 5½ hours nonstop, 6–7 hours via Miami; from Los Angeles, 8½ hours via Mexico; from Houston, 3½ hours nonstop; from Miami, 3 hours.

HOW TO COMPLAIN

If your baggage goes astray or your flight goes awry, complain right away. Most carriers require that you **file a claim immediately.**

➤ AIRLINE COMPLAINTS: U.S. Department of Transportation **Aviation Consumer Protection Division** (⊠ C-75, Room 4107, Washington, DC 20590, ☏ 202/366–2220, WEB www.dot.gov/airconsumer). **Federal Aviation Administration Consumer Hotline** (☏ 800/322–7873).

RECONFIRMING

Before leaving Costa Rica it's a good idea to **reconfirm your flight by phone within 72 hours of departure.** Failure to do so may result in cancellation of your reservation.

AIRPORTS

Besides the larger airports listed here, the other places where planes land aren't exactly airports. They more resemble a carport with a landing strip, at which a person with a SANSA clipboard arrives just minutes before a plane is due to land or take-off. The informality of domestic air service means you might want to **purchase your domestic airplane tickets in advance,** although you can buy them when you're in the country or directly from the SANSA Web site, too.

➤ AIRPORT INFORMATION: **Aeropuerto Internacional Daniel Oduber** (☏ 506/668–1032 in Liberia). **Aeropuerto Internacional Juan Santamaría**

(☏ 506/443–2622 or 506/443–2942 in San José). **Aeropuerto Internacional Tobías Bolaños** (⊠ Pavas, 3 km [2 mi] west of San José, ☏ 506/232–2820).

DUTY-FREE SHOPPING

San José's Aeropuerto Internacional Juan Santamaría has several duty-free shops, which sell mostly liquor and perfume.

AIRPORT TRANSFERS
AND TRANSPORTATION

Even though the San José airport has been recently renovated, all international passengers are funneled out one tiny doorway to an underground fume-filled parking area, which is flanked with hordes of tour operators waiting for arriving visitors and cab drivers calling out "taxi?" If you're in the first group, you need only look for a representative of your tour company with a sign that bears your name. Others should **take an orange cab,** called *taxi unidos,* which only work from the airport; avoid *collectivos,* or minivans—they're almost the same price as a taxi, the van is almost always crammed with other passengers, and you'll have to make stops at their hotels, which in San José traffic can really make your transfer another journey in itself. It's also safe to take any red or orange cab identified with a number and has a meter. Avoid *pirates* or unregulated cabs.

More than 90% of travelers spend the night in San José and leave for their domestic destination the first thing the next morning out of the SANSA terminal next to the international airport or out of tiny Tobias Bolaños Airport. Rarely does an international flight get into San José early enough to make a domestic connection, as the weather for flying is typically clear until about noon only. When given a choice, **always take earliest morning flight.** Also, domestic flights to the far south may not be direct. You might stop in Golfito first, then continue on to Puerto Jimenez, for example.

BIKE TRAVEL

You can rent mountain bikes in many resort areas, and they're actually a great way to get around town as well as explore off-road trails. The regional topographical maps sold at the San José department stores Universal and Lehmann include unpaved roads that are often perfect for mountain biking.

Several outdoor activities and sports tour operators lead organized mountain-bike tours, which take you to less-traveled areas and usually provide lunch and refreshments.

➤ BIKE MAPS: **Lehmann** (✉ Avda. Central between Cs. 1 and 3, Downtown, San José). **Universal** (✉ Avda. Central between Cs. 0 and 1, Downtown, San José).

BIKES IN FLIGHT

Most airlines accommodate bikes as luggage, provided they are dismantled and boxed. Airlines sell bike boxes, which are often free at bike shops, for about $5 (it's at least $100 for bike bags). International travelers can sometimes substitute a bike for a piece of checked luggage at no charge; otherwise, the cost is about $100. Domestic and Canadian airlines charge $25–$50. The Costa Rican airline SANSA allows disassembled mountain bikes (and 84 inch/7-ft surfboards) on board for $15 each way, space permitting. They cannot, however, confirm space availability ahead of time.

BOAT AND FERRY TRAVEL

WITHIN COSTA RICA

Regular passenger and/or car ferries connect Puntarenas with Playa Naranjo, Tambor, and Paquera, on the south end of the Nicoya Peninsula. These ferries take you to the southern and mid-Nicoya Peninsula. Traditionally, to get to Guanacaste, a car ferry crossed the Río Tempisque, about a one-hour drive northwest from Puntarenas, every 20 minutes from 5 AM to 11 PM in the high season (December–April), hourly in the green season (May–December). However, the new Río Tempisque bridge, officially called the Taiwan Friendship Bridge (guess who put up the funds?), is slated to open here at the end of 2002. The bridge, it is hoped, will eliminate the wait of up to three hours common for the 15-minute ferry trip. For the Southern Pacific Zone, the Arco Iris Passenger Ferry

makes daily runs between Golfito and Puerto Jiménez at 7 AM, 10:50 AM, 2:50 PM, and 7 PM, and the Zancudo ferry goes round-trip to Golfito hourly from 6 AM to 6 PM (if there are passengers).

FARES AND SCHEDULES

➤ INFORMATION: **Arco Iris Passenger Ferry** (506/661–1084). **Puntarenas–Playa Naranjo Ferry** (☎ 506/661–1069).**Río Tempisque Ferry** (506/661–8105). **Zancudo Ferry** (506/776–0012).

BUS TRAVEL

WITHIN COSTA RICA

Reliable, inexpensive bus service covers much of the country. Several different private companies leave San José from a variety of departure points. Buses range from huge, modern, air-conditioned beasts with lead-foot drivers, bathrooms, and an occasional movie to something a little less new and a whole lot more sweaty and crowded. For schedules and departure locations for your destination of choice, *see* Bus Travel *in* the A to Z sections of the appropriate chapter.

Tickets are sold at bus stations and on the buses themselves. The only way to reserve a seat is to buy your ticket ahead of time or, depending on the route, simply show up early for departure. On longer routes, buses stop midway at modest restaurants. Near the ends of their runs many nonexpress buses turn into large taxis, dropping passengers off one by one at their destinations; to save time, take a *directo* (express) bus.

➤ CENTRAL VALLEY BUS COMPANIES: **Empresarios Unidos** (☎ 506/222–0064). **Sacsa** (☎ 506/591–0636). **Transtusa** (☎ 506/222–4464). **Tuasa** (☎ 506/222–5325).

➤ NORTHERN GUANACASTE AND ALAJUELA BUS COMPANIES: **Tralapa** (☎ 506/221–7202). **Transportes La Cañera** (☎ 506/223–4242). **Transportes Tilarán** (☎ 506/222–3854).

➤ NICOYA PENINSULA BUS COMPANIES: **Empresa Alfaro** (☎ 506/685–5032). **Empresarios Unidos** (☎ 506/222–0064). **Pulmitan** (☎ 506/222–1650).

➤ CENTRAL PACIFIC BUS COMPANIES: **Transportes Delio Morales** (☎ 506/223–5567). **Transportes Jacó** (☎ 506/223–1109).

➤ SOUTHERN PACIFIC BUS COMPANIES: **Alfaro Tracopa** (☎ 506/221–4214). **Musoc** (☎ 506/222–2422). **Transportes Blanco Lobo** (☎ 506/257–4121).

➤ ATLANTIC LOWLANDS AND PACIFIC COAST BUS COMPANIES: **Autotransportes Sarapiquí** (☎ 506/259–8571). **Empresarios Guapilenos** (☎ 506/222–0610). **Transportes Caribeños** (☎ 506/221–2596). **Transportes Mepe** (☎ 506/257–8129).

PAYING

Bus companies accept cash only.

RESERVATIONS

In high season, bus tickets to most popular beaches should be purchased ahead of time. Reservations are not taken over the phone; you have to buy a ticket in person.

BUSINESS HOURS

BANKS AND OFFICES

Most state banks are open weekdays 9–3, and many are open Saturday morning. Several branches of Banco Nacional are open until 6. Private banks—Scotia, Banco Banex, and Banco de San José—tend to keep longer hours and are usually the best places to change U.S. dollars and traveler's checks.

GAS STATIONS

There are 24-hour gas stations near most cities, especially along the Pan-American Highway. Most other stations are open from about 7 to 7, sometimes until midnight.

MUSEUMS AND SIGHTS

Most of Costa Rica's public museums are closed on Monday.

PHARMACIES

Pharmacies throughout the country are generally open 8 AM–8 PM, though it's best to consult with your hotel's staff to be sure. Some pharmacies in San José, affiliated with clinics, stay open 24 hours. In the Central Valley the **Fischel Pharmacy** chain (☎ 506/257–7979) stays open until 10 PM.

SHOPS

Most shops are open weekdays 8–6 and Saturday 8–1.

CAMERAS
AND PHOTOGRAPHY

You will not be allowed to take pictures when watching turtles nest, as any light can deter them from nesting. Always ask permission before taking pictures of locals.

The *Kodak Guide to Shooting Great Travel Pictures* (available at bookstores everywhere) is loaded with tips.

➤ PHOTO HELP: **Kodak Information Center** (☎ 800/242–2424).

EQUIPMENT PRECAUTIONS

Don't pack film and equipment in checked luggage, where it is much more susceptible to damage. Try to **ask for hand inspection of film,** which becomes clouded after repeated exposure to airport X-ray machines, and **keep videotapes and computer disks away from metal detectors.** Always **keep film, tape, and computer disks out of the sun.** Carry an extra supply of batteries, and **be prepared to turn on your camera, camcorder, or laptop** to prove to airport security personnel that the device is real.

FILM AND DEVELOPING

Most film costs at least 20% more in Costa Rica than in the United States, so try to **bring along enough film for your trip.** Plenty of shops in San José develop film, usually the same day, but they tend to change the chemicals less often than they should, so you risk getting prints of poor quality. Kodachrome slide film cannot be developed in Costa Rica.

➤ LOCAL LABS: **Dima Color** (✉ 300 m (325 yards) east of U.S. Embassy, Pavas, ☎ 506/231–4130). **Rapi Foto** (✉ C. Central at Avda. 5, Downtown, San José, ☎ 506/223–7640).

CAR RENTAL

Many travelers shy away from renting a car in Costa Rica, if only for fear of the road conditions. Indeed, this is not an ideal place to drive—in San José, traffic is bad and car theft is rampant (look for guarded parking lots or hotels with lots); in rural areas, roads are often unpaved or dotted with potholes. The greatest deterrent of all might be the extremely high rental rates and gas prices (about $1.50 per gallon).

Still, having your own wheels gives you more control over your itinerary and the pace of your trip. If you decide to go for it, you'll have to choose which type of vessel to rent: a standard vehicle, fine for most destinations, or a *doble-tracción* (four-wheel-drive), often essential to reach the more remote parts of the country, especially during the rainy season. These can cost roughly twice as much as an economy car and should be booked well in advance. If you plan to rent any kind of vehicle between December 15 and January 3, or during Holy Week, **reserve several months ahead of time.**

Costa Rica has around 50 international and local car-rental firms, the larger of which have several offices around San José. At least a dozen rental offices line San José's Paseo Colón, and most large hotels have representatives. For a complete listing, look in the local phone directory once you arrive, under *alquiler de automóviles.*

➤ MAJOR AGENCIES: **Alamo** (☎ 800/327–9633, WEB www.alamo.com). **Avis** (☎ 800/331–1084; 800/879–2847 in Canada; 02/9353–9000 in Australia; 09/525–1982 in New Zealand; 0870/606–0100 in the U.K.). **Budget** (☎ 800/527–0700; 0870/607–5000 in the U.K., through affiliate Europcar). **Dollar** (☎ 800/800–6000; 0124/622–0111 in the U.K. through affiliate Sixt Kenning; 02/9223–1444 in Australia). **Hertz** (☎ 800/654–3001; 800/263–0600 in Canada; 020/8897–2072 in the U.K.; 02/9669–2444 in Australia; 09/256–8690 in New Zealand). **National Car Rental** (☎ 800/227–7368; 020/8680–4800 in the U.K. where it is known as National Europe).

CUTTING COSTS

To get the best deal, **book through a travel agent who will shop around.**

Do **look into wholesalers,** companies that do not own fleets but rent in bulk from those that do and often offer better rates than traditional car-rental operations. Payment must be made before you leave home.

➤ SAN JOSÉ AGENCIES: **Ada** (☎ 506/233–7733). **American** (☎ 506/221–5353). **Avis** (☎ 506/293–2222). **Budget** (☎ 506/255–4750). **Dollar** (☎ 506/257–1585). **Economy** (☎ 506/231–5410). **Elegante** (☎ 506/257–0026). **Hertz** (☎ 506/221–1818). **Hola** (☎ 506/231–5666). **National** (☎ 506/290–8787).

➤ WHOLESALERS: **Auto Europe** (☎ 207/842–2000 or 800/223–5555, FAX 800/235–6321, WEB www.autoeurope.com). **Kemwel Holiday Autos** (☎ 800/678–0678, FAX 914/825–3160, WEB www.kemwel.com).

INSURANCE

When driving a rented car you are generally responsible for any damage to or loss of the vehicle as well as for any property damage or personal injury that you may cause. Insurance issued by car-rental agencies in Costa Rica usually has a very large deductible. Before you rent, see what coverage your personal auto-insurance policy and credit cards provide.

RATES

High-season rates in San José begin at $45 a day and $290 a week for an economy car with air-conditioning, manual transmission, unlimited mileage, and obligatory insurance; but rates fluctuate considerably according to demand, season, and company. Rates for a four-wheel-drive vehicle during high season are $80 a day and $500 per week. When renting a car in San José, **ask whether the rate includes the mandatory $15 daily fee for collision insurance.**

REQUIREMENTS AND RESTRICTIONS

To rent a car with an international agency you need a driver's license, a valid passport, and a credit card; you must also be at least 25 years of age. If you use a local company, you must be 21.

SURCHARGES

Before you pick up a car in one city and leave it in another, **ask about drop-off charges or one-way service**

fees, which can be substantial. Note, too, that some rental agencies charge extra if you return the car before the time specified in your contract. To avoid a hefty refueling fee, **fill the tank just before you turn in the car,** but be aware that gas stations near the rental outlet may overcharge.

CAR TRAVEL

Driving in a developing nation can be a challenge, but it's a great way to explore certain regions, especially Guanacaste, the Atlantic Lowlands, and the Caribbean Coast (apart from Tortuguero and Barra del Colorado). Keep in mind that mountains and poor road conditions make most trips longer than you'd normally expect. If you want to visit a few different far-flung areas and have a short amount of time, domestic flights are a better option.

AUTO CLUBS

➤ IN AUSTRALIA: **Australian Automobile Association** (☎ 02/6247–7311).

➤ IN CANADA: **Canadian Automobile Association** (CAA; ☎ 613/247–0117).

➤ IN NEW ZEALAND: **New Zealand Automobile Association** (☎ 09/377–4660).

➤ IN THE U.K.: **Automobile Association** (AA; ☎ 0990/500–600). **Royal Automobile Club** (RAC; ☎ 0990/722–722 for membership; 0345/121–345 for insurance).

➤ IN THE U.S.: **American Automobile Association** (AAA; ☎ 800/564–6222).

DRIVING OVER THE BORDER

You can drive over Costa Rica's borders into Panama and Nicaragua, but not in a rental car—vehicles rented in one country cannot be taken into the next.

EMERGENCY SERVICES

In Costa Rica, 911 is the nationwide number for accidents. Traffic police are scattered around the country, but Costa Ricans are very good about stopping for people with car trouble. Local car-rental agencies can give you with a list of numbers to call in case of accidents or car trouble.

GASOLINE

Gas costs about $1.50 per gallon.

PARKING

Park overnight in a locked garage or guarded lot, as Central American insurance may hold you liable if your rental car is stolen. Most hotels, barring the least expensive, offer secure parking with a guard or locked gates, as car theft is rife.

ROAD CONDITIONS

Road conditions in Costa Rica are lamentable: you'll run into plenty of potholes and long stretches with no pavement at all.

RULES OF THE ROAD

There are plenty of questionable drivers on Costa Rican highways; **be prepared for harebrained passing on blind corners, tailgating, and failure to signal.** Watch, too, for two-lane roads that feed into one-lane bridges with specified rights of way. And finally, look out for potholes, even in the smoothest sections of the best roads. The highway speed limit in Costa Rica is usually 90 kph (54 mph), which drops to 60 kph (36 mph) in residential areas. Seat belts are required, though drunk-driving laws tend to be less severe than in other parts of the world. You may not drive out of Costa Rica in a rental car.

CHILDREN IN COSTA RICA

Thanks to its generally high safety and health standards, Costa Rica is popular with traveling families. Most of the health problems you might associate with the tropics are rare or nonexistent in Costa Rica (though they do exist in neighboring Nicaragua), and the country's most popular destinations have plenty to offer kids. However, many popular beaches have dangerous currents when the surf is up.

If you are renting a car, don't forget to **arrange for a car seat** when you reserve. For general advice about traveling with children, check out the family travel tips in the Family Travel section of www.fodors.com and consult *Fodor's FYI: Travel with Your Baby* (available in bookstores everywhere).

FLYING

If your children are two or older, **ask about children's airfares.** As a general rule, infants under two not occupying a seat fly at greatly reduced fares or even for free. When booking, **confirm carry-on allowances** if you're traveling with infants. In general, for babies charged 10% of the adult fare you are allowed one carry-on bag and a collapsible stroller; if the flight is full, the stroller may have to be checked or you may be limited to less.

Experts agree that it's a good idea to use safety seats aloft for children weighing less than 40 pounds. Airlines set their own policies: U.S. carriers usually require that the child be ticketed, even if he or she is young enough to ride free, since the seats must be strapped into regular seats. Do **check your airline's policy about using safety seats during takeoff and landing.** And since safety seats are not allowed everywhere in the plane, get your seat assignments early.

When reserving, **request children's meals or a freestanding bassinet** if you need them. But note that bulkhead seats, where you must sit to use the bassinet, may lack an overhead bin or storage space on the floor.

FOOD

U.S fast-food chains are plentiful in San José but not elsewhere in the country. Typical Costa Rican restaurants will serve plain grilled chicken, fish, or beef and french fries to hungry tykes.

LODGING

Most hotels in Costa Rica allow children under a certain age to stay in their parents' room at no extra charge, but others charge for them as extra adults; be sure to **find out the cutoff age for children's discounts.**

➤ BEST CHOICES: **Marriott Los Suenos** (✉ Playa Herradura, ☎ 506/630–9000). **Melia Conchal** (✉ Playa Conchal, ☎ 506/654–4123; 800/336–3542 in the U.S.). **Selva Verde Lodge** (✉ Puerto Viejo de Sarapiquí, ☎ 506/776–6800).

SIGHTS AND ATTRACTIONS

Places that are especially appealing to children are indicated by a rubber-duckie icon (🛁) in the margin.

COMPUTERS ON THE ROAD

Many hotels in Costa Rica have data ports. Batteries and stabilizers are hard to come by, however, and since the electrical current fluctuates significantly in these countries, a stabilizer is usually necessary. It's best to call your hotel in advance for details.

Cyber cafés are popping up all over metropolitan San José; ask around for the one nearest you. The ones we list below are centrally located and accustomed to international travelers.

➤ INTERNET CAFÉS: **CyberCafé Searchcostarica.com** (✉ Avda. 2 between Cs. 1 and 3, ground floor of Las Arcadas building, Downtown San José, ☎ 506/233–3558). **Internet Café Costa Rica** (✉ 91 m [100 yds] west of the Banco Popular, Avda. Central, San Pedro, ☎ 506/224–7295). **Racsa office** (✉ C. 1 at Avda. 5, Downtown, San José, ☎ 506/287–0087).

CONSUMER PROTECTION

Whenever shopping or buying travel services in Costa Rica, **pay with a major credit card,** if possible, so you can cancel payment or get reimbursed if there's a problem. If you're doing business with a particular company for the first time, **contact your local Better Business Bureau and the attorney general's offices** in your state and (for U.S. businesses) the company's home state as well. Have any complaints been filed? Finally, if you're buying a package or tour, always **consider travel insurance** that includes default coverage (☞ Insurance, *below*).

➤ BBBs: **Council of Better Business Bureaus** (✉ 4200 Wilson Blvd., Suite 800, Arlington, VA 22203, ☎ 703/276–0100, FAX 703/525–8277, WEB www.bbb.org).

CRUISE TRAVEL

Cruises are the most restful way to travel. The U.S.–Costa Rica cruise season runs September–May, with trips lasting from three days to a week. A travel agent can explain prices, which range from $1,000 to $5,000. Luxury liners equipped with pools and gyms sail from Fort Lauderdale, Florida, to Limón, or through the Panama Canal to Caldera, south of Puntarenas. Some cruises sail from Los Angeles to Caldera, continuing to the canal. On board the ship you can sign up for shore excursions and tours. Cruise packages include the cost of flying to the appropriate port.

To learn how to plan, choose, and book a cruise-ship voyage, check out Cruise How-to's on www.fodors.com and consult *Fodor's FYI: Plan & Enjoy Your Cruise* (available in bookstores everywhere).

➤ CRUISE LINES: **Carnival** (☎ 800/ 327–9501). **Crystal Cruises** (☎ 800/ 446–6645). **Cunard** (☎ 800/221– 4770). **Holland America** (☎ 800/ 426–0327). **Ocean Cruise** (☎ 800/ 556–8850). **Royal Viking** (☎ 800/ 422–8000). **Seabourn** (☎ 800/351– 9595). **Sitmar Cruise** (☎ 305/523– 1219). **Temptress Adventure Cruises** (☎ 800/580–0072).

CUSTOMS AND DUTIES

When shopping, **keep receipts** for all purchases. Upon reentering the country, **be ready to show customs officials what you've bought.** If you feel a duty is incorrect or object to the way your clearance was handled, note the inspector's badge number and ask to see a supervisor. If the problem isn't resolved, write to the appropriate authorities, beginning with the port director at your point of entry.

IN COSTA RICA

Visitors entering Costa Rica may bring in 500 grams of tobacco, 3 liters of wine or spirits, 2 kilograms of sweets and chocolates, and the equivalent of $100 worth of merchandise. Two cameras, six rolls of film, binoculars, and electrical items for personal use only are also allowed. Customs officials at San José's international airport rarely examine tourists' luggage, but if you enter by land, they'll probably look through your bags.

IN AUSTRALIA

Australian residents who are 18 or older may bring home $A400 worth of souvenirs and gifts (including jewelry), 250 cigarettes or 250 grams of tobacco, and 1,125 milliliters of alcohol (including wine, beer, and spirits). Residents under 18 may bring back $A200 worth of goods. Prohibited items include meat products. Seeds, plants, and fruits need to be declared upon arrival.

➤ INFORMATION: **Australian Customs Service** (Regional Director, ✉ Box 8, Sydney, NSW 2001, ☎ 02/9213– 2000 or 1300/363263; 1800/020504 quarantine-inquiry line, FAX 02/9213– 4043, WEB www.customs.gov.au).

IN CANADA

Canadian residents who have been out of Canada for at least seven days may bring home C$500 worth of goods duty-free. If you've been away fewer than seven days but more than 48 hours, the duty-free allowance drops to C$200; if your trip lasts 24–48 hours, the allowance is C$50. You may not pool allowances with family members. Goods claimed under the C$500 exemption may follow you by mail; those claimed under the lesser exemptions must accompany you. Alcohol and tobacco products may be included in the seven-day and 48-hour exemptions but not in the 24-hour exemption. If you meet the age requirements of the province or territory through which you reenter Canada, you may bring in, duty-free, 1.14 liters (40 imperial ounces) of wine or liquor *or* 24 12-ounce cans or bottles of beer or ale. If you are 16 or older you may bring in, duty-free, 200 cigarettes and 50 cigars. Check ahead of time with Revenue Canada or the Department of Agriculture for policies regarding meat products, seeds, plants, and fruits.

You may send an unlimited number of gifts worth up to C$60 each duty-free to Canada. Label the package UNSOLICITED GIFT—VALUE UNDER $60. Alcohol and tobacco are excluded.

➤ INFORMATION: **Canada Customs and Revenue Agency** (✉ 2265 St. Laurent Blvd. S, Ottawa, Ontario K1G 4K3, ☎ 204/983–3500, 506/636–5064, or 800/461–9999, WEB www.ccra-adrc. gc.ca/).

Smart Travel Tips A to Z

IN NEW ZEALAND

Homeward-bound residents 17 or older may bring back $700 worth of souvenirs and gifts. Your duty-free allowance also includes 4.5 liters of wine or beer; one 1,125-milliliter bottle of spirits; and either 200 cigarettes, 250 grams of tobacco, 50 cigars, or a combination of the three up to 250 grams. Prohibited items include meat products, seeds, plants, and fruits.

➤ INFORMATION: **New Zealand Customs** (Head office: ✉ The Customhouse, 17–21 Whitmore St., Box 2218, Wellington, ☎ 09/300–5399 or 0800/428–786, WEB www.customs.govt.nz).

IN THE U.K.

From countries outside the European Union, including Costa Rica, you may bring home, duty-free, 200 cigarettes or 50 cigars; 1 liter of spirits or 2 liters of fortified or sparkling wine or liqueurs; 2 liters of still table wine; 60 milliliters of perfume; 250 milliliters of toilet water; plus £145 worth of other goods, including gifts and souvenirs. Prohibited items include meat products, seeds, plants, and fruits.

➤ INFORMATION: **HM Customs and Excise** (✉ Portcullis House, 21 Cowbridge Rd. E, Cardiff CF11 9SS, ☎ 029/2038–6423 or 0845/010–9000, WEB www.hmce.gov.uk).

IN THE U.S.

U.S. residents who have been out of the country for at least 48 hours may bring home $600 worth of foreign goods duty-free, as long as they have not used the $600 allowance or any part of it in the past 30 days. This allowance, higher than the standard $400 exemption, applies to the 24 countries in the Caribbean Basin Initiative (CBI)—including Costa Rica. If you visit a CBI country and a non-CBI country, you may still bring in $600 worth of goods duty-free, but no more than $400 may be from the non-CBI country.

U.S. residents 21 and older may bring back 2 liters of alcohol duty-free, as long as one of the liters was produced in a CBI country. In addition, regardless of your age, you are allowed 200 cigarettes and 100 non-Cuban cigars.

Antiques, which the U.S. Customs Service defines as objects more than 100 years old, enter duty-free, as do original works of art done entirely by hand, including paintings, drawings, and sculptures. You may also send packages home duty-free, with a limit of one parcel per addressee per day (except alcohol or tobacco products or perfume worth more than $5). You can mail up to $200 worth of goods for personal use; label the package PERSONAL USE and attach a list of its contents and their retail value. If the package contains your used personal belongings, mark it PERSONAL GOODS RETURNED to avoid paying duties. You may send up to $100 worth of goods as a gift; mark the package UNSOLICITED GIFT. Mailed items do not affect your duty-free allowance on your return.

➤ INFORMATION: **U.S. Customs Service** (✉ 1300 Pennsylvania Ave. NW, Washington, DC 20229, WEB www.customs.gov; inquiries ☎ 202/354–1000;complaints c/o ✉ 1300 Pennsylvania Ave. NW, Room 5.4D, Washington, DC 20229; registration of equipment c/o ✉ Resource Management, ☎ 202/927–0540).

DINING

Costa Rican food is straightforward—plenty of simply seasoned and grilled fish, steaks, and chicken—and not spicy (although you may choose to add hot sauces that are provided). **Don't skimp on the fresh fruit** when it's served; it won't taste this good at home.

Prevalent at breakfast are eggs and *gallo pinto* ("spotted rooster," a mix of black beans and rice, often topped with a dollop of *natilla* (sour cream) and squeezed juices, from carrot to fresh-picked star fruit, that would cost a fortune at home. Always at lunch, and sometimes at dinner, you can depend on a *casado,* the *típico* Costa Rican meal of rice and black beans served with meat, chicken, or fish. Salads with avocado *aguacate* and *palmito* (hearts of palm) are also common. Note that lettuce is almost always served shredded.

Seafood is plentiful close to the coast, less so farther inland: *camarones* (shrimp), sautéed in garlic and butter and served with fries and salad; *langostinos* (a kind of lobster); and a fine variety of fish, like corvina, dorado, and guapote are available in most restaurants at reasonable prices (langostinos aside). Meat lovers, rejoice: the northwest, whose plains are covered with cattle ranches, produces the country's best steak.

There are also plenty of restaurants serving everything from French and Italian to Cantonese and Peruvian cuisine. The restaurants we list are the cream of the crop in each price category.

CATEGORY	COST*
$$$$	over $20 (over 6,930 colones)
$$$	$10–$20 (3,465–6,930 colones)
$$	$5–$10 (1,733–3,465 colones)
$	under $5 (under 1,733 colones)

per person for main course at dinner.

MEALTIMES

Dining hours in Costa Rica are usually noon–3 and 6–9. Unless otherwise noted, the restaurants listed in this guide are open daily for lunch and dinner.

PAYING

Cash is the rule at local restaurants. In Costa Rica, 23% is added to all menu prices—13% for tax and 10% for service. Because the gratuity is included, there is no need to tip, but if service is good, it's nice to add a little money to the obligatory 10%.

RESERVATIONS AND DRESS

Reservations are always a good idea: we mention them only when they're essential or not accepted. Book as far ahead as you can, and reconfirm as soon as you arrive. We mention dress only when men are required to wear a jacket or a jacket and tie.

WINE, BEER, AND SPIRITS

Costa Rica's one brewery makes half a dozen brands of beer, including the popular Imperial, a dark brew called Steinbrau, and a local version of Heineken. All wine is imported; the best deals are usually from Chile and Argentina, particularly the Chilean Castillero del Diablo and Sangre de Toro. Costa Rica's best rum is Centenario, but most Ticos drink a rot-gut rum called *guaro*. All of the above is served at restaurants and bars and sold in supermarkets and liquor stores. Café Britt makes a refined coffee liqueur that is sold at supermarkets and liquor stores, as well as the airport.

DISABILITIES AND ACCESSIBILITY

Accessibility in Central America is extremely limited. Wheelchair ramps are practically nonexistent, and streets are often unpaved outside major cities, making wheelchair travel difficult. Exploring most attractions involves walking down cobblestone streets, steep trails, or muddy paths. Buses are not equipped to carry wheelchairs, so people using wheelchairs should hire a van to get around and bring someone along to help out. There is some growing awareness of the needs of people with disabilities, and some hotels and attractions in Costa Rica have made the necessary provisions; the **Costa Rican Tourist Institute**, known locally as the ICT, has more information.

➤ LOCAL RESOURCES: **Costa Rican Tourist Institute** (✉ Avda. 4 and Cs. 5 and 7, 11th floor, Centro Colón, San José, Costa Rica, ☎ 506/223–1733).

LODGING

Very few hotels in Costa Rica are equipped for travelers in wheelchairs. In San José, the Hampton Inn and Hacienda El Rodeo, both near the international airport, have some wheelchair accommodations; and Wilson Botanical Gardens, in San Vito (Southern Pacific), has one room equipped for a wheelchair.

RESERVATIONS

When discussing accessibility with an operator or reservations agent, **ask hard questions.** Are there any stairs, inside *or* out? Are there grab bars next to the toilet *and* in the shower/tub? How wide is the doorway to the room? To the bathroom?

For the most extensive facilities meeting the latest legal specifications, **opt for newer accommodations.**

SIGHTS AND ATTRACTIONS

Unfortunately, most Costa Rican attractions are inaccessible for travelers with wheelchairs, as are restaurant bathrooms. Volcán Poás National Park is probably the most wheelchair-friendly site, with Volcán Irazú the runner-up. The Orosí Valley and Sarchí also have limited exploring options for travelers using wheelchairs. The Rain Forest Aerial Tram is a real challenge but might be a possibility for some.

TRANSPORTATION

Developed areas, especially San José and the Central Valley, can be managed in a wheelchair more easily than rural areas. The tour company **Vaya con Silla de Ruedas** (Go with Wheelchair) provides transportation and guided tours.

➤ CONTACT INFORMATION: **Vaya con Silla de Ruedas (Go with Wheelchair)** (☎ 506/391–5045, WEB www. gowithwheelchairs.com).

➤ COMPLAINTS: **Aviation Consumer Protection Division** (☞ Air Travel, *above*) for airline-related problems. **Civil Rights Office** (✉ U.S. Department of Transportation, Departmental Office of Civil Rights, S-30, 400 7th St. SW, Room 10215, Washington, DC 20590, ☎ 202/366–4648, FAX 202/366–9371, WEB www.dot.gov/ost/docr/index.htm) for problems with surface transportation. **Disability Rights Section** (✉ U.S. Department of Justice, Civil Rights Division, Box 66738, Washington, DC 20035-6738, ☎ 202/514–0301 or 800/514–0301; 202/514–0383 or 800/514–0383 TTY, FAX 202/307–1198, WEB www. usdoj.gov/crt/ada/adahom1.htm) for general complaints.

TRAVEL AGENCIES

In the United States, the Americans with Disabilities Act requires that travel firms serve the needs of all travelers. Some agencies specialize in working with people with disabilities.

➤ TRAVELERS WITH MOBILITY PROBLEMS: **Access Adventures** (✉ 206 Chestnut Ridge Rd., Scottsville, NY 14624, ☎ 716/889–9096, dltravel@prodigy.net), run by a former physical-rehabilitation counselor. **Care-Vacations** (✉ 5-5110 50th Ave., Leduc, Alberta T9E 6V4, Canada, ☎ 780/986–6404 or 877/478–7827, FAX 780/986–8332, WEB www. carevacations.com), for group tours and cruise vacations. **Flying Wheels Travel** (✉ 143 W. Bridge St., Box 382, Owatonna, MN 55060, ☎ 507/451–5005 or 800/535–6790, FAX 507/451–1685, WEB www.flyingwheelstravel. com).

DISCOUNTS AND DEALS

Be a smart shopper and **compare all your options** before making decisions. A plane ticket bought with a promotional coupon from travel clubs, coupon books, and direct-mail offers or on the Internet may not be cheaper than the least expensive fare from a discount ticket agency. And always keep in mind that what you get is just as important as what you save.

DISCOUNT RESERVATIONS

To save money, **look into discount reservations services** with toll-free numbers, which use their buying power to get a better price on hotels, airline tickets, even car rentals. When booking a room, always **call the hotel's local toll-free number** (if one is available) rather than the central reservations number—you'll often get a better price. Always ask about special packages or corporate rates.

When shopping for the best deal on hotels and car rentals, **look for guaranteed exchange rates,** which protect you against a falling dollar. With your rate locked in, you won't pay more, even if the price goes up in the local currency.

➤ HOTEL ROOMS: **Players Express Vacations** (☎ 800/458–6161, WEB www.playersexpress.com). **Turbotrip.com** (☎ 800/473–7829, WEB www.turbotrip.com).

PACKAGE DEALS

Don't confuse packages and guided tours. When you buy a package, you travel on your own, just as though you had planned the trip yourself. Fly-drive packages, which combine airfare and car rental, are often a good deal.

ECOTOURISM

Ecotourism, green tourism, environmental tourism: the buzzwords have been flying around Costa Rica for more than a decade. Many tour companies have incorporated a high level of environmental awareness into their business practices. **Find out whether or not your prospective tour company has "eco-friendly" policies,** such as hiring and training locals as guides, drivers, managers, and office workers; teaching people as much as possible about the plant and animal life, geography, and history that surrounds them; controlling the numbers of people allowed daily onto a given site; restoring watersheds and anything else damaged by trail-building, visiting, or general overuse; and discouraging wildlife feeding or any other unnatural or disruptive behavior (i.e., making loud noises to scare birds into flight). All these practices can mitigate the effects of intense tourism. After all, it's better to have a hundred people walking through a forest than to cut the forest down.

Whether you travel on your own or with a tour group, try to make your visit beneficial to those who live near protected areas: **use local guides or services,** eat in local restaurants, and buy local crafts or produce. To ensure land preservation for future generations, you can donate to local conservation groups or a few foreign environmental organizations—including Conservation International, the Nature Conservancy, and the World Wide Fund for Nature—that aid ecological efforts in Costa Rica.

➤ LOCAL CONSERVATION GROUPS: **ANAI** (☎ 506/224–3570). **APREFLOFAS** (☎ 506/240–6087). **Monteverde Institute** (☎ 506/645–5053). **Neotropica Foundation** (☎ 506/253–2130).

➤ INT. CONSERVATION GROUPS: **Conservation International** (✉ 2501 M St. NW, Suite 200, Washington, DC 20037, ☎ 800/429–5660 or 202/973–2227, WEB www.conservation.org). **Nature Conservancy** (✉ 4245 Fairfax Dr.,

Arlington, VA 22203, ☎ 703/841–5300, WEB www.tnc.org). **World Wide Fund for Nature** (✉ Av. du Mont-Blanc, CH 1196 Gland, Switzerland, ☎ 4122/364–9111, WEB www.panda.org).

NATIONAL PARKS

For specific information on Costa Rican parks and protected areas, call the environment ministry's national park information line (192). For specific requests, such as reserving camping or cabin space, call the regional office of the park in question. Practical information on parks, including limited literature, is available at the Fundación de Parques Nacionales.

The price of admission to Costa Rica's national parks is $6 per day.

➤ COSTA RICA PARK CONTACTS: **Fundación de Parques Nacionales** (✉ 300 m [328 yds] north and 300 m [328 yds] east of Church of Santa Teresita, San José, ☎ 506/257–2239). **Ministry of Environment and Energy** (MINAE; ☎ 192).

TOURS

If you park yourself at a beach hotel or an all-inclusive you'll miss what Costa Rica does best: nature. To get the most out of your trip, **pair yourself with a professional, bilingual nature guide,** who knows well the country's diverse landscapes, birds, animals, and where to find them. Costa Rica Expeditions, known for their commitment to conservation, has high-quality tours led by knowledgable, professional guides. Horizontes is also a top-notch natural-history tour operator with some of the country's best guides. Aventuras Naturales runs terrific adventure tours (including white-water rafting and bicycling) either as a one-day trip or multiday package. Sun Tours trips are well organized and guides are informative and friendly; they do a superb job of planning trips that hit all the country's highlights. There are many tour companies and guides out there (and many lodges staff their own naturalist).

"Soft adventure" travelers are well catered to aboard the 185-ft M.V.

Temptress, run by Temptress Adventure Cruises and Cruise West, with multiday natural-history cruises along the Southern Pacific coast.

➤ COSTA RICA: **Aventuras Naturales** (✉ Box 10736-1000 San José, ☎ 506/ 225–3939 or 800/514–0411, FAX 506/ 253–6934, WEB www.toenjoynature. com). **Costa Rica Expeditions** (☎ 506/222–0333, FAX 506/257–1665, WEB www.expeditions.co.cr). **Horizontes** (☎ 506/222–2022, FAX 506/ 255–4513, WEB www.horizontes.com). **Sun Tours** (☎ 506/296–7757, FAX 506/ 290–2723, WEB www.crsuntours.com). **Temptress Adventure Cruises** (Cruise West, 2401 4th Ave., Suite 700, Seattle, WA 98121-1438, ☎ 800/580– 0072, FAX 206/441–4757, WEB www. cruisewest.com).

WILDLIFE

Travelers are often surprised by how hard it can be to see animals in the rain forest; despite their frequent appearances in advertisements and brochures, many endangered species are practically impossible to spot. Between the low density of mammals, their shyness, and the fact that thick vegetation often obstructs your view, you must **be patient and stay attentive.** Because the tropical dry forest is less overgrown than the rain forest, it's one of the best life zones for animal observation; river trips, too, can make for great viewing. **Don't give up hope**: if you take the time to explore a few protected areas, you're almost certain to spy dozens of interesting critters.

ELECTRICITY

The electrical current in Central America is 110 volts (AC), with two prong outlets. Converters or adapters are required only for three-prong plugs. It's also advisable to bring a surge protector if you plan to use computer equipment.

EMBASSIES

Most embassies are on the western end of San José or in nearby suburbs. Citizens of Australia and New Zealand should contact the British Embassy.

➤ CANADA: (✉ Sabana Sur, next to tennis club, ☎ 506/296–4149).

➤ UNITED KINGDOM: (✉ Centro Colón, Paseo Colón between Cs. 38 and 40, ☎ 506/258–2025).

➤ UNITED STATES: (✉ Pavas, ☎ 506/ 220–3939).

EMERGENCIES

Costa Ricans are usually quick to respond in emergencies. In a hotel or restaurant, the staff will usually offer immediate immediate assistance, and in a public area, passersby can be counted on to stop and help.

➤ EMERGENCIES: **General emergencies** (☎ 911). **Ambulance** (☎ 128). **Police** (☎ 117; 127 outside cities).

ENGLISH-LANGUAGE MEDIA

English is practically everywhere in Costa Rica, from abundant publications to the cable TV beamed into most San José hotels.

BOOKS

Several San José bookstores carry a good selection of new and used English-language books, at prices slightly higher than those in the United States. Some large hotels and other shops also sell English-language books, particularly titles on the tropical outdoors.

➤ MAJOR BOOKSTORES: **Lehmann** (✉ Avda. Central between Cs. 1 and 3, Downtown, San José, ☎ 506/223– 1212). **Librería Internacional** (✉ 328 m [300 yds] west of Taco Bell, Barrio Dent, San José, ☎ 506/ 253–9553). **7th Street Books** (✉ C. 7 between Avdas. Central and 1, Downtown, San José, ☎ 506/256–8251).

NEWSPAPERS AND MAGAZINES

American newspapers and magazines are widely distributed at newsstands and hotels in San José, and sold in some resorts outside the capital. The English-language weekly the *Tico Times,* published every Friday, has local news and information on entertainment and travel.

RADIO AND TELEVISION

Most mid- to high-priced hotels in San José have cable TV in guest rooms, with at least a dozen English-language channels. Some hotels outside the capital have satellite dishes. **Don't expect remote lodges or smaller hotels to have in-room TVs.** Local TV is in Spanish and not worth writing home about. There is one exclusively English-language radio station, which plays rock (107.5 FM); a few others (99.5 and 102.3 FM) play some tunes in English.

ETIQUETTE AND BEHAVIOR

On the whole, Costa Ricans are extremely polite, quick to shake hands and place a soft kiss on the left cheek. Ticos (the name Costa Ricans use for themselves) tend to use formal Spanish, preferring, for example, *con mucho gusto* (with much pleasure) instead of *de nada* for "you're welcome". At the same time, an unsettlingly large portion of Costa Rican men make a habit of ogling or making gratuitous comments when young women pass on the street. Family is very important in Costa Rica. It is considered polite to ask about one's married status and family—don't confuse this for prying.

As you would anywhere, **dress and behave respectfully when visiting churches.**

BUSINESS ETIQUETTE

Northerners are bound to find business meetings friendlier and more relaxed in Costa Rica and its neighbors than at home. Dress is usually casual, and tardiness is common.

FLIGHTSEEING

San José–based pilot **Jenner Rojas** (☎ 506/385–5425) will take you anywhere in Costa Rica for "flightseeing" and picture-taking. The rate is $230 per hour, or less if you arrange a trip of several hours' duration.

GAY AND LESBIAN TRAVEL

While harassment of gays and lesbians is infrequent in Costa Rica, so are public displays of affection. Discretion is advised. Ticos, for whom religion and family are very important, tend to simply assume everyone is straight. As a result of its history of tolerance, Costa Rica has attracted many gay people from other Latin American nations and consequently has a large gay community. San José and Manuel Antonio are probably the most gay-friendly towns, with some gay-and-lesbian bars and hangouts. The beach at the northern end of Playa Espadilla in Manuel Antonio National Park is a small, secluded cove known as a gay nude beach. There are no anti-gay laws.

➤ GAY- AND LESBIAN-FRIENDLY TRAVEL AGENCIES: **Different Roads Travel** (✉ 8383 Wilshire Blvd., Suite 902, Beverly Hills, CA 90211, ☎ 323/651–5557 or 800/429–8747, FAX 323/651–3678, lgernert@tzell.com). **Kennedy Travel** (✉ 314 Jericho Turnpike, Floral Park, NY 11001, ☎ 516/352–4888 or 800/237–7433, FAX 516/354–8849, WEB www.kennedytravel.com). **Now Voyager** (✉ 4406 18th St., San Francisco, CA 94114, ☎ 415/626–1169 or 800/255–6951, FAX 415/626–8626, WEB www.nowvoyager.com).

GAY AND LESBIAN RESOURCES

San José's 1@10 Café Internet serves as a gay and lesbian resource center. Its web page (www.1en10.com) is a wealth of whom-to-contact, where-to-go info. ILPES, a private organization that promotes the rights of gays and lesbians, staffs a hot line weekdays 8–4. *Gente* magazine is a bimonthly gay Costa Rican magazine that has bilingual, LGBT–friendly tour and hotel listings. You can find it, and the community paper, *Gayness,* in gay-friendly hotels, bars, and bookshops. The informal Gay and Lesbian Guide to Costa Rica Web site, www.hometown.aol.com/GayCRica/guide.html, has some good travel information, including hotels that are listed with the Costa Rican Gay Business Association.

➤ LOCAL CONTACTS: **Agua Buena** (✉ San Pedro, ☎ 506/234–2411). **Costa Rica Human Rights Commission** (✉ San Pedro, ☎ 506/234–0581). **ILPES** (☎ 506/280–5225 hot line). **1@10 Café Internet** (Uno@Diez, ✉ Calle 1 at Av. 9, Barrio Amón, San José ☎ 506/258–4561).

GUIDEBOOKS

Plan well and you won't be sorry. Guidebooks are excellent tools—and you can take them with you. You may want to check out the full-color

Fodor's Exploring Costa Rica, available at on-line retailers and bookstores everywhere.

HEALTH

ENGLISH-SPEAKING DOCTORS

Many of the doctors at San José's Clinica Biblica and Clinica Catolica, and Escazú's CIMA Hospital speak English well, and some studied medicine in the United States. Many of these clinics have 24-hour pharmacies.

➤ LOCAL MEDICAL HELP: **CIMA Hospital** (✉ next to PriceSmart, Escazú, ☎ 506/208–1000). **Clinica Biblica** (✉ Avda. 14 at C. 1, San José, ☎ 506/257–5252). **Clinica Catolica** (✉ San Antonio Guadalupe, ☎ 506/ 283–6616).

FOOD AND DRINK

Most food and water here are sanitary. In rural areas, you run a mild risk of encountering drinking water, fresh fruit, and vegetables contaminated by fecal matter, which causes intestinal ailments known variously as Montezuma's Revenge (traveler's diarrhea) and leptospirosis (another disease borne in contaminated food or water that can be treated by antibiotics if detected early). Although it may not be necessary, you can stay on the safe side and **watch what you eat**—avoid ice, uncooked food, and unpasteurized milk (including milk products), and **drink bottled water.** Mild cases of Montezuma's Revenge may respond to Imodium (known generically as loperamide) or Pepto-Bismol (not as strong), both of which can be purchased over the counter. Paregoric, another antidiarrheal agent, requires a doctor's prescription in Costa Rica. Drink plenty of purified water or tea; chamomile is a good folk remedy. In severe cases, rehydrate yourself with a salt-sugar solution (½ teaspoon salt and 4 tablespoons sugar per quart of water).

HAZARDS

Mild insect repellents, like the ones in some skin softeners, are no match for the intense mosquito activity in the hot, humid regions of the Atlantic Lowlands, Osa Peninsula, and Southern Pacific. Moreover, perfume, aftershave, and other lotions and potions can actually attract mosquitoes. Poisonous snakes, scorpions, and other pests pose a small (overrated) threat.

The greatest danger to your person actually lies off this region's popular beaches—riptides are common wherever there are waves, and several tourists drown in them every year. If you see waves, ask the locals where it's safe to swim; and if you're uncertain, don't go in deeper than your waist. If you get caught in a rip current, swim parallel to the beach until you're free of it, and then swim back to shore.

MEDICAL PLANS

No one plans to get sick while traveling, but it happens, so **consider signing up with a medical-assistance company.** Members get doctor referrals, emergency evacuation or repatriation, hot lines for medical consultation, cash for emergencies, and other assistance.

➤ MEDICAL-ASSISTANCE COMPANIES: **International SOS Assistance** (WEB www.internationalsos.com; ✉ 8 Neshaminy Interplex, Suite 207, Trevose, PA 19053, ☎ 215/245–4707 or 800/523–6586, FAX 215/244–9617; ✉ 12 Chemin Riantbosson, 1217 Meyrin 1, Geneva, Switzerland, ☎ 4122/785–6464, FAX 4122/785– 6424; ✉ 331 N. Bridge Rd., 17-00, Odeon Towers, Singapore 188720, ☎ 65/338–7800, FAX 65/338–7611).

OVER-THE-COUNTER REMEDIES

Most drugs for which you need a prescription back home are sold over the counter in Central America. Pharmacies (*farmacias*) are abundant, and most sell aspirin and sunscreen in a wide range of SPFs, though the latter is relatively pricey.

SHOTS AND MEDICATIONS

According to the U.S. Centers for Disease Control, travel to Central America poses some risk of malaria, hepatitis A and B, dengue fever, typhoid fever, rabies, Chagas' disease, and *E. coli.* The CDC recommends getting vaccines for hepatitis A and typhoid fever, especially if you are going to be in the country or in remote areas or plan stay for more than six weeks. Check with the CDC for detailed health advisories and recommended vaccinations. In areas with malaria and dengue, both of which are carried by mosquitoes, **bring mosquito nets, wear clothing that covers your body, apply repellent containing DEET, and use insect spray** in living and sleeping areas. Malaria is not a problem in Costa Rica except for in the North Caribbean coast near the Nicaraguan border. It is not necessary to take malaria pills before your trip unless it will involve a prolonged stay or camping on the North Atlantic Coast.

Children traveling to Central America should have current inoculations against measles, mumps, rubella, and polio.

➤ HEALTH WARNINGS: **National Centers for Disease Control and Prevention** (CDC; National Center for Infectious Diseases, Division of Quarantine, Traveler's Health Section, ✉ 1600 Clifton Rd. NE, M/S E-03, Atlanta, GA 30333, ☎ 888/232–3228 or 800/311–3435, FAX 888/232–3299, WEB www.cdc.gov).

HOLIDAYS

National holidays are known as *feriados*. On these days government offices, banks, and post offices are closed, and public transport is restricted. Religious festivals are characterized by colorful processions.

Except for those in hotels, most restaurants and many attractions close between Christmas and New Year's Day and during Holy Week (Palm Sunday to Easter Sunday). Those that do stay open may not sell alcohol between Holy Thursday and Easter Sunday.

2003 dates: New Year's Day; February 12, Shrove Tuesday; April 11, Juan Santamaría Day; March 29–31, Good Friday–Easter Sunday; May 1, Labor Day; July 25, Annexation of Guanacaste; August 2, Virgin of the Angels (Costa Rica's patron saint); September 15, Independence Day; October 12, Columbus Day (Día de la Raza); Christmas.

INSURANCE

The most useful travel-insurance plan is a comprehensive policy that includes coverage for trip cancellation and interruption, default, trip delay, and medical expenses (with a waiver for preexisting conditions).

Without insurance you will lose all or most of your money if you cancel your trip, regardless of the reason. Default insurance covers you if your tour operator, airline, or cruise line goes out of business. Trip-delay covers expenses that arise because of bad weather or mechanical delays. Study the fine print when comparing policies.

If you're traveling internationally, a key component of travel insurance is coverage for medical bills incurred if you get sick on the road. Such expenses are not generally covered by Medicare or private policies. U.K. residents can buy a travel-insurance policy valid for most vacations taken during the year in which it's purchased (but check preexisting-condition coverage). British and Australian citizens need extra medical coverage when traveling overseas.

Always **buy travel policies directly from the insurance company**; if you buy them from a cruise line, airline, or tour operator that goes out of business you probably will not be covered for the agency or operator's default, which is a major risk. Before making any purchase, **review your existing health and home-owner's policies** to find what they cover away from home.

➤ TRAVEL INSURERS: In the United States: **Access America** (✉ 6600 W. Broad St., Richmond, VA 23230, ☎ 804/285–3300 or 800/284–8300, FAX 804/673–1586, WEB www. accessamerica.com/). **Travel Guard International** (✉ 1145 Clark St., Stevens Point, WI 54481, ☎ 715/345–0505 or 800/826–4919, FAX 800/955–8785, WEB www.travelguard. com).

➤ INSURANCE INFORMATION: In Australia: **Insurance Council of Australia** (✉ Level 3, 56 Pitt St., Sydney, NSW 2000, ☎ 03/9614–1077, FAX 03/9614–7924). In Canada: **Voyager**

Insurance (✉ 44 Peel Center Dr., Brampton, Ontario L6T 4M8, ☎ 905/791–8700; 800/668–4342 in Canada). In New Zealand: **Insurance Council of New Zealand** (✉ Box 474, Wellington, ☎ 04/472–5230, FAX 04/473–3011, WEB www.icnz.org.nz). In the United Kingdom: **Association of British Insurers** (✉ 51–55 Gresham St., London EC2V 7HQ, ☎ 020/7600–3333, FAX 020/7696–8999, WEB www.abi.org.uk).

LANGUAGE

Spanish is the official language, although tour guides and many people also speak English, especially along the Caribbean coast. You'll have a better time if you learn some basic Spanish before you go, and bring a phrase book with you. When possible, choose the more formal phrasing, such as *¿Cómo está usted?* (How are you?) rather than the North American or Mexican *¿Cómo está?*, which is not done here. At the very least, **learn the rudiments of polite conversation**—niceties like *por favor* (please) and *gracias* (thank you) will be warmly appreciated. A brief Spanish Vocabulary glossary appears in Chapter 9.

In the Caribbean province of Limón a creole English called Mekatalyu is widely spoken by older generations. English is understood by most everyone in these parts.

LANGUAGES FOR TRAVELERS

A phrase book and language-tape set can help get you started. *Fodor's Spanish for Travelers* (available at bookstores everywhere) is excellent.

SPANISH-LANGUAGE PROGRAMS

Thousands of people travel to Costa Rica every year to study Spanish. Dozens of schools in and around San José offer professional instruction and home stays, and there are several smaller schools outside the capital.

➤ CONTACTS: **Conversa** (✉ Apdo. 17–1007, Centro Colón, San José, ☎ 506/221–7649; 800/354–5036 in U.S. and Canada) also has a school in Santa Ana, west of San José. **IPEE** (✉ 23 m (25 yards) south of Pops, Curridabat, ☎ 506/283–7731; 813/988–3916 in U.S.). **ILISA** (✉ Dept. 1420, Box 25216, Miami, FL 33102, ☎ 506/225–2495; 800/454–7248 Ext. 3000 in U.S.). **La Escuela D'Amore** (✉ Apdo. 67, Quepos, ☎ 506/777–1143) is in beautiful Manuel Antonio.

LODGING

At Costa Rica's popular beach and mountain resorts **reserve well in advance for the dry season** (mid-December–April). You'll need to give credit-card information or send a deposit to confirm the reservation. Try to do this with the hotel and not a third-party reservations network. During the rainy season, May to mid-December, most hotels drop their rates considerably, which sometimes sends them into a lower price category than the one we indicate.

Luxury hotels are found mainly in San José, Guanacaste, and the Central Valley. Except for the most popular Pacific beaches, lodging in outlying areas is usually in simple *cabinas* (cabins). Cabinas range from basic cement boxes with few creature comforts to flashier units with all the modern conveniences. Costa Rica also has an abundance of nature lodges (often within private biological reserves) with an emphasis on ecology; most of these are entirely rustic, but a few of the newest are quite luxurious. About half the national parks in this region have campgrounds with facilities.

Nature lodges may be less expensive than they initially appear, as the price of a room usually includes three hearty meals a day. Since many of the hotels are remotely set and have an eco-friendly approach (even to luxury), air-conditioning, in-room telephones, and TVs are an exception to the rule. If these amenities are important to you, **ask about air-conditioning or phones when making your reservations.** We mention when they're not offered.

The lodgings we review are the cream of the crop in each price category. We always list facilities, but we don't specify whether they cost extra—when pricing hotel rooms, always ask what's included and what costs extra.

CATEGORY	COST*
$$$$	over $90 (over 31,500 colones)
$$$	$50–$90 (17,500–31,500 colones)
$$	$25–$50 (8,750–17,500 colones)
$	under $25 (under 8,750 colones)

*for a double room, excluding service and tax (16.4%)

APARTMENT AND VILLA RENTALS

If you want a home base that's roomy enough for a family and comes with cooking facilities, **consider a furnished rental.**In addition to accommodating your crowd, these can save you money. Look through classified ads in the Real Estate section of Costa Rica's English-language weekly, *The Tico Times*. Home-exchange directories sometimes list rentals as well as exchanges. Costa Rica Rentals International has rental homes and apartments in the San José area and elsewhere; Tropical Waters arranges short-term rentals in the Dominical area. Marina Trading Post, an affiliate of Century 21, arranges house and condominium rentals near Playa Flamingo.

➤ INTERNATIONAL AGENTS: **Hideaways International** (⊠ 767 Islington St., Portsmouth, NH 03801, ☎ 603/430–4433 or 800/843–4433, FAX 603/430–4444, WEB www.hideaways.com; membership $99). **Vacation Home Rentals Worldwide** (⊠ 235 Kensington Ave., Norwood, NJ 07648, ☎ 201/767–9393 or 800/633–3284, FAX 201/767–5510, WEB www.vhrww.com). **Villas and Apartments Abroad** (⊠ 1270 Ave. of the Americas, 15th floor, New York, NY 10020, ☎ 212/897–5045 or 800/433–3020, FAX 212/897–5039, WEB www.vaanyc.com). **Villas International** (⊠ 4340 Redwood Hwy., Suite D309 San Rafael, CA 94903, ☎ 415/499–9490 or 800/221–2260, FAX 415/499–9491, WEB www.villasintl.com).

➤ LOCAL AGENTS: **Costa Rica Rentals International** (⊠ Apdo. 1136–1250, Escazú, ☎ 506/228–6863). **Marina Trading Post** (⊠ Suites Presidenciales, Playa Flamingo, Guanacaste, ☎ 506/654–4004). **Tropical Waters** (⊠ 3½ km [2¼ mi] north of Dominical, ☎ 506/787–0031).

CAMPING

Many national parks have camping areas; it's best to contact the park rangers for information. Some popular beaches, including Manuel Antonio, Jacó, Sámara, Tamarindo, and Puerto Viejo, have private camping areas with bathrooms and showers. If you camp on the beach or in other unguarded areas, **don't leave belongings unattended in your tent.**

HOME EXCHANGES

If you would like to exchange your home for someone else's, **join a home-exchange organization,** which will send you its updated listings of available exchanges for a year and will include your own listing in at least one of them. It's up to you to make specific arrangements.

➤ EXCHANGE CLUBS: **Home Exchange International Group** (⊠ Box 1084, Canton, CT 06019, WEB www.heig.com; $35 yearly fee). **Intervac U.S.** (⊠ Box 590504, San Francisco, CA 94159, ☎ 800/756–4663, FAX 415/435–7440, WEB www.intervacus.com; $93 yearly fee includes one catalogue and on-line access).

HOSTELS

No matter what your age, you can **save on lodging costs by staying at hostels.** In Costa Rica, information and reservations for any of the country's six hostels are available at the Toruma Youth Hostel in San José. In some 5,000 locations in more than 70 countries around the world, Hostelling International (HI), the umbrella group for a number of national youth-hostel associations, offers single-sex, dorm-style beds and, at many hostels, rooms for couples and family accommodations. Membership in any HI national hostel association, open to travelers of all ages, allows you to stay in HI-affiliated hostels at member rates; one-year membership is about $25 for adults (C$26.75 in Canada, £9.30 in the United Kingdom, $30 in Australia, and $30 in New Zealand);

hostels run about $10–$25 per night. Members have priority; they're also eligible for discounts around the world, even on rail and bus travel in some countries.

➤ ORGANIZATIONS: **Australian Youth Hostel Association** (✉ 10 Mallett St., Camperdown, NSW 2050, Australia, ☎ 02/9565–1699, FAX 02/9565–1325, WEB www.yha.com.au). **Hostelling International—American Youth Hostels** (✉ 733 15th St. NW, Suite 840, Washington, DC 20005, ☎ 202/783–6161, FAX 202/783–6171, WEB www. hiayh.org). **Hostelling International—Canada** (✉ 400–205 Catherine St., Ottawa, Ontario K2P 1C3, Canada, ☎ 613/237–7884, FAX 613/237–7868, WEB www.hostellingintl.ca). **Youth Hostel Association of England and Wales** (✉ Trevelyan House, 8 St. Stephen's Hill, St. Albans, Hertfordshire AL1 2DY, U.K., ☎ 0870/870–8808, FAX 01727/844126, WEB www. yha.org.uk). **Youth Hostels Association of New Zealand** (✉ Box 436, Christchurch, New Zealand, ☎ 03/379–9970, FAX 03/365–4476, WEB www. yha.org.nz).

HOTELS

There are a few large hotels on the outskirts of San José and on some of the more popular beaches, but most Costa Rican hotels are smaller, with more personalized service. Outside San José, rooms are in great demand between the week after Christmas and the week before Easter; reserve one to three months in advance for those times. Most hotels drop their rates during the "green season" (May to December), and during this time—barring July—it's quite feasible to show up without reservations and haggle over rates, a process that can bring your hotel budget down to nearly half what it might be in the high season. All hotels listed have private bathrooms unless we indicate otherwise. If you want a double bed, request a *cama matrimonial*. There are a surprising number of rooms with single beds in them.

➤ TOLL-FREE NUMBERS: **Best Western** (☎ 800/528–1234, WEB www. bestwestern.com). **Choice** (☎ 800/221–2222, WEB www.hotelchoice. com). **Holiday Inn** (☎ 800/465–4329, WEB www.basshotels.com). **Inter-Continental** (☎ 800/327–0200, WEB www.interconti.com). **Marriott** (☎ 800/228–9290, WEB www.marriott. com). **Radisson** (☎ 800/333–3333, WEB www.radisson.com).

MAIL AND SHIPPING

Mail from the United States or Europe can take two to three weeks to arrive in Costa Rica (occasionally it never arrives at all). Within the country, mail service is even less reliable. Outgoing mail is marginally quicker, with delivery in five days to two weeks, especially when sent from San José. **Always use airmail for overseas cards and letters.** Mail theft is a chronic problem, so **do not mail checks, cash, or anything else of value.**

OVERNIGHT SERVICES

If you need to send important documents, checks, or other noncash valuables, you can use an international courier service, such as Federal Express, DHL, or Jetex, or any of various local courier services with offices in San José. (Look in the yellow pages under "Courier.") If you've worked with international couriers before, you won't be surprised to hear that, for any place farther away than Miami, "overnight" is usually a misnomer—shipments to most North American cities take two days, to Britain, three, and to Australia and New Zealand, four or five.

POSTAL RATES

Letters from **Costa Rica** to the United States and Canada cost the equivalent of U.S. 25¢, postcards to the United States 18¢; to the United Kingdom, letters cost 31¢, postcards 23¢; and to Australia or New Zealand, letters cost 33¢, postcards 30¢.

RECEIVING MAIL

You can have mail sent poste restante (*lista de correos*) to any Costa Rican post office. There is no house-to-house mail service—indeed, no house numbers—in Costa Rica; most residents pick up their mail at the post office itself. In written addresses, *apartado*, abbreviated *apdo.*, indicates a P.O. box.

Anyone with an American Express card or traveler's checks can receive mail at the American Express office in San José.

SHIPPING PARCELS

Packages can be sent from any post office, with rates spanning U.S. $6–$12 per kilogram and shipping time ranging from a week to a month, depending on destination. A quicker, more expensive alternative is United Parcel Service, which has offices in Costa Rica—prices are about 10 times what you'd pay at the post office, but packages arrive in a matter of days.

MONEY MATTERS

Here's an idea of the cost of living in Costa Rica: 750-milliliter (¾-liter) bottle of Coca-Cola, U.S. 65¢–95¢; cup of coffee, 50¢–95¢; bottle of beer, $1–$1.50; sandwich, $2–$3; daily U.S. newspaper, $1.25–$2.25. Prices throughout this guide are given for adults. Substantially reduced fees are almost always available for children, students, and senior citizens. For information on taxes, *see* Taxes, *below.*

ATMS

If you bring some cash (U.S. currency) with you and use ATMs, you can get by without traveler's checks. ATMs on the Plus system can be accessed at branches of the Banco Popular in Alajuela, Cartago, Heredia, Limón, Puntarenas, Quepos and half a dozen other cities. In San José, the main Banco Popular is at Avenida 2 and Calle 1, near the National Theater. Cash advances are also available in the Credomatic office, on Calle Central between Avenidas 3 and 5, or the Banco de San José, across the street, which also has an American Express office on the third floor. All offices of the Banco de San José (in Liberia, Puerto Limón, San Isidro, and other towns) have ATMs on the Cirrus system, and the bank has more than a dozen locations in San José, including the Centro Omni, one block north of the Gran Hotel Costa Rica.

CREDIT CARDS

Credit cards are accepted at most major hotels and restaurants in this book. As the phone system improves and expands, many budget hotels, restaurants, and other properties have begun to accept plastic; but plenty of properties, some in the expensive range, still require payment in cash. **Don't count on using plastic all the time**—once you venture outside San José **carry enough cash or traveler's checks** to patronize the many businesses without credit-card capability. Note that some hotels, restaurants, tour companies, and other businesses add a surcharge (around 5%) to the bill if you pay with a credit card, or give you a 5%–10% discount if you pay in cash.

Throughout this guide, the following abbreviations are used: **AE,** American Express; **DC,** Diner's Club; **MC,** MasterCard; and **V,** Visa.

➤ REPORTING LOST CARDS: **American Express** (☎ 0800/012–3211 collect to U.S.). **Diner's Club** (☎ 702/797–5532 collect to U.S.). **MasterCard** (☎ 0800/011–0184 toll-free to U.S.). **Visa** (☎ 0800/011–0030 toll-free to U.S.).

CURRENCY

All prices in this book are quoted in U.S. dollars.

The Costa Rican currency, the colón (plural: colones), is subject to continual, small devaluations. At press time, the colón had topped 350 to the dollar, 307 to the Euro, 219 the Canadian dollar, 187 to the Australian dollar, and 121 to the New Zealand dollar. Banks in Costa Rica won't change Australian or New Zealand dollars, so these currencies should be changed to U.S. dollars before arrival.

CURRENCY EXCHANGE

For the most favorable rates, **change money through banks or use local ATMs.** Although ATM transaction fees may be higher than at home, ATM rates are excellent because they are based on wholesale rates offered only by major banks. You won't do as well at exchange booths in airports, in hotels, in restaurants, or in stores, though their hours are often more convenient than those of the banks. To avoid surcharges and lines at airport exchange booths, you might want to **get a bit of local currency before you leave home.** But the cabbies at Costa Rica's international airport accept dollars and most hotels change them, so it's not necessary that you buy colones before you leave for Costa Rica.

Avoid people on the city streets who offer to change money. San José's outdoor money-changers are notorious for shortchanging people and passing counterfeit bills. The guys who change money at the airport aren't quite as shady, but they might not be above shortchanging you, and they don't offer great rates in any case.

➤ EXCHANGE SERVICES: **International Currency Express** (☎ 888/278–6628 for orders, WEB www.foreignmoney. com). **Thomas Cook Currency Services** (☎ 800/287–7362 for telephone orders and retail locations, WEB www. us.thomascook.com).

TRAVELER'S CHECKS

Do you need traveler's checks? It depends on where you're headed. If you're going to rural areas and small towns, go with cash; traveler's checks are best used in cities, and **it's best to ask if traveler's checks are accepted where you're lodging** when you make your reservations. Lost or stolen checks can usually be replaced within 24 hours. To ensure a speedy refund, buy your own traveler's checks— don't let someone else pay for them: irregularities like this can cause delays. The person who bought the checks should make the call to request a refund.

If you have an American Express card and can draw on a U.S. checking account, you can buy dollar traveler's checks at the American Express office in San José for a 1% service charge.

OUTDOORS AND SPORTS

BIKING

Costa Rica is a combination of mountainous terrain and cycle-friendly flatlands. A number of tour operators run bike tours. You can also rent bikes in most Costa Rican mountain and beach resorts.

➤ TOUR OPERATORS: **BiCosta Rica** (✉ Atenas, ☎ FAX 506/446–7585).

Coast to Coast (✉ San José, ☎ 506/ 280–8054). **Jungle Man Adventures** (✉ Hotel Don Fadrique, San José, ☎ 506/225–8186). **Río Escondido Mountain Bikes** (✉ Rock River Lodge, Tilarán, ☎ 506/695–5644).

BIRD-WATCHING

➤ TOUR OPERATORS: **Birding Club of Costa Rica** (✉ San Rafael, Heredia, Costa Rica, ☎ 506/267–7197). **Costa Rica Expeditions** (✉ San José, Costa Rica, ☎ 506/222–0333). **Horizontes** (✉ San José, Costa Rica, ☎ 506/ 222–2022).

CANOPY TOURS

If you not only want to see monkeys in Costa Rica but also want the perspective of one, **take a canopy tour.** Using rock climbing equipment, you slide along cables strung between treetops in the canopy. It's a unique experience that's easier to manage than you might think—even for the slightly fearful. (Children are not permitted.) One reputable company is The Original Canopy Tour, with branches in Monteverde, Tabacón (near Arenal), Drake Bay, and four other destinations. Their well-trained guides are bilingual and their safety record is good. **Don't go with the less-expensive competitors** unless you've acquainted yourself with their safety practices and feel comfortable; and **be prepared to walk away** if the trip doesn't look or feel professionally handled. It's still an unregulated business and many companies cut corners on safety to save a buck.

Sky Trek tours are similar to canopy tours, but may include suspension bridges, cable flights across valleys, and a hilltop tower (not necessarily located in the rain or cloud forest). Sky Walk tours are for those not necessarily up for the "Me Tarzan, you Jane" routine, with less strenuous canopy exploration options. (Older children are permitted.) Here you can tiptoe through the treetops on a series of six suspension bridges, which provide a monkey's-eye view of the aerial garden of the cloud-forest canopy. Get here early if you're into bird-watching.

➤ CANOPY TOUR CONTACTS: **The Original Canopy Tour** (☎ 506/257–

5149, WEB www.canopytour.com). **Sky Trek and Sky Walk** (☎ 506/645–5238, WEB www.skywalk.co.cr).

WATER SPORTS

Costa Rica is worth visiting for its water sports alone. Wild rivers churn plenty of white water for rafting, and Lake Arenal is one of the world's best places to windsurf. You can make skin-diving excursions from Drake Bay, Playa Flamingo, Playa Ocotal, and Playa del Coco, but Costa Rica's best dive spot, Cocos Island, can only be visited on a 10-day scuba safari on the *Okeanos Aggressor* or *Undersea Hunter.* Popular surfing beaches include Tamarindo, Jacó, Hermosa, and Dominical. Airlines generally allow surfboards on board for a nominal fee of around $15.

➤ DIVE OPERATORS—COSTA RICA: **Bill Beard's Diving Safaris** (✉ Playa Hermosa, ☎ 506/672–0012). **El Ocotal Diving Safaris** (✉ Playa del Ocotal, ☎ 506/670–0321). *Okeanos Agressor* (✉ Plaza Colonial, Escazú, ☎ 506/257–4948). *Undersea Hunter* (✉ ½ km (650 yards) north and 200 m (220 yards) west of Rosti Pollos, San Rafael de Escazú, ☎ 506/228–6535).

➤ RAFTING OUTFITTERS: **Aventuras Naturales** (✉ San Pedro, Costa Rica, ☎ 506/225–3939). **Costa Rica Expeditions** (✉ San José, Costa Rica, ☎ 506/222–0333). **Ríos Tropicales** (✉ San José, Costa Rica, ☎ 506/233–6455).

➤ WINDSURFING OUTFITTERS: **Tilawa** (✉ Lake Arenal, ☎ 506/695–5050, WEB www. windsurf-costarica.com).

PACKING

Pack light: Bring comfortable, hand-washable clothing. T-shirts and shorts are acceptable near the beach and in tourist areas; loose-fitting long-sleeve shirts and pants are good in smaller towns (where immodest attire is frowned upon) and to protect your skin from ferocious sun and, in some regions, mosquitoes. **Leave your jeans behind**—they take forever to dry and can't be worn out in the evenings like khakis. **Bring a large hat** to block the sun from your face and neck. **Pack a waterproof, lightweight jacket** and a light sweater for cool nights, early mornings, trips up volcanoes, and to the Atlantic coast; you'll need even warmer clothes for trips to Chirripó National Park or Volcán Baru and overnight stays in San Gerardo de Dota or La Providencia Lodge. Sturdy sneakers or hiking boots are essential for sightseeing on foot. Waterproof hiking sandals such as Tevas are good for boat rides, beach walks, streams (should you need to ford one), and light hiking trails. Bring at least one good (and wrinkle-free) outfit for going out at night. Costa Ricans tend to dress up a bit more than Americans. Remember to bring a small day-trip bag.

Insect repellent (if you're going to Tortuguero), sunscreen, sunglasses, and umbrellas (during the rainy season) are crucial. Women might have a tough time finding tampons, so bring your own. Other handy items—especially if you'll be roughing it—include toilet paper, facial tissues, a plastic water bottle, and a flashlight (for occasional power outages or inadequately lit walkways at lodges). **Don't forget binoculars** and a comfortable carrying strap. Snorkelers staying at budget hotels should consider bringing their own equipment; otherwise, you can rent gear at most beach resorts. If you're surfing, consider buying your board here; Tamarindo has a good shop. Some beaches, such as Playa Grande, do not have shade trees, so if you're planning to linger at the beach you might consider investing in a sturdy tarpaulin.

In your carry-on luggage, **pack an extra pair of eyeglasses or contact lenses and enough of any medication** you take to last the entire trip. You may also ask your doctor to write a spare prescription using the drug's generic name, since brand names may vary from country to country. In luggage to be checked, **never pack prescription drugs or valuables.** To avoid customs delays, carry medications in their original packaging. And don't forget to carry with you the addresses of offices that handle refunds of lost traveler's checks. Check *Fodor's How to Pack* (available in bookstores everywhere) for more tips.

CHECKING LUGGAGE

If you're flying from San José to any other domestic points in Costa Rica, the tiny, domestic passenger planes (seating about 6 to 12 people) require that you pack light. A luggage weight limit of 11.3 kilograms or 25 pounds (*including* carry-ons) is almost always enforced. For the same reason, two lighter bags are preferable to one heavy bag.

You are allowed one carry-on bag and one personal article, such as a purse or a laptop computer. Make sure that everything you carry aboard will fit under your seat or in the overhead bin. Get to the gate early, so you can board as soon as possible, before the overhead bins fill up.

If you are flying internationally, note that baggage allowances may be determined not by piece but by weight—generally 88 pounds (40 kilograms) in first class, 66 pounds (30 kilograms) in business class, and 44 pounds (20 kilograms) in economy.

Airline liability for baggage is limited to $2,500 per person on flights within the United States. On international flights it amounts to $9.07 per pound or $20 per kilogram for checked baggage (roughly $640 per 70-pound bag) and $400 per passenger for unchecked baggage. You can buy additional coverage at check-in for about $10 per $1,000 of coverage, but it excludes a rather extensive list of items, shown on your airline ticket.

Before departure, **itemize your bags' contents** and their worth, and label the bags with your name, address, and phone number. (If you use your home address, cover it so potential thieves can't see it readily.) Inside each bag, **pack a copy of your itinerary.** At check-in, **make sure that each bag is correctly tagged** with the destination airport's three-letter code. If your bags arrive damaged or fail to arrive at all, file a written report with the airline before leaving the airport.

PASSPORTS AND VISAS

When traveling internationally, **carry your passport** even if you don't need one (it's always the best form of ID) and **make two photocopies of the data page** (one for someone at home and another for you, carried separately from your passport). If you lose your passport, promptly call the nearest embassy or consulate and the local police.

AUSTRALIAN AND NEW ZEALAND CITIZENS

Citizens of Australia and New Zealand need only a valid passport to enter Costa Rica for stays of up to 30 days (and once you're here, you can go to the Migracion office in La Uruca and extend the visa to 90 days).

CANADIAN CITIZENS

Canadians need only a valid passport to enter Costa Rica for stays of up to 90 days.

U.K. CITIZENS

Citizens of the United Kingdom need only a valid passport to enter Costa Rica for up to 90 days.

U.S. CITIZENS

Although U.S. citizens technically do not need a valid passport to enter Costa Rica for stays of up to 30 days, the only alternative is to get a tourist card upon entry, which requires a photo ID and copy of your birth certificate. **Bring your passport**—for passage from Costa Rica into Panama or Nicaragua, for emergencies, for longer stays, and because it's an indisputable form of identification for changing currency, renting hotel rooms, and just about any other transaction. U.S. citizens with valid passports may stay in Costa Rica for 90 days, after which they must leave for at least 72 hours.

PASSPORT OFFICES

The best time to apply for a passport or to renew is in fall and winter. Before any trip, check your passport's expiration date, and, if necessary, renew it as soon as possible.

➤ AUSTRALIAN CITIZENS: **Australian Passport Office** (☎ 131–232, WEB www.dfat.gov.au/passports).

➤ CANADIAN CITIZENS: **Passport Office** (☎ 819/994–3500; 800/567–6868 in Canada, WEB www.dfait-maeci.gc.ca/passport).

➤ NEW ZEALAND CITIZENS: **New Zealand Passport Office** (☎ 04/494–0700, WEB www.passports.govt.nz).

➤ U.K. CITIZENS: **London Passport Office** (☎ 0870/521–0410, WEB www.ukpa.gov.uk) for fees and documentation requirements and to request an emergency passport.

➤ U.S. CITIZENS: **National Passport Information Center** (☎ 888/362–8668; $4.95 per call; must have credit card; WEB www.travel.state.gov/npicinfo.html).

SAFETY

Although crime is not a serious problem in Costa Rica, thieves can easily prey on tourists, so be alert and take precautions including: always roll up car windows and lock car doors when you leave your car, and keep windows rolled up and doors locked all the time in cities. Park in designated parking lots, or if that's not possible, accept the offer of men or boys who ask if they can watch your car while you are gone. Give them the equivalent of a dollar when you return. **Never leave valuables visible in a car.** Take them inside with you whenever possible, and if that's not possible, lock them in the trunk. Talk with locals or your hotel's staff about crime whenever you arrive in a new location. They will be able to tell you if it's safe to walk around after dark, and what areas to avoid.

Don't wear expensive jewelry or watches. Backpacks should be carried on your front. Likewise, wallets go in your front pocket. **Avoid carrying a waist or fanny pack,** which distinguishes you from the locals. The incapacitating drug Rohypnol is still afoot, and is being used on men and women, so never leave a drink unattended. When on a crowded bus, keep your hand on your wallet or your eyes on your purse. Never leave your belongings unattended anywhere, including at the beach or in a tent. Many hotel rooms have safes, which should be used (even if it's an extra charge). If your room doesn't have one, ask the manager to put your valuables in the hotel safe. Ask him or her to sign a list of what you put in the safe. Do not carry expensive cameras or much cash in cities.

Most importantly, **don't bring anything you can't stand to lose.**

Scams are common in San José, where a drug addict tells tales of having been recently robbed, then asks you for donations; a distraction artist squirts you with cream or chocolate sauce, then tries to clean you off while his partner steals your backpack; pickpockets and bag slashers work buses and crowds; and street money changers pass off counterfeit bills. To top it all off, car theft is rampant. Beware of anyone who seems overly friendly, aggressively helpful, or disrespectful of your personal space.

SENIOR-CITIZEN TRAVEL

Older travelers are flocking to Costa Rica, and many businesses are making an effort to cater to the specific comforts of this demographic. Some senior citizens may encounter more challenges to mobility than they do at home—especially on those muddy jungle trails—but should otherwise find Costa Rica most hospitable.

To qualify for age-related discounts, **mention your senior-citizen status up front** when booking hotel reservations (not when checking out) and before you're seated in restaurants (not when paying the bill). When renting a car, ask about promotional car-rental discounts, which can be cheaper than senior-citizen rates.

➤ EDUCATIONAL PROGRAMS: **Elderhostel** (✉ 11 Ave. de Lafayette, Boston, MA 02111-1746, ☎ 877/426–8056, FAX 877/426–2166, WEB www.elderhostel.org). **Interhostel** (✉ University of New Hampshire, 6 Garrison Ave., Durham, NH 03824, ☎ 603/862–1147 or 800/733–9753, FAX 603/862–1113, WEB www.learn.unh.edu/interhostel).

STUDENTS IN COSTA RICA

Although prices are on the rise, you can still travel on $25 to $30 a day if you put your mind to it. There are youth hostels and hotels affiliated with Hostelling International all over Costa Rica, though one of the cheapest ways to spend the night in this region is to camp; as long as you have your own tent, it's easy to set up house almost anywhere. Still, don't ever leave your belongings or a campfire unattended.

➤ IDS AND SERVICES: **STA Travel** (☎ 212/627–3111 or 800/781–4040, FAX 212/627–3387, WEB www.sta.com) for mail orders only, in the United States. **Travel Cuts** (✉ 187 College St., Toronto, Ontario M5T 1P7, Canada, ☎ 416/979–2406 or 888/838–2887, FAX 416/979–8167, WEB www. travelcuts.com).

STUDYING ABROAD

The University of Costa Rica has exchange programs with at least half a dozen American universities, the oldest of which is the University of Kansas program. Many private language institutes offer Spanish courses for college credit (☞ Spanish-Language Programs *under* Language).

TAXES

When you fly out of Costa Rica, you'll have to pay a $17 airport departure tax at Juan Santamaría Airport. (This fee may be going up to $21.) Although people may offer to sell it to you the moment you climb out of your taxi, it's best to **buy your exit stamp inside the airport**; look for airport-employee identification. If you buy elsewhere, you'll have no recourse if someone sells you fake stamps or gives you the wrong change or conversion rate.

VALUE-ADDED TAX

All Costa Rican businesses charge a 13% sales tax, and hotels charge an extra 4% tourist tax. Tourists do not get refunds on sales tax paid in Central American countries.

TELEPHONES

The Costa Rican phone system is very good by the standards of other developing countries. However, phone numbers change and are handed out willy-nilly and phone books are not updated regularly.

AREA AND COUNTRY CODES

The country code for Costa Rica is 506. There are no area codes. Phoning home: the country code for the United States and Canada is 001,

Australia 61, New Zealand 64, and the United Kingdom 44.

DIRECTORY AND OPERATOR ASSISTANCE

In Costa Rica, dial ☎ 113 for domestic directory inquiries and ☎ 110 for domestic collect calls.

INTERNATIONAL CALLS

Costa Rica's *guía telefónica* (phone book) lists the rates for calling various countries. To call overseas directly, dial 00, then the country code, the area code, and the number. Calls to the United States and Canada are discounted on weeknights between 10 PM and 7 AM and on weekends; calls to the United Kingdom are only discounted on weekends, from Friday at 10 PM to Monday at 7 AM.

It's cheapest to call from a pay phone using an international phone card, sold in shops; call from a pay phone using your own long-distance calling card; or call from a telephone office. Dialing directly from a hotel room is very expensive, as is recruiting an international operator to connect you.

LOCAL CALLS

Pay phones are abundant, though they always seem to be in use. Some phones accept coins; others require phone cards, which are sold in various shops.

LONG-DISTANCE SERVICES

AT&T, MCI, and Sprint access codes make calling long distance relatively convenient, but you may find the local access number blocked in many hotel rooms. First ask the hotel operator to connect you. If the hotel operator balks, ask for an international operator, or dial the international operator yourself. One way to improve your odds of getting connected to your long-distance carrier is to travel with more than one company's calling card (a hotel may block Sprint, for example, but not MCI). If all else fails, call from a pay phone.

➤ ACCESS CODES: **AT&T Direct** (☎ 0800/011–4114). **MCI WorldPhone** (☎ 0800/012–2222). **Sprint International Access** (☎ 0800/013–0123).

➤ TELEPHONE OFFICES: **Radiográfica Costarricense** (✉ Avda. 5 between Cs. 1 and 3), open weekdays 8 AM–7 PM and Saturday 8 AM–noon also has phone, fax, and Internet facilities.

PHONE CARDS

Costa Rica has two kinds of phone cards: domestic cards, which record what you spend, and international cards, which have codes that you have to punch into the telephone. Both cards are sold in an array of shops.

TIME

Costa Rica is in the Central Standard time zone, and observes Daylight Savings.

TIPPING

Restaurant bills include a 13% tax and 10% service charge—sometimes these amounts are included in prices on the menu, and sometimes they aren't. Additional gratuity is not expected, especially in cheap restaurants; but people often leave something extra when service is good. Leave a tip of about 50¢ per drink for bartenders, too.

In hotels, if you're not toting your bags to your room, tip the person who does $1; give more in $$$$ hotels. At the end of your stay, leave the equivalent of at least $2 per night for maid service.

At some point on a trip, most visitors to Costa Rica are in the care of a naturalist guide, who can show you the sloths and special hiking trails you'd never find on your own. **Give $10 per day to guides,** if they've transported and guided you individually or in small groups. Give less to guides on bigger tours, or if they're affiliated with the hotel or lodge where you're staying.

TOURS AND PACKAGES

Because everything is prearranged on a prepackaged tour or independent vacation, you spend less time planning—and often get it all at a good price.

For hundreds of out-of-the-ordinary tour options click on "Adventure" at www.fodors.com.

BOOKING WITH AN AGENT

Travel agents are excellent resources. But it's a good idea to collect brochures from several agencies as some agents' suggestions may be influenced by relationships with tour and package firms that reward them for volume sales. If you have a special interest, **find an agent with expertise in that area**; ASTA (☞ Travel Agencies, *below*) has a database of specialists worldwide.

Make sure your travel agent knows the accommodations and other services of the place he or she is recommending. Ask about the hotel's location, room size, beds, and whether it has a pool, room service, or programs for children, if you care about these. Has your agent been there in person or sent others whom you can contact?

Do some homework on your own, too: local tourism boards can provide information about lesser-known and small-niche operators, some of which may sell only direct.

BUYER BEWARE

Each year consumers are stranded or lose their money when tour operators—even large ones with excellent reputations—go out of business. So **check out the operator.** Ask several travel agents about its reputation, and try to **book with a company that has a consumer-protection program.** (Look for information in the company's brochure.) In the United States, members of the National Tour Association and the United States Tour Operators Association are required to set aside funds to cover your payments and travel arrangements in the event that the company defaults. It's also a good idea to choose a company that participates in the American Society of Travel Agents' Tour Operator Program (TOP); ASTA will act as mediator in any disputes between you and your tour operator.

Remember that the more your package or tour includes the better you can predict the ultimate cost of your vacation. Make sure you know exactly what is covered, and **beware of hidden costs.** Are taxes, tips, and transfers included? Entertainment and excursions? These can add up.

➤ TOUR-OPERATOR RECOMMENDATIONS: **American Society of Travel Agents** (☞ Travel Agencies, *below*). **National Tour Association** (NTA; ✉ 546 E. Main St., Lexington, KY 40508, ☎ 859/226–4444 or 800/682–8886, WEB www.ntaonline.com). **United States Tour Operators Association** (USTOA; ✉ 275 Madison Ave., Suite 2014 New York, NY 10016, ☎ 212/599–6599 or 800/468–7862, FAX 212/599–6744, WEB www.ustoa.com).

TRAIN TRAVEL

Costa Rica's train system has been defunct for years due to recurring earthquakes.

TRANSPORTATION
WITHIN COSTA RICA

The most common form of public transportation is the bus. All Costa Rican towns are connected by regular, inexpensive bus service. Buses are $5–$10 from the capital to Quepos and $5–$9 to Monteverde, for example, the more expensive being the *directo* (express) service rate. Buses between major cities are modern and air-conditioned, however, once you get into the rural areas, you may get the school-bus equilavent. Because buses can be a slow and uncomfortable way to travel, domestic flights are a desirable and practical option. Most major destinations are served by daily domestic flights, most costing a reasonable US$40–US$90 one way (round-trips are double the one-way fare). Renting a car gives you the most freedom, but rates can be expensive, especially since you'll probably (depending on where you're headed) need four-wheel drive.

TRAVEL AGENCIES

A good travel agent puts your needs first. Look for an agency that has been in business at least five years, emphasizes customer service, and has someone on staff who specializes in your destination. In addition, **make sure the agency belongs to a professional trade organization.** The American Society of Travel Agents (ASTA), with 24,000 agents in some 140 countries, is the largest and most influential in the field. Operating under the motto "Integrity in Travel," it maintains and enforces a strict code of ethics and will step in to help mediate any agent-client disputes if necessary. ASTA also maintains a Web site that includes a directory of agents. (If a travel agency is also acting as your tour operator, *see* Buyer Beware *in* Tours and Packages, *above*.)

➤ LOCAL AGENT REFERRALS: **American Society of Travel Agents** (ASTA; ☎ 800/965–2782 24-hr hot line, FAX 703/739–3268, WEB www.astanet.com). **Association of British Travel Agents** (✉ 68–71 Newman St., London W1T 3AH, U.K., ☎ 020/7637–2444, FAX 020/7637–0713, WEB www.abtanet.com). **Association of Canadian Travel Agents** (✉ 130 Albert St., Suite 1705, Ottawa, Ontario K1P 5G4, Canada, ☎ 613/237–3657, FAX 613/237–7502, WEB www.acta.ca). **Australian Federation of Travel Agents** (✉ Level 3, 309 Pitt St., Sydney NSW 2000, Australia, ☎ 02/9264–3299, FAX 02/9264–1085, WEB www.afta.com.au). **Travel Agents' Association of New Zealand** (✉ Box 1888, Wellington 6001, New Zealand, ☎ 04/499–0104, FAX 04/499–0827, WEB www.taanz.org.nz).

VISITOR INFORMATION

Instituto Costarricense de Turismo in San José staffs a tourist information office beneath the Plaza de la Cultura, next to the Museo de Oro. Pick up free maps, bus schedules, and brochures weekdays 9–12:30 and 1:30–5.

➤ COSTA RICA—U.S. AND CANADA: **Costa Rica Tourist Board** (☎ 800/343–6332).

➤ COSTA RICA—U.K.: **Costa Rica Tourist Services** (✉ 47 Causton St., London SW1P 4AT, ☎ 020/7976–5511, FAX 020/7976–6908).

➤ IN COSTA RICA: **Instituto Costarricense de Turismo** (ICT; ✉ C. 5 between Advas. Central and 2, Barrio del Catedral, San José, ☎ 222–1090, WEB www.tourism-costarica.com).

➤ U.S. GOVERNMENT ADVISORIES: **U.S. Department of State** (✉ Overseas Citizens Services Office, Room 4811

N.S., 2201 C St. NW, Washington, DC 20520, ☎ 202/647–5225 interactive hot line or 888/407–4747, WEB www.travel.state.gov); enclose a business-size SASE.

WEB SITES

Do check out the World Wide Web when planning your trip. You'll find everything from weather forecasts to virtual tours of famous cities. Be sure to **visit Fodors.com** (www.fodors. com), a complete travel-planning site. You can research prices, check out bargains, read late-breaking travel news, and book plane tickets, hotel rooms, rental cars, vacation packages, and more. In addition, you can post your pressing questions in the Travel Talk section. Other planning tools include a currency converter and weather reports, and there are loads of links to travel resources.

Start with www.costarica.tourism.co.cr and www.infocostarica.net/english for general information. For current events, check out the English-language Tico Times on-line at www.ticotimes. net and La Nación's English-language "supersite" www.incostarica.net. To explore nature-tour options, see the commercial sites at www.horizontes. com and www.expeditions.co.cr.

WHEN TO GO

The most popular time to visit Costa Rica is the dry season, which runs from mid-December through April. From mid-December until early February in particular, you have the combined advantages of good weather and lush vegetation. Of course, hotels are more likely to be full during this time of year, making advance planning all but essential; and some areas, especially Guanacaste, are dry and dusty by April, for lack of enriching rains.

In the rainy season, beaches are often wet in the afternoon but sunny and dry in the morning. Much of Costa Rica gets some sunny weather in July, August, and early September; and the Caribbean coast tends to enjoy a short dry season in September and October, while the Pacific slope is being drenched by daily storms.

To avoid crowds and high prices, come to Costa Rica in the rainy season, which is sometimes promoted as the "green" season. Green it is—the vegetation is lush and most gorgeous—but some roads, especially those without asphalt, are washed out, and require four-wheel drive and patience. Come in July or August, when the storms let up a bit, or mid-December, when the rains are tapering off but the high tourist season has yet to kick in. While some rural hotels shut down for the rainiest months, September and October, most stay open and have rooms to spare. You'll even have the beaches to yourself.

It can be useful to know that Costa Ricans call their dry season (mid-December–April) *verano* (summer), and the rainy season (May–mid-December) *invierno* (winter).

CLIMATE

Central America's climate varies greatly between the lowlands and the mountains. Tropical temperatures generally hover between 70°F and 85°F; high humidity, especially in the dense jungle of the Caribbean coast, is the true culprit in any discomfort. Guanacaste, on the more arid Pacific coast, is perhaps Costa Rica's hottest region, with frequent temperatures in the 90s during the dry season. Drink plenty of bottled water to avoid dehydration.

➤ FORECASTS: **Weather Channel Connection** (☎ 900/932–8437), 95¢ per minute from a Touch-Tone phone.

SAN JOSÉ

San José weather is typical of other highland towns.

Average daily high and low temperatures:

Jan.	75F	24C	May	80F	27C	Sept.	79F	26C
	58	14		62	17		61	16
Feb.	76F	24C	June	79F	26C	Oct.	77F	25C
	58	14		62	17		60	16
Mar.	79F	26C	July	77F	25C	Nov.	77F	25C
	59	15		62	17		60	16
Apr.	79F	26C	Aug.	78F	26C	Dec.	75F	24C
	62	17		61	16		58	14

GOLFITO

Positioned at sea level, Golfito has a climate similar to that of most coastal and lowland towns, such as Manuel Antonio, Jacó, Puntarenas, and most of Guanacaste.

Average daily high and low temperatures:

Jan.	91F	33C	May	91F	33C	Sept.	91F	33C
	72	22		73	23		72	22
Feb.	91F	33C	June	90F	32C	Oct.	90F	32C
	72	22		73	23		72	22
Mar.	91F	33C	July	90F	32C	Nov.	91F	32C
	73	23		72	22		72	22
Apr.	91F	33C	Aug.	90F	32C	Dec.	91F	33C
	73	23		72	22		72	22

1 DESTINATION: COSTA RICA

COSTA RICA: NATURE'S DISNEYLAND

High on the "must visit" lists of seasoned and armchair travelers, Costa Rica is riding a wave of well-deserved popularity as an ecological wonderland. Just a few years ago the whereabouts of the country, situated between Panama and Nicaragua in the Central American isthmus, would have been a moderately challenging question suitable for contestants on Jeopardy!™. Now, the mere mention of the country conjures up visions of rain forests, volcanoes, tropical beaches, and exotic wildlife. And it delivers on all these and more. For a country that's about the same size as the state of West Virginia, it's packed with incredible biological diversity, varied landscapes, and a seemingly endless selection of outdoor diversions, from bird-watching and beach trips to rigorous rafting and rain forest hiking trips.

Costa Rica's raw natural beauty and accessibility gives it a broad range of visitors. Some are "soft adventure" types, looking to explore the wildlife reserves within the country's exemplary system of national parks and perhaps the luxe hotels along the sun-drenched Pacific beaches. (It doesn't hurt that you can also drink the water straight from the tap.) However, the beaches might also be the stomping ground of more serious adventurers on a mission to surf some of North Americas best waters. Whichever type you are, and whether you visit the tropical jungles of the Caribbean coast or the modern cities of the Central Valley, or both, it's apparent that from nearly every angle the country is downright gorgeous. It seems no one is passing up the opportunity to see for themselves.

As full-time residents, Costa Ricans—or Ticos, as they call themselves—know just how good they have it. Fiercely proud of their history, culture, and achievements, Ticos are also a remarkably polite and accommodating people. They will go to great lengths to "quedar bien"—to leave a good impression, especially with foreigners, and are known throughout Latin America for their friendliness and willingness to be helpful. Many Costa Ricans, especially younger people who live in the Central Valley, speak English well,

and most visitors return to their home countries impressed with Ticos' warmth and hospitality.

History explains some of the reasons Costa Rica has managed to avoid the turmoil that has engulfed much of Central America in the last half century, and has achieved a higher standard of living than its neighbors. Never an important part of the Spanish empire, Costa Rica was largely neglected during the colonial era and experienced most of its growth after independence from Spain. It is consequently a nation of immigrants, who came to work and prospered. Although most Latin American countries remain dominated by families that were granted vast tracts of land by the Spanish Crown, Costa Rica is more of a workingman's republic. Most Ticos are middle class by Latin American standards, and are the descendents of independent small farmers. Ticos have a strong sense of national identity and pride themselves first on being Costa Ricans rather than Central Americans, or even Latin Americans.

The strife that rocked Central America during much of the past two decades painted a less-than-rosy picture of the area in the minds of most North Americans and Europeans, and people not well acquainted with Costa Rica often equate the problems in countries such as El Salvador and Nicaragua with all of the isthmus. In the midst of political unrest, Costa Rica managed to remain an island of stability and peace. The country has no army, for example—it was abolished in 1949. Costa Rica is also the region's most sturdy democracy, and the country has a deep-rooted respect for human rights. Ticos love to quote oft-repeated expressions about the country's achievements, such as "Costa Rica has more teachers than policemen" and "Why have tractors without violins?," among others. In education, for example, Costa Rica ranks with many developed countries (the literacy rate is about 93%). Its telecommunications system, although quirky by North American standards, is probably the best in the region, as is its health-care system.

The country's most impressive quality, however, is its biological diversity, seen in the variety of flora, fauna, landscapes, and microclimates within its frontiers. National parks and preserves cover about 15% of the country and are home to 850 species of birds, 205 species of mammals, 376 types of reptiles and amphibians, and more than 9,000 different species of flowering plants, among them 1,200 varieties of orchids. Landscapes include cool mountain valleys and massive volcanoes emitting tufts of smoke, hilly coffee *fincas* (farms) and flat banana groves, and sultry mangrove forests and palm-strewn beaches.

The many rivers that wind down the country's valleys churn through steep stretches that are popular white-water-rafting routes, and some end up as languid jungle waterways appropriate for both animal-watching and sportfishing. With mile upon mile of beaches backdropped by coconut palms and thick forest, the Caribbean and Pacific coasts are ideal for swimming and sunbathing, and when the sun goes down, many beaches are visited by nesting sea turtles. The oceans that hug those coasts hold intricate coral formations, rugged islands, colorful schools of fish, and plentiful waves, enticing anglers, surfers, and sea kayakers. What more could you want?

A BRIEF HISTORY

First Encounters

In mid-September 1502, on his fourth and last voyage to the New World, Christopher Columbus was sailing along the Caribbean coast of Central America when his ships were caught in a violent tropical storm. Seeking shelter, he found sanctuary in a bay protected by a small island; ashore, he encountered native people wearing heavy gold disks and gold bird-shape figures who spoke of great amounts of gold in the area. Sailing farther south, Columbus encountered more natives, also wearing pendants and jewelry fashioned in gold. He was convinced that he had discovered a land of great wealth to be claimed for the Spanish empire. The land itself was a vision of lush greenery; popular legend has it that, on the basis of what

he saw and encountered, Columbus named the land Costa Rica, the rich coast.

The Spanish Colonial Era

The first Spaniard to attempt conquest of Costa Rica was Diego de Nicuesa in 1506. But his sick and starving troops were not able to surmount the resistance of the indigenous population and the Spanish were unsuccessful. Similar hardships were encountered by other Spaniards who visited the region. The first "successful" expedition to the country was made by Gil González de Ávila in 1522. Exploring the Pacific coast, he converted more than 6,000 people of the Chorotega tribe to Catholicism. A year later he returned to his home port in Panama with the equivalent of $600,000 in gold, but more than 1,000 of his men had died on the exhausting journey. Of course, just as many native peoples, if not more, died due to disease and skirmishes with the Europeans. Many other Spanish expeditions were undertaken, and, fortunately for the people indigenous to the area, all were less than successful at colonization, often because of rivalries between various expeditions. By 1560, almost 60 years after its discovery, no permanent Spanish settlement existed in Costa Rica (this name was then in general use, although it incorporated an area far larger than its present-day boundaries), and the indigenous peoples had not been subdued.

Costa Rica remained the smallest and poorest of Spain's Central American colonies, producing little wealth for the empire. Unlike other countries around it, Costa Rica tended to be largely ignored in terms of conquest and instead began to receive a wholly different type of settler—hardy, self-sufficient individuals who had to work to maintain themselves. Costa Ricans, both settlers and native peoples, endured the difficult living conditions of an agriculture-based existence in exchange for Spain's lack of interest. The population stayed at fewer than 20,000 for centuries (even with considerable growth in the 18th century) and was mainly confined to small, isolated farms in the highland Central Valley and the Pacific lowlands.

By the end of the 18th century, however, Costa Rica began to emerge from isolation. Some trade with neighboring Spanish colonies was carried out—in spite of constant harassment by English pirates, both at sea and on land—and the population had begun to expand across the Central Valley.

Seeds of political discord, which were soon to affect the colony, had been planted in Spain when Napoléon defeated and removed King Charles IV in 1808 and installed his brother Joseph on the Spanish throne. Costa Rica pledged support for the old regime, even sending troops to Nicaragua in 1811 to help suppress a rebellion against Spain. By 1821, though, sentiment favoring independence from Spain was prevalent throughout Central America, and Costa Rica supported the declaration of independence issued in Guatemala on September 15 of that year. Costa Rica did not become a fully independent sovereign nation until 1836, after annexation to the Mexican empire and 14 years as part of the United Provinces of Central America. The only major threat to that sovereignty took place in 1856, when the mercenary army of U.S. adventurer William Walker invaded the country from Nicaragua, which it had conquered the year before. Walker's plan to turn the Central American nations into slave states was cut short by Costa Rican president Juan Rafael Mora, who raised a volunteer army and repelled the invaders, pursuing them into Nicaragua and joining troops from various Central American nations to defeat the mercenaries.

Foundations of Democracy

The 19th century saw dramatic economic and political changes in Costa Rica. For the major part of that century, the country was ruled by a succession of wealthy families whose grip was partially broken only toward the end of the century. The development of agriculture included the introduction of coffee in the 1820s and bananas in the 1870s, both of which became the country's major sources of foreign exchange.

In 1889 the first free popular election was held, characterized by full freedom of the press, frank debates by rival candidates, an honest tabulation of the vote, and the first peaceful transition of power from a ruling group to the opposition. This event provided the foundation of political stability that Costa Rica enjoys to this day.

During the early 20th century each successive president fostered the growth of democratic liberties and continued to expand the free public school system, started during the presidency of Bernardo Soto in the late 1880s. By the 1940s economic growth was healthy due to agricultural exports, but the clouds of discontent were again gathering. In 1948 the president, Rafael Angel Calderón Guardia, refused to hand over power after losing the election; the result was a civil uprising by outraged citizens, led by the still-revered José Figueres Ferrer. In a few short weeks the rebellion succeeded and an interim government was inaugurated.

New Beginnings

On May 8, 1948, Figueres accepted the position of president of the Founding Junta of the Second Republic of Costa Rica. One of his first acts was to disband the army, creating in its stead a national police force.

Significant changes took place during the 1950s and 1960s, including the introduction of social-welfare policies, greater expansion of the public school system, and greater involvement by the state in economic affairs. The early 1970s saw further growth, but then an economic crisis introduced Costa Ricans to hyperinflation. By the mid-1980s, Costa Rica had begun pulling out of its economic slump, in part thanks to efforts to diversify the economy, which had long been dominated by coffee and bananas. In 1994, tourism surpassed bananas as the country's largest earner of foreign exchange. Two years later, Intel opened a microchip assembly plant in the suburbs of San José, and other high-tech companies including Dell Electronics and Motorola also opened customer service call centers in Costa Rica, providing relatively well-paying jobs for educated, bilingual Ticos.

Recent years have seen the continued growth of the tourism industry, and the establishment of new industries, including thriving but controversial Internet-based gambling operations tied to U.S. sporting events. Still, inflation hovers around 12% annually, the per capita income in Costa Rica is only $3,300 per year, and the country's currency continues to be devalued on a regular basis.

Today the challenge facing Costa Rica is how to conserve its natural resources while still permitting modern development. Urban sprawl in the Central Valley, and the development of megaresorts along both coasts, threaten forests, wildlife, and the slower pace of life which makes Costa Rica so enjoyable for visitors. Although tourism provides a much-needed injection of foreign exchange into the economy, it has yet to be fully decided which direction it should take. The buzzwords now are "ecotourism" and "sustainable development," and it is hoped that Costa Rica will find it possible to continue down these roads rather than opt for something akin to the Acapulco or Cancún style of development.

WHAT'S WHERE

San José

In the shadow of emerald mountain slopes, in the middle of the country, Costa Rica's capital is the center of national political, cultural, and economic life. A third of Costa Rica's 4 million people live in San José, its surrounding suburbs, and the neighboring cities of Heredia, Alajuela, and Cartago. Urban sprawl in the last decade has led these formerly separate cities to merge with the outskirts of the capital or *chepe,* as locals call it. For a destination at more than 914 m (3,000 ft) above sea level, San José has a surprisingly pleasant climate for the capital of a tropical country.

The city has a varied cultural calendar and a handful of good restaurants offering cuisine from all over the world. Many of the city's upscale restaurants and charming bed-and-breakfasts are older homes and mansions. Shops here selling clothing and electronics, for example, don't really exist elsewhere in the country. (Try to take care of practical needs—including shopping, medical problems, and buying medicines—while you are here.) There are also several good museums, raucous bars, and discos. A stroll around downtown's lively plazas and parks, an evening at the symphony, or a visit to the University of Costa Rica in the San Pedro area will show you how Ticos live, play, and work. Most visitors spend only a day or two in the city before or after heading off to the mountains or beaches. Since the capital is the country's transportation hub, it's often nec-

essary to return to San José when traveling between destinations.

Central Valley: Around San José

The Meseta Central, or Central Valley, is a broad bowl planted with neat rows of coffee and dotted with traditional towns. The valley, which includes the capital and is the most densely populated region of the country, is surrounded by a ring of stunning volcanoes and mountains. Its altitude assures a pleasant mixture of warm days and cool nights; the upper slopes can often become quite cold. In the mountainous areas are active volcanic craters, luxuriant cloud forests, and some of the country's best hotels and restaurants, many with unforgettable vistas. This region includes the upscale suburbs of San José including Escazú and Heredia, where Costa Rica's wealthy have sprawling estates dotted with shimmering swimming pools and tropical fruit orchards. Heredia "The City of Flowers" and sunny Alajuela are smaller cities that are increasingly becoming bedroom communities of San José. So, too, is Cartago, the former colonial capital until 1823, and the site of a national pilgrimage that takes place each year in August.

Costa Rica's most accessible volcanoes, Poás and Irazú, define the valley's northern edge, and are two of the country's most visited destinations. To the east lies the smaller Orosi Valley, a coffee-growing region with historic monuments and lovely scenery, and the agricultural community of Turrialba, near which is the country's most important archaeological site, the Monumento Nacional Guayabo. The golden (coffee) bean forms the backbone of the Costa Rican economy, and the valley around San José is the heart of the industry.

Northern Guanacaste and Alajuela

If, having come to Costa Rica to get away from it all, you want to get farther away from it all, head to the country's untrammeled northwestern corner, where nature is pretty much untouched. Birds and birders flock here—up in the Monteverde Cloud Forest and the many other preserves and parks that grace the region, you can flesh out your life list with once-in-a-lifetime sightings. The accessible La Paz

Waterfall Gardens, with its colossal *cataratas* (waterfalls), and butterfly and hummingbird gardens, guarantees you'll see some beautiful wildlife. Down by the sea, at Santa Rosa National Park, the cast of characters is different, and the critter-watching not a jot less sublime. Volcanoes, too, loom large on the ethereal landscape: Lake Arenal sits in the shadow of the great Volcán Arenal, whose molten show, as long as the clouds are out of the way, will humble you. A stay at the Arenal Observatory Lodge will give you the closest views of smoke spirals and lava flows. Lake Arenal, in the shadow of the volcano, has winds that create conditions for some of the best windsurfing in the Americas. The beautifully landscaped Tabacón Resort, also near Arenal, makes for a relaxing day in the hot springs. The Caño Negro Wildlife Refuge, in the far north, lies in the migratory flyway of hundreds of thousands of birds. Northern Guanacaste and Alajuela—with a few notable exceptions including La Fortuna and Monteverde—is one of the least developed regions of the country, and thus one of the most authentic. Agriculture remains the dominant way of life, and what tourism there is focuses on nature.

Nicoya Peninsula

With world-class surfing at Playa Avellanas, the first-rate beach resorts of Tamarindo, and scads of nesting sea turtles, the Nicoya Peninsula is for many the best of all Costa Rican worlds. It's drier here than in the rest of the country, so when it's inconveniently rainy elsewhere, you can still get voluntarily wet in this sun-drenched region. One of the best places to submerge yourself is Playa Pelada, where the rocks create surreal snorkeling landscapes. Likewise, whoever named Playa Hermosa—Beautiful Beach—was telling it like it is. As for the coastal hotels, many large, all-inclusive beach resorts are increasingly focusing on golf, and many charter flights arriving at Liberia's tiny airport carry golf bags in their cargo holds. Private cabanas concealed in the forest are not too hard to come by, if it's solace you seek. For something a little more wild, visit the party town of Montezuma, near the private reserve Curú National Wildlife Refuge and Cabo Blanco Nature Reserve, Costa Rica's first protected area. The port city of Puntarenas, on the mainland, is the gateway to the Nicoya Peninsula—ferries leave almost

hourly. Once the most popular beach resort in Costa Rica, the seaside city has seen better days, but recent efforts to spruce it up have helped. Whether you surf, turtle-watch, or sightsee, Nicoya will keep you breezily occupied.

Central Pacific Coast

Some of the country's most popular destinations are in this region—from the surfing town of Jacó to gorgeous Manuel Antonio National Park, home to diminutive, endangered squirrel monkeys, sloths, iguanas, many birds, and three white-sand beaches. The glowing sunsets and sparkling water are reason enough to visit the coast, and every year brings new private reserves, dolphin-watching tours, swaying bridges suspended high in the forest canopy, and other nature-based attractions. Sea-kayaking, hiking, rafting, and horseback riding are all first class here, and the large number of tour operators running these activities means prices are competitive. The area is also known for its seafood, and menus are based around fresh-caught yellowfin tuna, dorado, and crustaceans. Quepos, a town adjacent to Manuel Antonio, lives off tourism, and has several discos, decent restaurants, and cheaper hotels. (Although during the lush and green May-to-November rainy season, prices in the chichi park area drop.) Just north, the surf town of Jacó is a young person's paradise with plenty of activity day and night. The most overdeveloped of all Costa Rican beach towns, Jacó is funky, fun, and unabashedly tacky, with casinos, discos, and bars for when sun goes down.

Southern Pacific Coast

Home to some of Costa Rica's wildest country, even by local standards, the Southern Pacific is perfect for those who like their settings heavy on outdoor beauty, hold the civilization. In the lush and enormous Corcovado National Park, hikers scamper past swamplands, jungle-thick riverbanks, unspoiled beaches, and heavenly virgin rain forest. If you want to bond with nature but don't fancy sleeping outdoors in it, make for one of the sybaritic lodges in the heart of the Osa Peninsula. A boat ride in Drake Bay, meanwhile, shows you the same rugged coastline that Sir Francis saw when he paid a call, and some of the country's most beautiful underwater scenery at Isla del Caño. Several luxurious lodges in Drake Bay cater to amateur naturalists, anglers, and scuba divers. Puerto Jiménez and Golfito are air transportation hubs, with a few hotels and restaurants, mostly catering to anglers and shoppers in the latter's duty-free zone. South of Golfito lie some of Costa Rica's most remote beaches including Playa Pavones and Playa Zancudo, which are also world-class surfing destinations, with a few less hedonistic lodges of their own.

Atlantic Lowlands and the Caribbean Coast

Northeastern Costa Rica marches more to Caribbean drummers than to the Central American rhythms of San José. You'll find reggae, johnnycakes, and fluent English-speakers in Puerto Limón. Natural sights explode here, both above and below sea level; experience both at Cahuita National Park, where you can snorkel or ride a glass-bottom boat around the coral reef or stroll the snowy-white, forest-edged beach. At Tortuguero National Park, majestic green sea turtles come ashore to nest, having beaten nature's ferocious odds to make it as far as adulthood; the park also hides crocodiles, manatees, and a host of other species. Rustic Barra del Colorado welcomes avid anglers. Inland and up in the clouds, the sprawling Braulio Carrillo National Park is the lush, comfortable home of still more plants and animals, and you can soar above them all in the Rain Forest Aerial Tram. While visitors to Costa Rica tend to favor the Pacific Coast, partly because the Atlantic has fewer luxury accommodations and a more unpredictable rainy season, biologists, backpackers, and budget travelers have realized that many of Costa Rica's most beautiful spots—and true bargains—are found here on the Atlantic.

PLEASURES AND PASTIMES

Archaeology

Though Costa Rica was never part of the Maya empire and has nothing to compare with the ruins of Guatemala and Mexico, Monumento Nacional Guayabo, a partially excavated and large ancient city (with around 20,000 inhabitants) cover-ing 49 acres, the country's only ruins, is worth a visit. It's surrounded by protected rain forest, on the slopes of Volcán Turrialba, and was abandoned about AD 1400. (It was discovered in 1968 when a local resident was walking her dog.) Abstract patterns carved on the stones continue to baffle archaeologists, although some clearly depict jaguars, which were revered as deities. A guided tour (in Spanish only) takes visitors through the ruins. In general, Costa Rica artifacts—including pottery, techniques for building dwellings, tools, and jewelry—show both South American and Mesoamerican influences, due to the country's strategic position at a crossroads between several trading empires. The gold, jade, ceramics, and stonework created by the area's ancestral people can also be admired at several San José museums.

Bird-watching

Many of Costa Rica's creatures are named after their homes: for example, the wild turkey–like Highland Tinamou, the melodious Riverside Wren, or the Volcano Hummingbird. You may be surprised to encounter a Canadian Warbler, Baltimore Oriole, or Kentucky Warbler—some of the 200 North American birds found in Costa Rica. Some species stay year-round and others come and go during the winter migration. In addition to the tourist species, Costa Rica also has the requisite tropical birds, including six kinds of toucans, 16 parrots and parakeets, and more than 50 hummingbirds. Other tropical groups, such as ant birds, are well represented. The birds of Costa Rica represent close to 10% of the total species in the world.

Dining

While it's possible to order everything from sushi to crepes in Costa Rica, most Ticos have a simple but delicious diet built around rice, beans, and the myriad fruits and vegetables that flourish here. Costa Rican food isn't spicy, and many dishes are seasoned with the same five ingredients—onion, salt, garlic, cilantro, and red bell pepper. Specialties include *arroz con pollo* (chicken with rice), *ensalada de palmito* (heart of palm salad), *sopa negra* (black bean soup), *gallo pinto* (rice with black beans for breakfast), and *casados* (plates of rice, beans, fried plantains, salad, cheese, and fish, chicken, or meat). *Sodas*—inexpensive restaurants comparable to diners—offer these choices for lunch and dinner. The Pacific Coast areas are known for seafood including corvina, a sea bass, yellowfin tuna, dorado, and mahimahi. Other dishes include *arroz con mariscos* (fried rice with fish, shrimp, octopus, and clams), lobster and *langostino* (like a lobster but smaller), and ceviche, a raw fish appetizer made from fresh corvina and lots of lime juice—the lime juice actually "cooks" the fish. Most bars serve bocas ("mouthfuls") with drinks, in the same tradition as Spanish tapas, which may include small portions of fried chicken, *carne en salsa* (meat stewed in a tomato sauce), or ceviche. Don't be surprised if you see men slurping down raw turtle eggs in tomato juice; they're believed to increase sexual potency.

When you can, take advantage a *fresco natural*, a fresh-squeezed fruit drink (including carrot, orange, mango, star fruit, and more) that's inexpensive by North American standards. Coffee—which in the countryside may come heavily presweetened—is usually served with steamed milk, if you order it *con leche*. For dessert, *tres leches*, a sinfully rich cake of condensed and evaporated milk and sugar, or flan, a caramel-flavor custard, are customary. Make sure you try some of the native fruits colorfully displayed at open-air stands along the highway. *Mamones chinos* are red spiky balls protecting a white fruit similar to a lichi, guavas are huge bean pods containing large seeds covered in sweet white pulp, and tart green mangoes cut into slivers and served with salt are a local favorite.

Fishing

Costa Rica is a freshwater and saltwater angler's dream. Marlin, sailfish, tuna, and dorado abound in the Pacific and fishing folk fill the Golfito-area fishing lodges all the way up the coast in search of them. Tarpon and snook are the highlights of the Caribbean and its lodges. The Barra del Colorado River is in the heart of the rain forest (and gets more than 200 inches of annual rainfall) and the best fishing is from December to early May, as well as late July to late August. *Guapote* (sea bass), catfish, and *gaspar* (alligator gar) can also be caught here. Lake Arenal, in the northern central part of the country, has many rainbow bass and gaspar, and several mountain lodges offer trout fishing in

tumbling streams. Good fishing is also found in the Río Frío, which passes through Los Chiles near Nicaragua. Tarpon, snook, white drum, gar, and other species bite here. You can fish from the municipal dock in Los Chiles or rent a *panga* (small boat) driven by a local guide. At press time, a full day of deep-sea fishing costs about $975 and a half day about $575.

Horseback Riding

Because horseback riding remains a common form of transportation in rural Costa Rica, you can ride just about everywhere. Experienced equestrians should be pleased with the frisky spirit of some Costa Rica horses. But even if you can't remember when you were last in the saddle, exploring a bit of the countryside on horseback is recommended. Horses can be rented in most of the popular beach towns and mountain resorts, and guided trail rides often head to waterfalls, scenic overlooks, and other landmarks that you might otherwise not see. The most interesting places to ride are the many farms and ranches that have been converted to nature lodges, several of which border national parks. Several companies in Monteverde, Montezuma, and other towns offer overnight horseback trips, which involve camping. Costa Rican *criollos*, a small, sturdy and extremely surefooted breed used for roping cattle, is the most common rental horse. Many criollos are gaited and thus very comfortable to ride. Large Americans and Europeans are often too big for criollos—if your feet are within a foot and a half of the ground, ask for a larger horse.

Lodging

Costa Rica has accommodations to fit every taste and budget, from modern luxury resorts complete with golf courses to rustic nature lodges with private cabanas surrounded by jungle. Away from cities, hotels in small towns and rural areas aim to be more than just a place to rest your head for the night. Many have nature preserves with hiking trails, butterfly gardens, hot-springs spas, private beaches, and adventure tours. Some employ resident guides who are experts in local flora and fauna and lead interpretive trips. Although most visitors stay a night or two in the capital, the most interesting places to stay are not in San José, although there are some charming colonial homes that have been

GOING FISHING?

IF YOU'VE COME ALL THIS WAY to fish, you won't be out of luck. Costa Rica teems with a constant supply of *pescado* (fish), some of which might seem unique to North Americans. Below are some local catches and where you'll find them.

Gaspar (alligator gar), found in Barra del Colorado river and Lake Arenal, look like a holdover from prehistoric times and have a long narrow snout full of sharp teeth; they make great sport on light tackle. Gar meat is firm and sweet (some people say it tastes like shrimp), but the fish's eggs should never be eaten because they are toxic to humans.

Guapote (rainbow bass) make their home in Lake Arenal, a man-made and beautiful 35-km-long (22-mi-long) lake with views of the Arenal volcano. It's a hard-hitting catch, though; 5- to 6-pounders are common. Taxonomically, guapote are not related to bass, but are caught similarly, by casting or flipping plugs or spinner bait. It's difficult to fish from the shore at Lake Arenal; area hotels and tour operators can arrange boats. Alternatively, lodges offering trout fishing are near the Cerro de la Muerte, off the Pan-American Highway leading south from San José. The streams are stocked, and the fish tend to be small. However, the scenery in this area makes a day spent here worthwhile.

Marlin and sailfish migrate northward through the year, beginning about November when they are plentiful in the Golfito region. From December into April they spread north to Quepos, which has some of the country's best deep-sea fishing, and are present in large numbers along Nicoya Peninsula at Carrillo and Sámara from February to April, and near Tamarindo and Flamingo, from May to September. Pacific Ocean sailfish average over 45 kilos (100 pounds), and are usually fought on a 15-pound line or less. Costa Rican laws require that all sails, except record catches, are released. Sportfishing operators run full-service charters out of the towns mentioned above, and all of the country's travel agencies and larger hotels can arrange fishing trips.

Tarpon and snook fishing is big on the Caribbean coast, centered at the mouth of the Barra del Colorado River, which hosts several world-renowned fishing lodges. The acrobatic tarpon, which averages about 85 pounds here, is able to swim freely between saltwater and freshwater and is considered by many to be the most exciting catch on earth. Tarpon sometimes strike like a rocket, hurtling 5 m (16 ft) into the air, flipping, and twisting left and right. Anglers say the success rate of experts is to land about one out of every 10 tarpon hooked. In the Colorado, schools of up to 100 tarpon following and feeding on schools of small, sardinelike fish called *titi* travel for more than 160 km (100 mi) to Lake Nicaragua. Tarpon are in greatest abundance just outside the river mouth, but are also present on the river itself, and in its backwaters and lagoons. Snook also make the long swim up the Barra del Colorado River following the titi. The long-standing International Game Fishing Association all-tackle record was taken in this area.

converted to elegant and mid-price-range inns. (Neighboring Escazú and Heredia have several upscale inns with excellent restaurants, which overlook coffee farms and are near the airport.)

Around the country are wonderful hotels and lodges (some with or without modern amenities) that also have a Central American flavor. Price tends to depend not just on amenities or the size of room or cabin, but upon how remote a property is and whether meals, activities, and tours are included. The Costa Rican government recently adopted a rating system that awards from one to five leaves based on ecological and social criteria. A guide to the program is available from the Costa Rica Tourism Institute (Instituto Costarricense de Turismo).

Rain Forests

The lowland rain forests of Costa Rica and the rest of the New World tropics are the most complex biological communities that exist. A typical hectare (2½ acres) of Costa Rican rain forest might be home to nearly 100 species of trees, for example— 30 is typical in the richest forests of the United States. In addition to trees, you'll see giant rain forest versions of orchids, epiphytes and other plants common to U.S. households, as well as sloths, monkeys, copious birds, and more.

Good places for hiking are Braulio Carrillo National Park, near San José which contains rain forest and cloud forest, and the hot and humid rain forest in La Selva Biological Station. On the Pacific coast, Corcovado National Park and Marenco Wildlife Refuge have well-maintained— but muddy and steep—trails where you can meander for hours through impressive primary forests. Filled with giant strangler figs and dripping with moss, Monteverde's private reserve is a good places to hike through primeval cloud forests. Even a quick walk through Manuel Antonio on the way to the beach will reveal all kinds of wildlife. For a closer look at the canopy, ride the Rain Forest Aerial Tram, near the Guápiles Highway or, for an adventurous angle, take a canopy tour. Whenever possible, it's best to walk or hike with a local guide—a good one will point out plants and animals you will surely miss if you go on your own, and will explain the complex interactions between flora, fauna, and climate.

Shopping

Many of the colorful goods sold in Costa Rica are actually made in Guatemala, Nicaragua, or Panama, but some local crafts are still practiced. Featured in many art forms, the oxcart is the national symbol of Ticos' hardworking, self-reliant character and rural roots. The brightly painted wooden carts come in all dimensions—from the size of a matchbook to life-size. Sarchí, in the Western Central Valley, is one of the country's centers for crafts and carpentry, and the art of making oxcarts here has been passed down through generations. In addition, Sarchí's artisans work native hardwoods into bowls, boxes, toys, platters, and jewelry. Stores in this small town, and many in San José, will ship your purchase anywhere in the world.

In the capital, art galleries near the downtown Parque Morazón and the northern suburb of Moravia have the best shopping. Popular items sold in both districts include wood-framed mirrors in the shape of toucans and other forest creatures, bamboo mobiles of tropical fish, and leather rocking chairs. Also in San José, the outdoor crafts market beside the Museo Nacional is a fun place to browse, although most items here are overpriced. A good place to buy gifts is the Annemarie Souvenir shop inside the Hotel Don Carlos, in downtown San José, near the National Library. The two-story store has everything from local music CDs to hand-painted ceramic tiles. Coffee and rum make good gifts, and you can save money by buying them in a supermarket. Most tourists buy Café Britt, however, Volio and Café Rey Tarrazú are much cheaper and almost as good. As for rum, look for Ron Centenario or better still, the Nicaraguan brand, Flor de Caña.

Snorkeling and Scuba Diving

The options for observing marine life range from simple snorkeling sessions off the beach near your hotel to a full-fledged scuba-diving safari. Several dive schools in San José offer PADI open-water diving courses for about $375. Some beach hotels will allow noncertified divers to use scuba equipment for shallow dives of 15 m (49 ft) or less. Underwater excursions are available from several Caribbean beach towns, from Puerto Viejo to Gandoca-Manzanillo Wildlife Refuge, which borders Panama, and from Limón to Isla Uvita. The

Caribbean is clearest in October and November, when visibility can reach 30 m (100 ft). Pacific excursions depart from the southern zone's Drake Bay, and Flamingo, Ocotal, and Playa del Coco in the northern province of Guanacaste.

The Pacific Coast has less colorful coral but more big animals, such as manta rays, sea turtles, and even whale sharks. The best Pacific diving spot is Isla del Caño, near Drake Bay. The snorkeling is excellent around the rocky points that flank spots called Bajo del Diablo and Paraiso, where you are guaranteed to encounter thousands of big fish. Lodges in Drake Bay offer day trips. The country's largest reef, which has been severely damaged but still has plenty to admire, is now protected within the Parque Nacional Cahuita. The northwest is a popular diving area, too, with dozens of dive spots around Santa Catalina, which can be visited from the area's resorts.

Costa Rica's best dive spot, Cocos Island, can only be visited on 9- or 10-day scuba trips. Two live-aboard dive boats, the *Okeanos Aggressor* and the *Undersea Hunter,* take experienced divers to this remote, spectacular destination 600 km (375 mi) southwest of the mainland. Waters at Cocos Island teem with eight shark species including hammerheads and whale sharks, and a host of other marine life including mantas.

Surfing

Though Costa Rica is now one of the world's most popular surfing destinations, the waves—from the radical, experts-only reef break at Puerto Viejo on the Atlantic Coast to the mellower waves off the town of Tamarindo on the Pacific—remain relatively uncrowded. The water is deliciously warm on both coasts and there are good waves year-round.

The Central Pacific is the most popular surfing destination because it's closest to San José and offers plenty of diversity. The party town of Jacó has a fun beach break, is home to some of Costa Rica's best surfers, and has several surf shops and ding repair facilities. Surfers often use Jacó as a base for trips to other area beaches south of Jacó, like Playa Hermosa, with a long beach and surfing competitions, and less-crowded Playa Panama. Near Puntarenas, the sand spit at the mouth of the Barranca River produces one of the world's longest left-breaking waves, although the water here is quite polluted.

About a dozen popular surf spots are scattered along the coast to the south of Tamarindo. Because Tamarindo has an excellent surf shop and many hotels and restaurants, it's frequently a base for surfers as they sample area beaches: Playas Langosta, Avellanas, and Negra. Playa Avellanas is a favorite weekend destination of Tico surfers, and has eight different surf spots ranging from beach breaks to rock-reef breaks to river-mouth sandbar breaks. A spectacular and well-known break is Witches Rock at Playa Naranjo, inside Parque Nacional Santa Rosa. Getting here requires a boat ride or long, bumpy journey over a rutted dirt road, but the reward is worth the trip.

Those willing to make the journey to Pavones and Matapalo, on Costa Rica's southern Pacific coast, will get to ride some of the world's longest waves. Dominical has also long drawn surfers to its consistent beach breaks, and a surf shop here rents, sells, and repairs surfboards. Though Costa Rica's short Atlantic coast has few surf spots, Puerto Viejo's Salsa Brava is one of the country's best breaks. The water starts deep and runs quickly onto a shallow reef, forming some seriously huge waves.

Volcanoes

Molten lava and incandescent rocks regularly spill out of Costa Rica's most spectacular volcano, Volcán Arenal, making it and others incredibly popular attractions. Seven of the country's 100 or so volcanoes are still active today. Near San José, paved roads run right to the summit of Poás and Irazú volcanos, which are also two of Costa Rica's most visited national parks. Volcán Irazú, Costa Rica's highest at 3,753 m (12,313 ft), last erupted on the day of U.S. President John F. Kennedy's visit in 1963. Ash showers followed by rain left the Central Valley covered in black soot and sludge for months. Dormant Volcán Barva, in the southern section of Braulio Carrillo National Park north of San José, is cloaked in cloud forest, has two crater lakes, and spectacular scenic overlooks as rewards for a steep all-day hike to the summit.

Nothing in Costa Rica rivals the sheer mass and power of Volcán Arenal, which is often ringed with an ominous haze by day. At night, you can see red hot molten lava oozing from the cone, a flirtatious dance with disaster. In August 2000, an eruption sent poisonous gases spilling down the eastern side of the mountain, killing a tour guide from San José and two tourists from Texas who were watching from a supposedly safe distance. Geologists who scrutinized the area after the tragedy found the popular Tabacón hot-springs resort and a camping area to be in a high-risk zone, but this hasn't stopped visitors from flocking to them. The government has since posted warning signs at the hot springs and various other points around the volcano. Not quite as active, the steaming crater at Rincón de la Vieja National Park, also in the country's northern zone, is worth the hard hike to get to it. In the park, steaming fumaroles bubble on the ground, and a cold river collides with a warm sulfur spring to provide excellent swimming.

White-Water Rafting

Wild rivers provide plenty of water for rafting in Costa Rica, where a half dozen Olympic kayak teams spend the winter and white-water enthusiasts flock from all over the globe. More than 20 rafting companies offer single and multiday trips marked by gorgeous scenery, a variety of difficulty levels, and year-round warm water. The largest companies, Ríos Tropicales, Costa Rica Expeditions, and Adventuras Naturales, observe rigorous safety standards and treat the country's rivers with the respect they deserve. The country's rafting center is Turrialba, a hospitable, medium-size town on the banks of the Reventazón River and home to many of the country's best rafting guides and kayakers. The Reventazón and nearby Pacuare rivers are the most popular because they have exciting runs and are close enough to San José for a day trip. Several La Fortuna operators, near Volcán Arenal, also offer Class III and IV white-water trips on the Río Peñas Blanca and Río Toro. The narrow shape of these rivers requires the use of special, streamlined U.S.-made boats that seat four people and go very fast. Nearby, the tamer Sarapiquí River is also gorgeous, and several rafting companies use it for half-day trips through verdant rain forest and tranquil towns. Near Quepos, rafting companies run three white rivers—the Parrita, Naranjo,

and Savegre—that have rather limited seasons. Starting in San Isidro in southern Costa Rica, the country's longest white-water run is the Río General, a rousing raft or kayak trip that includes long stretches of flat water.

Wildlife

Costa Rica covers less than 0.03% of the earth's surface but contains nearly 4% of the planet's animal species. The country is home to more than 100 kinds of bats, 4 species of monkeys, 6 kinds of wild cats, and more than 870 bird species—more bird species than are found in the United States and Canada combined. Many of the animals, including sloths, poison dart frogs, toucans, and monkeys with prehensile tails are found only in the American tropics. This abundance of wildlife is due in part to the country's geographical position on a land bridge between North America and South America. South American monkeys and sloths met North American squirrels and raccoons in the tropical forest canopy, making Costa Rica a unique animal habitat.

Insects—while not most people's favorites—are important for rain forest ecology, and their interactions with plants are fascinating. Leaf-cutter ants, found marching methodically through the forest, don't eat the leaves they carry back to their nests; their food is a fungus they cultivate on the leaves. Flitting around Costa Rica are more than 2,000 species of butterflies, including the huge and incandescent blue morpho. The country's many enclosed butterfly gardens, some of which export live pupae to butterfly exhibits in North America and Europe, offer visitors the chance to see them up close and learn about their life cycles. Five of the world's seven species of sea turtles nest in Costa Rica, including the green, leatherback, loggerhead, Olive Ridley, and hawksbill. More than 30 of the world's 80 species of dolphins, whales, and porpoises inhabit Costa Rican waters, and tour companies near the south Caribbean Gandoca Manzanillo National Wildlife Refuge and in the Central Pacific beach town of Quepos offer dolphin- and whale-watching excursions.

Visitors to Costa Rica may be frustrated by the difficulty of seeing mammals in the wild. Forests with dense foliage combined with the animals' skittish nature and excellent camouflage make them hard to see. Come expecting a National Geographic–style safari and you surely will be disappointed. Realistically, you can expect to see coatis (a long-nose, long-tailed relative of the raccoon), monkeys, and perhaps a sloth or agouti (largish rodent). The majority of the country's mammals are bats; including bats that eat fruit, insects, fish, and even other bats. White bats, a giant bat with a wingspan of ½ m (2 ft), and two species of vampire bats (one for birds and one for mammals) live in Costa Rica. Sightings of large mammals, including wildcats and tapirs, are extremely rare. On the plus side for most people, you probably won't see any of Costa Rica's 18 species of poisonous snakes either. (Snakes will always try to flee unless cornered or protecting a nest.) As you move through the country, you will have continuous opportunities to see wildlife. It's mostly a matter of luck, although talking with locals, and hiring local guides, will increase your chances of being at the right place at the right time.

Windsurfing

Champion windsurfers have called Costa Rica's Lake Arenal one of the world's top five windsurfing spots. The man-made lake, which has spectacular view's of the country's most active volcano, is 35 km (22 mi) long and the water temperature averages 23° C (73° F) from December to April. Unusually stable winds average 40 kph (25 mph); windsurfers typically sail one sail all day. Tilawa Marina and windsurfing center on the lake rents equipment, offers all levels of lessons, and has rescue boats. The best windsurfing spots are in the north and northwest sides of the lake. Coto Lake, a small, remote lake just north of Arenal, also offers excellent windsurfing conditions during the same months.

Bolaños Bay, in Guanacaste near the border with Nicaragua, is the place for ocean windsurfing, with winds as strong and consistent as Arenal's. However, the closed bay combined with side-onshore winds makes this a very safe spot. Conditions for windsurfing are best from November to April. Bolaños Bay Resort caters to windsurfers, offers lessons, and rents boards and sails. Also near the border with Nicaragua, the beautiful beaches and good windsurfing spots Cuajiniquil and Puerto Soley have tranquil waters with direct offshore

winds during the December-to-April dry season. Farther south, Tamarindo and Playa Flamingo also have good windsurfing conditions. Ocean windsurfing is not very popular in Costa Rica, so windsurfers should bring their own equipment unless they are staying near Bolaños Bay.

FODOR'S CHOICE

Dining

Ambrosia, San José. Fifteen minutes from downtown, this eclectic restaurant has long been popular among local epicureans thanks to its delicious inventions. $$$

The Garden, Puerto Viejo de Talamanca. Chef-owner Vera Mabon's Indian-Canadian-Trinidadian background inspires sophisticated Costa Rican fusion cooking. $$–$$$

Nogui's (Sunrise Café), Tamarindo. Local expats swear by this scruffy little joint, saying Nogui's langostino (small lobster) is the best in Guanacaste. Hearty American-style breakfast is also served. $$–$$$

Café Mundo, San José. From its lovely old wooden house in historic Barrio Amón, this popular café serves pastas, salads, meat and seafood dishes at reasonable prices. The pastries are to die for. $$–$$$

Chubascos, Volcán Poás. It's a winning combination: brisk mountain air, delicious refrescos, green surroundings, and platters packed with traditional Costa Rican taste treats. $$

Miss Edith, Cahuita. The outrageous Caribbean menu includes a variety of vegetarian dishes and herbal teas that owner Miss Edith claims will cure whatever ails you. $$

Lodging

Bosque del Cabo, Cabo Matapalo. The rustic and yet world-class bungalows (love the garden showers) afford breathtaking views of the ocean, and the lodge's nonstop activities in and around the private nature reserve make a hum-drum vacation unlikely. $$$$

Hotel Punta Islita, Guanacaste, Nicoya Peninsula. Overlooking the Pacific, this isolated resort offers comfortable rooms, splendid views, good food, and abundant peace and quiet. $$$$

Lapa Ríos, Cabo Matapalo. Perched on a ridge in a private rain forest reserve, with views of the surrounding jungle and the ocean beyond, Lapa Ríos is a small hotel that brings you close to nature without skimping on the amenities. $$$$

La Mariposa, Manuel Antonio. Set high on a promontory, this elegant Spanish-style villa and series of private bungalows mixes luxury, tranquility, and the best view in Manuel Antonio. $$$$

Villa Caletas, Tárcoles. Each of these exquisite bungalows on a forested promontory seems to enjoy a better view than the next. The scenery and isolation are only enhanced by the architecture, interior design, and cuisine. $$$$

Xandari, Alajuela. Whether you fix your vision on the clever design of the spacious villas or just watch birds and butterflies flit through the surrounding tropical gardens, its hard not to be enchanted by this unique inn and spa. $$$$

Le Bergerac, San José. Deluxe rooms and extensive gardens have long kept this quiet, friendly hotel a notch above the competition, and the presence of L'Ile de France, one of the city's best restaurants, makes it that much more compelling.$$$

Grano de Oro, San José. Built at the turn of the 20th century, this pink wooden house is now one of the capital's finest hotels, with interior gardens, a sundeck, and a first-class restaurant. $$$$

Hotel Capitán Suizo, Tamarindo. Many consider this Swiss-run gem the finest beachfront lodging in Guanacaste. Its lush gardens provide a wonderful sense of seclusion not far from Tamarindo's resort-town amusements and gorgeous beach. $$$–$$$$

Sueño del Mar, Playa Langosta. A sweet little Mexican-style B&B, with Balinese outdoor showers, fantastic breakfasts, charming gardens, and a perfect beach, sleeps just a handful for an intimate getaway. It can also accommodate a larger gathering of family or friends. $$$–$$$$

Fonda Vela, Monteverde. Built with local hardwoods, these spacious rooms have plenty of windows, the better to enjoy the surrounding forest and distant Gulf of Nicoya. The restaurant serves food to match the view. $$$

Hotel Aranjuez, San José. Lush gardens, abundant common areas, hearty breakfasts, and low prices make this little B&B in the quiet Barrio Aranjuez a real bargain. $$

Natural Wonders

Guayabo National Monument, Turrialba. More of an archaeological wonder, Guayabo was once home to 20,000 people. This ancient city was abandoned in the 15th century, and lay undiscovered until 1968.

Jungle rivers. Slip into the rain forest the old-fashioned way. Adventures range from heart-stopping paddles down the hair-raising rapids of the Pacuare to lazy navigation of Caribbean canals or Pacific estuaries. With luck you'll spot a roseate spoonbill, purple gallinule, howler monkey, crocodile, or caiman along the way.

Pacific sunsets. There's something about the cloud formations, colors, and settings that makes these exemplary crepuscular productions. Flocks of frolicking, diving pelicans, scarfing up sardines, often add foreground action.

Volcán Arenal erupting at night. Arenal's perfectly conical profile dominates the southern end of a lake, and thrills onlookers with regular incendiary performances. (Check safety conditions at this active volcano before going.)

Outdoor Activities

Bird-watching on the Osa Peninsula. If you already own a few field guides, then you've probably planned your trip with our feathered friends in mind. If you don't, sign up for a tour, borrow some binoculars, and get up at dawn—you won't regret your search for a keel-billed toucan or red-rump tanager.

Monkeying around on an Original Canopy Tour, Monteverde. Do as the monkeys, and swing from tree to tree on a canopy tour, with locations in Monteverde and around the country. With mountain climbing gear fastening you in, you'll have a perspective of the Costa Rican rain forest from the top down.

Soaking in the Tabacón hot springs. From the Tabacón Resort's gorgeously landscaped hot-springs streams, you can soak away your cares and take in views of magnificent and rumbling Volcán Arenal. Check safety conditions at this active volcano before going.

GREAT ITINERARIES

On the Crater's Edge
5–7 days

Don't spend much time in San José—instead quickly head to the Central Valley and one of the luxe resorts. In the morning go for a hike up to the crater lakes at Volcán Barva, or take a high-altitude horseback ride. Continue exploring the western Central Valley, spending the morning at Volcán Poás, or go as far as the majestic and active Volcán Arenal, stopping en route for a soak at Tabacón hot springs. After a night in this area, return to San José for a flight to a Pacific Coast beach resort, like Tamarindo or Manuel Antonio National Park, or a remote jungle lodge, and spend the rest of your time here.

A Walk in the Clouds
7 days

From San José head to one of the Central Valley inns for a night or two to acclimatize to Costa's Rica's *pura vida*—the good life—philosophy. Then head to La Paz Waterfall Gardens en route to Volcán Arenal. Spend a night or two in the area, take a hike, a white-water rafting trip on the Sarapiquí, or a bird-watching boat trip through Caño Negro Wildlife Refuge. Then continue to Monteverde Cloud Forest and consider a canopy tour. Via San José, make for the Drake Bay area for snorkeling or sportfishing or the gorgeous and remote Osa Peninsula for jungle living, allowing two nights. End your trip with a relaxing stint on the beach—choose the upscale beach areas of Tamarindo or Manuel Antonio National Park, or one of the less-touristed areas along the Pacific. Note that you can buy one-way tickets back to the capital, if your coastal destination changes.

A Caribbean Caper
9 days

Follow the Walk in the Clouds itinerary, and when you've returned to San José from your beach stay, fly to the rustic Caribbean Coast, a beautiful and less-developed area, which feels more like Jamaica than Costa Rica. Base yourself near Tortuguero and visit Tortuguero National Park. Look for green sea turtles coming ashore to nest and other marine wildlife. If time is not an issue, anglers should head north to Barra del Colorado; others should head south for a Cahuita National Park, for snorkeling or a ride in a glass-bottom boat around the coral reef. Return to Tortuguero for a flight back to the capital.

2 SAN JOSÉ

Most trips to Costa Rica begin and
end in its capital, San José, center for
transportation, commerce, and cultural
attractions. From San José you can explore
nearby coffee-producing towns in the
Central Valley and points beyond: drive to
the top of a volcano, raft white-water rapids,
or zoom out to a Pacific Ocean island.

S HADY PARKS, QUIET MUSEUMS, LIVELY PLAZAS, and a cobblestone pedestrian boulevard that cuts through downtown make
up for the city's less impressive attributes—its disproportionate
share of potholes, traffic jams, and unimpressive gray office blocks that
dominate the downtown grid. Fortunately, many of San José's older
neighborhoods and its more affluent suburbs are downright charming. Some 1 million Ticos (as Costa Ricans call themselves) live and
work in the greater metropolitan area, where such urban activities as
fine dining and nightlife exist alongside such urban problems as petty
crime and exhaust fumes.

Updated
by George
Soriano

Downtown San José is a mere 40-minute drive from verdant, tranquil
countryside. The city stands in a broad, fertile bowl at an altitude of
more than 914 m (2,998 ft) bordered to the southwest by the jagged
Cerros de Escazú (Escazú Hills), to the north by Volcán Barva (Barva
Volcano), and to the east by lofty Volcán Irazú. In the dry season (mid-
December–April), these green uplands are almost never out of sight,
and during rainy-season afternoons they're usually enveloped in cloudy
mantles. Temperatures ranging from 15°C to 26°C (59°F to 79°F) create cool nights and pleasant days. The rainy season lasts from May to
December, though mornings during this time are often sunny and brilliantly clear.

San José was founded in 1737 and replaced nearby Cartago as the capital of Costa Rica in 1823, shortly after the country won independence
from Spain. San José grew relatively slowly during the following century, as revenues from the coffee and banana industries financed the
construction of stately homes, theaters, and a trolley system that was
later abandoned. The city mushroomed after World War II, when
many old buildings were razed to make room for cement monstrosi-
ties, and it eventually sprawled to the point of connection to nearby
cities. Industry, agribusiness, the national government, and the international diplomatic corps are headquartered here, and all the institu-
tions required of a capital city—good hospitals, schools, the country's
main university, theaters, restaurants, and nightclubs—flourish in close
quarters.

Pleasures and Pastimes

Dining

Costa Rican specialties include *arroz con pollo* (chicken with rice), *ensalada de palmito* (heart-of-palm salad), *sopa negra* (black-bean soup),
gallo pinto (rice with black beans), and *casados* (plates of rice, beans,
fried plantains, salad, cheese, and fish or meat). Take advantage of the
plato del día (plate of the day), a cheap lunch special that often includes
a main course, *fresco natural* (fresh fruit drink), soup, and dessert. The
most popular fish on Tico menus is *corvina*, a white flaky fish, which
is usually breaded and panfried or sautéed with garlic. Tico food is often
mild, but the capital has a smorgasbord of international restaurants,
should you need some variety. You might also want to try one of the
superlative Central Valley restaurants west of the city.

CATEGORY	COST*
$$$$	over $20
$$$	$10–$20
$$	$5–$10
$	under $5

per person for main course at dinner.

Excursions

San José's central position in the Central Valley, and its relative proximity to both the Pacific coast and the mountains, invite day trips—you can be out in the countryside in just 20 to 30 minutes. The Central Valley is a boon for quick outdoor adventures, among them treks to waterfalls and volcanoes, horseback tours on private ranches, mountain hikes, and white-knuckle rafting excursions down the Sarapiquí, Reventazón, and Pacuare rivers. Most tours will pick you up at your San José hotel and drop you off the same day.

Festivals

Every other year the two-week Festival Internacional de las Artes brings dancers, theater groups, and musicians from Costa Rica and elsewhere to a dozen city venues in late March. The Festival de Coreógrafos is a dance festival held each December, and the Festival Internacional de Música enlivens July and August. A carnival parade heads down Avenida 2 every December 26, and a horse parade gets under way December 27. During Semana Universitaria (University Week), usually in April, students at the University of Costa Rica put their studies on hold to concentrate on drinking and dancing. The Día de la Virgen de Los Angeles honors Costa Rica's patron saint every August 2 with processions and a well-attended mass. On the eve of this holiday, nuns, athletes, families, and friends walk *la romaría*, a 22-km (14-mi) trek along the highway from San José to Cartago.

Lodging

San José packs every kind of accommodation, from luxury to bare necessity. You'll find massive hotels with all the modern conveniences and amenities, historic buildings with traditional architecture, a convenient location, but fewer creature comforts, and smaller establishments with the simplicity (and prices) beloved of backpackers. Dozens of former homes in the city's older neighborhoods, such as Barrio Amón, Barrio Otoya, and surrounding towns such as San Pedro, have been converted to moderately priced bed-and-breakfasts.

CATEGORY	COST*
$$$$	over $90
$$$	$50–$90
$$	$25–$50
$	under $25

for a double room, excluding service and tax (16.4%)

EXPLORING SAN JOSÉ

Costa Rica's capital is laid out on a grid: *avenidas* (avenues) run east and west, while *calles* (streets) run north and south. Avenidas north of the Avenida Central have odd numbers, and those to the south have even ones. On the western end of the city, Avenida Central becomes Paseo Colón; on the eastern end, at about Calle 31, it becomes an equally busy, though nameless, four-lane boulevard. Calles to the east of Calle Central have odd numbers; those to the west are even. This would be straightforward enough, except that Costa Ricans do not use street addresses. They rely instead on an archaic system of directions that makes perfect sense to them but tends to confuse foreigners. A typical Tico address could be "200 m (218 yards) north and 50 m (54 yards) east of the post office." The key to interpreting such directions is to keep track of east and west, and remember that a city block is 100 m (109 yards) long.

Beyond the block and street level, downtown San José is divided into numerous *barrios* (neighborhoods), which are also commonly cited in directions. Some barrios are worth exploring; others you'll want to avoid.

Barrio Amón and Barrio Otoya, northeast of the town center, are two of the city's oldest sections; some of their historic buildings are being transformed into charming hotels. Los Yoses and Barrio Escalante, east of downtown, are basically residential neighborhoods with some nice restaurants and galleries, and a few B&Bs. San Pedro, another pleasant area even farther east, is the home of the University of Costa Rica and numerous youth-oriented bars and restaurants.

San José's northwest quarter (everything west of Calle Central and north of Avenida 3) is a very different story. Called the Zona Roja, or red-light district, it's a rough area, frequented by prostitutes and alcoholics, and is best avoided unless you're headed to one of the bus companies there, in which case you should take a taxi. Much of the city's southern half—south of Avenida 4 between Calles Central and 14—is equally undesirable. If you follow Avenida Central west to where it becomes Paseo Colón, you'll enter an affluent area, with plenty of restaurants, cinemas, and hotels. The farther west you head, the more exclusive the neighborhoods become. Escazú, in the hills west of San José, is a traditional town that has become a favorite among U.S. expatriates. Surrounding neighborhoods are packed with relatively upscale, U.S.-style restaurants and a few cozy inns.

Most museums, shops, and restaurants are within walking distance of each other. If you're headed for a far-flung spot, or need to get from one end of the city to another, grab a taxi—they're abundant and inexpensive (U.S. $3–$4 for most trips). On the whole, San José is a relatively safe city, but a growing influx of tourists has resulted in an increase in the number of thieves to prey on them, such as bag and backpack slitters, pickpockets, and distraction artists who usually work in pairs—one person hassles you, or sprays something on you and helps you clean it off, while his or her partner gets your purse, wallet, backpack, camera, and so on. Make sure you keep a photocopy of your passport and a list of credit-card phone numbers in your luggage, and never leave anything in an unguarded car.

Numbers in the text correspond to numbers in the margin and on the San José map.

Great Itineraries

San José has several interesting museums and theaters, more shops than you can shake a credit card at, and pleasant sidewalk amenities like newsstands and ice cream vendors. If you're here during the rainy season, head out to the countryside in the morning and return to the city to shop and visit museums in the afternoon.

IF YOU HAVE 1 DAY
Devote day one to exploring San José. Wander down the Avenida Central mall, pop into the Teatro Nacional and the Catedral Metropolitana, and visit the Museo Nacional, Museo de Oro, or Museo de Jade.

IF YOU HAVE 3 DAYS
After you've surveyed the sights on the walking tour, on the morning of day two, you should get out of the capital. Some nearby sights include a visit to La Paz Waterfall Gardens, INBio parque, or tour the Café Britt coffee plantation in Heredia in the Central Valley, saving the afternoon for shopping. (☞ *See* Chapter 3.) On day three you'll want to head up a volcano, take a trip to the rain forest and aerial tram near Santa Clara, or explore the historic Orosí Valley southeast of town. The moderately adventurous should consider a white-water rafting trip on the Class III and IV rapids of the Río Pacuare (thrilling, but not so thrilling as to induce heart failure), with swimmable warm water and spectacular scenery.

Downtown San José

A Good Walk

Start at the eastern end of the **Plaza de la Cultura** ①, where wide stairs lead down to the **Museo de Oro** ②, whose gold collection deserves a good hour or two. Next to the museum entrance, pop into the Instituto Costarricense de Turismo (ICT tourist office) for a free map, bus schedule, and brochures. Wander around the bustling plaza and slip into the **Teatro Nacional** ③ for a look at the elegant interior and perhaps a cup of coffee in the lobby café. Leaving the theater, you'll be facing west, with the city's main eastbound corridor, Avenida 2, to your left. Walk 1½ blocks west along Avenida 2 to the **Parque Central** ④ and **Catedral Metropolitana** ⑤. Cross Avenida 2 and head north one block on Calle Central to Avenida Central, where you should turn left and follow the pedestrian zone to the small plaza next to the **Banco Central** ⑥. Continue west along the pedestrian zone to the **Mercado Central** ⑦, and shop or browse at your leisure. Head back east two blocks on the Avenida Central pedestrian zone, then turn left on Calle 2, and walk one block north to the green-and-gray stuccoed **Correos** ⑧, the central post office. From there, return to Avenida Central and walk east along the mall back to the Plaza de la Cultura.

From the eastern end of the Plaza de la Cultura, near the Museo de Oro, walk two blocks east on Avenida Central, turn left onto Calle 9, walk one block north, turn right, and slither halfway down the block to the **Serpentario** ⑨, which has an interesting collection of creepy crawlers. Turn left when you leave and head 1½ blocks west on Avenida 1 and one block north to **Parque Morazán** ⑩. Walk across the park— be careful crossing busy Avenida 3—and walk along the yellow metal school building to shady **Parque España** ⑪. On the north side of the park, on Avenida 7, is the modern Instituto Nacional de Seguros (INS) building, whose 11th-floor **Museo de Jade** ⑫ has an extensive American-jade collection and great city views.

From the INS building, continue east on Avenida 7 two blocks, passing the Cancilleria, or Foreign Ministry, and the Embajada de México (Mexican Embassy) on your left; then turn right on Calle 15 and walk a block south to the corner of **Parque Nacional** ⑬. Take a look at the Monumento Nacional at the center of the park, and then head two blocks south to the entrance of the **Museo Nacional** ⑭, housed in the old Bellavista Fortress. On the west side of the fortress lies the terraced **Plaza de la Democracia** ⑮; from here you can walk west down Avenida Central to return to the Plaza de la Cultura.

TIMING

This walk can take an entire day if you pause to absorb each museum and monument and stop to shop here and there. You can, however, easily split the tour in half: see all the sights west of the Plaza de la Cultura (①–⑧) one day and the remaining places (⑨–⑮) on another. Every stop on this tour is open Tuesday to Friday; if you're here on Monday or a weekend, check the hours listed below to make sure the sights you want to see are open.

Sights to See

❻ **Banco Central** (Central Bank). Outside the western end of Costa Rica's unattractive, modern federal reserve bank are 10 sculpted figures of bedraggled *campesinos* (peasants). The small, shady plaza south of the bank is popular with hawkers, money changers, and retired men, and can be a good place to get a shoe shine and listen to street musicians. Beware: the money changers here are notorious for circulating counterfeit bills and using doctored calculators to shortchange unwitting tourists. ⊠ *Between Avdas. Central and 1 and Cs. 2 and 4, Barrio La Merced.*

❺ Catedral Metropolitana (Metropolitan Cathedral). To the east of the park stands this not terribly interesting neoclassic structure, built in 1871, with a corrugated tin dome; inside, however, the cathedral has patterned floor tiles and framed polychrome bas-reliefs. The interior of the small chapel (Sagrario) on the cathedral's north side is even more ornate than the cathedral itself, but it's usually closed. Masses are held throughout the day on Sunday starting at 6 AM. ⊠ *Between Avdas. 4 and 2 and Cs. Central and 1, Barrio La Catedral,* ☎ *221–3820.* ⊙ *Weekdays 6 AM–noon and 3–6 PM, Sun. 6 AM–9 PM.*

❽ Correos (Central Post Office). The handsome, carved exterior of the post office, dating from 1917, is hard to miss among the bland buildings surrounding it. There's a display of first-day stamp issues upstairs, from where you can see the loading of *apartados* (post-office boxes) going on below: Ticos covet these hard-to-get boxes, as the city's lack of street addresses makes mail delivery a challenge. A small café on the first floor of the Correos overlooks the bustling pedestrian boulevard and a small park shaded by massive fig trees. Behind the park is the marble facade of the exclusive, members-only Club Unión. The large building behind the Correos is the Banco Nacional, a state-run bank. ⊠ *C. 2 between Avdas. 1 and 3, Barrio La Merced.* ⊙ *Weekdays 8– 6:30, Sat. 8–noon.*

❼ Mercado Central (Central Market). This block-long melting pot is a warren of dark, narrow passages flanked by stalls packed with spices (some purported to have medicinal value), fish, fruit, flowers, pets, and wood and leather crafts. You'll also see dozens of cheap restaurants and snack stalls, including the country's first ice cream vendor. Be warned: the concentration of shoppers makes this a hot spot for pickpockets, purse snatchers, and backpack slitters. ⊠ *Avdas. Central and 1 and Cs. 6 and 8, Barrio La Merced.* ⊙ *Mon.–Sat. 6–6.*

NEED A
BREAK?

Ice cream is an art in this country, and after a long walk on crowded sidewalks, it may just save your sanity. The crème de la cream is dished out by two prolific chains, Pop's and Wall's (formerly Mönpik). You'll find a **Pop's** on Avenida Central between Calles 11 and 13. Everyone loves the mango. There are two **Wall's** on Avenida Central, one at Calle 6 and one at Calle Central. Beware the blue *pitufo* (Smurf) flavor but do try the *trits*, a chocolate-swirl sandwich with a crumbly cookie crust.

★ **⓬ Museo de Jade** (Jade Museum). This is the world's largest collection of American jade—that's "American" in the hemispheric sense. Nearly all the items on display were produced in pre-Columbian times, and most of the jade dates from 300 BC to AD 700. In the spectacular Jade Room, pieces are illuminated from behind so you can appreciate their translucency. A series of drawings explains how this extremely hard stone was cut using string saws with quartz-and-sand abrasive. Jade was sometimes used in jewelry designs, but it was most often carved into oblong pendants. The museum also has other pre-Columbian artifacts, such as polychrome vases and three-legged metates (small stone tables for grinding corn), and a gallery of modern art. The final room on the tour has a startling display of ceramic fertility symbols. ⊠ *11th floor of INS building, Avda. 7 between Cs. 9 and 11, Barrio Carmen,* ☎ *223–5800 or 223–2584.* ⊡ *$5.* ⊙ *Weekdays 8:30–3.*

★ **❷ Museo de Oro** (Gold Museum). The dazzling, modern museum of gold, in a three-story underground building, contains the largest collection of pre-Columbian gold jewelry in Central America—20,000 troy ounces

San José

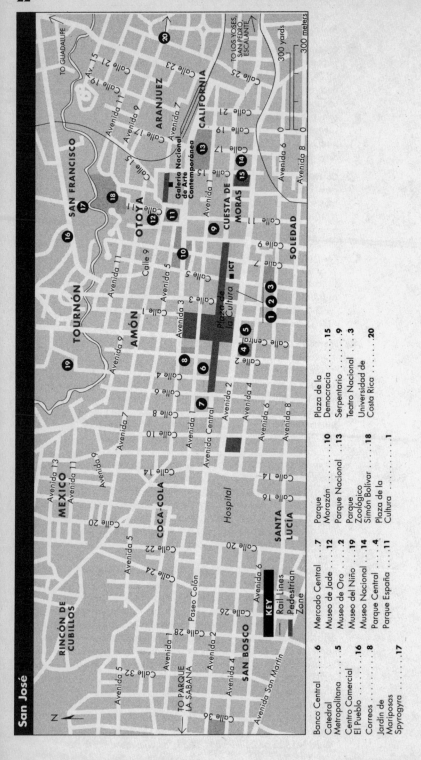

KEY
— Rail Lines
— Pedestrian Zone

Banco Central **6**
Catedral
Metropolitana ...**5**
Centro Comercial
El Pueblo **16**
Correos **8**
Jardín de
Mariposas
Spyrogyra **17**

Mercado Central ...**7**
Museo de Jade ...**12**
Museo de Oro ...**2**
Museo del Niño ...**19**
Museo Nacional ...**14**
Parque Central ...**4**
Parque España ...**11**

Parque
Morazán **10**
Parque Nacional ...**13**
Parque
Zoológico
Simón Bolívar ...**18**
Plaza de la
Cultura **1**

Plaza de la
Democracia **15**
Serpentario ...**9**
Teatro Nacional ...**3**
Universidad de
Costa Rica **20**

in more than 1,600 individual pieces—all owned by the Banco Central. Many pieces are in the form of frogs and eagles, two animals perceived by the region's pre-Columbian cultures to have great spiritual significance. Most spectacular are the varied shaman figurines, which represent the human connection to animal deities. ⊠ *Eastern end of Plaza de la Cultura, Barrio La Catedral,* ☎ *243–4202.* ⚟ *$5.* ☉ *Tues.–Sun. 10–4:30.*

⑭ Museo Nacional (National Museum). Set in the whitewashed colonial interior of the Bellavista Fortress, dating from 1870, the National Museum gives you a quick and insightful lesson in Costa Rican culture from pre-Columbian times to the present. Glass cases display pre-Columbian artifacts, period dress, colonial furniture, and photographs. Outside are a veranda and a pleasant, manicured courtyard garden. A former army headquarters, this now-tranquil building saw fierce fighting during the 1948 revolution, as the bullet holes pocking its turrets attest. ⊠ *C. 17 between Avdas. Central and 2, Barrio La Catedral,* ☎ *257–1433.* ⚟ *$5.* ☉ *Tues.–Sun. 8:30–4:30.*

❹ Parque Central (Central Park). Technically the city's nucleus, this simple tree-planted square has a gurgling fountain and cement benches. In the center of the park is a spiderlike, mango-color gazebo donated by former Nicaraguan dictator Anastasio Somoza. Several years ago a referendum was held to decide whether to demolish the despot's gift, but Ticos voted to preserve the bandstand for posterity. Across Avenida 2, to the north, stands the **Teatro Melico Salazar,** San José's second major performance hall (after the Teatro Nacional). The fast-food outlet between the two was once a major movie theater. ⊠ *Between Avdas. 2 and 4 and Cs. 2 and Central, Barrio La Catedral.*

⑪ Parque España. This shady little park is one of the most pleasant spots in the capital. A bronze statue of Costa Rica's Spanish founder, Juan Vasquez de Coronado, overlooks an elevated fountain on its southwest corner; the opposite corner has a lovely tiled guardhouse. A bust of Queen Isabel of Castile stares at the yellow compound to the east of the park—once a government liquor factory, this is now the **Centro Nacional de la Cultura** (National Center of Culture). Covering a double block, the complex houses the Ministry of Culture, two theaters, and the extensive **Museo de Arte y Diseño Contemporáneo** (Museum of Contemporary Art and Design), which hosts changing exhibits of work by artists and designers from all over Latin America. To the west of the park is a two-story, metal-sided school made in Belgium and shipped to Costa Rica in pieces more than a century ago. The yellow colonial-style building to the east of the modern INS building is the **Casa Amarilla,** home of Costa Rica's Foreign Ministry. The massive ceiba tree in front, planted by John F. Kennedy and the presidents of all the Central American nations in 1963, gives you an idea of how quickly things grow in the tropics. A few doors east is the elegant Mexican Embassy, once a private home. ⊠ *Between Avdas. 7 and 3 and Cs. 11 and 17, Barrio del Carmen.*

⑩ Parque Morazán. Anchored by a neoclassic bandstand, the largest park in downtown San José is somewhat barren, though the tabebuia trees on its northwest corner brighten things up when they bloom in the dry months. Avoid the park late at night, when a rough crowd and occasional muggers appear. Along the southern edge are a public school and two lovely old mansions, both with beautiful facades—one is a private home, the other a prostitute pickup bar. There's a park annex with a large fountain to the northeast, across busy Avenida 3, in front of the metal school building. ⊠ *Avda. 3 between Cs. 5 and 9, Barrio del Carmen.*

★ ⑬ **Parque Nacional** (National Park). A bronze monument commemorating Costa Rica's battle against American invader William Walker in 1856 forms the centerpiece of this large and leafy park. The park paths are made of cobblestone rescued from downtown streets and tall trees shading concrete benches often hide colorful parakeets in their branches. The modern pink building west of the park houses the Registro Público (National Registry) and the Tribunal Supremo de Elecciones (Electoral Tribunal), which keep track of voters and oversee elections. The tall gray building to the north is the Biblioteca Nacional (National Library), beneath which, on the western side, is the **Galería Nacional de Arte Contemporánea,** a small gallery exhibiting the work of contemporary artists, mostly Costa Rican. Quality varies, but since admission is free, it's always worth taking a peek. The walled complex to the northwest is the Centro Nacional de Cultura. Across from the park's southwest end is the Moorish **Asamblea Legislativa** (Legislative Assembly), where Costa Rica's congress meets. Next door is the Casa Rosada, a colonial-era residence now used for Congressional offices, and behind that is a more modern house used by the government for parties and special events. One block northeast of the park is the former Atlantic Railway Station. The park is best avoided at night, despite ample lighting and security patrol. ⊠ *Between Avdas. 1 and 3 and Cs. 15 and 19, Carmen district.*

★ ❶ **Plaza de la Cultura.** This large cement square surrounded by shops and fast-food restaurants is somewhat sterile, but it's a nice place to feed pigeons and buy some souvenirs. It's also a favored performance spot for local marimba bands, clowns, jugglers, and colorfully dressed South Americans playing Andean music. The stately **Teatro Nacional** dominates the plaza's southern half, and its western edge is defined by the venerable Gran Hotel Costa Rica with its 24-hour Café Parisienne. ⊠ *Between Avdas. Central and 2 and Cs. 3 and 5, Barrio La Catedral.*

⑮ **Plaza de la Democracia.** President Oscar Arias built this terraced open space west of the Museo Nacional to mark 100 years of democracy and to receive dignitaries during the 1989 hemispheric summit. The view west toward the dark-green Cerros de Escazú is nice in the morning and fabulous at sunset. The plaza is dominated by a statue of José "Pepe" Figueres, three-time president and leader of the 1948 revolution. Along the western edge jewelry, T-shirts, and crafts from Costa Rica, Guatemala, and South America are sold in a string of stalls. ⊠ *Between Avdas. Central and 2 and Cs. 13 and 15, Catedral district.*

🖐 ❾ **Serpentario** (Serpentarium). Don't be alarmed by the absence of motion within the display cases here—the inmates are very much alive. Most notorious in this collection of snakes and lizards is the terciopelo, responsible for more than half the poisonous snakebites in Costa Rica. The menagerie includes boa constrictors, Jesus Christ lizards, poison dart frogs, iguanas, and an aquarium full of deadly sea snakes, as well as such exotic creatures as king cobras and Burmese pythons. ⊠ *Avda. 1 between Cs. 9 and 11, Barrio del Carmen,* ☎ *255–4210.* 🎟 *$6.* ☉ *Weekdays 9–6, weekends 10–5.*

★ ❸ **Teatro Nacional** (National Theater). Easily the most enchanting building in Costa Rica, the National Theater stands at the southwest corner of the Plaza de la Cultura. Chagrined that touring prima donna Adelina Patti bypassed San José in 1890, wealthy coffee merchants raised import taxes to hire Belgian architects to design this building, lavish with cast iron and Italian marble. The sandstone exterior is marked by Italianate arched windows, marble columns with bronze capitals, and statues of strange bedfellows Ludwig van Beethoven (1770–1827) and

17th-century Spanish golden-age playwright Pedro Calderón de la Barca (1600–81). The Muses of Dance, Music, and Fame are silhouetted in front of an iron cupola. Given the provenance of the building funds, it's not surprising that frescoes on the stairway inside depict coffee and banana production. The theater was inaugurated in 1897 with a performance of Gounod's *Faust*, featuring an international cast. The sumptuous neo-Baroque interior sparkles thanks to an ongoing restoration project. The theater closes occasionally for rehearsals. The stunning **Café del Teatro Nacional** just off the vestibule serves upscale coffee concoctions, good sandwiches, and exquisite pastries. ⊠ *Plaza de la Cultura, Barrio La Catedral,* ☎ *221–1329.* ⊡ *Entry $2.50, performance tickets $4–$40 ($10 average).* ⊙ *Weekdays 9–5, Sat. 9–noon.*

⓴ **Universidad de Costa Rica.** The University of Costa Rica, in San Pedro just east of San José, is a great place to hang out and meet people, especially if your Spanish is pretty good. The open-air gallery at the **Facultad de Bellas Artes** (College of Fine Arts), on the east side of campus, hosts free music recitals on Tuesday nights.If the Serpentario doesn't satisfy your thirst for the yucky, scurry on over to the **Museo de Insectos** (⊠ north of Bellas Artes, in the basement of the Artes Musicales Building, ☎ 207–5318), open weekdays 1–4:45. The $2 admission buys you a good look at dead insects in re-created habitats and information in English and Spanish on everything from insect sex to the diseases these little buggers cause.

Aficionados of Spanish literature should browse around the many off-campus bookstores. Anyone who appreciates cheap grub (you know who you are) will enjoy the vast selection of inexpensive lunch places around the university. Weeknights at the university are mellow, but nearby bars are packed with students and intellectuals on weekends. To get to San Pedro, walk a few miles east along Avenida Central's strip of shops and bars or take a $2 taxi ride from downtown and get off in front of Banco Nacional, just beyond the rotunda with the fountain in the middle of it. ⊠ *Avda. Central and C. Central, Barrio Montes de Oca, San Pedro.*

North of Downtown

A Good Tour
The first two of these destinations are north of the city center, very close to each other. Take a taxi to the **Centro Comercial El Pueblo** ⑯, in Barrio Tournón. One block east and half a block south of El Pueblo is the **Jardín de Mariposas Spyrogyra** ⑰, a butterfly garden overlooking the greenery of Costa Rica's zoo, the **Parque Zoológico Simón Bolívar** ⑱. The best way to reach the zoo, however, is to walk north from the bandstand in the Parque Morazán along Calle 7 to the bottom of the hill, then turn right. The **Museo del Niño** ⑲, a children's museum and scientific and cultural center housed in an old jail, lies several blocks to the west. It's surrounded by dubious neighborhoods, so take a taxi there.

TIMING
You can visit all four of these sights in one morning.

Sights to See
⓰ **Centro Comercial El Pueblo** (El Pueblo Shopping Center). This shopping center was built to resemble the kind of colonial village that Costa Rica lacks. *Pueblo* means "town," of course, and the cobbled passages, adobe walls, and tiny plazas are surprisingly convincing. Most of the commercial spaces are occupied by bars, restaurants, and discos that attract a twentysomething crowd. El Pueblo gets very busy at

night, especially on weekends—but there are a few shops worth checking out during the day. ⊠ *Avda. 0, Barrio Tournón.* ☉ *Daily.*

★ ☾ ⑰ **Jardín de Mariposas Spyrogyra** (Butterfly Garden). An hour or two at this magical garden is entertaining and educational for nature lovers of all ages. Self-guided tours enlighten you on butterfly ecology and give you a chance to see the winged creatures close up. Following an 18-minute video introduction, you're free to wander screened-in gardens along a numbered trail. Some 30 species of colorful butterflies flutter about, accompanied by six types of hummingbirds. Try to come when it's sunny, as butterflies are most active then. A small, moderately priced café borders the garden and serves sandwiches and Tico fare. Spyrogyra abuts the northern edge of Parque Zoológico Simón Bolívar, but you enter on the outskirts of Barrio Tournón, near El Pueblo Shopping Center. ⊠ *½ block east and 1½ blocks south of main entrance to El Pueblo, Barrio Tournón,* ☏ *222–2937.* ⊡ *$7.* ☉ *Daily 8–4.*

☾ ⑲ **Museo del Niño.** San José's Children's Museum is housed in a former jail, and big kids may want to check it out just to marvel at the castle-like architecture and the old cells that have been preserved in an exhibit about prison life. Three halls in the complex are filled with eye-catching seasonal exhibits for kids, ranging in subject from local ecology to outer space. The exhibits are annotated in Spanish, but most are interactive, so language shouldn't be much of a problem. The museum's **Galería Nacional,** adjoining the main building, is more popular with adults; it usually shows fine art by Costa Rican artists free of charge. Adjoining the museum is the **Auditorio Nacional,** in which the National Symphony plays morning concerts at 10 from March to November. ⊠ *North end of C. 4, Barrio del Carmen,* ☏ *222–7485.* ⊡ *$5.* ☉ *Weekdays 8–5, weekends 9:30–4:30.*

☾ ⑱ **Parque Zoológico Simón Bolívar.** Considering Costa Rica's mind-boggling diversity of wildlife, San José's zoo is rather modest in scope. It does, however, provide an introduction to some of the animals you might see in the jungle. The park is set in a forested ravine in historical Barrio Amón, offering soothing green space in the heart of the city. ⊠ *Avda. 11 and C. 11, Barrio Amón,* ☏ *233–6701.* ⊡ *$2.* ☉ *Weekdays 8–3:30, weekends 9–4:30.*

DINING

Wherever you eat in San José, be it a small *soda* (café) or a sophisticated restaurant, dress is casual. Meals tend to be taken earlier than in other Latin American countries; few restaurants serve past 10 PM. Note that 23% is added to all menu prices—13% for tax and 10% for service. Because a gratuity is included, there's no need to tip; but if your service is good, it's nice to add a little money to the obligatory 10%. Except for those in hotels, most restaurants close between Christmas and New Year's Day and during Holy Week (Palm Sunday to Easter Sunday). Call before heading out. Those that do stay open may not sell alcohol between Holy Thursday and Easter Sunday. Even if you keep your base in San José, consider venturing to the Central Valley towns for a meal or two.

Downtown San José

CAFÉS

Costa Rican coffee is strong, and a few places still serve it the old-fashioned way: hot milk in one pitcher and hot coffee in the other. Coffee is not generally taken alone but with bread or a sweet.

$ ✕ Café Britt Teatro Nacional. The country's foremost purveyor of gourmet coffee just took over the concession stand at Teatro Nacional. It wins the prize for most relaxed atmosphere. Have a cup of mocha with hazelnut and rest your weary head against cool marble while gazing at the frescoes on the ceiling. Atmosphere comes at a reasonable price here—coffees run anywhere from $1 to $2, depending on how much alcohol or ice cream is added. Sandwiches and cakes will set you back $3 to $4. ⊠ *Teatro Nacional, on Plaza de la Cultura, Barrio La Catedral,* ☎ *221–3262. Closed Sun. Open during evening performances.*

$ ✕ La Esquina del Café. Okay, so it looks a little like a tourist trap, and it does have a souvenir shop, but this is the place for cappuccinos and lattes made with frothed milk. The coffee, roasted fresh daily from six different coffee zones of the country, is the smoothest you'll ever drink. It can also be bought in bean form for $10 a kilo. Drinks and pastries are about $1 each. ⊠ *Av. 9 and C. 3 Bis, Barrio Amón,* ☎ *257–9868.*

CHINESE

$ ✕ Fulusu. Some like it hot, and this Chinese place near local landmark Hotel Presidente is one of the very few Costa Rica restaurants where you can get a spicy food fix. The menu is full of authentic and delicious dishes, making it easy to forgive the mundane Asian prints and checkered tablecloths. Start with some *empanadas chinas* (dumplings similar to pot stickers); then move on to a main course like *vainicas con cerdo* (green beans with pork) or *carne estilo sichuan* (Szechuan beef). One entrée and two orders of rice are usually enough for two. ⊠ *C. 7 between Avdas. Central and 2, Barrio La Catedral,* ☎ *223–7568. AE, MC, V.*

COSTA RICAN

$$–$$$ ✕ La Cocina de Leña. La Cocina serves up traditional Costa Rican fare
★ amid white walls hung with old tools and straw bags to make you feel like you're down on the farm. Popular Tico dishes such as black-bean soup, ceviche, tamales, oxtail with cassava, and plantains cost a bit more here than at small cafés downtown, but the restaurant makes up for the price with live marimba music several nights a week during the high season. Although the kitchen closes at 11, you're welcome to stay as long as the band keeps playing. It is one of the few places that doesn't close during Holy Week. ⊠ *Centro Comercial El Pueblo, Barrio Tournón,* ☎ *223–3704. AE, MC, V.*

$$ ✕ El Cuartel de la Boca del Monte. Although it's one of San José's more popular late-night bars, El Cuartel is actually a nice place to have a meal, too. The restored brick walls, wood beams, and simple wood tables lend a rustic feel in one room, and you'll find a more finished room to the left of the entrance, decorated with original art. Best on the menu is arroz con pollo, but you can also order plates of delicious *bocas* (snacks), such as the *plato de gallos* (corn tortillas topped with beef, potatoes, and other fillings) and *piononos* (sweet plantains stuffed with cheese or beans and served with sour cream). ⊠ *Avda. 1 between Cs. 21 and 23, Barrio La California,* ☎ *221–0327. AE, MC, V. No lunch weekends.*

$ ✕ Mama's Place. Mama's is a Costa Rican restaurant with a difference: the owners are Italian, so in addition to corvina *al ajillo* (sautéed with garlic) and other staple Tico fare, they serve homemade seafood chowder, traditional pastas, and meat dishes with delicate wine sauces. The brightly decorated coffee shop opens onto busy Avenida 1; the more subdued restaurant is upstairs. At lunchtime, it's usually packed with business types drawn to the delicious and inexpensive daily specials and perhaps the macrobiotic fruit shakes, another menu item that sets this place apart. ⊠ *Avda. 1 between Cs. Central and 2, Barrio del Carmen,* ☎ *223–2270. MC, V. Closed Sun.*

San José Dining and Lodging

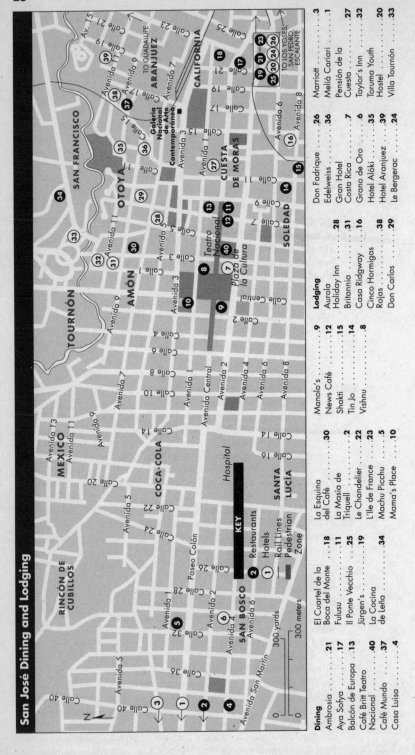

KEY

- ② Restaurants
- ① Hotels
- ▬ Rail Lines
- Pedestrian Zone

Dining

Ambrosia	21
Aya Sofya	17
Balcón de Europa	13
Café Britt Teatro Nacional	40
Café Mundo	37
Casa Luisa	4
El Cuartel de la Boca del Monte	18
Fulusu	11
Il Ponte Vecchio	25
Jürgen's	19
La Cocina de Leña	34
La Esquina del Café	30
La Masía de Triquell	2
Le Chandelier	22
L'Ile de France	23
Machu Picchu	5
Mama's Place	10
Manolo's	9
News Café	12
Shakti	15
Tin Jo	14
Vishnu	8

Lodging

Aurola Holiday Inn	28
Britannia	31
Casa Ridgway	16
Cinco Hormigas Rojas	38
Don Carlos	29
Don Fadrique	26
Edelweiss	36
Gran Hotel Costa Rica	7
Grano de Oro	6
Hotel Aloki	35
Hotel Aranjuez	39
Le Bergerac	24
Marriott	3
Meliá Cariari	1
Pensión de la Cuesta	27
Taylor's Inn	32
Toruma Youth Hostel	20
Villa Tournón	33

$ ✕ **Manolo's.** This 24-hour eatery has been popular with travelers for years, both for its convenient location on the bustling pedestrian thoroughfare and for its great sandwiches, espressos, and *churros con chocolate* (fried dough with hot fudge sauce). A few outdoor tables allow for some of the city's best people-watching. Inside, however, the place feels more like a diner than a café, down to its plastic-coated menu and its promise of breakfast food at any hour. The owner always prepares a few Spanish favorites in addition to the typical Tico fare, such as *tortilla española* (a thick potato and onion omelet). ⊠ *Avda. Central between Cs. Central and 2, Barrio La Catedral,* ☎ *221–2041. AE, MC, V.*

ECLECTIC

$$$–$$$$ ✕ **Jürgen's.** Decorated in gold and terra-cotta with leather and wood accents, the dining room of this contemporary and chic restaurant feels more like a lounge than a fine restaurant. In fact, the classy bar with a large selection of good wine and good cigars, is a prominent feature. But the inventive menu, with such delicacies as medallions of roast duck and tuna fillet encrusted with sesame seeds, sets this place apart from the city's more traditional venues. Service here is tops and the feel is trendy and relaxed. ⊠ *800 yards north of the Subaru dealership, on Barrio Dent Blvd., Barrio Dent,* ☎ *283–2239. AE, MC, V. Closed Sun.*

$$$ ✕ **Ambrosia.** The navy-blue canopy in an open-air shopping plaza her-
★ alds this chic restaurant. The international menu draws the customers. Expect inventive salads, soups, pasta, and fish dishes. Start with *sopa Neptuna* (a creamy fish soup with tomato and bacon), and follow with either the light fettuccine ambrosia (in a rich cream sauce with ham and oregano) or the corvina *troyana* (covered with a shrimp and tarragon sauce). The dining room is relaxed, with subdued watercolors, crisp white tablecloths, wood and cane chairs, and plants. ⊠ *Centro Comercial de la C. Real, San Pedro,* ☎ *253–8012. AE, DC, MC, V. No dinner Sun.*

$$–$$$ ✕ **Café Mundo.** You could easily walk by this corner restaurant with-
★ out noticing its tiny sign behind the foliage. Walk in and upstairs, how-ever, and you'll discover an elegant eatery serving meals on the porch, on a garden patio, or in two dining rooms. Chicagoan chef Ray Johnson prepares creative salads, pastas, pizzas, hot and cold sandwiches at lunch, and grill dishes for dinner. Start with the soup of the day and some fresh-baked bread; then opt for penne in a shrimp and veg-etable cream sauce or *lomito en salsa de vino tinto* (tenderloin in a red-wine sauce). Save room for the best chocolate cake in town, driz-zled with homemade blackberry sauce. ⊠ *C. 15 and Avda. 9, Barrio Otoya,* ☎ *222–6190. AE, MC, V. Closed Sun.*

$$ ✕ **News Café.** Had your fill of rice and beans? You can get a Caesar salad and other American dishes here. Breakfasts and dinner fare are hearty, but the café is most popular at lunchtime and cocktail hour. It's one of the few eateries in the city with covered outdoor seating, and it's in the perfect place for it—right off the pedestrian boulevard's east end. Inside, the wrought-iron chairs, wood beams, and brick walls give the place an old-town tavern feel, though it's actually on the first floor of the 1960s landmark Hotel Presidente. ⊠ *C. 7 and Avda. Cen-tral, Barrio La Catedral,* ☎ *222–3022. AE, MC, V.*

FRENCH

$$$$ ✕ **Le Chandelier.** Formal service and traditional sauce-heavy French dishes are part of the experience at the city's classiest restaurant, Le Chandelier. The dining room is elegant, with wicker chairs, a tile floor, and original paintings. The Swiss chef, Claude Dubuis, might start you off with saffron ravioli stuffed with ricotta cheese and walnuts. His main courses include such unique dishes as corvina in a *pejibaye* (peach palm) sauce; hearts of palm and veal chops glazed in a sweet port-wine sauce; or the more familiar *pato a la naranja* (duck à l'orange). ✉ *1 block west and 1 block south of the ICE building, Los Yoses, San Pedro,* ☎ *225–3980. AE, MC, V. No lunch Sat.*

\$\$\$ ✕ **L'Ile de France.** Long one of San José's most popular restaurants,
★ L'Ile de France is in the Le Bergerac hotel in Los Yoses, where you can dine in a tropical garden courtyard. Chef and proprietor Jean-Claude Fromont offers a fairly traditional French menu with some interesting innovations. Start with the classic onion soup or with *pâté de lapin* (rabbit liver pâté); then sink your teeth into a pepper steak, broiled lamb with seasoned potatoes, or corvina in a spinach sauce. Save room for the profiteroles, puff pastries filled with vanilla ice cream and smothered in chocolate sauce, or the delicious crème brûlée. ✉ *Le Bergerac hotel, C. 35 between Avdas. Central and 2, first entrance to Los Yoses, Los Yoses, San Pedro,* ☎ *283–5812. Reservations essential. AE, MC, V. Closed Sun. No lunch.*

ITALIAN

\$\$\$ ✕ **Il Ponte Vecchio.** Italian owners have used eclectic artwork and candlelight to help create cozy spaces in which to sip wine and enjoy a quiet meal. Do as many foreign residents who favor the place: After a Caprese salad, tuck into one of the many homemade pasta specialties, such as seafood fettuccine with mussels and shrimp or traditional tomato lasagna. Cream sauces are excellent across the board. Portions are on the small side, so you can be sinful without being sorry. ✉ *100 yards east and 25 yards north of Fuente de la Hispanidad, San Pedro,* ☎ FAX *283–1810. AE, MC, V.*

\$\$–\$\$\$ ✕ **Balcón de Europa.** With old sepia photos and a strolling guitarist that seems to have been working the room for years, Balcón transports you to the era of its inception, 1909. Pasta specialties such as the *plato mixto* (mixed plate with lasagna, tortellini, and ravioli) are so popular that they haven't changed much, either. For something lighter, try the scrumptious heart-of-palm salad or sautéed corvina. ✉ *Avda. Central and C. 9, Barrio La Catedral,* ☎ *221–4841. AE, MC, V. Closed Sat.*

PAN-ASIAN

\$\$–\$\$\$ ✕ **Tin Jo.** You can eat in the Japan, India, China or Thailand rooms
★ at this wide-ranging Asian restaurant with a menu to match its varied dining areas. Tin Jo stands apart from the two other Chinese restaurants on this block with always exceptional food and whimsical decorations that add color to this former residence. Start with a powerful Singapore Sling (brandy and fruit juices) before trying such treats as *kaeng* (Thai shrimp and pineapple curry in coconut milk), *mu shu* (a beef, chicken, or veggie stir-fry with crepes), *samosas* (stuffed Indian pastries), and sushi rolls. ✉ *C. 11 between Avdas. 6 and 8, Barrio La Soledad,* ☎ *221–7605. AE, MC, V.*

PERUVIAN

\$\$–\$\$\$ ✕ **Machu Picchu.** A few travel posters and a fishnet holding crab and
★ lobster shells are the only props used to evoke Peru, but no matter: the food is anything but plain, and the seafood is excellent. The *pique especial de mariscos* (special seafood platter), big enough for two, presents you with shrimp, conch, and squid cooked four ways. The ceviche here is quite different from, and better than, that served in the rest of the country. A blazing Peruvian hot sauce served on the side adds zip to any dish, but be careful—apply it by the drop. ✉ *C. 32, 150 yards north of Kentucky Fried Chicken, Barrio Paseo Colón,* ☎ *222–7384. AE, DC, MC, V. Closed Sun.*

SPANISH

$$$–$$$$ ✕ **Casa Luisa.** The moment you enter this homey, upscale Catalan restaurant, you sense you're in for a special evening. It is eclectic and artful, with wood floors, arresting artwork, soft lighting, and flamenco music in the background. Start the meal with gazpacho or eggplant pâté, accompanied by a glass of top Spanish wine. The wonderful main dishes include rosemary lamb chops, suckling pig, and grilled lobster. Finish with a platter of nuts, dates, and figs drizzled with a wine sauce or the decadent *crema Catalana* with a *brûlée* glaze. Reservations are recommended. ✉ *Avda. 4 and C. 40, southeast of the Controlaria building, Barrio Sabana Sur,* ☎ *296–1917. MC, V. Closed Mon.*

$$$ ✕ **La Masía de Triquell.** San José's most traditional Spanish restaurant is appropriately housed in the Casa España, a Spanish cultural center. The dining room follows the theme with a tile floor; wood beams; red, green, and yellow walls; white tablecloths; and leather-and-wood Castilian-style chairs. *Champiñones al ajillo* (mushrooms sautéed with garlic and parsley) make a fine appetizer; *camarones Catalana* (shrimp in a tomato-and-garlic cream sauce) are a standout entrée. The long wine list is strongest in the Spanish and French departments. Reservations are a good idea. ✉ *50 yards west and 150 yards north of Burger King, Barrio Sabana Norte,* ☎ *296–3528. AE, DC, MC, V. Closed Sun.*

TURKISH

$$ ✕ **Aya Sofya.** Natives of Istanbul, the chef and one of the owners have imported excellent recipes for red peppers stuffed with spicy beef and rice, eggplant-tomato salad, and other Mediterranean treats. Vegetarians will find a good selection of vegetable and green salads. Desserts include a scrumptious yogurt-and-honey *revani* cake as well as the beloved baklava. Beyond the obligatory evil-eye motif and a few wall hangings, this is a no-frills place, but good food and a friendly staff make it a find. ✉ *Avda. Central and C. 21, Barrio La California,* ☎ *221–7185. MC, V. Closed Sun.*

VEGETARIAN

$ ✕ **Shakti.** Between the baskets of fruit and vegetables at the entrance and the wall of herbal teas, health food books, and fresh herbs for sale by the register, there's no doubt you're in a vegetarian-friendly joint. The bright and airy restaurant serves breakfast and lunch: homemade bread, soy burgers, pita sandwiches (veggie or chicken, for carnivorous dining companions), macrobiotic fruit shakes, and a hearty plato del día that comes with soup, green salad, and a fruit beverage. The *ensalada mixta* is a meal in itself, packed with root vegetables native to Costa Rica. ✉ *Avda. 8 between Cs. 13 and 11, Barrio Lujan,* ☎ *222–4475. Reservations not accepted. No credit cards. No dinner.*

$ ✕ **Vishnu.** Named after the Hindu god who preserves the universe, Vishnu has become a bit of an institution in San José. Even its dining area looks institutional—sterile booths with Formica tables and posters of fruit on the walls—but the attraction is the inexpensive vegetarian food. Your best bet is usually the plato del día, which includes soup, beverage, and dessert, but the menu also offers soy burgers, salads, fresh fruit juices, and a yogurt smoothie called *morir soñando* (literally, "to die dreaming"). ✉ *Avda. 1, west of C. 3, Barrio del Carmen,* ☎ *222–2549. Reservations not accepted. No credit cards.*

LODGING

Downtown San José

Staying downtown area allows you to travel around the city as most Ticos do: on foot. Stroll the city's parks, museums, and shops, and then retire in one of many small or historic hotels that have plenty in the way of character.

$$$$ ☷ **Aurola Holiday Inn.** The upper floors of this 17-story mirrored-glass building, three blocks north of the Plaza de la Cultura, have the best views in town. Ignoring the view of downtown San José and its surroundings, however, you could just as soon be in Ohio, as the interior decoration betrays no local influence. The high-ceiling lobby is modern and airy, with lots of shiny marble. The good restaurant and casino are on the top floor, making full use of their vantage points. ⊠ *Avda. 5 and C. 5, Barrio Amón,* ☎ *222–2424; 800/465–4329 in the U.S.,* FAX *222–2621,* WEB *www.aurolaholidayinn.com (mailing address: Apdo. 7802–1000, San José). 188 rooms, 12 suites. Restaurant, bar, cafeteria, indoor pool, hot tub, sauna, gym, casino. AE, DC, MC, V.*

$$$$ ☷ **Britannia.** Except for the addition of some rooms and the conversion of the old cellar into an intimate international restaurant, this stately pink home with a tiled porch has changed little since its construction in 1910. Rooms in the newer wing are slightly small, with carpeting and hardwood furniture. Deluxe rooms and junior suites in the original house are spacious, with high ceilings and windows on the street side; they're worth the extra money but are close enough to the street that noise might be a problem if you're a light sleeper. ⊠ *C. 3 and Avda. 11, Barrio Amón,* ☎ *223–6667,* FAX *223–6411,* WEB *www.centralamerica.com/cr/hotel/britania.htm (mailing address: Apdo. 3742–1000, San José). 19 rooms, 4 suites. Restaurant. AE, MC, V.*

$$$$ ☷ **Grano de Oro.** Two turn-of-the-20th-century wooden houses on ★ San José's western edge have been converted into one of the city's most charming inns. New rooms have been added to the attractive space, which is decorated with old photos of the capital and paintings by local artists. A modest restaurant, run by a French chef, is surrounded by a lovely indoor patio and gardens. The old rooms are the nicest, especially the Garden Suite, with hardwood floors, high ceilings, and private garden. The hotel's sundeck has a view of both the city and the far-off volcanoes. ⊠ *C. 30 between Avdas. 2 and 4, Barrio Paseo Colón,* ☎ *255–3322,* FAX *221–2782,* WEB *www.hotelgranodeoro.com (mailing address: 1701 N.W. 97 Ave., Box 025216, SJO 36, Miami, FL 33102–5216). 31 rooms, 3 suites. Restaurant, hot tub. AE, MC, V.*

$$$–$$$$ ☷ **Hotel Alóki.** Guest rooms in this elegant turn-of-the-20th-century manor house surround a covered courtyard restaurant, whose wicker furniture and potted tropical plants spill onto multicolored glazed tiles. The antique furniture, gilt mirrors, and old prints in the rooms make this small, quiet place one of the most tasteful in San José. The Presidential Suite has a large drawing room. Breakfast is included. ⊠ *C. 13 between Avdas. 9 and 11, Barrio Otoya,* ☎ *222–6702,* FAX *221–2533,* WEB *www.tropicalcostarica.com. 6 rooms, 1 suite. Restaurant, bar; no air-conditioning. MC, V.*

$$$ ☷ **Don Carlos.** As one of the city's first guest houses, Don Carlos has ★ been in the same family for four generations. Most rooms in the rambling villa have ceiling fans, big windows, and original art. Those in the Colonial Wing have a bit more personality, and several newer rooms on the third floor have volcano views. Abundant public areas are adorned with orchids, pre-Columbian statues, and paintings depicting Costa Rican life. The on-site souvenir shop, Boutique Annemarie, has the city's largest selection of crafts and curios. Complimentary cocktails and breakfast are served on the garden patio; the small restaurant serves lunch and dinner. ⊠ *C. 9 and Avda. 9, Barrio Amón,* ☎ 221–6707, FAX 255–0828, WEB *www.doncarlos.com (mailing address: Box 025216, Dept. 1686, Miami, FL 33102-5216). 21 rooms, 12 suites. Restaurant, hot tub, travel services; no air-conditioning in some rooms. AE, MC, V.*

$$$ ⊞ **Edelweiss.** Never mind that the interior may look more European than Latin American (one of the owners is Austrian). This elegant little inn has comfortable rooms in a charming area, near the Parque España. Rooms have carved doors, custom-made furniture, and small bathrooms. Most have hardwood window frames and floors; several have bathtubs. Complimentary breakfast is served in the garden courtyard, which doubles as a bar. ⊠ *Avda. 9 and C. 15, Barrio Otoya,* ☎ 221–9702, FAX 222–1241, WEB *www.edelweisshotel.com. 27 rooms. Bar, fans; no air-conditioning. AE, MC, V.*

$$$ ⊞ **Gran Hotel Costa Rica.** Opened in 1930, the grande dame of San José hotels remains a focal point of the city and is the first choice of travelers who want to be where the action is. It's a good deal for the money, but the flow of nonguests who frequent the 24-hour casino, Café Parisienne, restaurant, and bar reduces the intimacy quotient to zero. Rooms are large and somewhat lackluster, with small windows and tubs in the tiled baths. Most overlook the Plaza de la Cultura, which can be a bit noisy, and the quieter interior rooms are pretty dark. Breakfast is complimentary. ⊠ *Avda. 2 and C. 3, Barrio La Catedral,* ☎ 221–4000, FAX 221–3501 (mailing address: Apdo. 527–1000, San José). 106 rooms, 4 suites. Restaurant, bar, café, fans, casino; no air-conditioning. AE, DC, MC, V.

$$$ ⊞ **Taylor's Inn.** As a converted early 20th-century brick house, the inn's old charm makes up for such small flaws as cracking window sills and an uninspiring courtyard garden. Its comfortable, clean rooms and proximity to downtown attractions are also selling points. Rooms upstairs have pleasant views. First-floor rooms have original wood floors and adjoin a central courtyard with a high ceiling and handsome wood beams. Three rooms have bathtubs, a rarity in city hotels. Especially attractive to families is the suite in the front of the inn with a sitting area that connects to a standard double room. ⊠ *Avda. 13, C. 3 Bis, Barrio Amón,* ☎ 257–4333, FAX 221–1475. 12 rooms. Travel services; no air-conditioning. AE, MC, V.

$$$ ⊞ **Villa Tournón.** North of downtown, just two blocks from El Pueblo shopping center, the Tournón is popular with traveling businesspeople, who appreciate the peace, security, and reasonable rates. Sloping wooden ceilings and bare, redbrick walls may recall a ski chalet, but the kidney-shape pool out back is surrounded by tropical foliage. The carpeted rooms are snug and tastefully decorated, with pastel shades and prints. The restaurant is highly regarded, and the buffet breakfast is big enough to make you skip lunch. ⊠ *Avda. 0, east side of traffic circle, Barrio Tournón,* ☎ 233–6622, FAX 222–5211, WEB *www.cool.co.cr/usr/villa-tournon (mailing address: Apdo. 6606–1000, San José). 80 rooms. Restaurant, cable TV, pool, gym, outdoor hot tub, bar. AE, MC, V.*

$$ ⊞ **Cinco Hormigas Rojas.** The name of this whimsical little lodge translates as "Five Red Ants." Behind the wall of vines that obscures it from the street is a wild garden that leads to an interior space filled with original artwork. Color abounds, from the bright hues on the walls right down to the toilet seats. Sure enough, the resident owner is an artist—Mayra Güell turned the house she inherited from her grandmother into San José's most original B&B–cum–art gallery. It's in the historic Barrio Otoya, one of San José's few pleasant neighborhoods, and the room price includes a hearty breakfast. ⊠ *C. 15 between Avdas. 9 and 11, Barrio Otoya,* ☎ FAX 257–8581, WEB *www.crtimes.com/tourism/cincohormigasrojas/*

maincinco.htm. 6 rooms, 2 with bath. No air-conditioning, no room phones, no room TVs. AE, MC, V.

$$ ★ 🏨 **Hotel Aranjuez.** Several 1940s-era houses, with extensive gardens and cozy common areas, constitute this family-run B&B. Every room is comfortable, but each is different—it pays to check out a few, as some have private gardens or little sitting rooms. Aranjuez is a short walk from most San José attractions and offers such perks as discount tour service. The complimentary breakfast buffet makes lunch unthinkable. Reserve well in advance during high season. ⊠ *C. 19 between Avdas. 11 and 13, Barrio Aranjuez,* ☎ *256–1825,* FAX *223–3528,* WEB *www.hotelaranjuez.com. 35 rooms, 25 with bath. In-room safes, travel services; no air-conditioning. MC, V.*

$$ 🏨 **Pensión de la Cuesta.** Rooms in this laid-back, centrally located wooden villa in sloping Cuesta de Nuñez have hardwood floors, brightly painted walls, and original art. Rooms in back are quieter, but those in front are brighter. You can lounge and read in the sunken sitting area (also used as the breakfast room), which has a high ceiling, a wall of windows, and cable TV. Breakfast is included in the price, and you're welcome to use the kitchen at other times. The nine rooms share four baths. A furnished apartment is also for rent. ⊠ *Avda. 1 between Cs. 11 and 15, Apdo. 1332, Barrio Cuesta de Nuñez,* ☎ *256–7946,* FAX *255–2896,* WEB *www.arweb.com/lacuesta. 9 rooms without bath, 1 apartment. No air-conditioning, no room TVs. AE, MC, V.*

$ ★ 🏨 **Casa Ridgway.** Affiliated with the Quaker Peace Center next door, Casa Ridgway is the budget option for itinerants concerned with peace, the environment, and social issues in general. Set in an old villa on a quiet street, the bright, clean premises include a planted terrace, a lending reference library, and a kitchen where you can cook your own food. There are three rooms with two bunk beds each, three rooms with single beds, and one with a double bed, all of which share three bathrooms. ⊠ *Avda. 6 Bis and C. 15, Barrio Lujan,* ☎ FAX *233–6168 (mailing address: Apdo. 1507–1000, San José). 7 rooms without bath. Library, meeting room; no air-conditioning, no room phones, no room TVs. No credit cards.*

Northeast of San José

The small properties beyond downtown, toward the university, offer personalized service and lots of peace and quiet. Plenty of restaurants and bars are within easy reach, although downtown is just a 10-minute cab ride away.

$$$ ★ ✕🏨 **Le Bergerac.** Le Bergerac, surrounded by extensive green grounds, is the cream of a growing crop of small, upscale San José hotels. French owned and managed, it occupies two former private homes and is furnished with antiques. All rooms have custom-made wood-and-stone dressers and writing tables; deluxe rooms have two beds, private garden terraces or balconies, and large bathrooms. The hotel's restaurant, L'Ile de France, is one of the city's best, so dinner reservations are essential, even for guests. Complimentary breakfast is served on a garden patio. ⊠ *C. 35 between Avdas. Central and 2, first entrance to Los Yoses, Los Yoses, San Pedro,* ☎ *234–7850,* FAX *225–9103,* WEB *www.bergerac.com (mailing address: Apdo. 1107–1002, San José). 18 rooms. Restaurant, meeting room, travel services. AE, MC, V.*

$$$ ✕🏨 **Don Fadrique.** This tranquil, family-run B&B on the outskirts of San José was named after Fadrique Guttierez, an illustrious great-uncle of the owners. A collection of original Costa Rican art decorates the lobby and rooms, most of which have hardwood floors, peach walls, and pastel bedspreads. Several carpeted rooms downstairs open onto the garden. There is also an enclosed garden patio, where meals are served. ⊠ *C. 37 at Avda. 8, Los Yoses, San Pedro,* ☎ *225–8186,* FAX *224–9746,*

WEB *www.centralamerica.com/cr/hotel/fadrique.htm. 20 rooms. Restaurant; no air-conditioning. AE, MC, V.*

$–$$ ▣ **Toruma Youth Hostel.** The headquarters of Costa Rica's expanding hostel network is housed in an elegant colonial bungalow, built around 1900, in the eastern suburb of Escalante. The tiled lobby and veranda are ideal places for backpackers to hang out and exchange travel tales and enjoy a light complimentary breakfast. Beds on the ground floor are in little compartments with doors; rooms on the second floor have standard bunks. There are also two private rooms for couples. The on-site information center offers discounted tours. ⊠ *Avda. Central between Cs. 29 and 31, Escalante,* ☎ FAX *224–4085 (mailing address: 6 Apdo. 1355–1002, San José). 2 rooms without bath, 95 beds in 17 rooms. Dining room; no air-conditioning, no room phone, no room TVs. MC, V.*

Northwest of San José

These rather luxe properties cater to business travelers or those looking for something familiar or closer to the airport.

$$$$ ▣ **Marriott.** Towering over a coffee plantation west of San José, the
★ stately Marriott evokes an unusual colonial splendor. The building's thick columns, wide arches, and central courtyard are straight out of the 17th century, and hand-painted tiles and abundant antiques complete the historic appearance. Guest rooms are more contemporary, but they're elegant enough, with hardwood furniture and sliding glass doors that open onto tiny Juliet-type balconies. ⊠ *765 yards west of Firestone, off Autopista General Cañas, San Antonio de Belén,* ☎ *298–0000; 800/228–9290 in the U.S.,* FAX *298–0011,* WEB *www.marriotthotels.com/marriott/sjocr. 245 rooms, 7 suites. 2 restaurants, café, lobby lounge, 2 pools, hair salon, driving range, putting green, 3 tennis courts, health club, business services, meeting room, travel services, car rental. AE, DC, MC, V.*

$$$$ ▣ **Meliá Cariari.** The low-rise Meliá Cariari was San José's original luxury hotel, and it remains popular for its excellent service and out-of-town location. Just off the busy General Cañas Highway, about halfway between San José and the international airport, the Cariari is surrounded by thick vegetation that buffers it from traffic noise. Spacious, carpeted guest rooms in back overlook the pool area. The relaxed poolside bar, with cane chairs and colorful tablecloths, and nearby casino are popular spots. ⊠ *Autopista General Cañas, 600 yards east of intersection for San Antonio de Belén, Cariari,* ☎ *239–0022; 800/227–4274 in the U.S.,* FAX *239–2803 (mailing address: Apdo. 737–1007, San José. 200 rooms, 20 suites. 2 restaurants, bar, cafeteria, pool, hot tub, golf privileges, 11 tennis courts, gym, casino. AE, DC, MC, V.*

NIGHTLIFE AND THE ARTS

The Arts

Film

Dubbing is rare in Costa Rica; films are screened in their original language, usually English, and subtitled in Spanish. There are theaters all over downtown San José, as well as in the malls outside the city. Check the local papers *La Nación* or the *Tico Times* (in English) for current listings. **Sala Garbo and Laurence Olivier** (⊠ Avda. 2 and C. 28, Barrio Paseo Colón, ☎ 222–1034) shows arty films, often in languages other than English (with, of course, Spanish subtitles). **Cine Variedades** (⊠ C. 5 between Avdas. Central and 1, Barrio del Carmen, ☎ 222–6108) shows art movies. **Outlet Mall Cinemas** (⊠ in front of San Pedro's Catholic Church, San Pedro, ☎ 234–8868) is a San José art house, near the university.

Theater and Music

The baroque **Teatro Nacional** (⊠ Plaza de la Cultura, Barrio del Catedral, ☎ 221–1329) is the home of the excellent National Symphony Orchestra, which performs on Friday evening and Sunday morning between April and December. The theater also hosts visiting musical groups and dance companies. San José's second main theater is the **Teatro Melico Salazar** (⊠ Avda. 2 between Cs. Central and 2, Barrio del Catedral, ☎ 221–4952). There are frequent dance performances and concerts in the Teatro FANAL and the Teatro 1887, both in the **Centro Nacional de la Cultura** (⊠ C. 13 between Avdas. 3 and 5, Barrio Otoya, ☎ 257–5524). The **Eugene O'Neill Theater** (⊠ Avda. 1, C. 37, Barrio Vásquez Dent, San Pedro, ☎ 207–7500) at the Costa Rican–North American Culture Center has chamber concerts and plays most weekend evenings. The center is a great place to meet expatriate North Americans. Dozens of theater groups (most of which perform slapstick comedies) hold forth in smaller theaters around town. An English-language troupe, the **Little Theatre Group,** performs four plays a year; check the English-language *Tico Times* for the latest.

Nightlife

Bars

No one could accuse San José of having too few watering holes, but outside the hotels, there aren't many places to have a quiet drink—Tico bars tend to be on the lively side. For a little taste of Mexico in Costa Rica, head to **La Esmeralda** (⊠ Avda. 2 between Cs. 5 and 7, Barrio del Catedral), a popular late-night spot where locals enjoy live mariachi music until the wee hours. The second floor of the **Casino Colonial** (⊠ Avda. 1 between Cs. 9 and 11, Barrio del Carmen, ☎ 258–2827) is a good place to watch a game. **Mac's Bar** (⊠ Sabana Park S., next to the Tennis Club, Sabana Sur, ☎ 234–3145) is a quiet spot for a drink.

The **Centro Comercial El Pueblo** (⊠ Avda. 0, Barrio Tournón) has a bar for every taste, from quiet pubs to thumping discos. Several bars have live music on weekends; it's best to wander around and see what sounds good. A trendy place to see and be seen is **El Cuartel de la Boca del Monte** (⊠ Avda. 1 between Cs. 21 and 23, Barrio La California), a large bar where young artists and professionals gather to sip San José's fanciest cocktails and share plates of tasty *bocas* (snacks). It has live music Monday and Wednesday night. The **Jazz Café** (⊠ Avda. Central next to Banco Popular, San Pedro), draws big crowds, especially for live jazz on Tuesday and Wednesday nights.

The highly recommended restaurant, **Café Mundo** (⊠ C. 15 and Avda. 9, Barrio Otoya, ☎ 222–6190), is also quiet spot for a drink frequented by gay and bohemian crowds. **El Bochinche** (⊠ C. 11 between Avdas. 10 and 12, Barrio Soledad) is another of San José's upscale gay bars that doubles as a restaurant.

Casinos

The 24-hour **Casino Colonial** (⊠ Avda. 1 between Cs. 9 and 11, Barrio del Carmen, ☎ 258–2827) has a complete casino, cable TV, bar, and restaurant and a betting service for major U.S. sporting events. **Jungle Casino** (⊠ Avda. Central between Cs. 7 and 9, Barrio del Catedral, ☎ 222–5022) in the Balmoral Hotel downtown is a casino, bar, and restaurant in one. Most of the city's larger hotels also have casinos, including the Aurola Holiday Inn (the view from the casino is breathtaking), Meliá Cariari, Radisson Europa, and Gran Hotel Costa Rica.

Discos

El Tobogan, just outside town on the road north to Guápiles, is the place to watch the best in Latin dancing. Its oversize hall is always packed with a mature crowd who swivel to live music on the weekends. For a more international scene, **Planet Mall,** on the top floor of the massive San Pedro Mall, is one of the city's most expensive dance bars. The **Centro Comercial El Pueblo** has two full-fledged discos: Cocoloco has Latin music, and Inifnito plays mostly techno, pop, and funk on one dance floor and Latin music on the other. Across the parking lot from the Centro Comercial El Pueblo is **La Plaza,** a larger, slightly more upscale disco that plays a good mix of pop and Latin music.

Déjà Vu (⊠ C. 2 between Avdas. 14 and 16A, Barrio El Pacífico) is a mostly gay, techno-heavy disco with two dance floors. Take a taxi to and from here; the neighborhood's sketchy. A gay and lesbian crowd also frequents **La Avispa** (⊠ C. 1 between Avdas. 8 and 10, Barrio del Catedral), which has two dance floors and a quieter upstairs bar with pool tables.

OUTDOOR ACTIVITIES AND SPORTS

Participant Sports

Fitness Centers and Day Spas

The Radisson Europa Hotel (⊠ Avda. 15 between Cs. Central and 3, next to La Republica newspaper office, Barrio Tournón, ☎ 257–3257) houses the downtown branch of the upscale, full-service gym **Multi Spa,** which offers daily rates (about $4) for drop-ins. Other luxury hotels, like the Aurola Holiday Inn, Marriott, and the Meliá Cariari, have modern gyms for guests only. **Gimnasio Perfect Line** (⊠ C. 1 and Avda. Central, 6th floor, Barrio del Carmen) is a full gym with inexpensive one-month memberships (about $35). For a complete listing, look under *"Gimnasios"* in the local *Páginas Amarillas* (Yellow Pages).

The **Harmony Day Spa** at Hotel Amón Plaza (⊠ Avda. 11 and C. 3 Bis, Barrio Amón, ☎ 257–0191) offers massages, manicures, pedicures, and sunburn relief treatments. The hotel also lends its hot tub, pool, and modest exercise equipment to nonguests for about $3 a day.

Running

Once San José's airport but now a eucalyptus-shaded park, **Parque La Sabana,** at the end of the Paseo Colón, is the city's best place to run, with 5-km (3-mi) routes on cement paths. Within the park are a sculpture garden and duck ponds. Free **aerobics classes** on La Sabana's west end start at 9 on Sunday morning and usually draw scores.

White-Water Rafting

White-water trips down the Reventazón, Pacuare, Sarapiquí, and General rivers all leave from San José. Nearly half a dozen licensed, San José–based tour companies operate similar rafting and kayaking trips of varying lengths and grades. The Reventazón's Class III and IV–V runs are both day trips, as are the Sarapiquí's Class II–IV runs. You descend the General (Class III–IV) on a three-day camping trip. You can run the Pacuare (Class III–IV) in one, two, or three days, the Sarapiquí (Class II–IV) in one day.

Accommodations for overnight trips on the General or Pacuare River are usually in tents, but Aventuras Naturales and Riós Tropicales have comfortable lodges on the Pacuare, making them the most popular outfitters for overnight trips on that river. Costa Rica Expeditions runs day trips. The cost is around $75–$95 per day, depending on the river. Two- and three-day river rafting or kayaking packages with overnight stays are considerably more expensive.

Aventuras Naturales (⊠ behind Banco Nacional, Barrio Roosevelt, San Pedro, ☎ 225–3939 or 224–0505, FAX 253–6934) is a popular outfitter with high-adrenaline rafting adventures on the Pacuare, Reventazón, and Sarapiquí rivers. **Ríos Tropicales** (⊠ 50 yards south of Centro Colón, Barrio Paseo Colón, San José, ☎ 233–6455, FAX 255–4354) is the largest outfitter running white-water tours in the area. **Costa Rica Expeditions** (⊠ Avda. 3 and C. Central, Barrio María Auxiliadora, San José, ☎ 257–0766, FAX 255–4354) has been offering rafting tours to the Pacuare, Reventazón, and Sarapiquí rivers for more than 20 years.

Spectator Sports

Soccer

Professional soccer matches are usually played on Sunday morning or Wednesday night in either of two San José stadiums. The **Estadio Nacional** is on the western end of La Sabana park. The **Estadio Ricardo Saprissa** is in the northern suburb of Tibás. Consult the Spanish-language daily *La Nación* or ask at your hotel for details on upcoming games—you simply buy a ticket at the stadium box office. Prices range from $2 to $12—the most expensive are reserved seats in the shade (ask for *sombra numerado*).

SHOPPING

Specialty Items

Antiques

Antigüedades Chavo (⊠ C. Central between Avdas. Central and 1, Barrio del Carmen, ☎ 258–3966) sells mostly furniture but has some smaller antiques. **Antigüedades El Museo** (⊠ Avda. 7 and C. 3 Bis, Barrio Amón, ☎ 223–9552) sells antique paintings, ceramics, jewelry, and other small items.

Books and Maps

Lehmann (⊠ Avda. Central between Cs. 1 and 3, Barrio del Catedral, ☎ 223–1212) has some books in English and a stock of large-scale topographical maps. **Librería Internacional** (⊠ 330 yards west of Taco Bell, Barrio Dent, ☎ 253–9553) has English translations of Latin American literature and myriad coffee-table books on Costa Rica. **7th Street Books** (⊠ C. 7 between Avdas. Central and 1, Barrio del Catedral, ☎ 256–8251) has an excellent selection of new and used books in English and is particularly strong on Latin America and tropical ecology.

Coffee and Liquor

You can buy coffee in any souvenir shop or supermarket, where you'll get the best price. The best brand is Café Rey Tarrazú; the second-best is Café Britt. Good, fresh-roasted coffee is also sold at **La Esquina del Café** (⊠ Avda. 9, C. 3 Bis, Barrio Amón, ☎ 257–9868), which has a great selection of coffee souvenirs and hand-rolled Costa Rican cigars that can be enjoyed at La Esquina's bar and café. Costa Rica's best rum is the aged Centenario—pick up a bottle for about $8. There are also several brands of coffee liqueurs, the oldest of which is Café Rica but the best of which is Britt. Buy these at any of San José's abundant supermarkets and liquor stores.

Crafts

Atmosfera (⊠ C. 5 between Avdas. 1 and 3, Barrio del Carmen, ☎ 222–4322) has three floors of crafts and local art, including wooden bowls, jewelry, and paintings and sculptures by Costa Rican artists. **Galería Namu** (⊠ Avda. 7 between Cs. 5 and 7, behind Aurola Holiday Inn, Barrio Amón, ☎ 256–3412) has Costa Rican folkloric art and some of the best indigenous crafts in town. Its inventory brims with colorful creations by the Guaymí, Boruca, Bribri, Chorotega, Hueter, and Maleku peoples from Costa Rica. You'll also find exquisitely carved ivory nut "Tagua" figurines made by Wounan Indians from Panama's Darien region. Take note of carved balsa masks, woven cotton blankets, and hand-painted ceramics.

Souvenirs

Boutique Annemarie (⊠ C. 9 and Avda. 9, Barrio Amón, ☎ 221–6707) in the Don Carlos hotel has a huge selection of popular souvenirs and CDs of Costa Rican musicians, including Grammy-winning Editus. The boutique carries comical figurines, cards, stationery, and standard, kitschy tourist gear.

The **gift shop** at Aeropuerto Internacional Juan Santamaría has coffee ($5 per pound), and a terrific selection of good-quality merchandise, such as hand-carved bowls and jewelry, Aveda-esque aromatherapy candles, banana paper stationery, and Costa Rica travel books. There's nary another store in the country carrying such desirable items all in one place. But you'll pay U.S. prices.

SAN JOSÉ A TO Z

To research prices, get advice from other travelers, and book travel arrangements, visit www.fodors.com.

AIRPORTS AND TRANSFERS

There are two airports in the San Jose area—Aeropuerto Internacional Juan Santamaría, 16 km (10 mi) northwest of downtown San José, the destination for all international flights, and Aeropuerto Internacional Tobías Bolaños in Pavas, 3 km (2 mi) west of the city center, from which some domestic flights depart.

➤ AIRPORT INFORMATION: **Aeropuerto Internacional Juan Santamaría** (☎ 443–2942). **Aeropuerto Internacional Tobías Bolaños** (☎ 232–2820).

AIRPORT TRANSFERS

A taxi from the airport to downtown San José costs around $12. Drivers wait at the airport exit in a startling mass. They do not expect tips, but beware of drivers eager to take you to a particular hotel—their only motive is a hefty commission. Far cheaper (about 40¢), and almost as fast, is the bus marked RUTA 200 SAN JOSÉ, which drops you at the west end of Avenida 2, close to the heart of the city. If you rent a car at the airport, driving time to San José is about 20 minutes, 40 minutes if traffic is heavy or you get lost. Note that some hotels provide a free shuttle service—inquire when you reserve.

BUS TRAVEL TO AND FROM SAN JOSE

A handful of private companies operate from San José, providing reliable, inexpensive bus service throughout much of Costa Rica from several departure points (San José has no central bus station). For bus stops and companies, *see* Chapter 3.

BUS TRAVEL WITHIN SAN JOSE

Bus service within San José is absurdly cheap (30¢–50¢) and easy to use. For Paseo Colón and La Sabana, take buses marked SABANA-CEMENTERIO from stops on the southern side of the Parque Morazán, or on Avenida 3 next to the Correos building. For the suburbs of Los Yoses and San Pedro near the university, take one marked SAN PEDRO, CURRIDABAT, or LOURDES from Avenida Central, between Calles 9 and 11.

CAR RENTAL

Contact any of the major agencies below to rent a car in San José. It's virtually impossible to rent a car in Costa Rica between December 20 and January 3. If you want to do so, reserve far in advance. Any other time of year, shop around for the best rate.

➤ MAJOR AGENCIES: **Alamo** (✉ Avda. 18 between Cs. 11 and 13, Barrio González-Viques, ☎ 233–7733 or 800/570–0671). **Budget** (✉ Paseo Colón and C. 30, Barrio Paseo Colón, ☎ 223–3284 or 800/224–4627). **Dollar** (✉ Paseo Colón and C. 32, Barrio Paseo Colón, ☎ 257–1585 or 800/800–4000). **Hertz** (✉ Paseo Colón and C. 38, Barrio Paseo Colón, ☎ 221–1818 or 800/654–3001). **National** (✉ 1 km [½ mi] north of Hotel Best Western Irazú, Barrio La Uruca, ☎ 290–8787 or 800/227–7368).

CAR TRAVEL

San José is the hub of the national road system. Paved roads fan out from Paseo Colón south to Escazú and northwest to the airport and Heredia. For the Pacific coast, Guanacaste, and Nicaragua, take the Carretera Interamericana (Pan-American Highway) north (CA1). Calle 3 runs east into the highway to Guápiles, Limón, and the Atlantic coast through Braulio Carrillo National Park, with a turnoff to the Sarapiquí region. If you follow Avenida Central or 2 east through San Pedro, you'll enter the Pan-American Highway south (CA2), which has a turnoff for Cartago, Volcán Irazú, and Turrialba before it heads southeast over the mountains toward Panama.

Almost every street in downtown San José is one-way. Try to avoid driving at peak hours (8 AM–9 AM and 5 PM–6:30 PM), as traffic gets horribly congested. Parking lots, scattered throughout the city, charge around $1 an hour. Outside the city center, you can park on the street, where *cuidacarros* (car guards) usually offer to watch your car for a 100-colón tip. Even so, never leave shopping bags or valuables inside your parked car.

EMBASSIES

The British Embassy handles inquiries for citizens of Australia and New Zealand.

➤ CONTACTS: **British Embassy** (✉ Centro Colón, Paseo Colón between Cs. 38 and 40, Barrio Paseo Colón, ☎ 258–2025). **Canadian Embassy** (✉ Oficentro La Sabana, Sabana Sur, Sabana Sur ☎ 296–4149). **United States Embassy** (✉ in front of Centro Comercial del Oeste, Apdo. 920–1200, Pavas, ☎ 220–3939).

EMERGENCIES

You can dial ☎ 911 for just about any emergency. Your embassy can provide you with a list of recommended doctors and dentists. Hospitals open to foreigners include Clínica Bíblica, which has a 24-hour pharmacy, and Clínica Católica.

➤ EMERGENCY SERVICES: **Ambulance** (☎ 128). **Fire** (☎ 118). **Police** (☎ 117; 127 outside major cities). **Traffic Police** (☎ 222–9245).

➤ HOSPITALS: **Clínica Bíblica** (✉ Avda. 14 between Cs. Central and 1, Barrio El Pacífico, ☎ 257–0466 emergencies). **Clínica Católica**

(✉ Guadalupe, attached to San Antonio Church on C. Esquivel Bonilla St., Barrio Guadalupe, ☎ 283–6616).

TOURS

Everyone is setting up tours these days, but a few companies have more experience than most. Prescheduled half-day and full-day bus tours to waterfalls, Central Valley volcanoes, coffee plantations, botanical gardens, and San José sights can be arranged through Eclipse Tours. You can also tour San José and the surrounding area on a mountain bike, in a raft, in a sea kayak or on horseback. Aventuras Naturales leads rafting and mountain-biking tours. Costa Rica Expeditions is one of the country's most experienced rafting outfitters. Expediciones Tropical arranges horseback riding tours. Sun Tours and Horizontes will customize natural-history and adventure trips with expert guides to any Costa Rican itinerary. Ríos Tropicales offers rafting, sea-kayaking, and mountain-biking tours. The Rain Forest Aerial Tram takes you floating through the treetops on a modified ski lift. Tropical Bungee runs bungee-jump trips daily from San José to an old bridge on the way to the Central Pacific. For a day trip to the beach at Punta Coral and Isla Tortuga, try Calypso.

The popular coffee tour run by Café Britt, in Heredia, presents the history of coffee harvesting and drinking via skits, a coffee-farm tour, and a tasting. Most of San José's travel agencies can arrange one-day horseback tours to farms in the surrounding Central Valley.

➤ TOUR COMPANIES: **Aventuras Naturales** (✉ Avda. 5 at C. 33, Barrio Escalante, ☎ 225–3939, FAX 253–6934). **Café Britt** (✉ 900 yards north and 400 yards west of Comandancia, Barva de Heredia, Heredia, ☎ 261–0707, FAX 260–1456). **Calypso** (✉ Arcadas building, 3rd floor, next to Gran Hotel Costa Rica, Barrio del Catedral, San José, ☎ 256–2727, FAX 256–6767). **Camino Travel** (✉ C. 1 between Avdas. Central and 1 Barrio del Carmen, San José, ☎ 257–0107, FAX 257–0243). **Costa Rica Expeditions** (✉ Avda. 3 at C. Central, Barrio del Carmen, San José, ☎ 222–0333, FAX 257–1665). **Eclipse Tours** (✉ Villa Tournón, Avda. 0, east side of traffic circle, Barrio Tournón, San José, ☎ 223–7510, FAX 233–3672). **Expediciones Tropical** (✉ C. 3 between Avdas. 11 and 13, Barrio Amón, San José, ☎ 257–4171, FAX 257–4124). **Horizontes** (✉ 150 yards north of Pizza Hut, Barrio Paseo Colón, San José, ☎ 222–2022, FAX 255–4513). **Rain Forest Aerial Tram** (✉ Avda. 7 between Cs. 5 and 7, Barrio Amón, San José, ☎ 257–5961). **Ríos Tropicales** (✉ 50 yards south of Centro Colón, Barrio Paseo Colón, San José, ☎ 233–6455, FAX 255–4354). **Sun Tours** (✉ 200 yards south of Burger King, Barrio La Uruca, San José, ☎ 296–7757, FAX 296–4307). **Tropical Bungee** (✉ Sabana Sur, 100 yards west and 50 yards south of Controlaria, Sabana Sur, San José, ☎ 232–3956).

TAXIS

Taxis are a good deal within the city. You can hail one on the street (all taxis are red with a gold triangle on the front door) or have your hotel or restaurant call one for you, as cabbies tend to speak only Spanish and addresses are complicated. A 3-km (2-mi) ride costs around $2, and tipping is not the custom. Taxis parked in front of expensive hotels charge about twice the normal rate. By law, all cabbies must use their meters—called *marias*—when operating within the metropolitan area; if one refuses, negotiate a price before setting off, or hail another. Cab companies include San Jorge, Coopetaxi and, if you need to go to the airport, Taxis Unidos.

➤ TAXI COMPANIES: **Coopetaxi** (☎ 235–9966). **San Jorge** (☎ 221–3434). **Taxis Unidos** (☎ 221–6865).

TRAVEL AGENCIES

➤ LOCAL AGENT REFERRALS: **Aviatica** (✉ Avda. 1 and C. 1, Barrio del Carmen, ☎ 222–5630). **Galaxy** (✉ C. 3 between Avdas. 5 and 7, Barrio Amón, ☎ 233–3240). **Intertur** (✉ 50 yards west of Kentucky Fried Chicken, Avda. Central between Cs. 31 and 33, Barrio Francisco Peralta, ☎ 253–7503).

VISITOR INFORMATION

➤ TOURIST INFORMATION: **Instituto Costarricense de Turismo** (ICT; ✉ C. 5 between Advas. Central and 2, Barrio del Catedral, ☎ 222–1090) staffs a tourist information office beneath the Plaza de la Cultura, next to the Museo de Oro. Pick up free maps, bus schedules, and brochures weekdays 9–12:30 and 1:30–5.

3 THE CENTRAL VALLEY: AROUND SAN JOSÉ

Distinctive hotels in the Central Valley hills offer what the capital can't—quiet and luxurious accommodations surrounded by awesome volcanoes and working coffee *fincas* (farms). The Valley is a no-less convenient base for heady excursions: Peer into the crater of a volcano, marvel at rushing waterfalls, wander through butterfly gardens, or visit colonial-era towns that prosper thanks to the *grano de oro* (golden bean).

Updated
by George
Soriano

COUNTRY ROADS WINDING UP THE HILLS of the Meseta Central, or Central Valley, lead past an abundance of charming hotels and restaurants set among cloud forests, coffee fields, and volcano villages. When skies are clear, sweeping views from these properties are yet another reason to base yourself here for a while.

Hovering more than 3,000 ft above sea level, the valley is Costa Rica's approximate geographic center, sandwiched between hulking mountain chains—the foothills of the Cordillera de Talamanca define the valley's southern edge, and the Cordillera Central sweeps across its northern border. Three fuming volcanoes along these chains are within easy reach: Volcán Irazú, Costa Rica's highest, towers to the east of San José; Poás, whose active crater often spews a plume of sulfuric smoke, stands to the northwest; and the older, dormant Volcán Barva looms between the two. Dramatic craters and thick cloud forests at their summits are protected within national parks, while the slopes in their shadows are coffee communities and quaint agricultural hamlets.

Though most of the region's colonial architecture has been destroyed by earthquakes and the ravages of time, several smaller cities preserve a bit more history than you'll find in San José. The central squares of Alajuela, Escazú, and Heredia, for example, are surrounded by architectural mixtures of old and new. Cartago, the country's first capital, has scattered historical structures and the impressive Basílica de Nuestra Señora de Los Angeles. Beyond these small cities lie dozens of tiny farming communities, where lovely churches and adobe farmhouses look out onto coffee fields. You can easily tackle the Central Valley's attractions on a series of half- or full-day excursions from San José, but the abundance of excellent food and lodging in the valley's other towns invites you to base yourself here for a spell.

Pleasures and Pastimes

Dining

Restaurants in the Central Valley run the gamut, from rustic mountain lodges, where hearty meals are enhanced by the beauty of the natural surroundings, to the exceptional eateries in the hills above Escazú—fine dining with a backdrop of San José by night. Even if you keep your base in San José, consider venturing to this bedroom community for a meal or two.

CATEGORY	COST*
$$$$	over $20
$$$	$10–$20
$$	$5–$10
$	under $5

per person for main course at dinner.

Festivals

The Día de la Virgen de Los Angeles, which honors Costa Rica's patron saint, is celebrated in Cartago on August 2 with processions and a well-attended mass. The night before, tens of thousands of faithful worshipers walk *la romaría*, a 22-km (14-mi) trek east down the highway from San José to Cartago. April 11 is Día de Juan Santamaría in Alajuela, when a loud parade and other festivities get under way. July's Festival de los Mangoes, also in Alajuela, celebrates this tropical fruit with nine days of music, parades, markets, and general merrymaking. On the second Sunday in March, the Día del Boyero (Oxcart-Driver

Day) is marked with a colorful procession of carts through San Antonio de Escazú.

Lodging

The accommodations scattered across this area range from rustic *cabinas* (cottages) to elegant suites. Many are family-run enterprises with unique, sometimes whimsical designs that take advantage of exceptional countryside locations. If you want to get away from it all, and be close to the transportation hub, lodgings outside the capital are a very attractive option.

CATEGORY	COST*
$$$$	over $90
$$$	$50–$90
$$	$25–$50
$	under $25

for a double room, excluding service and tax (16.4%)

Volcanoes

Some of Costa Rica's most accessible volcanoes stand on the northern edge of the Central Valley, and paved roads run right to the summits of two, Poás and Irazú. Volcán Poás is very popular, as it has an extensive visitor center, an active crater, a luxuriant forest, and a jewel-like blue-green lake. Volcán Irazú, Costa Rica's highest, is topped by a desolate landscape (the result of violent eruptions in the early 1960s), but on a clear day the view is unparalleled. Barva, in the southern section of Braulio Carrillo National Park north of San José, is cloaked in an extensive cloud forest that resounds with the songs of colorful birds, such as the emerald toucanet and resplendent quetzal. You can visit all three volcanoes on day trips from San José; Poás and Irazú require only a morning, the summit of Barva a full day.

Exploring the Central Valley

The region has an extensive network of paved roads, many of which are in relatively good shape. The Pan-American Highway runs east–west through the valley (through the center of San José) and turns south at Cartago. Dozens of roads head off of this well-marked highway, but if you stray from the main travelers' routes, you may find a lack of road signs. If you do, don't despair—locals are always happy to point you in the right direction.

Numbers in the text correspond to numbers in the margin and on the Central Valley: Around San José map.

Great Itineraries

Most Central Valley towns stand in the shadows of volcanoes, so try to stop in one or two towns on your way down from the summit of any volcano you visit. To reach Volcán Poás, for example, you have to drive through Alajuela; Heredia lies on the road to Volcán Barva, and Cartago sits at the foot of Irazú. From Irazú you can take the serpentine roads eastward to Volcán Turrialba, Turrialba, and Guayabo National Monument, Costa Rica's most important archaeological site. Paraíso, just southeast of Cartago, is the gateway to the Valle de Orosi (Orosi Valley), southeast of San José.

IF YOU HAVE 2 DAYS

Drive up ⛰ **Volcán Poás** ⑤, where you can also visit nearby **La Paz Waterfall Gardens** ⑥, and then settle in for a night near the summit or just have a good lunch before returning to warmer ⛰ **Alajuela** ④ or San José. The next day, explore the Orosi Valley, stopping at the fascinating **Jardín Lankester** ⑫ on the way.

The Central Valley: Around San José

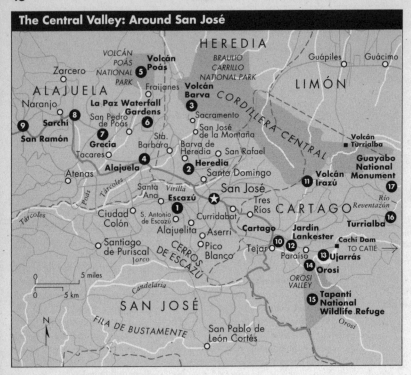

IF YOU HAVE 4 DAYS

Head to ⊡ **Heredia** ② and the adjacent coffee communities, continuing up the slopes of **Volcán Barva** ③ for a picnic in the cool mountain air. The energetic can hike up to the crater lakes at the volcano's peak, or take a high-altitude horseback ride before retiring in the hills for the night. Continue exploring the western Central Valley, spending the morning at ⊡ **Volcán Poás** ⑤, and the afternoon visiting the towns of ⊡ **Grecia** ⑦ and **Sarchí** ⑧. On day 3, head southeast for a hike in **Tapantí National Wildlife Refuge** ⑮, stopping in Cartago and spending the night in the East Valley. ⑭. Drive early the next morning to the summit of **Volcán Irazú** ⑪, and then wind your way down its slopes to **Guayabo National Monument** ⑰ and ⊡ **Turrialba** ⑯. Devote day four to white-water rafting.

When to Tour the Central Valley

From January to May it tends to be sunny and breezy here. On the upper slopes of the volcanoes, January and February nights can get quite cold. Afternoon downpours are common starting mid-May, dropping off a bit between July and September; from mid-September to December, precipitation picks up again. But don't rule out travel to Costa Rica during the rainy season (May to December)—some days are spared rain, and when it does rain, it's usually during what you might call the siesta hours. Because few travelers visit during this period, you probably won't need reservations. The valley is swathed in green after the rains, but come January the sun begins to beat down, and by April the countryside is parched. Costa Ricans generally take their vacations during Holy Week (the week before Easter) and the last two weeks of the year, so it's essential to reserve cars and hotel rooms in advance for these periods.

THE WESTERN CENTRAL VALLEY

As you drive north or west out of San José, the city's suburbs and industrial zones quickly give way to arable land, most of which is given over to vast coffee plantations. Coffee has come to symbolize the prosperity of both the Central Valley and the nation as a whole; as such, this all-important cash crop has inspired a fair bit of folklore. Costa Rican artists, for example, have long venerated coffee workers, and the painted oxcart, once used to transport coffee to the coast, has become a national symbol.

Within Costa Rica's coffee heartland are plenty of tranquil agricultural towns and two provincial capitals, Alajuela and Heredia. Both cities owe their relative prosperity to the coffee beans cultivated on the fertile lower slopes of the Poás and Barva volcanoes. The upper slopes, too cold for coffee crops, are dedicated to dairy cattle, strawberries, ferns, and flowers, making for markedly different and thoroughly enchanting landscapes along the periphery of the national parks. Since the hills above these quaint valley towns hide some excellent restaurants and lodgings, rural overnights are a wonderful way to stretch out your exploration, before, after, or instead of a trip to the coast.

Escazú

❶ *5 km (3 mi) southwest of San José.*

A 15-minute drive west of San José takes you to Escazú, a traditional coffee-farming town and now a bedroom community at the foot of a small mountain range. Local lore has dubbed it the City of Witches, as it's thought to be popular with those spell-casting women. Escazú's ancient church faces a small plaza, surrounded in part by weathered adobe homes. Scattered amid the coffee fields that cover the steep slopes above town are well-tended farmhouses, often painted blue and white, with tidy gardens and the occasional oxcart parked in the yard—precisely the kind of scene that captured the attention of many a Costa Rican painter in the 20th century. There are also plenty of fancy homes between the humble farmhouses, especially in the San Antonio and San Rafael neighborhoods.

High in the hills above Escazú stands the tiny community of **San Antonio de Escazú,** famous for its annual oxcart festival held the second Sunday of March. The view from here—of nearby San José and distant volcanoes—is impressive by both day and night. If you head higher than San Antonio de Escazú, brace yourself for virtually vertical roads that wind up into the mountains toward **Pico Blanco,** the highest point in the Escazú Cordillera.

Dining and Lodging

$$$$ ✕ **Hostaría Cerutti.** This little Italian restaurant on a busy intersection is the diva of San José's Italian eateries. Within a lovely, century-old adobe house, its whitewashed walls are adorned with antique prints. The extensive menu is heavy on seafood: start with octopus and asparagus in pesto, or ravioli with mushrooms in a truffle sauce; then sink your teeth into some *cordero al horno* (rack of lamb roasted with vegetables). Reservations are recommended. ⊠ *Cruce de San Rafael de Escazú,* ☎ *228–4511. AE, MC, V. Closed Tues.*

$$$–$$$$ ✕ **Le Monastère.** A former monastery turned formal restaurant high in the San Rafael hills has the best view of the Central Valley. The dining room is dressed up in antiques, with tables set for a five-course meal; waiters don friar robes. The Belgian owner prepares outstanding classic French dishes and some original Costa Rican items, such as a grilled

caiman appetizer. Or try the more conventional grilled corvina smothered in a Provençal herb sauce. The restaurant serves dinner only, from 7 to 11 PM—reservations are recommended—but the bar beneath the dining room, La Cava, has live music Tuesday through Saturday and is open into the wee hours. ⊠ *San Rafael de Escazú (take old road to Santa Ana, turn left at the Paco Shopping Center, and follow signs),* ☎ *289–4404. AE, DC, MC, V. Closed Sun. No lunch.*

$–$$ ✕ **Café de Artistas.** The "Warhol's Sandwich" (a bagel loaded with bacon, eggs, and cheese) or "Monet's Morning" (thickly sliced French toast with real maple syrup) are two inventively named dishes on the breakfast menu at this bohemian-chic café–cum–art gallery. Lunch begets the veggie-based "Torte Da Vinci" (a vegetable and tofu dish). Walls washed in ocher create perfect backdrop for the many whimsical paintings and antique furniture. Nifty novelty items lying around the dining area, include hand-tooled cigar boxes from Cuba. Plus everything's for sale. ⊠ *San Rafael de Escazú, 100 yards west of Rolex Plaza,* ☎ *228–6045. MC, V. Closed Mon. No dinner.*

$$$$ ☷ **Alta.** Perhaps it's lofty location befits the lofty price (well, by Costa
★   Rican standards). Views from the Iberian-style hotel, which has barrel-tile roofs, ocher stuccoed walls, and hand-painted bathroom tiles, are breathtaking. A sloping stairway lined with tall columns and palms runs through the property, reminiscent of a narrow street in southern Spain. Guest rooms have beautiful terra-cotta tile floors, earth-tone fabrics and walls, colonial-style furniture, and a few paintings. Rooms on floors two through five have small balconies; ground-floor rooms have garden terraces and direct pool access. Its eclectic restaurant, La Luz, is popular with the expat crowd. ⊠ *Old road to Santa Ana, Escazú,* ☎ *282–4160,* FAX *282–4162,* WEB *www.thealtahotel.com (mailing address: Interlink 964, Box 02–5635, Miami, FL 33102,* ☎ *888/388–2582). 19 rooms, 4 suites. Restaurant, pool, hot tub, sauna, gym. AE, DC, MC, V.*

$$$ –$$$$ ☷ **Tara Resort Hotel.** Modeled after the famous fictitious mansion from *Gone With the Wind* and decorated in antebellum style, this luxurious little inn is near the top of Pico Blanco. Throughout the three-story white-and-green building, hardwood floors are covered with patterned area rugs. Guest rooms are decorated with floral spreads and lace curtains; French doors open onto the public veranda. At the Atlanta Dining Gallery, try the beef tenderloin in green-peppercorn sauce. After dinner, try your hand at poker in the the parlor-style casino. ⊠ *600 yards south of the cemetery of San Antonio de Escazú,* ☎ *228–6992,* FAX *228–9651 (mailing address: Apdo. 1459–1250, Escazú). 12 rooms, 1 suite, 1 bungalow. Restaurant, pool, hot tub, massage, spa. AE, MC, V.*

$$$ ☷ **Costa Verde Inn.** Rooms at this attractive B&B on the outskirts of Escazú make nice use of local hardwoods in their furniture and trim, and their white walls display traditional Peruvian art. South American art adorns the main building, where a large sitting area has comfortable chairs and a fireplace. The inn is surrounded by gardens, and at night you can see the lights of San José twinkling to the east. Complimentary breakfast is served on the shady patio. ⊠ *From southeast corner of second cemetery, 200 yards west and 100 yards north,* ☎ *228–4080,* FAX *289–8591,* WEB *www.costaverdeinn.com (mailing address: SJO 1313, Box 025216, Miami, FL 33102-5216). 15 rooms. Pool, hot tub, tennis court; no air-conditioning. AE, MC, V.*

$$$ ☷ **Posada El Quijote.** At this friendly, family-run B&B perched on a hill in the Bello Horizonte neighborhood (on the San José side of Escazú), you'll find the best vantage point on the sundeck. The living room has big windows, a couch, a fireplace, and lots of modern art. Deluxe rooms have city views; superior rooms overlook the gardens. The inn is a pet-friendly, so guest dogs, cats, and birds are often seen on the property; complimentary breakfast is served on a covered interior patio.

☒ *Bello Horizonte de Escazú,* ☎ *289–8401,* FAX *289–8729,* WEB *www. quijote.co.cr (mailing address: Dept. 239–SJO, Box 025216, Miami, FL 33102-5216). 9 rooms, 2 apartments. Travel services; no air-conditioning. AE, MC, V.*

Heredia

➋ *15 km (9 mi) north of Escazú, 9 km (6 mi) north of San José.*

With a population of around 30,000, Heredia is the capital of one of Costa Rica's most important coffee provinces and perhaps the country's best-preserved colonial town. It bears witness, however, to how little preservation can mean in an earthquake-prone country: Heredia has lost many of its colonial structures over the years. Still, the city retains an historic feel, with old adobe buildings scattered throughout downtown, and you'll see more in the charming nearby villages of Barva de Heredia, Santo Domingo, and San Rafael de Heredia.

The tree-studded **Parque Central** holds some colonial appeal. At the park's eastern end stands the impressive stone **Catedral de Heredia,** dating back to 1797, whose thick walls, small windows, and squat buttresses have kept it standing through countless quakes and tremors. Unfortunately, the church's stained-glass work has not fared as well. The park has a simple kiosk and a cast-iron fountain imported from England in 1897. ☒ *Parque Central,* ☎ *237–0779.* ☉ *Daily 6–6.*

Surrounding the park are some interesting buildings. The 1843 barrel-tile-roof **Casa de la Cultura,** often houses art exhibits. Behind the brick **Municipalidad** (municipal building) stands a strange, decorative tower called the fortín, or small fort.

Between Heredia and Barva is the **Museo de Cultura Popular** (Museum of Popular Culture), an early 20th-century farmhouse built with an adobe-like technique called *bahareque.* Run by the National University, the museum is furnished with antiques and surrounded by a small garden and coffee fields. An inexpensive, open-air lunch restaurant serves authentic Costa Rican cuisine and can be a lively spot on weekends, when a more extensive menu is sometimes paired with marimba music and folk dancing. ☒ *Between Heredia and Barva, follow signs for right turn,* ☎ *260–1619.* ☒ *$2.* ☉ *Daily 9–4, restaurant daily 11–2. No credit cards.*

☏ The producer of Costa Rica's most popular export-quality coffee, **Café Britt,** offers a lively tour of its working coffee plantation, which highlights Costa Rica's history of coffee cultivation through a theatrical presentation. (You have to see it to believe it.) Take a short walk through the coffee farm and processing plant, and learn how professional tasters distinguish a fine cup of java in a coffee-tasting session from a not-so nice one. On an additional tour ($10) you can learn how espresso beans are roasted and then make your own cappuccino after lunch. ☒ *900 yards north and 400 yards west of the Comandancia, Heredia,* ☎ *260–2748,* FAX *260–1456.* ☒ *$20, $27 with transportation from San José.* ☉ *Dec.–May, tours daily at 9, 11, and 3; June–Nov., tours daily at 11.*

☏ The guided tour of **INBio Parque** is an excellent introduction to three of the country's ecosystems before you head out to see them for real. After watching short videos, wander trails through climate-controlled wetlands and out to tropical dry forest. Along the way, stop at the butterfly farm, snake and insect exhibits, and a bromeliad garden. English-speaking guides end the tour with a discussion on biodiversity and INBio (Biodiversity Institute). A pleasant restaurant serves typical Costa

Rican fare and an extensive bookstore and shop has eco-friendly souvenirs. ⊠ *400 yards north and 250 yards west of Shell gas station in Santo Domingo, Heredia,* ☎ *244–4790.* 🖃 *$16.* ☉ *Daily 8–5.*

The small community of **Barva de Heredia,** about 2 km [1 mi] north of Heredia proper, has a wonderful Parque Central surrounded by old Spanish-tiled adobe houses on three sides and a white stucco church to the east. Flanked by royal palms, the stout, handsome church dates from the late 18th century; behind it is a lovely little garden shrine to the Virgin Mary. On a clear day you can see verdant Volcán Barva towering to the north, and if you follow the road that runs in front of the church, veering to the right, you'll reach the village of Sacramento. Here the road turns into a steep, dirt track leading to the Barva sector of Braulio Carrillo National Park.

Lodging

$$$ 🏨 **Hotel Bougainvillea.** Here you'll soon forget that you're only 15 min-
★ utes from San José. Set amid the coffee farms of Santo Domingo de Heredia, the Bougainvillea has extensive grounds filled in with tall trees and brightened by one of the country's most impressive bromeliad gardens. The spacious, carpeted guest rooms are furnished with local hardwoods; the tiled bathrooms come with tub and hair dryer. Decorating the lobby and excellent restaurant are original pre-Columbian pieces and paintings by local artists. ⊠ *Guápiles Hwy. to Tibas exit, then road to Santo Domingo, and follow signs,* ☎ *244–1414,* 𝖥𝖠𝖷 *244–1313,* 𝖶𝖤𝖡 *www.bougainvillea.co.cr (mailing address: Apdo. 69–2120, San José). 76 rooms, 4 suites. Restaurant, bar, pool, hot tub, sauna, tennis court. AE, MC, V.*

Volcán Barva

❸ *20 km (12 mi) north of Heredia, 30 km (19 mi) north of San José.*

North of Barva de Heredia the road grows narrow and steep as it winds its way up the verdant slopes of Barva Volcano, whose 3,166-m (9,500-ft) summit is the highest point in **Braulio Carrillo National Park.** To the east a similar road climbs the volcano from San Rafael de Heredia, ending atop **Monte de la Cruz,** which borders the national park. Dormant for 300 years now, Barva is massive: its lower slopes are almost completely planted with coffee fields and hold about a dozen small towns. The upper slopes consist of pastures divided by exotic pines and the occasional native oak and cedar, giving way to the botanical diversity of the cloud forest near the top. The air is usually cool at the summit. Combined with the pines and pastures, the flora here will surprise you if you've presumed that only rain forest plants, bananas, and coffee beans can grow in Costa Rica.

Any vehicle can make the trip past San Rafael de Heredia to the Monte de la Cruz, and even buses follow the loop above Barva via **San José de la Montaña;** but it's rough going if you want to get much higher than this. From San José de la Montaña to the crater, you can, in the dry months, take a four-wheel-drive vehicle over the extremely rocky road to the park entrance; alternately, leave your car and hike up on foot, a four-hour trip.

Barva's misty, luxuriant summit is the only part of the park where camping is allowed, and it's a good place to see the rare resplendent quetzal if you're here early in the morning. Because it's somewhat hard to access, Barva receives a mere fraction of the crowds that flock to the summits of Poás and Irazú. A 30-minute hike in from the ranger station takes you to the main crater, which is about 200 yards in diameter; its almost vertical sides are covered in poor man's umbrellas, a plant

COSTA RICA'S GOLDEN BEAN

WHEN COSTA RICA'S FIRST elected president, Juan Mora Fernandez, began encouraging his compatriots to cultivate coffee back in 1830, he could hardly have imagined how profound an impact the crop would have on his country. Over the last hundred years, coffee has transformed Costa Rica from a colonial backwater into a relatively affluent and cosmopolitan republic.

It was the "golden bean" that financed the construction of most of the nation's landmarks. Founding families owned the largest plantations, creating a coffee oligarchy that has produced the majority of Costa Rican presidents. The bean also provided an economic incentive for tens of thousands of immigrant families from Europe and elsewhere in the Americas, who, during the 1800s and early 1900s, were given land in exchange for cutting down the forest and planting coffee. These farmers formed the backbone of a middle-class majority that has long distinguished Costa Rica from most of Latin America. Whether you credit the power of caffeine or the socioeconomic factors surrounding the crop, the tidy homes, colorful gardens, and orderly farms of the Central Valley make Costa Ricans look like the original coffee achievers.

Thanks to its altitude and mineral-rich volcanic soil, the Central Valley is ideal for growing coffee, and the crop covers nearly every arable acre of this region. Strangely, since it dominates the Central Valley's physical and cultural landscape, coffee is not actually native to Costa Rica: biologists claim the plant evolved in the mountains of Ethiopia. Arab nations were sipping the aromatic beverage as early as the 7th century—its scientific name is *Coffea arabica*—but it didn't catch on in Europe until the 1600s. Coffee plants first arrived in Costa Rica from the Caribbean, probably in the early 1820s.

The coffee-growing cycle begins in May, when the arrival of annual rains makes the dark-green bushes explode into a flurry of white blossoms—as close as it comes to snowing in Costa Rica. By November, the fruit starts to ripen, turning from green to red, and the busy harvest begins as farmers race to get picked "cherries" to *beneficios,* processing plants where the beans—two per fruit—are removed, washed, dried by machine, and packed in burlap sacks for export. Costa Rica's crop is consistently among the world's best, and most of the high-grade exports wind up in Europe and the United States.

Traditionally, coffee bushes are grown in the shade of trees, such as citrus or the nitrogen-fixing members of the bean family. Recently, however, many farmers have switched to sun-resistant varieties, cutting down shade trees to pack more coffee bushes into each acre. Shade farms provide habitats for migratory birds and other animals, but the new shadeless farms are practically biological deserts, which is why environmentalists are promoting a return to the old system by labeling shade coffee ECO-OK.

Ticos are fueled by an inordinate amount of coffee. They generally filter it through cloth bags, a method that makes for a stronger cup of java than your average American brew. The mean bean is even used in a favorite local dish: chicken roasted with coffee wood. Sadly, many Ticos drink the low-grade stuff, often mixed with molasses, peanuts, or corn for bulk—and roasted too long; you're best off buying such reliable brands as Café Rey's Tarrazú, Café Britt, Américo, Volio, and Montaña.

that thrives in the highlands, and oak trees laden with epiphytes (non-parasitic plants that grow on other plants). At the crater's lower edge is an otherworldly black lake; farther down the track into the forest lies another crater lake. Bring rain gear, boots, and a warm shirt, and stick to the trails—even experienced hikers who know the area have lost their way up here. ☎ *283–5906 or 192 for National Parks Service information.* ☒ *$6.* ☉ *Tues.–Sun. 7–4.*

Just northeast (about 2 km [1 mi]) of Heredia lies **San Rafael de Heredia,** a quiet, mildly affluent coffee town with a large church notable for its stained-glass windows and bright interior. The road north from the church winds its way up Volcán Barva to hotels Chalet Tirol and La Condesa and to Monte de la Cruz lookout point. **Santo Domingo,** southeast of Heredia, is another attractive agricultural community with two churches, an abundance of adobe houses, and some traditional coffee farms on its outskirts.

Lodging

$$$$ ⊞ **Clarion Hotel Real La Condesa.** Suggestive of a lodge in a more northern latitude, the La Condesa lobby has a stone fireplace surrounded by couches, armchairs, and a small bar. The central courtyard, topped by a giant skylight, is occupied by one of the hotel's three restaurants. A tropical garden is similarly enclosed in the pool area. Guest rooms are carpeted and tastefully furnished, and each has a picture window. Suites have bedroom lofts, sitting areas, and the hotel's best views. Families should consider the log cabin villas with full kitchens. ☒ *Next to the Castillo Country Club, 10 km (6 mi) north of Heredia, San Rafael de Heredia,* ☎ *267–6001,* FAX *267–6200. 47 rooms, 36 suites, 4 villas. 3 restaurants, 2 bars, indoor pool, hot tub, horseback riding, squash, meeting room, travel services, car rental. AE, MC, V.*

$$$$ ⊞ **Finca Rosa Blanca Country Inn.** There's nothing common about
★   this luxurious little B&B overlooking coffee farms; you need only step through the front door of the Gaudíesque main building to marvel at its soaring ceiling, white-stucco arches, and polished wood. Each guest room is different, but all have original art, local hardwoods, and colorful fabrics. The spacious, two-story suite is out of a fairy tale, with a spiral staircase leading up to a window-lined tower bedroom. Out on the grounds—planted with tropical flowers and shaded by massive fig trees—are two villas, each with two bedrooms. Four-course dinners are optional. ☒ *Barrio Jesus, 6 km (4 mi) west of Santa Barbara de Heredia,* ☎ *269–9392,* FAX *269–9555,* WEB *www.fincarosablanca.com (mailing address: SJO 1201, Box 025216, Miami, FL 33102-5216). 6 rooms, 2 villas. Dining room, pool, horseback riding, travel services, airport shuttle; no air-conditioning. AE, MC, V.*

$$$ ⊞ **Las Ardillas.** Surrounded by old pines on a country road, these unpretentious log cabins are inviting retreats for those looking to lock themselves up in front of a fireplace and tune out the world. The small on-site spa is one reason to venture from the comfortable, romantic rooms; the other is a meal at the restaurant, which specializes in meats roasted over a wood fire and has a nice selection of Spanish wines. Breakfast is complimentary. All rooms have modest wood furniture, kitchenettes, and queen-size beds. ☒ *Main road, Guacalillo de San José de la Montaña,* ☎ *260–2172,* FAX *266-1993 (mailing address: Apdo. 44–309, Barva). 15 cabins. Restaurant, bar, kitchenettes, hot tub, massage, sauna, spa; no air-conditioning, no room phones. AE, MC, V.*

$$$ ⊞ **Hotel Chalet Tirol.** Amazingly enough, the Chalet Tirol's Austrian design doesn't seem out of place amid the pines, pastures, and cool air of Volcán Barva's upper slopes. The replica of a cobbled Tirolean town square—complete with fountain and church—may be a bit much, but the cozy, bright, two-story wooden chalets are quite charming, as

is the restaurant, with its ivy, wooden ceiling, and elegant murals. Quality French cuisine makes this a popular weekend destination for Costa Ricans. The suites have fireplaces and are more private than the separate chalets. Breakfast is complimentary. ⊠ *Main road, 10 km (6 mi) north of Heredia, San Rafael de Heredia,* ☎ *267–6222,* FAX *267– 6229. 13 suites, 10 chalets. Restaurant, bar, tennis court; no air-conditioning. AE, DC, MC, V.*

Outdoor Activities and Sports

HIKING

The upper slopes of Volcán Barva have excellent hiking conditions: cool air, vistas, and plentiful birds. The crater lakes topping the volcano can only be reached on foot, and if you haven't got a four-wheel-drive vehicle, you'll also have to trek from Sacramento up to the entrance of Braulio Carrillo National Park. **Hotel Chalet Tirol** (☎ 267–6222) leads an early morning walk on a 4-km (2½-mi) trail through the cloud forest—an excellent trip for bird-watchers.

HORSEBACK RIDING

Horseback-riding tours along the upper slopes of Volcán Barva, near Braulio Carrillo National Park, combine views of the Central Valley with close exposure to the cloud forest and resident bird life. You can reserve a horseback excursion through **Hotel Chalet Tirol** (☎ 267–6222). Otherwise try booking a horseback tour through travel agencies in San José.

Alajuela

❹ *20 km (13 mi) northwest of San José.*

Despite being Costa Rica's second-largest city (population 50,000) and a mere 30-minute bus ride from the capital, Alajuela has a decidedly provincial air. Architecturally it differs little from the bulk of Costa Rican towns: it's a grid plan of low-rise structures painted in primary colors. Alajuela's picturesque **Parque Central** is filled with royal palms and mango trees, has a lovely fountain imported from Glasgow, and cement benches where locals gather to chat. Surrounding the plaza is an odd mix of charming old buildings and sterile cement boxes. The large, neoclassic **cathedral,** badly damaged by a 1990 earthquake, has interesting capitals decorated with local agricultural motifs and a striking red dome. The interior, though spacious, is rather plain except for the ornate dome above the altar. ⊠ *C. Central between Avdas. 1 and Central,* ☎ *441–0769.* ☉ *Daily 8–6.*

To the north of the park stands the **old jail,** which now houses the local offices of the Ministry of Education—an appropriate metaphor for a country that claims to have more teachers than police.

Alajuela was the birthplace of Juan Santamaría, the national hero who lost his life in a battle against the mercenary army of U.S. adventurer William Walker (1824–60) when the latter invaded Costa Rica in 1856. A statue of the youthful Santamaría stands in Alajuela's **Parque Juan Santamaría,** one block south of the Parque Central. Juan Santamaría's heroic deeds are celebrated in the **Museo Juan Santamaría,** one block north of Parque Central. The museum contains maps, compasses, weapons, and paintings, including an image of Walker's men filing past to lay down their weapons. The colonial building that houses the museum is more interesting than the displays, however. ⊠ *C. 2 and Avda. 3,* ☎ *441–4775.* 🎟 *Free.* ☉ *Tues.–Sun. 10–6.*

Spread over the lush grounds of ♻ **Zoo Ave** (Bird Zoo) is a collection of large cages holding macaws, toucans, hawks, and parrots, not to mention crocodiles, monkeys, and other interesting critters. The zoo runs a breeding project for rare and endangered birds and mammals, all of which are destined for eventual release. An impressive mural bordering part of the facility shows Costa Rica's 850 bird species painted to scale. To get here, head west from the center of Alajuela past the cemetery; then turn left after the stone church in Barrio San José. Kids under 10 get in for $2. ⊠ *La Garita de Alajuela,* ☎ *433–8989.* ☞ *$9.* ☉ *Daily 9–5.*

☺ The **Finca de Mariposas** (Butterfly Farm), in the suburb of La Guácima, offers a regular lecture on the ecology of these delicate insects and gives you a chance to observe and photograph them up close. In addition to an apiary exhibit, the farm's several microclimates keep comfortable some 40 rare species of butterflies. Try to come here when it's sunny, as that's when butterflies are most active. The farm offers transportation from San José for $10. ⊠ *From San José, turn south (left) at the intersection just past Cariari Hotel, then right at church of San Antonio de Belén, then left, and then follow butterfly signs,* ☎ *438–0115.* ☞ *$15.* ☉ *Daily 8:30–5.*

Lodging

$$$$ 🏨 **Pura Vida Retreat Center.** Yoga classes and workshops are as much a part of the stay as the accommodations themselves. A weekly rate includes two daily yoga classes, tours, transfers, all meals, and one massage. If you like privacy, upgrade to the minimalist Japanese pagoda, with a Balinese-style outdoor shower and its own hot tub and sun deck. Three suites and a villa have large windows and bamboo furniture, and more creature comforts than the unique "tentalows" or luxury tents set within surrounding tropical gardens. A stay in the carpeted tents (furnished with a chair, night tables, and small wood desk) is meant to strengthen the connection with the outdoors, which means you're up with the sun, when the first yoga activity begins. The retreat serves delicious and healthy meals, and the spa offers many treatments from massage to guided meditation. ⊠ *700 yards south of cantina Salon Apolo 15, Pavas de Carrizal,* ☎ *392–8099,* ℻ *483–0041,* 🌐 *www.puravidaspa.com (mailing address: Apdo. 1112, Alajuela 4050; reservations: R & R Resorts, Box 1496, Conyers, GA 30012,* ☎ *888/767–7375). 45 tent bungalows, 3 suites, 1 villa, 1 pagoda. Dining room, spa, travel services; no air-conditioning, no room phones, no room TVs. AE, MC, V.*

$$$$ 🏨 **Xandari.** The tranquil and colorful Xandari is a strikingly original
★ inn. Its bold design is the brainchild of a talented couple—he's an architect, she's an artist. Contemporary pueblo-esque villas, along a ridge overlooking Alajuela, are spacious, with plenty of windows, colorful paintings, creatively placed tile showers, large terraces, and secluded lanais (sunbathing patios). Ultra villas are independent; the two Prima villas share one building. The attractive restaurant serves low-fat food, using some ingredients grown on the grounds. The slow enjoyment of meals is emphasized. A trail through the hotel's forest reserve winds past five waterfalls. ⊠ *3 km (1.8 mi) north of Alajuela, turn left after small bridge, follow signs,* ☎ *443–2020,* ℻ *442–4847,* 🌐 *www.xandari.com (mailing address: Apdo. 1485–4050, Alajuela). 17 villas. Restaurant, bar, 2 pools, hot tub, spa; no air-conditioning, no room TVs. AE, MC, V.*

$$$ 🏨 **Orquídeas Inn.** Once the home of a coffee farmer, this Spanish-colonial residence has some quirky additions that make it a lively retreat in otherwise tranquil surroundings: a bar dedicated to Marilyn Monroe, an outdoor grill-your-own steak house, and a geodesic dome that contains one of the hotel's four suites. Standard rooms have terra-cotta tile floors, Guatemalan bedspreads, and paintings by Central American artists. Rooms in a newer wing are more in keeping with a tropical theme, with bamboo headboards and colorful floral bedspreads. Pet toucans, parrots, and macaws inhabit the wooded grounds, which means there's lots of squawking by the light of day. ⊠ *5 km (3 mi) west of cemetery,* ☎ *433–9346,* FAX *433–9740 (mailing address: Apdo. 394, Alajuela). 29 rooms, 4 suites. Restaurant, bar, pool. AE, MC, V.*

Volcán Poás

❺ *37 km (23 mi) north of Alajuela, 57 km (35 mi) north of San José.*

The main crater of the Poás volcano, at nearly 1½ km (1 mi) across and 333 m (1,000 ft) deep, is one of the largest active craters in the world. The sight of this vast, multicolored pit, gurgling with smoking fumaroles and a greenish-turquoise sulfurous lake, is simply breathtaking. All sense of scale is absent here, as the crater is devoid of vegetation. A paved road leads all the way to the 2,933-m (8,800-ft) summit: the road from Alajuela winds past coffee fields, pastures, screened-in fern plantations, and, near the summit, thick cloud forest.

The peak is frequently enshrouded in mist, and many who come here see little beyond the lip of the crater. If you're faced with pea soup, wait a while, especially if some wind is blowing—the clouds can disappear quickly. The earlier in the day you go, the better your chance of a clear view. If you're lucky, you'll see the famous geyser in action, spewing a column of gray mud high into the air. Poás last had a major eruption in 1953 and is thought to be approaching another active phase; at any sign of danger, the park is closed to visitors. It can be very cold and wet up top, so dress accordingly. If you come ill equipped, you can duck under the poor man's umbrella plant. No one is allowed to venture onto the edge of the crater.

The 57-square-km (22-square-mi) **Volcán Poás National Park** protects the epiphyte-laden cloud forest on the volcano's slopes and the dwarf shrubs near the summit. One trail, which leads some 15 minutes off to the right of the main crater trail, winds through shrubs and dwarf trees toward the large and eerie **Laguna Botos** (Botos Lake), which occupies an extinct crater. **Sendero Escalonia** leads through a taller stretch of cloud forest from the picnic area back to the parking lot; boards along the way bear sentimental eco-poetry. Mammals are rare in this area, but you should see various birds, including insect-size hummingbirds and larger sooty robins. Quetzals have also been spotted in this park on occasion. Note that Volcán Poás is a popular sight and gets quite crowded, especially on Sunday. It's not a good choice if you want to commune with nature in solitude. Poás also has a modest gift shop and a cafeteria that serves hot coffee to help warm up from the high-altitude chill. ⊠ *From San José, take Pan-American Hwy. to Alajuela, Rte. 130 to Poás and follow signs,* ☎ *484–2424 or 192 for National Parks Service information.* ☜ *$6.* ☉ *Daily 7–4.*

★ **❻** **La Paz Waterfall Gardens.** Self-guided brick-lined trails through this landscaped high-elevation park lead past five magnificent rushing waterfalls—the park's main attractions. Arm yourself with a raincoat, as it's easy to get sprayed upon from the observation decks, which put the cascades within arm's reach. The main trail from the visitor center, complete with an attractive gift shop and open-air cafeteria with a view, leads first to a huge multilevel butterfly observatory and continues past a garden where hummingbird feeders attract swarms of the playful little birds. Take an alternate trail through a fern and orchid garden before winding back to the visitor center for hot tea or coffee. A free shuttle van transports you from the trail exit and back to the main building, if you'd prefer to avoid the hike back uphill. The tour takes about 1½ hours. ☒ *On the road to Poás Volcano, turn right at the sign to Poasito and continue for 1½ km (1 mi). Turn left at the sign for Vara Blanca, continue for 5 km (3 mi); it's 20 km (12 mi) from Alajuela,* ☏ *482–2720,* WEB *www.waterfallgardens.com.* ☒ *$24.* ☉ *Daily 8:30 –4.*

Dining and Lodging

$$ ✕ **Chubascos.** Set amid tall pines and colorful flowers on the upper
★ slopes of Poás Volcano, this popular restaurant has a small menu of traditional Tico dishes and delicious daily specials. Pick from the full selection of *casados* (plates of rice, beans, fried plantains, salad, cheese, and meat, chicken, or fish) and platters of *gallos* (homemade tortillas with meat, cheese, or potato fillings). The *refrescos* (fresh fruit drinks) are top-drawer, especially the ones made from locally grown *fresas* (strawberries) and *moras* (blackberries), blended with milk. ☒ *1 km (½ mi) north of Fraijanes,* ☏ *482–2280. AE, MC, V.*

$$$ ⛉ **Poás Volcano Lodge.** The rustic architecture of this former dairy farmhouse, with rough stone walls and pitched beam roof, fits perfectly into the rolling pastures that surround this retreat, inspired by English and Welsh country homes. The interior mixes Persian rugs with textiles from Latin America, and Guaitil Indian pottery with North American pieces. The lodge's most alluring feature is its oversize sunken fireplace, followed closely by the view of the Caribbean Lowlands from its 2,077m (6,232-ft) perch. All rooms are different, so look at a few before you decide: one has an exquisite stone bathtub. A small dairy farm and garden supply the kitchen with ingredients for the hearty breakfasts. ☒ *6 km (4 mi) east of Chubascos Restaurant, on road to Vara Blanca,* ☏ *482–2194,* FAX *482–2513,* WEB *www.poasvolcanolodge.com (mailing address: Apdo. 5723–1000, San José). 9 rooms, 7 with bath. Dining room, Ping-Pong, billiards, Internet, laundry service; no room phones. MC, V.*

$$ ⛉ **La Providencia Lodge.** These wood cabins scattered along the hill-
★ side have colorful quilts for chilly mornings and nights, but not much else in the way of creature comforts. If you're looking for outdoor adventure, tranquillity, and close contact with nature—and you've rented a four-wheel-drive vehicle—this rustic, remote lodge perched on the northern edge of Poás Volcano National Park is just the place. From the lodge's 500-acre forest reserve, you can look for quetzals and dozens of other birds while either hiking or horseback riding on the lodge's popular tour. The property is spectacular and the lodge is a great example of what ecolodges can be. ☒ *2 km (1 mi) to the left, from the Poás Volcano National Park entrance,* ☏ FAX *380–6315 or 389–5842 (mailing address: Apdo. 10240–1000, San José). 6 cabins. Restaurant, hiking, horseback riding; no air-conditioning, no room phones, no room TVs. No credit cards.*

Outdoor Activities and Sports

HIKING

The footpaths in Poás Volcano National Park are rather short. Nearby La Providencia Lodge has more extensive trails for exploring the cloud forest.

HORSEBACK RIDING

La Providencia Lodge offers three different horseback tours, one of which leads around Volcán Poás to views of waterfalls and charred forests. You don't need to be a guest to join a tour, but you do have to call a day in advance to reserve your horse(s).

Shopping

A number of roadside stands on the way up Poás sell strawberry jam, *cajeta* (a pale fudge), and corn crackers called *biscochos*. The **Neotrópica**

Foundation sells nature-theme T-shirts, cards, and posters in the national park's visitor center and devotes a portion of the profits to conservation projects.

Grecia

7 *26 km (16 mi) northwest of Alajuela, 46 km (29 mi) northwest of San José.*

Grecia's brick-red, prefabricated iron **Gothic church** overlooks a small **Parque Central,** where you might spot one of the resident sloths in the trees. The church was one of two buildings in the country imported from Belgium in the 1890s (the other is the metal schoolhouse next to San José's Parque Morazán), when some prominent Costa Ricans decided that metal structures would better withstand the periodic earthquakes that had taken their toll on so much of the country's architecture. The pieces of metal were shipped from Antwerp to Limón, then transported by train to Alajuela—from which point the church was carried, appropriately, by oxcarts.

At the **Mundo de las Serpientes** (World of Snakes), 50 varieties of serpents are kept in large outdoor cages. If you want to take one out for petting or photographing, just ask. ⊠ *2 km (1 mi) east of Grecia, on road to Alajuela,* ☎ *494–3700.* ☜ *$11.* ☉ *Daily 8–4.*

Lodging

$$$$ ⊡ **Vista del Valle Plantation Inn.** This B&B on an orange and coffee
★ plantation outside Grecia overlooks the canyon of the Río Grande and is popular with honeymooners. Cottages are decorated in minimalist style with simple wooden furniture and sliding French doors that open onto small porches. Each has its own personality; the Nido is the most romantic. The hotel's forest reserve has an hour-long trail leading down to a waterfall. Breakfast is served by the pool or in the main house, where you can relax in a spacious living room. The American owners are excellent cooks who can accommodate special requests with advance notice. ⊠ *On highway 1 km (½ mi) west of Rafael Iglesia bridge (follow signs),* ☎ *450–0800,* ℻ *451–1165,* ⓦⓔⓑ *www.vistadelvalle.com (mailing address: Apdo. 1485–4050, Alajuela). 2 rooms, 10 cottages. Restaurant, pool, hot tub, horseback riding; no air-conditioning, no room phones, no room TVs. MC, V.*

Sarchí

8 *8 km (5 mi) west of Grecia, 53 km (33 mi) northwest of San José.*

Tranquil little Sarchí is spread over a collection of hills surrounded by coffee plantations. Though many of its inhabitants are farmers, Sarchí is also one of Costa Rica's centers for crafts and carpentry. People drive here from all over the Central Valley to shop for furniture, and caravans of tour buses regularly descend upon the souvenir shops outside town. Local artisans work native hardwoods into bowls, boxes, toys, platters, and even jewelry, but the area's most famous products are its brightly colored oxcarts—replicas of those traditionally used to transport coffee. Trucks and tractors have largely replaced oxcarts on Costa Rican farms, but the little wagons retain their place in local folklore and can be spotted everywhere from small-town parades to postcards.

The vast majority of people who visit Sarchí spend all their time wandering through a crafts bazaar (8 km [5 mi] northwest of Grecia, which is 53 km [33 mi] northwest of San José, just off the Pan-American Highway), but if you have some time, this traditional community is worth poking around. The **church** (on Grecia's main road) dates only from the

1950s and is not particularly elaborate, but it is a colorful structure with several statues of angels alighted on its facade and a simple interior with some nice woodwork. Flanked by small gardens, the church faces a multilevel park in which a brightly decorated oxcart is displayed under its own roof. If you turn right from the church, walk two blocks north, turn right again, and walk another block and a half, you'll see the town's only real oxcart factory on your left. **Taller Eloy Alfaro e Hijos** (Eloy Alfaro and Sons Workshop) was founded in 1923, and its carpentry methods have changed little since then. The two-story wooden building housing the wood shop is surrounded by trees and flowers—usually orchids—and all the machinery on the ground floor is powered by a waterwheel at the back of the shop. Carts are painted in back, and although the factory's main product is a genuine oxcart—which sells for about $2,000—they also make some smaller mementos that can easily be shipped home. ⊠ *2 blocks north and 1½ blocks east of church,* ☏ *no phone.* ▨ *Donation suggested.* ◷ *Weekdays 8–4.*

Shopping

Sarchí is the best place in Costa Rica to buy miniature oxcarts, the larger of which are designed to serve as patio bars and can be broken down for easy transport or shipped to your home. Another popular item is a locally produced rocking chair with a leather seat and back. There's one store just north of town, and several larger complexes to the south. The nicest is the **Chaverri Factory** (☏ 454–4944), a little over 2 km (1 mi) south of Sarchí on the main road, and you can wander through its workshops (in back) to see the artisans in action. Chaverri is a good place to buy wooden crafts, but nonwood products, not to mention coffee and T-shirts, are cheaper in San José. Chaverri also runs a restaurant next door, Las Carretas, which serves international meals all day and offers a good lunch buffet. The street behind the Taller Eloy factory comes alive on Friday for the local **farmers' market.**

San Ramón

◉ *23 km (14 mi) west of Sarchí, 59 km (36 mi) northwest of San José.*

Having produced a number of minor bards, San Ramón is known locally as the City of Poets, and you may well be tempted to wax lyrical yourself as you gaze at the facade of its church or stroll through its tidy Parque Central. As pleasant a little town as it may be, however, San Ramón hides its real attractions in the countryside to the north, on the road to La Fortuna, where comfortable nature lodges offer access to private nature preserves. Aside from the poets, the massive **Iglesia de San Ramón,** built in a mixture of the Romanesque and Gothic styles, is the city's claim to fame. In 1924 an earthquake destroyed the smaller adobe church that once stood here, and the city lost no time in creating a replacement—this great gray cement structure took a quarter of a century to complete, from 1925 to 1954. To ensure that the second church would be earthquake-proof, workers poured the cement around a steel frame that was designed and forged in Germany (by Krupp). Step past the formidable facade and you'll discover a bright, elegant interior. ⊠ *Across from Parque Central,* ☏ *445–5592.* ◷ *Daily 6–11:30 AM and 1:30–7 PM.*

Lodging

$$$$ ⊞ **Villablanca.** Owned by former Costa Rican president Rodrigo Carazo, who is often around, this charming hotel is on a working dairy and coffee farm. The farmhouse contains the reception desk, bar, and restaurant; down the hill are lovely *casitas* ("little houses"), which are tiny replicas of traditional adobe farmhouses complete with whitewashed walls, tile floors, cane ceilings, and fireplaces. Resident guides lead nature walks through the adjacent cloud-forest reserve, where you can take a pulse-quickening canopy tour. Horses are available for exploring the rest of the farm. ✉ *20 km (12 mi) north of San Ramón on road to La Fortuna,* ☎ *228–4603,* ℻ *228–4004,* ⓦⓔⓑ *www.villablanca-costarica. com (mailing address: Apdo. 247–1250, Escazú). 48 casitas. Restaurant, bar, horseback riding; no air-conditioning, no room TVs. AE, DC, MC, V.*

$$$ ⊡ **Valle Escondido.** "Hidden Valley" lies within an ornamental plant farm at the edge of a 250-acre forest preserve. You could spend days exploring the 20 km (12 mi) of trails, which wind through primary forest past waterfalls and giant trees. The spacious rooms have panoramic views and small covered porches. The restaurant serves good international fare, particularly Italian. You're welcome to hike in the preserve even if you stop in just for lunch. ✉ *32 km (19 mi) north of San Ramón,* ☎ *231– 0906 or 460–1227,* ℻ *232–9591,* ⓦⓔⓑ *www.valleescondido.com. 33 rooms. Restaurant, fans, pool, hot tub, hiking, horseback riding; no air-conditioning, no room TVs. AE, MC, V.*

THE EASTERN CENTRAL VALLEY

East of San José are Costa Rica's highest volcano and the remains of both the country's most important archaeological site and its oldest church. Ecological attractions include a botanical garden and a protected cloud forest. Cartago, the country's first capital, has scattered historical structures and the impressive Basílica de Los Angeles.

Cartago

❿ *22 km (14 mi) southeast of San José.*

Although it's a small city, Cartago, was the country's first capital and held that title for almost three centuries. It's much older than San José, but earthquakes have destroyed most of its colonial structures, leaving just a few interesting buildings among the concrete boxes. Cartago became Costa Rica's second most prominent city in 1823, when the seat of government was moved to the emerging economic center of San José. You'll see some attractive old buildings as you move through town, most of them erected after the 1910 quake. The devastating earthquake prevented completion of the central Romanesque cathedral. **Las Ruinas** (the ruins) of this unfinished house of worship now stand in a pleasant central park planted with tall pines and bright bougainvillea. The majority of the architecture in tiny Cartago is bland, with one impressive exception: the gaudy Basílica de Nuestra Señora de Los Angeles.

Basílica de Nuestra Señora de Los Angeles. The gaudy Basilica of Our Lady of the Angels, 10 blocks east of the central square, is a hodge-podge of architectural styles from Baroque to Byzantine, with a dash of Gothic. The interior is even more striking, with a colorful tile floor, intricately decorated wood columns, and lots of stained glass. It's also the focus of an amazing annual pilgrimage: the night of August 1 and well into the early morning hours of the 2nd, the road from San José clogs with worshipers, some of whom have traveled from as far away as Nicaragua, on their way to celebrate the 1635 appearance of La Negrita (the Black Virgin), Costa Rica's patron saint. At a spring behind the church, people fill bottles with water believed to have curative properties. Miraculous healing powers are attributed to the saint herself, and devotees have placed thousands of tiny symbolic crutches, ears, eyes, and legs next to her diminutive statue in recognition of her gifts. The constant arrival of tour buses and school groups, along with shops selling candles and bottles of holy water in the shape of La Negrita, make the scene a bit of a circus. The statue has twice been stolen, most recently in 1950 by José León Sánchez, now one of Costa Rica's best-known novelists, who spent 20 years on the prison island of San Lucas for having purloined the Madonna. ⊠ *C. 16 between Avdas. 2 and 4, Cartago,* ☎ *551–0465.* ⊘ *Daily 6–7.*

Volcán Irazú

⑪ *31 km (19 mi) northeast of Cartago, 50 km (31 mi) east of San José.*

Volcán Irazú is Costa Rica's highest volcano, at 3,753 m (11,260 ft), and its summit has long been protected as a national park. The mountain looms to the north of Cartago, and its eruptions have dumped considerable ash on the city over the centuries. The most recent eruptive period lasted from 1963 to 1965, beginning the day John F. Kennedy arrived in Costa Rica for a presidential visit. Boulders and mud-rained down on the countryside, damming rivers and causing serious floods. Although farmers who cultivate Irazú's slopes live in fear of the next eruption, they're also grateful for the soil's richness, a result of the volcanic deposits.

The road to the summit climbs past vegetable fields, pastures, and native oak forests. You'll pass through the villages of Potrero Cerrado and San Juan de Chicoá before reaching the summit's bleak but beautiful **crater.** Irazú is currently dormant, but the gases and steam that billow from fumaroles on the northwestern slope are sometimes visible from the peak above the crater lookouts. Head up as early in the morning as possible—before the summit is enveloped in clouds—to see the chartreuse crater lake and, if you're lucky, views of nearby mountains and either the Pacific or Caribbean in the distance. There are no trails or visitor centers at the summit, but a paved road leads all the way to the top where a small coffee shop offers hot beverages to warm up intrepid visitors. Before reaching the park's main entrance, about 1 km (½ mi) from the village of Potrero Cerrado, Volcán Irazú's **Area Recreativa de Prusia** (Prusia Recreation Area) has hiking trails through oak and pine forest and picnic areas in case you've packed your own supplies. Admission at either entrance allows entry to both sectors of Volcá Irazú. Bring warm, waterproof clothing for your time on the summit. ☎ *551–9398 or 192 for National Parks Service information.* ⊡ *$6.* ⊘ *Daily 8–3:30.*

Dining

$$ ✕ **Restaurant 1910.** Decorated with vintage photos of turn-of-the-20th-century buildings and landscapes, this restaurant documents the disastrous 1910 earthquake that rocked this area and all but destroyed the colonial capital of Cartago. The menu is decidedly Costa Rican, featuring traditional specialties like *pozol* (stew of corn and pork)—hard to find in modern Tico kitchens. ⊠ *300 yards north of Cot–Pacayas turnoff on the way to Volcán Irazú,* ☎ **FAX** *536–6063. AE, MC, V.*

Jardín Lankester

⑫ *7 km (4½ mi) east of Cartago, 57 km (35 mi) southeast of San José.*

If you're into plants, especially orchids, you'll definitely want to visit the Lankester Botanical Garden. Created in the 1950s by the English naturalist Charles Lankester to help preserve the local flora, it's now maintained by the University of Costa Rica. The lush garden and greenhouses contain one of the largest orchid collections in the world—more than 800 native and introduced species. Orchids are mostly epiphytes, meaning they use other plants for support without damaging them in the process. Bromeliads, heliconias, and aroids also abound, along with 80 species of trees including rare palms, bamboo, torch ginger, and other ornamentals. The diversity of plant life attracts many birds. The best time to come here is January through April, when the most orchids are in bloom. To reach the gardens, drive through the center of Cartago, turn right at the Basílica, then left on the busy road to Paraíso and Orosi. After 6 km (4 mi), an orange sign on the right marks the garden's short dirt road. ⊠ *Dulce Nombre, Cartago,* ☎ *552–3247.* ☜ *$5.* ⊙ *Daily 9–3:30.*

Shopping

The gift shop in Jardín Lankester is one of the few places in Costa Rica where you can buy orchids that you can take home legally: along with the endangered plants comes a CITES certificate—a sort of orchid passport—that lets you ferry them across international borders without any customs problems.

THE OROSI VALLEY

The Orosi Valley, an area of breathtaking views and verdant landscapes 30 km (19 mi) south of San José, holds remnants of both the colonial era and the tropical forest that covered the country when the Spanish first arrived. The valley was one of the earliest parts of Costa Rica to be settled by Spanish colonists—in the 17th century, as ruins and a colonial church attest. Rich soil and proximity to San José have combined to make this an important agricultural area, with extensive plantations of coffee, chayote, and other vegetables. The valley is fed in the west by the confluence of the Navarro and Orosi rivers and drained in the east by the ferocious Reventazón. A dam built in the 1970s to create one of the country's first hydroelectric projects formed the Lago de Cachí, or Cachí Reservoir.

Two roads descend into the valley from Paraíso, an unattractive town 8 km (5 mi) east of Cartago. Both lead to a loop around the reservoir, passing tidy patchworks of cultivated crops, small towns, and the Represa de Cachí (Cachí Dam). Find the roads by turning right just before Paraíso's shady Parque Central. If you turn left at the *bomberos* (fire station), which houses some splendid old-style fire engines, you'll be on your way to Ujarrás; if you go straight, the road will lead you toward the town of Orosi and Tapantí National Park. Whichever route you choose, you'll eventually end up back at the same intersection. As you snake down into the valley, past coffee plantations, pastures, and patches of forest, keep your eyes open for the *mirador,* or lookout point, with covered picnic tables perched on top of the canyon.

Ujarrás

⓭ *10 km (6 mi) southeast of Paraíso, 18 km (11 mi) southeast of Cartago.*

The ruins of Costa Rica's oldest church, **Iglesia de Ujarrás,** stand in a small park at the site of the former town of Ujarrás, on the floor of the Orosi Valley, just down the hill from Paraíso. Built between 1681 and 1693 in honor of the Virgin of Ujarrás, the church, together with the surrounding village, was abandoned in 1833 after a series of earthquakes and floods. An unlikely Spanish victory in 1666 over a superior force of invading British pirates was attributed to a prayer stop here. Today it's a pleasant monument surrounded by well-kept gardens and large trees, which often attract flocks of parakeets and parrots. ⊠ *Ujarrás.* ⊙ *Daily 8–5.*

Dining

$$\text{-}$$$

★ ✕ **La Casona del Cafetal.** The valley's best lunch stop is on a coffee plantation overlooking the Cachí Reservoir. The spacious brick building has a high, barrel-tile roof, with tables indoors and on a tiled portico on the lake side. Inventive twists on the local fare include *arroz tucurrique* (baked rice with cheese and heart of palm) and corvina *jacaranda* (stuffed with shrimp), as well as traditional casados. A gift shop sells local wood sculptures. ✉ *2 km (1 mi) south of Cachí Dam,* ☎ *577–1414. AE, MC, V. No dinner.*

Shopping

The unique **Casa del Soñador** (House of the Dreamer; ☎ 533–3297), 1 km (½ mi) south of the Cachí Dam on the main road through the valley, was built by local wood sculptor Macedonio Quesada. Though Macedonio died several years ago, his son and a former apprentice are still here, carving interesting, often comical little statues out of coffee wood. The **Casona del Cafetal** (2 km (1 mi) south of Cachí Dam, ☎ 577–1414) sells similar sculptures to those fashioned at Casa del Soñador, which have been carved from coffee roots by yet another apprentice of Macedonio Quesada. His name is José Luís Sojo and he also carves the huge totem poles depicting coffee harvesting that are displayed at the restaurant.

Orosi

⑭ *7 km (4 mi) south of Paraíso, 35 km (22 mi) southeast of San José.*

The town of Orosi, in the heart of the valley, has but one major attraction: a beautifully restored **colonial church.** Built in 1743, the structure has a low-slung whitewashed facade; the roof is made of cane overlaid with terra-cotta barrel tiles. Inside are an antique wooden altar and ancient paintings of the stations of the cross and the Virgin of Guadelupe, all brought to Costa Rica from Mexico. The **museum** in the cloister annex has a small collection of old religious regalia, polychromed wood carvings, and colonial furniture. ✉ *Across from soccer field,* ☎ *no phone.* 🎟 *Museum 50¢.* ☉ *Church daily 9–5; museum hrs vary (ask around for someone to open it).*

South of town, some **balneario** (thermal pools) fed by a hot spring are open to the public for a nominal fee. The pools are closed on Tuesday.

Lodging

$$ 🏨 **Orosi Lodge.** Run by a German couple who have built a warm, familiar rapport with the community, the little lodge blends in with Orosi's pretty, old-town architecture, with whitewashed walls trimmed in blue, high ceilings, and lovely use of natural wood. Local artisans provided some of the furnishings, such as the clay lamps in each room. The lodge's bright, airy coffee shop looks out onto the town's main square, and Latin music usually plays from an authentic 1960s jukebox in the foyer. The simple rooms have wood floors and wicker headboards, but common areas are colorful, with lots of painting and sculpture by local artisans. Rooms on the second floor have views of the Orosi Valley and Volcán Irazú. ✉ *50 yards east of the balneario (thermal pools),* ☎ FAX *533–3578,* WEB *www.orosilodge.com. 6 rooms. Mountain bikes; no air-conditioning, no room phones, no room TVs. MC, V.*

Tapantí National Wildlife Refuge

🖲 *12 km (7 mi) south of Orosi, 28 km (17 mi) southeast of Cartago.*

Tucked into the steep southern end of the Orosi Valley, Refugio Nacional de Fauna Silvestre Tapantí encompasses a 47-square-km (18-square-mi) preserve. Drained by countless streams, this cloud forest provides refuge for more than 200 bird species, including the graceful, endangered quetzal. Quetzals are most readily visible in the dry season (mid-December to April), when they mate; ask the park rangers where to look for them. The 10-km (6-mi) track to Tapantí follows the course of the Río Grande de Orosi past coffee plantations, elegant *fincas* (farmhouses), and seasonal barracks for coffee pickers before it's hemmed in by the steep slopes of thick jungle. Stop at the rangers' office and visitor center, on the right as you enter the park, to pay the entry fee. You can leave your vehicle 1½ km (1 mi) up the road, at a parking area where trails head off into the woods on both sides. The Sendero Oropéndola trail leads to two loops. The first loop passes a picnic area and several swimming holes with brisk but inviting emerald waters. The trail on the other side of the parking lot forms a loop along a forested hillside. Farther up from the parking area, about 2½ km (1½ mi), is an entrance to the La Pava Trail on the right. This trail leads down a steep hill to the riverbank. Several miles farther up the road from La Pava is a lovely view of a long, slender cascade on the far right of the valley.

Since the park clouds up in the afternoon, it's best to get an early start. Taxis carrying up to six people make trips to the reserve from Orosi's soccer field. Camping is not permitted. ☎ *192 for National Parks Service information; 758–3996 Amistad Atlántico branch of the National Parks Service.* ⌷ *$6.* ⊙ *Daily 7–4.*

TURRIALBA AND GUAYABO NATIONAL MONUMENT

The tranquil town of Turrialba and the nearby Guayabo ruins lie considerably lower than the rest of the Central Valley, so they enjoy more tropical climates. There are two ways to reach this area, both of which pass spectacular scenery. The more direct route, accessible by heading straight through both Cartago and Paraíso, winds through coffee and sugar plantations before descending abruptly into Turrialba. For the second route, turn off the road between Cartago and the summit of Irazú near the town of Cot. That narrow route twists along the slopes of Irazú and Turrialba volcanoes, passing some stunning scenery—pollarded trees line the road to form stately avenues, and white-girdered bridges cross crashing streams. From Santa Cruz a trail leads up within hiking distance of the 3,633-m (10,900-ft) summit of Volcán Turrialba. As you begin the descent to Turrialba town, the temperature rises and neatly farmed coffee crops blanket the slopes.

Turrialba

🖲 *58 km (36 mi) east of San José.*

The relatively well-to-do agricultural center of Turrialba (population 30,000) suffered when the main San José–Puerto Limón route was diverted through Guápiles. The demise of the famous Jungle Train that connected these two cities was an additional blow. Though pleasant enough, Turrialba doesn't have much to offer, but the surrounding countryside hides some spectacular scenery, patches of rain forest, and a few excellent lodges. Turrialba is also near two of Costa Rica's best white-water rivers—the Pacuare and Reventazón—which explains why kayakers and rafters flock here. Serious water enthusiasts, including the white-water Olympic kayaking teams from a handful of countries, stay all winter.

OFF THE
BEATEN PATH

CATIE – Just outside Turrialba, on the road to Siquirres, is the Centro Agronómico Tropical de Investigación y Enseñanza (Center for Tropical Agricultural Research and Education), known by its Spanish acronym, CATIE. One of the leading tropical research centers in the world, CATIE draws students and experts from all over the Americas. The 8-square-km (3-square-mi) property includes modern labs and offices, landscaped grounds, seed-conservation chambers, greenhouses, orchards, experimental agricultural projects, a large swath of rain forest, and lodging for students and teachers. A muddy trail leads down into the forest behind the administration building, where you can see some of the biggest rapids on the Reventazón River. CATIE is also a good place to bird-watch; you might even catch sight of the yellow-winged jacana or purple gallinule in the lagoon near the main building. Call ahead to reserve a free tour. ☎ 556-6431, FAX 556-1533. ☉ Daily 7–4.

Lodging

$$$$ 🏨 **Casa Turrire.** Standing at the edge of a sugar plantation that's bordered by an artificial lake, this timeless hotel looks like a manor house that has survived mysteriously intact from the turn of the 20th century. In fact, it's the product of more recent imaginations. From the royal palms that line the driveway to the tall columns and tile floors, Casa Turrire is an exercise in elegance and attention to detail. High-ceiling guest rooms have tropical hardwoods, small balconies, and bright bathrooms with tubs. The classy central courtyard is a civilized spot in which to relax after a day's adventure. ✉ *12 km (7 mi) north on the Carretera a la Suiza from Turrialba,* ☎ *531-1111,* FAX *531-1075,* WEB *www.hotelcasaturire.com. (mailing address: Apdo. 303–7150, Turrialba). 12 rooms, 4 suites. Restaurant, bar, pool, hot tub, tennis court, horseback riding; no kids. AE, MC, V.*

$$$$ 🏨 **Rancho Naturalista.** Customized guided horseback and bird-watching tours within a 125-acre private nature reserve are the reasons to come and stay here. Three hundred species of birds and thousands of different kinds of moths and butterflies live on the reserve, and a resident ornithologist helps you see and learn as much as you want. The two-story lodge is upscale modern with rustic touches, as are its two separate cabins. Good home cooking is served in the indoor and outdoor dining rooms, both of which have beautiful views of Volcán Irazú and Turrialba Valley. Rates include all meals and guided tours. ✉ *Southeast of Turrialba, 2½ km (1½ mi) up an unpaved road from Tuís,* ☎ *430–0400,* ☎ FAX *531-1516,* WEB *www.ranchonaturalista.com (mailing address: Dept. 1425, Box 025216, Miami, FL 33102-5216). 9 rooms, 7 with bath. Dining room, horseback riding; no air-conditioning, no room phones, no room TVs. No credit cards.*

$$–$$$ 🏨 **Albergue Volcán Turrialba.** In the foothills of the volcano, accessible only by four-wheel-drive vehicle (which the lodge will arrange for a fee), the Volcán has comfortable rooms. You'll eat well, too: all meals are included in the room price, and the proprietors serve healthy, Costa Rican–style meals cooked on a wood-burning stove. Even more compelling are the tours, one of which goes deep into the Turrialba crater, and another of which visits the fumaroles and thermal waters of Volcán Irazú. Mountain-biking and horseback-riding trips as well as a 10-hour trek from the Volcán Turrialba to Guápiles via Braulio Carrillo National Park can also be arranged. ✉ *20 km (12 mi) east of Cot, turn right at Pacayas on the road to Volcán Turrialba,* ☎ FAX *273-4335,*

WEB *www.volcanturrialbalodge.com (mailing address: Apdo. 1632–2050, San José). 12 rooms. Dining room, bar, parking (fee); no air-conditioning, no room phones, no room TVs. MC, V.*

$$ 🏠 **Turrialtico.** From the Caribbean town of Siquirres, a hedged drive winds its way up to this dramatically positioned, open-sided hotel. The second-floor rooms, handsomely designed with wood floors and Guatemalan spreads on firm beds, might be the best bargain in Costa Rica. Ask for a room on the west side—these have dazzling views toward Turrialba and, if there are no clouds, Volcán Irazú. The restaurant serves a small selection of authentic Costa Rican cuisine cooked on a woodstove. A possible drawback is that Turrialtico is a breakfast stopover for tour and raft-trip buses. ⊠ *8 km (5 mi) south of Siquirres on the road to Siquirres,* ☎ *538–1111,* FAX *538–1575 (mailing address: Apdo. 121–7150, Turrialba). 14 rooms. Restaurant; no air-conditioning, no room phones, no room TVs. AE, MC, V.*

Outdoor Activities and Sports

RAFTING AND KAYAKING

It's no coincidence that half a dozen Olympic kayaking teams use Turrialba as their winter training ground: it lies conveniently close to two excellent white-water rivers, the Reventazón and the Pacuare. And despite their appeal to the experts, these rivers can also be sampled by neophytes. The **Río Reventazón** flows right past Turrialba and has several navigable stretches; the most popular stretch has unfortunately been cut short by the construction of a dam (the Tucurrique section, Class III). The Florida section (Class III), above Turrialba, is a rip-roaring alternative for inexperienced rafters.

Just southeast of here is the **Río Pacuare,** Costa Rica's most spectacular white-water route, which provides rafters with an unforgettable, exhilarating, adrenaline-pumping experience. The 32-km (20-mi) Pacuare run includes a series of Class III and IV rapids with evocative nicknames like Double Drop, Burial Grounds, and Magnetic Rock. The astoundingly beautiful scenery includes lush canyons where waterfalls plummet into the river, and vast expanses of rain forest—stretches of the Pacuare stood in for Africa in the otherwise forgettable 1995 film *Congo.* That riverine landscape is inhabited by toucans, kingfishers, Zaracaris, *oropéndolas* (golden orioles) and other birds—along with blue morpho butterflies, the odd river otter, and other interesting critters. The rafting outfitters Aventuras Naturales and Ríos Tropicales have their own lodges on the river, making them the best options for two- and three-day trips that include jungle hikes.

For details on rafting or kayaking both the Pacuare and Reventazón rivers, contact **Aventuras Naturales** (☎ 225–3939 or 224–0505, FAX 253–6934). **Costa Rica Ríos Aventuras** (☎ 556–9617) is a top local outfitter for white-water thrills on the Pacuare and Reventazón. White-water adventures on the Pacuare and Reventazón are also available through the San José–based **Costa Rica Whitewater** (☎ 257–0766, FAX 255–4354). **Rainforest World** (☎ 556–2678) also specializes in white-knuckle trips on Turrialba's Pacuare and Reventazón rivers. **Ríos Tropicales** (☎ 233–6455, FAX 255–4354) is another San José–based operator offering day tours and multiple-day rafting adventures on the Pacuare and Reventazón.

Guayabo National Monument

⑰ *19 km (12 mi) north of Turrialba, 72 km (45 mi) east of San José.*

On the slopes of Volcán Turrialba is Monumento Nacional Guayabo, Costa Rica's most significant archaeological site. In 1968 a local landowner was out walking her dogs when she discovered what she thought was a tomb. A friend, archaeologist Carlos Piedra, began excavating the site and unearthed the base wall of a chief's house in what eventually turned out to be the ruins of a large community (around 20,000 inhabitants) covering 49 acres. The city was abandoned in AD 1400, probably due to disease or starvation. A guided tour in Spanish takes you through the rain forest to a mirador from which you can see the layout of the excavated circular buildings. Only the raised foundations survive, since the conical houses themselves were built of wood. As you descend into the ruins, notice the well-engineered surface and covered aqueducts leading to a trough of drinking water that still functions today. Next you'll pass the end of an 8-km (5-mi) paved walkway used to transport the massive building stones—abstract patterns carved on the stones continue to baffle archaeologists, but some clearly depict jaguars, which were revered by Indians as deities. The hillside jungle is captivating, and the trip is further enhanced by bird-watching possibilities: sacklike nests of oropéndolas hang from many of the trees. The last few miles of the road are in such bad shape that you'll need a four-wheel-drive vehicle to get here. Camping is allowed near the ranger station. ☎ 290–8202 or 192 for National Parks Service information. 🎫 $6. ☉ Tues.–Sun. 8–4.

THE CENTRAL VALLEY A TO Z

To research prices, get advice from other travelers, and book travel arrangements, visit www.fodors.com.

AIRPORTS AND TRANSFERS

The Aeropuerto Internacional Juan Santamaría is 16 km (10 mi) northwest of downtown San José.

➤ AIRPORT INFORMATION: **Aeropuerto Internacional Juan Santamaría** (☎ 443–2622).

AIRPORT TRANSFERS

You can get taxis from the airport to any point in the Central Valley for between $10 and $50. Most upscale hotels can arrange a pickup for you when you reserve your room. Buses leave the airport for Alajuela several times an hour; from Alajuela you can catch buses to Grecia, Sarchí, and San Ramón. Less-frequent buses (one to three per hour) serve Heredia. To get from the airport to Escazú, Cartago, or Turrialba, you have to change buses in San José.

BUS TRAVEL TO AND FROM CENTRAL VALLEY

There are many buses that will take you into Western Central Valley. Buses leave for Escazú from San José (✉ Avda. 6 between Cs. 12 and 14) every 20 minutes. Buses begin the 25-minute trip to Heredia, from Calle 1 between Avenidas 7 and 9, every 10 minutes. For a 20-minute trip to Volcán Barva, take the Paso Llano bus from Heredia with the Rapidos Heredianos bus line, and get off at Sacramento crossroads; the first bus is at 6:30 AM. Note: some of these buses go only as far as San José de la Montaña, adding an hour to the hike; check first.

Departures for Alajuela, a 20-minute ride, are from Avenida 2 between Calles 12 and 14 with TUASA bus lines, daily every 10 minutes 6 AM– 7 PM, every 40 minutes 7 PM–10:30 PM. An excursion bus for Volcán Poás departs San José daily at 8:30 AM from Calle 12 between Avenidas 2 and 4 (a 90-minute ride) and returns at 2:30 PM. Departures for the 40-minute trip to Grecia, from the Coca-Cola station, Calle 16 at Avenida 1, on the TUAN bus line are every 30 minutes. Direct buses to Sarchí take 1½ hours and leave from San José's Coca-Cola station (✉ C. 16 between Avdas. 1 and 3) at 12:15 and 5:30. Buses for the one-hour ride to San

Ramón with Empresarios Unidos leave from the Puntarenas bus station (C. 16 between Avdas. 10 and 12) every hour 6 AM to 7 PM.

Other buses will take you to Eastern Central Valley. SACSA buses leave San José for the 45-minute trip to Cartago from Calle 5 and Avenida 18, every 10 minutes daily; going from Cartago to Orosi Valley, Autotransportes Mata buses leave hourly, weekdays 8 AM–2 PM, and weekends 2 PM–7 PM, from the southern side of the Cartago Ruinas. An excursion bus, run by Metropoli, departs San José for the two-hour ride to Volcán Irazú every Saturday and Sunday at 8 AM from Avenida 2 between Calles 1 and 3, across from the Gran Hotel Costa Rica; this bus returns at 1 PM.

TRANSTUSA buses leave for Turrialba and Guayabo National Monument, a two-hour trip, from Calle 13 between Avenidas 6 and 8 hourly 8–8.

➤ BUS INFORMATION: **Autotransportes Mata** (☎ 391–8268). **Empresarios Unidos** (✉ C. 16 at Avda. 12, ☎ 222–0064). **Metropoli** (☎ 272–0651). **Rapidos Heredianos** (✉ C. 1 and Avdas. 7 and 9, ☎ 233–8392). **SACSA** (☎ 233–5350). **TRANSTUSA** (☎ 556–0073). **TUAN** (☎ 494–2139). **TUASA** (☎ 222–5325).

BUS TRAVEL WITHIN CENTRAL VALLEY

Buses travel between Alajuela and Heredia's main bus stations every half hour. To reach Zoo Ave, take the bus to La Garita, which departs every hour from the main bus station in Alajuela. Direct buses to Sarchí depart from Alajuela (✉ C. 8 between Avdas. 1 and 3) every 30 minutes 6 AM–9 PM; the ride takes 90 minutes. Buses traveling between San José and Grecia or San Ramón pick up passengers on the southern edge of Alajuela, at the Tuasa Bus stop (Avda. 2 between Cs. 12 and 14). Departures for Grecia leave from Naranjo, from Naranjo's Central Park, hourly 6 AM–7 PM, a 15-minute hop.

To visit Jardín Lankester, take the Paraíso bus, which leaves the south side of Cartago's Parque Central every 15 minutes daily.

Hourly Autotransportes Mata buses depart from Cartago's southern side of Las Ruinas for a loop around the Orosi Valley, stopping at Orosi and Ujarrás. To reach Tapantí, you'll have to hire a taxi in Orosi.

The bus to Guayabo National Monument, a 50-minute ride, leaves once a day from one block south of the bus station in Turrialba, Monday to Saturday at 11 AM and Sunday at 9:30 AM.

CAR RENTAL

The closest car rental agencies are located in San José.

CAR TRAVEL

Many points in Western Central Valley can be easily reached by car. To reach Escazú from San José, turn left at the western end of Paseo Colón, take the first right, get off the highway at the first exit, and turn right at the traffic light. Turn right at the bottom of the hill for San Rafael and the old road to Santa Ana. Paseo Colón ends at Parque La Sabana, on the west end of San José; turn right here for Alajuela and Heredia. For Heredia, turn right off the highway just before it heads onto an overpass, where the Hotel Irazú stands on the right; follow the road for a couple of miles and then turn left at the Universidad Nacional for the center of Heredia, or continue straight for the town and volcano of Barva. The route to Volcán Barva heads north out of Heredia through the communities of Barva, San José de la Montaña, Paso Llano, and Sacramento. At Sacramento the paved road turns to dirt, growing worse as it nears the ranger station. A four-wheel-drive vehicle can make it all the way to the ranger station in the dry season. For Alajuela, take the highway all the way out to the airport and turn right. You can reach Grecia by continuing west on the highway past the airport—the turnoff is on the right—or by heading into Alajuela and turning left just before the Alajuela cemetery. For Sarchí, take the highway well past the airport to the turnoff for Naranjo; then veer right just as you enter Naranjo. San Ramón is on the Pan-American Highway west of Grecia; head straight through town and follow the signs to reach the hotels to the north.

All the attractions in the eastern Central Valley are accessible from San José by driving east on Avenida 2 through San Pedro, then following signs from the intersection to Cartago. Shortly before Cartago, a traffic light marks the beginning of the road up Irazú, with traffic to Cartago veering right. For the Jardín Lankester head straight through Cartago (entrance on right), turning right at the Basílica and left after two blocks.

For the Orosi Valley head straight through Cartago, turn right at the Basílica de Los Angeles, and follow the signs to Paraíso. Turn right at Paraíso's central plaza. A few blocks east, at the fire station, you can either turn left for Ujarrás or continue straight for Orosi and Tapantí National Park; either way takes you into the same loop around the valley.

The road through Cartago and Paraíso continues east to Turrialba, where you pick up another road a few blocks east of that town's central plaza. Marked by signs, this road leads north to the monument.

EMERGENCIES

In case of any emergency, dial 911, or one of the specific police or fire department numbers listed below.

➤ EMERGENCY SERVICES: **Ambulance** (☎ 128). **Fire** (☎ 118). **Police** (☎ 117). **Traffic Police** (☎ 222–9330).

TAXIS

Taxis parked near the central plazas in Alajuela, Cartago, and Heredia can take you to up Poás, Irazú, and Barva volcanoes, respectively, but the trips are quite expensive (about $50) unless you can assemble a group. If you don't have a car, the only way to get to Tapantí National Park is to take a cab from Orosi. Taxis parked near San Ramón's central plaza can take you to the nature lodges north of town. Consult with your hotel's front desk manager, who can sometimes recommend private drivers that charge less.

TOURS

Most San José tour offices can also set you up with guided tours to the Poás and Irazú volcanoes or the Orosi Valley. Swiss Travel is one of the oldest operators in the country. Horizontes offers expertly guided adventure and natural-history tours in the Central Valley and beyond. For white-water rafting outfitters, *see* Outdoor Activities and Sports *in* Turrialba, *above*.

➤ TOUR COMPANIES: **Horizontes** (✉ Paseo Colón, 150 yards north of Pizza Hut, San José, ☎ 222–2022). **Swiss Travel** (✉ Meliá Corobicí hotel lobby, San José, ☎ 231–4055).

VISITOR INFORMATION

Visitor Information services are based in San José, although Central Valley hotels are often a good, local source of information.

4 NORTHERN GUANACASTE AND ALAJUELA

The red lava of the Arenal Volcano and the green cloud forests of Monteverde loom over Costa Rica's northernmost reaches. This amazingly diverse region also takes in Caño Negro's remote, bird-filled waters; the windsurfing mecca of Laguna de Arenal; dusty, deforested uplands with cowboys and grazing cattle; jungles alive with birds, monkeys, and butterflies; and sparkling Pacific Coast beaches. And if you want to make like a bird, don't pass up the chance to glide through the treetops on one of the north's famed canopy tours.

Updated by
Jeffrey Van
Fleet

THERE AREN'T MANY PLACES ON GLOBE with cloud forests, miles of sun-drenched beaches, and an active volcano. But here in the northwest all are within proximity of each other. The northwest offers you far more than the myriad ecosystems of the dry coastal plain, with the lush cloud and rain forests of Monteverde; waterfalls, hot springs, and estuaries bursting with life; and the volcanoes and peaks of the Cordillera de Guanacaste, the Cordillera de Tilarán, and sections of the Cordillera Central. From the wetlands of Caño Negro National Wildlife Refuge in the far north, down to the green farmlands and foothills around La Fortuna and San Carlos, east of Volcán Arenal, this wealthy part of the country has a magnificent landscape and array of things to do in it.

Guanacaste is bordered by Nicaragua and the Pacific Ocean. The province derives its name from the broad ear-pod trees that shade the lounging white Brahman cattle so prevalent in the region. An independent province of Spain's colonial empire until 1787, when it was ceded to Nicaragua, Guanacaste became part of Costa Rica in 1814. After their independence in 1821, both Nicaragua and Costa Rica claimed Guanacaste for their own. The Guanacastecos themselves were divided: the provincial capital, Liberia, wanted to return to Nicaragua, while rival city Nicoya favored Costa Rica. Nicoya got its way, helped by the fact that at the time the vote was taken, Nicaragua was embroiled in a civil war.

Guanacaste's far-northwestern coastline, still for the most part unblemished, offers everything the Nicoya Peninsula does and more: the dry forests and pristine sands of Santa Rosa National Park, the bird sanctuary of Isla Bolaños, the endless beaches of the Gulf of Santa Elena, and breezy Bahía Salinas. A pair of beachfront resort hotels has set up camp on this part of the coast, but the high-rise tourist-driven development common farther south on the Nicoya has yet to materialize up here.

East of the Carretera Interamericana (Pan-American Highway), Guanacaste's dry plains and forests slope upward into volcano country and the northern sector of the province of Alajuela. Marching northwest to southeast in a rough, formidable line, the volcanoes of the Cordillera de Guanacaste include Orosi, Rincón de la Vieja and its nearby sister Santa María, Tenorio, and Arenal, looming over the southeast end of man-made Laguna de Arenal. The northernmost peak in the Cordillera de Tilarán, Arenal ranks as one of the world's most active volcanoes. Coughs that sound like thunder, tufts of smoke, lava flow, and mini avalanches are perceptible to those who come within 32 km (20 mi) of the place—and many do. Below and between these active and not-so-active craters and calderas, the terrain ranges from dry forest to impassable jungle, from agricultural plain to roadless swamp.

Parks in the province of Guanacaste protect some of the last remnants of the Mesoamerican tropical dry forest that once covered the Pacific lowlands from Costa Rica to the Mexican state of Chiapas. A few of the parks and destinations in this area are relatively accessible from San José, even for day trips. Others require grueling hours of driving over pothole-scarred roads. As you contemplate spending time in this region—or anywhere in Costa Rica, for that matter—be sure to allow plenty of time for excruciatingly slow driving. That brief hop from the smooth pavement of the Pan-American Highway up to the famous cloud forests of Monteverde, for example, looks like 30 minutes behind the wheel when measured on the map. In reality, it's two hours of bone-jarring road, although stretches of it are being repaved.

Pleasures and Pastimes

Cloud Forests and Wildlife Refuges

The far north encompasses high- and low-altitude, wetland and dry forest conservation areas. The lowland rainforest Caño Negro National Wildlife Refuge abounds with waterfowl, crocodiles, and *caimanes*. Contrast that with Santa Rosa National Park's dry forest, crawling with ocelots, armadillos, various species of small monkeys, and the Olive Ridley turtle, which comes to nest on the park's beaches August–November. World renowned, the Quaker-administered Monteverde Cloud Forest Reserve is one of Costa Rica's top tourist draws. Expect to see an incredible variety of mammal and bird life within its confines. If you're lucky, you'll catch a glimpse that bird-watcher's Holy Grail, the resplendent quetzal. Monteverde also affords you the opportunity to make like a bird and view the cloud forest via a canopy tour. With the aid of cables, secure harnesses, and platform landings, you'll glide through the air with the greatest ease.

Dining

Guanacaste's traditional foods derive from dishes prepared by pre-Columbian Chorotega Indians. Typical fare includes *frito guanacasteco* (black beans, rice, vegetables, and meat), *pedre* (carob beans, pork, chicken, onions, sweet peppers, salt, and mint), *sopa de albóndigas* (meatball soup with chopped eggs and spices), and *arroz de maíz* (a kind of corn stew, sometimes made *con pollo,* with chicken). Meat lovers, rejoice: the northwest, whose plains are covered with cattle ranches, produces the country's best steak.

CATEGORY	COST*
$$$$	over $20
$$$	$10–$20
$$	$5–$10
$	under $5

per person for main course at dinner.

Lodging

East and west of the mountains, Costa Rica's far northern zone offers a good mix of quality hotels, nature lodges, working ranches, and more basic *cabinas* (cottages). In the areas of Monteverde and La Fortuna, a range of low- and mid-price hotels, cabinas, and resorts fills the demand generated by visitors to Volcán Arenal and the cloud forest. Book ahead if you're headed to the coast during the dry season (December–April), especially for weekends—and absolutely for Christmas and Easter weeks—when Ticos flock to the beach.

CATEGORY	COST*
$$$$	over $90
$$$	$50–$90
$$	$25–$50
$	under $25

for a double room, excluding service and tax (16.4%)

Hot Springs and Waterfalls

After a day of heavy-duty sightseeing, pamper yourself and soak those tired muscles in one of the region's three hot springs complexes. The famed Tabacón resort complex and the smaller Baldi Termae, both near La Fortuna, as well as the Hotel Occidental El Tucano, outside San Carlos, all offer chances to take the waters. You're in for a more invigorating experience with a moderately strenuous hike to the *cataratas* (waterfalls) of La Fortuna.

Volcanoes

The sheer mass and power of Volcán Arenal, often ringed with an ominous haze, dominates Laguna de Arenal (Lake Arenal). The Volcano reiterates its presence at night, when you can sometimes see red-hot molten lava oozing from the cone, a flirtatious dance with disaster. Closest looks can be had from the Arenal Observatory Lodge which, according to those who monitor the volcano, is also thankfully out of the path of danger. It's easy to reach Arenal from the Pan-American Highway—watch for the turnoff at the town of Cañas—or from the east through La Fortuna. You may have to spend more than one day here, as the cone can be covered by clouds, especially during the rainy season. Farther northwest, experienced hikers can trek to the lip of the steaming Rincón de la Vieja crater on trails through the namesake national park; less-active travelers can check out Las Pailas, a cluster of miniature volcanoes, fumaroles, and mud pots encircled by a relatively easy trail. Among the other (inactive) volcanoes are Orosi, in Guanacaste National Park, and Tenorio, which shares its name with yet another national park. Guanacaste National Park is minimally developed for tourism, and Tenorio, though protected, as yet has no infrastructure.

Windsurfing

When winter arrives up north, serious American windsurfers look to the south. These days many of them head to Laguna de Arenal, which many world-champion windsurfers have called "one of the world's top five windsurfing spots." From December through April, Caribbean trade winds sneak through a pass in the Cordillera Central, crank up to 80 kph (50 mph) or more, and blow from the east toward the northwest end of the lake, creating perfect conditions for high-wind freshwater sailing. The scenery here, too, is unmatched: watch the frequent volcanic eruptions while you glide along. The lake is somewhat choppy due to its narrow shape, but strong winds, freshwater, and hassle-free rigging and launch sites on both shores make it worthwhile. On the far northwest Pacific coast, Bahía Salinas gives Lake Arenal a run for its money in windsurfing circles. The winds aren't quite as strong, but the November-through-August season makes Costa Rica close to a year-round windsurfing destination.

Exploring Northern Guanacaste and Alajuela

Northern Guanacaste and Alajuela encompass the volcanic mountains of the Cordillera de Guanacaste, the northern section of the Cordillera de Tilarán, and the plains stretching west to the sea and north to Nicaragua. Most destinations on the west side of the mountains, including the coastal beaches, national parks, and the northwestern end of Laguna de Arenal, lie within easy reach of the Pan-American Highway. To reach La Fortuna, Tabacón, Volcán Arenal, the east end of Laguna de Arenal, and points farther east—including Caño Negro and Upala—the easiest drive is by way of Zarcero and San Carlos (Ciudad Quesada). Several roads pass through the mountains, linking these two distinct zones. Though they're mostly paved, these roads—one follows the northern shore of Laguna de Arenal and the other skirts the volcanoes along the nation's northern edge—still have poorly surfaced stretches and are subject to washouts and other difficulties. Always get a report on road conditions before setting out on long trips.

Numbers in the text correspond to numbers in the margin and on the Northern Guanacaste and Alajuela map.

Great Itineraries

As you plan your travels in this region, know that a fair amount of your time will be spent on the road. That is simply the reality of travel in Costa Rica, and particularly in these spread-out parts.

IF YOU HAVE 3 DAYS

Head northeast out of San José and through the mountains around **Zarcero** ①, en route to ⊞ **La Fortuna** ③. The next day, hike to the La Fortuna waterfall, drive to ⊞ **Volcán Arenal** ⑤, checking out the Tabacón Resort's hot springs, or take a rafting trip on the Río Sarapiquí or the Río Toro. Arrange one of the taxi–boat–taxi connections across the lake for an early trip to Monteverde. Spend the afternoon taking in the unique area attractions—the frog pond, the butterfly garden, a canopy tour—and devote the next morning to exploring the cloud forest reserve, the earlier the better.

IF YOU HAVE 5 DAYS TO SEE PARKS

Start from San José with a predawn drive to the ⊞ **Monteverde Cloud Forest Biological Reserve** ⑧ and spend a day hiking in the cloud forest. If Monteverde is too crowded, the compelling but smaller Santa Elena Reserve is just down the road (north). After overnighting in the area, another crack-of-dawn drive will take you to ⊞ **Tilarán** ⑦ by way of the mountain track (four-wheel-drive vehicle only) or the Pan-American Highway for an active day on Laguna de Arenal. Stay in Tilarán or in one of the lodges at the lake's northwesterly end. An alternative to a direct trip to Tilarán is a taxi–boat–taxi connection from Monteverde to La Fortuna, where you can arrange a day tour of the **Caño Negro National Wildlife Refuge** ④. Early the next day return to the highway and drive north and then inland again for a day hike in ⊞ **Rincón de la Vieja National Park** ⑨. Stay at the mountain lodge, or return to the highway and head farther north for a night and a day at Hacienda Los Inocentes, the 100-year-old lodge on the northern border of ⊞ **Guanacaste National Park** ⑫. Stay a second night in the lodge, or late in the day head down to **Santa Rosa National Park** ⑩. For a break from parks, your four-wheel-drive vehicle will safely deliver you to Playa Naranjo for a day at the beach.

IF YOU HAVE 5 DAYS FOR PARKS AND THE BEACH

After a pass through **Zarcero** ①, spend a day and night in the Laguna de Arenal area—⊞ **La Fortuna** ③, ⊞ **Nuevo Arenal** ⑥, or ⊞ **Tilarán** ⑦—and see the volcano (and its nocturnal performance), lake, Tabacón Resort, and/or the La Fortuna waterfall. From La Fortuna, head north to spend a day touring the **Caño Negro National Wildlife Refuge** ④. Then take the road northwest that leads through the San Rafael de Guatuso area and continues around the Volcán Orosi. Stop for a mind-expanding look at Lago de Nicaragua from the *mirador* (lookout) at La Virgen, near Santa Cecilia, and then continue down the west slope of the mountains. Spend a night at Hacienda Los Inocentes, near ⊞ **Guanacaste National Park** ⑫, then a day hiking or horseback riding before continuing on to ⊞ **La Cruz** ⑬ and the resorts on the south shore of the half-moon-shape ⊞ **Bahía Salinas** ⑭. After a night (or two) here, work your way down to **Santa Rosa National Park** ⑩ for a day at the beach or take a day hike in the mixed environments of **Rincón de la Vieja National Park** ⑨. Either camp in the park or, more comfortably, tuck yourself into one of the nearby lodges or hotels.

When to Tour Northern Guanacaste and Alajuela

Given the larger numbers of tourists that visit Volcán Arenal and especially Monteverde, consider an off-season or edge-of-season trip to avoid the crowds. In terms of weather, the areas west of the Cordillera de Guanacaste are best toured in the dry season (December–April). How-

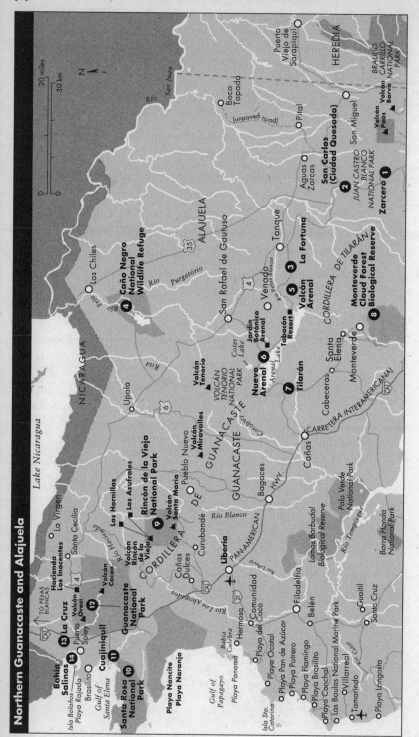

Northern Guanacaste and Alajuela

ever, during the wet season (May–November), rain generally falls for just an hour or two each day, so beyond the effect on the roads, problems with traveling are minimal. (Rainfall is about 65 inches per year here, the lowest in the country.) Farther inland, the northern uplands and lowlands offer a mixed climactic bag—the more easterly lowlands share the humid Caribbean weather of the east coast, and less distinct rainy and dry seasons, while the uplands partake of the drier, cooler mountain clime.

ARENAL AND THE CORDILLERA DE TILARÁN

Dense green cloud forests cloak the rugged mountains and rolling hills of the Cordillera de Tilarán extending northwest from San José. Great swaths of primary forest and jungle, including the marvelous cluster of reserves, straddle the continental divide at Monteverde. Farther north and west, Laguna de Arenal and the rolling green hills around it pay homage to the dark heart of this region—fiery, magnificent Volcán Arenal.

Laguna de Arenal has two distinct personalities: the northwest end is windsurf central—a row of power-generating windmills, with blades awhirl on the ridge above the Hotel Tilawa, signals another use for the relentless, powerful wind. The more sheltered southeast end, closer to the dam, is popular for other water sports, especially fishing for guapote (it looks like a rainbow bass). The southeast is also a marvelous place from which to view the volcano. If you took away the volcanoes, you might mistake the countryside of green, rolling hills for the English Lake District.

Zarcero

❶ *70 km (43 mi) northwest of San José.*

Ninety minutes from San José, the small town of Zarcero looks like it was designed by Dr. Seuss. Evangelisto Blanco, a local landscape artist, modeled cypress topiaries in fanciful animal shapes—motorcycle-riding monkeys, a lightbulb-eyed elephant—which enliven the park in front of the town church. The church interior is covered with elaborate pastel stencils and detailed religious paintings by Misael Solís, a local oldtimer.

Passing through Sarchí and Naranjo on your way here, you'll wind upward through miles of coffee plantations, with spectacular views of the mountains. There are some hair-raising roadside chasms, particularly on the east slopes, and the highway gets foggy by late afternoon, but the road is paved all the way.

Lodging

$$ 🏨 **Hotel Don Beto.** Flory Salazar, one of the country's most gracious hotel owners, opens her home on the central park to guests. The immaculate hotel is tastefully decorated with the mementos she has picked up in her travels. Rooms vary in size and all are decorated with bright, pastel drapes and bedspreads. Consummate traveler though Flory is, she's an expert on the home front, too, and is happy to advise. ✉ *Northeast corner of Central Park,* ☎ ℻ *463–3137. 8 rooms, 4 with bath. No air-conditioning, no room phone, no room TVs. MC, V.*

Shopping

Zarcero is renowned for its peach preserves and mild white cheese, both of which are sold in stores around town and along the highway. Stop at **El Tiesto Souvenir Shop,** across from the park, and talk politics with owner Rafael, a native Tico who lived in New Jersey for a while. He knows everything about the area and can arrange day trips to nearby waterfalls. At the tiny café-store **Super Dos** on the main road opposite the church in Zarcero, you can get a coffee and empanada *de piña* (of pineapple) while you mull over buying some of the excellent local peach preserves.

San Carlos (Ciudad Quesada)

❷ *45 km (28 mi) northwest of Zarcero.*

This lively, if not particularly picturesque, mountain market town serves a fertile dairy region and is worth a stop for a soak in the soothing thermal waters. Choose from a variety of sources. A visit to Hotel Occidental El Tucano ($4 per day; $10 weekends) is a private resort popular with travelers on tours. Aguas Termales, just west of El Tucano's grounds, but served by the same hot springs, lets you soak those tired muscles for $2 per day. The streams and pools on the beautifully landscaped grounds at the Tabacón Resort ($17 per day) are regulated for a variety of temperatures.

East of San Carlos, where foothills mark the transition from the coastal lowland to the central mountains, lies **Juan Castro Blanco National Park.** The park, which spans 142 square km (88 square mi), was created to protect large tracts of virgin forest around the headwaters of the Plantar, Toro, Aguas Zarcas, Tres Amigos, and La Vieja rivers. Unfortunately, the park has no facilities of any kind at present, though it's possible to explore some of the park's southern trails on foot or with four-wheel-drive vehicle.

Lodging

$$$ ☷ **Hotel Occidental El Tucano.** You come to El Tucano for the waters: the hotel abuts a river of hot, healing, marvelously invigorating natural springs. Two large outdoor hot tubs, the Olympic-size pool, natural sauna, and cool plunge are all fed by the Río Aguas Caliente, the cascading river that flows through the property. The hotel itself is somewhat overscale, and its public spaces suffer from too much concrete and the impersonality of any hotel subject to tour-group bookings. The food is ordinary at best, and air-conditioning and in-room safes cost extra. Spa treatments, including mud wraps, are brusque. ⊠ *8 km (5 mi) east of San Carlos on Hwy 140,* ☎ *460–6000,* ℻ *460–1692,* 🕸 *www.occidentaltucano.com (mailing address: Apdo. 434–1150, San José,* ☎ *221–9095). 90 rooms. Restaurant, bar, pool, sauna, spa, 2 tennis courts, gym, horseback riding, laundry service, meeting rooms. AE, MC, V.*

$$$ ☷ **Laguna del Lagarto Lodge.** One of Costa Rica's smaller eco-lodges is a hideaway in a 1,250-acre rainforest near the Nicaraguan border. Most of the rustic cabin rooms come with single beds. Some 380 bird species and counting have been logged here, including the endangered green macaw. Buffet style meals are extra, and are served on a patio with splendid river and forest views. Rates include one guided walk and use of canoes. Recommended extras include horseback riding and a boat trip on the San Carlos river. ⊠ *7 km (4 mi) north of Boca Tapada,* ☎ *289–8163,* ℻ *289–5295,* 🕸 *www.lagarto-lodge-costa-rica.com. 20 rooms, 18 with bath. Bar, restaurant, laundry service, horseback riding; no air-conditioning, no phones, no room TVs. MC, V.*

La Fortuna

❸ *40 km (25 mi) east of Volcán Arenal, 10 km (6 mi) northwest of San Carlos.*

At the foot of towering, overpowering Volcán Arenal, the small farming community of La Fortuna de San Carlos (commonly called La Fortuna) attracts visitors from around the world. The town overflows with restaurants, hotels, and tour operators. It's also the best place to arrange trips to the popular Caño Negro National Wildlife Refuge, since the town is on the road to that protected area. Tours vary in price and quality, so ask around, but all provide an easier alternative than busing up north to Los Chiles and hiring a boat to take you down through the rain forest on Río Frío.

Besides offering access to a multitude of outdoor adventures, La Fortuna also provides you with the opportunity for some serious soaking pampering. Where else can you lounge in a natural hot-springs waterfall with a volcano spitting fireballs overhead? Kick back at the **Tabacón Resort,** a busy day spa and hotel, with gorgeous gardens, waterfalls, mineral water soaking streams (complete with subtle ladders and railings and average 39° C [102 F°]), swimming pools, swim-up bars, and dining facilities, which mingle in a florid Latin interpretation of grand European baths. Nonguests of the hotel can purchase a day pass and move on. The best deal is to sign up for a zip-through-the-trees canopy tour ($45), the price of which includes access to the waters. If you're seeking an Iskandria Spa treatment, it's best to make an appointment a day in advance. ⊠ *13 km (8 mi) northwest of La Fortuna on highway toward Nuevo Arenal,* ☎ *460–2020 or 256–1500,* FAX *221–3075,* WEB *www.tabacon.com.* ⌦ *Entry $17, 45-min massage $40, mud-pack facial $20.* ⊙ *Daily noon–10. MC, V.*

If Tabacón is full or if you want a less expensive spa alternative, head to **Baldi Termae.** The complex's seven hot-spring-fed pools vary in temperature but share views of Volcán Arenal. There's also a swim-up snack bar. ⊠ *4 km (2½ mi) west of La Fortuna,* ☎ *479–9651.* ⌦ *$10.* ⊙ *Daily 10–10.*

A pleasant but steep day hike from La Fortuna takes you to the 54-m- (177-ft-) high waterfall **Cataratas de La Fortuna.** The 6-km (4-mi) walk to the falls begins off the main road toward the volcano; look for the yellow billboard marking the entrance. If you've got your own wheels, double-check road conditions in the rainy season. If you don't feel like walking, several operators in La Fortuna will take you to the falls by car or on horseback.

OFF THE BEATEN PATH
VENADO CAVERNS – In 1945 a farmer in the mountain hamlet of Venado fell in a hole, and thus were discovered the Cavernas de Venado (Venado Caverns). The limestone caves, 45 minutes (about 35 km [21 mi]) north of La Fortuna and 15 km [9 mi] southeast of San Rafael, contain a series of eight chambers with an assortment of stalactites, stalagmites, underground streams, and other subterranean formations. Sunset Tours normally runs trips from La Fortuna. ☎ *479–9415 Sunset Tours.* ⌦ *Tours $35.* ⊙ *Daily 7 AM–8 PM.*

Dining

$–$$ ✕ **La Choza de Laurel.** The tantalizing chicken turning on the rotisserie and the cloves of garlic and bunches of onions dangling from the roof always draw in passersby to this open-air Costa Rican–style restaurant near the center of town. These folks open early; it's a great place to grab a hearty breakfast on your way to the volcano. ⊠ *100 m northwest of town church,* ☎ 479–9231. *MC, V.*

$–$$ ✕ **Rancho la Cascada.** You can't miss its tall, palm-thatch roof in the center of town. The festive upstairs contains a bar, whose large TV, neon signs, and flashing lights give it the appropriate ambience. Downstairs, the spacious dining room—decorated with foreign flags—serves basic, mid-priced Costa Rican fare as well as hearty, American-style breakfasts. ⊠ *Across from northeast corner of Parque Central,* ☎ 479–9145. *AE, MC, V.*

$–$$ ✕ **La Vaca Muca.** It isn't a posh place, but the food is good and the servings are generous. The exterior is draped with foliage, and the interior has turquoise paneling and bamboo aplenty. Try the casado heaped with chicken, beef or fish, rice, beans, fried egg, fried banana, and cabbage salad—easily enough for two. ⊠ *2 km (1 mi) west of La Fortuna,* ☎ 479–9186. *V. Closed Mon.*

$ ✕ **Soda La Parada.** It's always busy but never crazy. Grab an open-air seat alongside the locals, under the canvas tarp (from which hangs a huge color TV), and let the waiters in neon-lime shirts bring you a fresh carrot-and-orange juice, a beef or chicken empanada, or one of the tasty casados. You and your wallet will leave full. ⊠ *Across from town church and regional bus stop,* ☎ 479–9546. *No credit cards.*

Lodging

$$$$ 🏨 **Tabacón Resort.** Without question, Tabacón, with its impeccably landscaped gardens and hot-spring rivers at the base of Volcán Arenal, is ★ one of Central America's most compelling resorts. The hot springs and small but lovely spa customarily draw visitors inland from the ocean with no regrets. All rooms have tile floors, a terrace or patio, and big bathrooms. Some have volcano views; others overlook the manicured gardens. The suites are some of the country's finest lodgings, with tile floors, plants, beautiful mahogany armoires and beds, and two-person Jacuzzi tubs. The hotel's intimacy is somewhat compromised by its scale and its popularity with day-trippers, so the hotel has some private areas (including a dining room and pool) for overnight guests only. ⊠ *13 km (8 mi) northwest of La Fortuna on highway toward Nuevo Arenal,* ☎ 256–1500, ſAX 221–3075, WEB *www.tabacon.com (mailing address: Apdo. 181–1007, San José). 73 rooms, 9 suites. Restaurant, 3 bars, dining room, cable TV, 9 pools, outdoor hot tub, mineral baths, spa, airport shuttle (fee). MC, V.*

$$$–$$$$ 🏨 **Arenal Observatory Lodge.** Once you're arrive at the end of the winding road leading to the lodge, originally founded by Smithsonian researchers in 1987, you're as close as anyone should be to an active volcano, a mere 1⅕ km (1½ mi) away. The isolated lodge is fairly rustic, emphasizing that outdoor activities are what it's all about. Rooms are simply furnished, but comfortable (comforters on beds are a cozy touch), and most have stellar views. After a hike, take a dip in the "infinity" pool or 12-person Jacuzzi, which face tall pines one side and the volcano on the other. The dining room, which serves tasty and hearty food, has great views of the volcano and lake. ⊠ *3 km (2 mi) east of dam on Laguna de Arenal; from La Fortuna, drive to Tabacón Resort and continue 4 km (3 mi) past the resort to turnoff at base of volcano; turn and continue for 9 km (5½ mi),* ☎ ſAX 695–5033, ☎ 290–7011 in San José, ſAX 290–8427 in San José, WEB *www.arenal-observatory.co.cr (mailing address: Apdo. 13411–1000, San José). 35 rooms, 2 suites. Restaurant, pool, outdoor hot tub, horseback riding, laundry service; no phones, no room TVs. AE, MC, V. CP*

$$$–$$$$ 🏨 **Montaña de Fuego Inn.** Set on a manicured grassy roadside knoll, this highly recommended collection of cabins affords utterly spectacular views of Volcán Arenal. The spacious, well-made hardwood structures are notable for their large porches. All rooms have ceiling fans and rustic decor. The friendly management can arrange tours of the area. ⊠ *8 km (5 mi) west of La Fortuna,* ☎ *460–1220,* FAX *460–1455,* WEB *www.montanadefuego.com. 52 cabinas. Restaurant, pool, hot tub, laundry service. AE, MC, V.*

$$$ 🏨 **Arenal Country Inn.** It doesn't quite approximate an English country inn, although it is a bit charming. Each brightly furnished, modern room has two queen-size beds and a private patio. The lush grounds have great views of the Arenal volcano. Rates include a big breakfast served in the restaurant, an open-air converted cattle corral. You can take lunch and dinner there as well. ⊠ *1 km south of church of La Fortuna, south end of town,* ☎ *479–9670,* FAX *479–9433,* WEB *www.costaricainn.com. 20 rooms. Bar, restaurant, in-room safes, minibars, pool, laundry service, meeting room, travel services; no room TVs. AE, MC, V.*

$$$ 🏨 **Las Cabañitas Resort.** Each of the red-roof cabinas here has a terrace that looks out over landscaped grounds toward the volcano; have a seat in a rocking chair and enjoy the view. Inside, you'll find solid wood furnishings and quilted bedspreads. ⊠ *1 km (½ mi) east of La Fortuna,* ☎ *479–9400,* FAX *479–9408 (mailing address: Apdo. 5–4417, La Fortuna). 30 cabinas. Restaurant, bar, pool, laundry service; no phones, no room TVs. AE, MC, V.*

$$$ 🏨 **Chachagua Rain Forest Lodge.** At this working ranch, intersected by a sweetly babbling brook, you can see caballeros at work, take a horseback ride into the rain forest, and look for toucans from the open-air restaurant, which serves beef, milk, and cheese produced on the premises. Each cabina has a pair of double beds and a deck with a picnic table. Large, reflective windows enclosing each cabina's shower serve a marvelous purpose: birds gather outside your window to watch their own reflections while you bathe and watch them. The lodge is 3 km (2 mi) up a rough track—four-wheel drive is recommended in rainy season— on the road headed south from La Fortuna to La Tigra. ⊠ *12 km (7 mi) south of La Fortuna,* ☎ *231–0356,* FAX *290–6506,* WEB *www.novanet.co.cr/chachagua (Apdo. 476–4005, Ciudad Cariari). 15 cabinas. Restaurant, bar, pool, sauna, tennis court, horseback riding, casino, meeting rooms; no phones, no room TVs. AE, MC, V.*

$$$ 🏨 **Lomas del Volcán.** You'd think you were right on top of the volcano, but Arenal is really a reassuring 6 km (4 mi) away. You need a four-wheel-drive vehicle to get here, but once you do, you can luxuriate in the splendid isolation. The simple cabins have hot water and come with two beds and throw rugs. Each has a volcano-viewing porch. ⊠ *Road entrance 1½ km (1 mi) west of La Fortuna,* ☎ *393–1361,* FAX *479–9770,* WEB *www.lomasdelvolcan.com. 8 cabins. Fans, refrigerators; no air-conditioning, no phones, no room TVs. AE, MC, V.*

$$$ 🏨 **Luigi's Lodge.** Every one of this hotel's rooms fronts a stunning view of the volcano: it's the only lodging in the center of town able to make that claim. Rooms also have high wooden ceilings and stenciled animal drawings. The green-and-white tiled bathrooms have bathtubs, a rarity in Costa Rica. The adjoining restaurant serves pizza. ⊠ *200 m northwest of town church,* ☎ *479–9636,* FAX *479–9898,* WEB *www.luigislodge.com. 22 rooms. Restaurant, pool, hot tub, gym. AE, MC, V.*

$$$ 🏨 **Tilajari Hotel Resort.** As a comfortable base from which to have outdoor or adventure tours, this 35-acre resort with a butterfly garden and orchard is a good choice. The hotel organizes horseback tours through its own rain forest preserve, kayak tours in the river that nudges up against the property, as well as other area tours. "Papaya on a stick" feeders hang outside the open-air dining room, attracting an array of raucous toucans and parrots to entertain you while you sip your morning coffee. The modest guest quarters have river-view balconies and satellite

TV; family suites have lofts. Tilajari is a half hour outside of town, and there's no shuttle service. ✉ *San Carlos Valley, just outside Muelle (follow signs), about 25 km (15 mi) from La Fortuna,* ☎ *469–9091,* FAX *469–9095,* WEB *www.arenallodge.com (mailing address: Apdo. 81, San Carlos, Alajuela). 60 rooms, 16 suites. Restaurant, bar, 2 pools, outdoor hot tub, 6 tennis courts, horseback riding, Ping-Pong, laundry service, meeting rooms. AE, MC, V.*

\$\$ 🏨 **Cabinas Los Guayabos.** A great budget alternative to the more expensive lodgings lining the road to the volcano is this group of basic but spotlessly clean cabins managed by a friendly family. The units have all the standard budget lodging furnishings, but each comes with its own porch facing Arenal, ideal for viewing the evening spectacle. ✉ *9 km (5½) west of La Fortuna,* ☎ *460–6644. 5 cabins. No air-conditioning, no phones, no room TVs. No credit cards.*

\$\$ 🏨 **Hotel San Bosco.** Covered in blue-tile mosaics, this two-story hotel
★ is certainly the most attractive and comfortable in the main part of town. Two kitchen-equipped cabinas (which sleep 8 or 14 people) are a good deal for families. The spotlessly clean, white rooms have polished wood furniture and firm beds and are linked by a long veranda lined with benches and potted plants. You pay a little more for air-conditioning. ✉ *220 m north of La Fortuna's gas station,* ☎ *479–9050,* FAX *479–9109,* WEB *www.arenal-volcano.com. 34 rooms, 2 cabinas. Pool, hot tub, laundry service; no phones. AE, MC, V.*

\$\$ 🏨 **La Pradera.** ìThe Prairieî is a simple roadside hotel with 10 comfortable guest rooms, all with high ceilings, spacious bathrooms, and verandas. Two rooms have Jacuzzis. Beef eaters should try the high thatched-roof restaurant next door. The steak with jalapeño sauce is a fine, spicy dish. ✉ *About 2 km (1 mi) west of La Fortuna,* ☎ *479–9597,* FAX *479–9167. 10 rooms. Restaurant; no air-conditioning in some rooms. AE, MC, V.*

Outdoor Activities and Sports

CANOPY TOURS

Want a bird's-eye view of the trees? Let the professionals at the **Original Canopy Tour** (✉ Tabacón Resort, 13 km [8 mi] northwest of La Fortuna on highway toward Nuevo Arenal, ☎ 460–2020 or 256–1500, FAX 221–3075, WEB www.canopytour.com) show you the canopy from a new perspective. You'll be securely strapped into a rock-climbing harness and attached to a pulley and horizontal zip line. Well-trained guides then send you whizzing between trees that stand about 100 m (328 ft) over the streams of Tabacón. (If it's a small tour, they may even be able to snap a picture of you.) Since a tour requires a certain amount of fearlessness, it's not for everyone, but it's for more folks than you might think. While it's not rigorous per se, it's certainly exhilarating and unique. Tours are at 7:30 AM, 10 AM, 1:30, and 4. The price of a tour (\$45) includes admission to Tabacón hot springs for the day.

FISHING

The eastern side of Laguna de Arenal has the best freshwater fishing in Costa Rica, with guapote aplenty, although it is difficult to fish from the shore. Arenal Observatory Lodge is one of many hotels and tour companies in the area offering boats and guides.

HIKING

To take the 6-km (4-mi) day hike from La Fortuna to the **Cataratas de la Fortuna,** look for the yellow entrance sign off the main road toward the volcano. After walking 1½ km (1 mi) and passing two bridges, turn right and continue straight ahead until you reach the river turnoff. You'll go 10 or 15 minutes down a steep but very well constructed step trail that has a few vertiginous spots along the way. Swimming in the pool under the waterfall is fairly safe. You can work your way around into the cavelike area behind the cataract for an unusual rear view, but you'll have to swim in turbulent waters and/or hike over slippery rocks. A $2 fee is collected at the head of the trail, which is open daily 7–4.

HORSEBACK RIDING

If you're interested in getting up to Monteverde from the Arenal–La Fortuna area without taking the grinding four-hour drive, there's an alternative: the ever-ingenious Suresh Krishnan, a transplant from California, offers a wonderful adventure out of his tour agency, **Desafío Tours** (✉ Central plaza [Apdo. 37–4417], La Fortuna, ☎ 479–9464, WEB www.desafiocostarica.com)—a 4½-hour guided horseback trip around the southern shore of Lake Arenal with continuing service to Monteverde. The trip involves taxi service on both ends, as well as a boat ride across Laguna de Arenal. They'll take your luggage and drive your car up there if need be, all for $65 per person. You leave La Fortuna at 7:30 AM and arrive in Monteverde around 2:30 PM. **Eagle Tours** (✉ north of gas station, La Fortuna, ☎ 479–9091) has horseback rides to Monteverde, with the caveat that rainy conditions and poor trail conditions could cancel the trip. Note that many other agencies in La Fortuna and Monteverde offer rides over a muddy, poorly maintained trail. Some riders have returned with stories of terrified horses barely able to navigate the way. It's best to avoid other tours.

RAFTING

Several La Fortuna operators offer Class III and IV white-water trips on the Río Toro. The narrow shape of this river requires the use of special, streamlined, U.S.-made boats that seat just four and go very fast.

Desafío Expeditions (✉ Central plaza [Apdo. 37–4417], La Fortuna, ☎ 479–9464, WEB www.desafiocostarica.com) has trips on the Río Toro for $59 per person.

SPELUNKING

Sunset Tours (✉ Across from Desafío Expeditions, La Fortuna, ☎ 479–9415) will take you to the Venado Caverns for $25, including an English-speaking guide, entrance fee, boots, and a lantern. Prepare to get wet and muddy.

Caño Negro National Wildlife Refuge

❹ *91 km (57 mi) northwest of La Fortuna.*

A lowland rain forest reserve in the far northern reaches of Alajuela, Refugio Nacional de Vida Silvestre Caño Negro covers 62 square km (38 square mi). Caño Negro has suffered severe deforestation over the years, but most of the Río Frío is still lined with trees, and the park's vast lake is an excellent place to watch such waterfowl as the roseate spoonbill, jabiru stork, and anhinga, as well as a host of resident exotic animals. In the dry season, you can ride horses; but the visit here chiefly entails a wildlife-spotting boat tour. Caño Negro can be reached from the Nuevo Arenal–La Fortuna area, or you can approach via Upala (a bus from here takes 45 minutes). Visiting with a tour company is the best way to see the park. ✉ $6. ☼ *Daily 7–4.*

Sunset Tours (☎ 479–9415), in La Fortuna, runs daylong tours down the Río Frío to Caño Negro for $45. Bring your jungle juice: the mosquitoes are voracious. Camping is permitted or you can stay in basic lodging for around $10, including meals.

Volcán Arenal

★ ❺ *17 km (11 mi) west of La Fortuna, 128 km (80 mi) northwest of San José.*

If you've never seen an active volcano, Arenal makes a spectacular first—its perfect conical profile dominates the southern end of Laguna de Arenal. Night is the best time to observe it, as you can clearly see rocks spewing skyward and red-hot molten lava enveloping the top of the cone. Phases of inactivity do occur, however, so it's wise to check ahead. The volcano is also frequently hidden in cloud cover, so you may have to stay more than one day to get in a good volcano-viewing session.

Arenal lay dormant for 400 years until 1968. On July 29 of that year an earthquake shook the area, and 12 hours later Arenal blew. Pueblo Nuevo to the west bore the brunt of the shock waves, poisonous gases, and falling rocks; 80 people perished. Since then, Arenal has been in a constant state of activity—eruptions, accompanied by thunderous grumbling sounds, are sometimes as frequent as one per hour. An enormous eruption in 1998 put the fear back into the local community and led to closure of Route 42 and the evacuation of several nearby hotels. This earth-shaking event reminded everyone what it really means to coexist with an active volcano.

Though folks here still do it, hiking is not recommended on the volcano's lower slopes; in 1988 two people were killed when they attempted to climb it. History repeated itself in 2000 with the death of an American traveler and her guide who were hiking on the lower slopes in a supposedly safe area. The conventional wisdom in these parts is that it's still safe to approach from the south and west, within the national park, although many recommend enjoying the spectacle from no closer than any of the lodges themselves.

Nuevo Arenal

❻ *40 km (25 mi) west of La Fortuna.*

There's little reason to stop in Nuevo Arenal itself. Off the main road, the pleasant, if nondescript, *nuevo* town was created in 1973 to replace the original Arenal, flooded when the lake was created. If you're staying overnight in the area make sure you find a hotel with a view of the volcano. On the north shore, between the dam and the town of Nuevo Arenal, there's one short stretch of road still unpaved, potholed, and at times quite dangerous; beware of deep, tire-wrecking washouts at all times. This stretch adds a bone-jarring hour to an otherwise lovely drive with spectacular lake and volcano views all the way.

Five kilometers (3 miles) east of Nuevo Arenal, the elegantly organized **Jardín Botánico Arenal** (Arenal Botanical Gardens) exhibits more than 2,000 plant species from around the world. Countless orchids, bromeliads, heliconias, and roses; varieties of ferns; and a Japanese garden with a waterfall are among the many floral splendors laid out along well-marked trails. An accompanying brochure describes everything in delightful detail; well-placed benches and a fruit-and-juice stand provide resting places along the paths. ☎ 694–4273. ⬚ *$5.* ☺ *Daily 9–5.*

Lodging

$$$–$$$$ ⬚ **Arenal Lodge.** Surrounded by macadamia trees and rain forest, this modern white bungalow is high above the dam, midway between La Fortuna and Nuevo Arenal. You need four-wheel drive to negotiate the steep 2-km (1-mi) drive, but the hotel will ferry you from the bottom. Bedroom suites, some in a newer annex, are pleasantly furnished, with

pretty green-tile baths; there are also cheaper, smaller, darker rooms without volcano views. Interiors are finished in natural wood, with walls of louvered windows. Hilltop chalets have floor-to-ceiling windows and kitchenettes. Perks include use of bicycles, a small snooker table, breakfast with the price of a room, and a free hour of horseback riding. ⊠ 18½ km (11½ mi) west of La Fortuna, past the Arenal Dam, then 2 km (1 mi) north, ☎ 383–3957, WEB www.arenallodge.com (mailing address: Apdo. 1139–1250, Escazú, ☎ 228–3189, FAX 289–6798). 6 rooms, 18 suites, 10 chalets. Dining room, hiking, horseback riding, fishing, library, Internet, laundry service. AE, MC, V.

$$$ 🏨 **Hotel Joya Sureña.** In the midst of a working coffee plantation, this Canadian-owned property with variously sized suites occupies a rather imposing three-story hacienda-style building surrounded by tropical gardens. It's fairly luxurious for up-country Costa Rica. Extensive trails in and around the place bring a rich diversity of plant, animal, and bird life to view. ⊠ 1½ km (1 mi) down a rocky road that leads east from Nuevo Arenal, ☎ 694–4057, FAX 694–4059. 28 rooms. Restaurant, pool, hot tub, massage, sauna, health club, hiking, boating, fishing, laundry service. AE, MC, V.

$$$ 🏨 **Lake Coter Eco-Lodge.** This ruggedly handsome mountain hideaway tucked into cloud forest offers lots to do, thanks to the setting. The lodge offers canopy tours on-site, hikes on 29 km (18 mi) of trails, kayaking and sailing on Laguna de Arenal, and an extensive stable of horses for trail rides through the cloud forest. Stay in comfortable ridgetop cabinas, if they're available. Clean, basic rooms are attached to the main brick-and-hardwood reception building, which has a friendly bar, dining facilities, a fireplace, and a pool table. ⊠ 3 km (2 mi) up a rough track off north shore of Laguna de Arenal, ☎ 694–4480 or 440–6768, FAX 694–4460 or 440–6725, WEB www.ecolodgecostarica.com. 23 rooms, 14 cabinas. Restaurant, bar, hiking, horseback riding, boating, laundry service, meeting room. AE, MC, V.

Shopping

Toad Hall (☎ 381–3662), an eclectic store on the road between Nuevo Arenal and La Fortuna, sells everything from indigenous art to maps to recycled paper. The owners can give you the lowdown on every tour and tour operator in the area; they also run a deli-café with stunning alfresco views of the lake and volcano. Toad Hall is open daily from 8:30 to 5.

Tilarán

❼ 22 km (14 mi) southwest of Nuevo Arenal, 62 km (38 mi) west of La Fortuna.

Heading west around Laguna de Arenal, you'll pass a couple of small villages and several charming hotels ranging from the Cretan-inspired fantasy Hotel Tilawa to the rustic Rock River Lodge. The quiet whitewashed town of Tilarán, on the southwest side of Laguna de Arenal, is used as a base by bronzed windsurfers.

Dining and Lodging

$$$ ✕🏨 **Hotel Tilawa.** Tilawa is a knockoff of the Palace of Knossos on Crete. And yet, even on the west of Laguna de Arenal, its neoclassic murals, columns, and plant-draped arches don't seem dramatically out of place. The spacious rooms have two queen-size beds with Guatemalan bedspreads and natural wood ceilings; the bathrooms are especially spacious. The property could use a renovation, but the sailing tours in a 12-m (39-ft) catamaran and windsurfing school and shop can make this a practical place to base yourself. Packages include the use of wind-

surfing gear. ✉ *8 km (5 mi) north of Tilarán,* ☎ *695–5050,* FAX *695–5766,* WEB *www.hotel-tilawa.com (mailing address: Apdo. 92–5710, Tilarán). 28 rooms. Restaurant, bar, pool, hiking, horseback riding, windsurfing, boating, mountain bikes, laundry service. AE, MC, V.*

$$ ✕⬚ **La Carreta.** Comfy, modern rooms—complete with cable TV, an option usually not found in hotels in this price category—and the best restaurant in town are the hallmarks of this cozy hotel. The restaurant dishes up Tico and Italian food on a front porch overlooking a leafy garden. The friendly U.S. owners also run an on-site art gallery, book exchange, souvenir shop, and bicycle and car rental service. ✉ *Behind cathedral,* ☎ *695–6654,* FAX *695–6654. 6 rooms. Restaurant, cable TV, hot tub. MC, V.*

$$$ ⬚ **Rock River Lodge.** A long, handsome building on a grassy hill above the road leading from Tilarán to Nuevo Arenal houses six rustic wooden cabinas. They share a shaded front porch with views of the volcano. Eight Santa Fe–style cabinas are farther up the hill. The restaurant, bar, and lobby occupy another building closer to the road, with plenty of porch space and lounging sofas, an open kitchen, and a welcoming fireplace. The hotel rents windsurfing gear; its launching site is across the lake from that of the Hotel Tilawa. The restaurant serves well-prepared food at reasonable prices. ✉ *Apdo. 95–5710, Tilarán,* ☎ FAX *695–5644,* WEB *www.rokriverlodge.com. 6 rooms, 8 cabinas. Restaurant, bar, horseback riding, windsurfing, fishing, mountain bikes, laundry service; no phones, no room TVs. V.*

$ ⬚ **Hotel Naralit.** Spell Tilarán backwards and you get the name of a great budget option in the center of town. It's very basic but comfortable, run by friendly folks, and spotlessly clean. A large glass door fronts a porch in each pleasantly furnished room letting in lots of light. The Naralit manages a small restaurant next door. ✉ *Opposite south side of cathedral, Tilarán,* ☎ *695–5393,* FAX *695–6767. 26 rooms. Some cable TV, some refrigerators. V.*

Outdoor Activities and Sports

HORSEBACK RIDING
Uncounted miles of good horse trails cover a marvelous mix of terrain. **Hotel Tilawa** (☎ 695–5050) and nearly every other reputable hotel can make arrangements for guided and unguided horseback treks.

MOUNTAIN BIKING
For those days when the windsurfers get "skunked" (the wind fails to blow), the **Hotel Tilawa** (☎ 695–5050) rents mountain bikes for riding a network of roads and trails in the area at the north end of Laguna de Arenal.

WINDSURFING
Rock River Lodge (☎ 695–5644) is one of several hotels that rent windsurfing equipment. The best selection of windsurfing equipment for rent or purchase can be found at **Tilawa Viento Surf** (☎ 695–5008), the lakefront shop associated with the Hotel Tilawa and the only outfitter here open year-round.

En Route   If your bones can take it, a very rough track leads from Tilarán via Cabeceras to Santa Elena, near the Monteverde Cloud Forest Biological Reserve, doing away with the need to cut across to the Pan-American Highway. You may well need a four-wheel-drive vehicle—inquire locally about the present condition of the road—but the views of Nicoya Peninsula, Lake Arenal, and Volcán Arenal reward those willing to bump around a bit. Note, too, that you don't really save much time—on a good day, it takes about 2½ hours as opposed to the 3 required via Cañas and Río Lagarto on the highway.

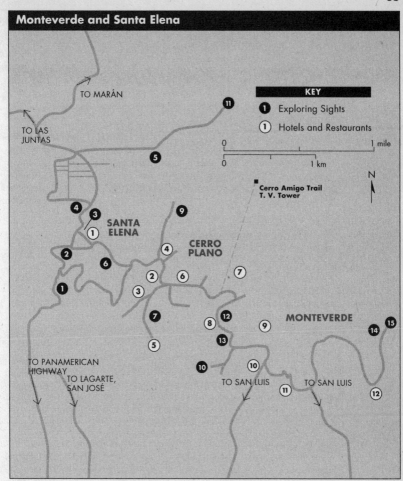

Monteverde and Santa Elena

KEY

1 Exploring Sights

(1) Hotels and Restaurants

0 _____ 1 mile
0 _____ 1 km

N

Cerro Amigo Trail
T. V. Tower

TO MARÁN

TO LAS JUNTAS

SANTA ELENA

CERRO PLANO

MONTEVERDE

TO PANAMERICAN HIGHWAY

TO LAGARTE, SAN JOSÉ

TO SAN LUIS

TO SAN LUIS

Exploring

Bajo del Tigre Trail **10**

CASEM **13**

Hummingbird Gallery **14**

Jardín de las Mariposas **7**

Meg's Stables **12**

Monteverde Cloud Forest Reserve **15**

Original Canopy Tour **9**

Original Canopy Tour Office **2**

Ranario de Monteverde **1**

Reserva Santa Elena **11**

Reserva Sendero Tranquilo **8**

Santa Elena Reserve Office **4**

Serpentario Monteverde **6**

Sky Trek/ Sky Walk **5**

Sky Trek/ Sky Walk Office . . .**3**

Dining & Lodging

Arco Iris Lodge **1**

De Lucía **3**

El Bosque **8**

El Establo Mountain Resort **6**

Fonda Vela **11**

Hotel Belmar **7**

Hotel El Sapo Dorado **4**

Jungle Groove Café **9**

La Colina **10**

Pensión Montverde Inn **5**

Pizzería de Johnny **2**

Trapp Family Lodge **12**

MONTEVERDE CLOUD FOREST BIOLOGICAL RESERVE

★ ⑧ *35 km (22 mi) southeast of Tilarán, 167 km (104 mi) northwest of San José.*

In close proximity to several fine hotels, the private Reserva Biológica Bosque Nuboso Monteverde is one of Costa Rica's best-kept reserves, with well-marked trails, lush vegetation, and a cool climate. The area's first residents were a handful of Costa Rican families fleeing the rough-and-ready life of nearby gold-mining fields during the 1940s. They were joined in the 1950s by Quakers from Alabama who came in search of peace, tranquillity, and good grazing, but the cloud forest that lay above their dairy farms was soon to attract the attention of ecologists. Educators and artisans followed, giving Monteverde and its "metropolis," the village of Santa Elena, a mystique all their own.

The collision of moist winds with the continental divide here creates a constant mist whose particles provide nutrients for plants growing at the upper layers of the forest. Giant trees are enshrouded in a cascade of orchids, bromeliads, mosses, and ferns, and, in those patches where sunlight penetrates, brilliantly colored flowers flourish. The sheer size of everything, especially the leaves of the trees, is striking. No less astounding is the variety: 2,500 plant species, 400 species of birds, 500 types of butterflies, and more than 100 different mammals have so far been cataloged at Monteverde. A damp and exotic mixture of shades, smells, and sounds, the cloud forest is also famous for its population of resplendent quetzals, which can be spotted feeding on the *aguacatillo* (like an avocado) trees; best viewing times are early mornings from January until September, and especially during the mating season of April and May. Other forest-dwelling inhabitants include hummingbirds and multicolor frogs.

For those who don't have a lucky eye, a short-stay aquarium is in the field station; captive amphibians stay here just a week before being released back into the wild. Although the reserve limits visitors to 100 people at a time, Monteverde is one of the country's most popular destinations and gets very busy, so come early and allow a generous slice of time for leisurely hiking to see the forest's flora and fauna; longer hikes are made possible by some strategically placed overnight refuges along the way. At the entrance to the reserve you can buy self-guide pamphlets and rent rubber boots; a map is provided when you pay the entrance fee. A two-hour guided night tour starts each evening at 7:30. Note that the Monteverde settlement has no real nucleus; houses and hotels flank a 6-km (4-mi) road from Santa Elena until you arrive at the reserve's entrance. ☎ 645–5122, 🌐 *www.cct.or.cr.* 🖾 *Reserve $12, guide $15.* ☉ *Daily 7–4.*

Greet 30 species of live Costa Rican reptiles and amphibians at the ☾ **Serpentario Monteverde.** ⌧ *Just outside Santa Elena on road to Monteverde,* ☎ 645–5238. 🖾 *$3.* ☉ *Daily 8–5.*

★ ☾ Only in Monteverde would visitors groove to the nightlife at the **Ranario de Monteverde,** an exhibition of 25 species of frogs, toads, and other amphibians. Bilingual biologist-guides take you through a 45-minute tour of the terrariums in the facility just outside Santa Elena. For the best show, come around dusk and stay well into the evening when the critters become more active and much more vocal. ⌧ *600 yards southeast of Supermercado La Esperanza,* ☎ 645–6320. 🖾 *$8.* ☉ *Daily 9–8:30.*

Several conservation areas that have sprung up near Monteverde make attractive day trips, particularly if the Monteverde reserve is too busy. The **Reserva Santa Elena,** just west of Monteverde, has a series of trails that can be walked alone or with a guide. ✉ *6 km (3½ mi) north of Santa Elena,* ☎ *645–5390,* WEB *www.monteverdeinfo.com.* 🎫 *$8.* ⏱ *Daily 7–4.*

With tours operating out of the El Sapo Dorado hotel (☎ 645–5010), the **Reserva Sendero Tranquilo** invites you to hike 200 acres containing four different stages of cloud forest, including one area illustrating the results of cloud-forest devastation. ✉ *3 km (2 mi) north of park entrance,* ☎ *645–5010.* 🎫 *$20 (2-person minimum, 10-person maximum).*

☾ The **Jardín de las Mariposas** (Butterfly Garden) displays tropical butterflies in three enclosed botanical gardens with stunning views of the Golfo de Nicoya. A guided tour helps you understand the stages of a butterfly's life. The private **bird farm** next door has several trails through secondary forest. More than 90 bird species have been sighted here, from the crowned motmot to the resplendent quetzal. ✉ *Near Pensión Monteverde Inn (take right-hand turnoff 4 km [2½ mi] past Santa Elena on road to Monteverde; continue for 2 km [1 mi]),* ☎ *645–5512.* 🎫 *$7.* ⏱ *Daily 9:30–4.*

Dining and Lodging

$$–$$$ ✕ **De Lucía.** Cordial Chilean owner José Belmar is the walking, talking (five languages) menu in this elegant restaurant. He's always on hand to explain with enthusiasm such masterfully prepared dishes as sea bass with garlic sauce and orange chicken. All the entrées are served with an impressive assortment of grilled vegetables and fried plantains. The handsome wooden restaurant with red mahogany tables is given a distinct South American flavor by an array of Andean tapestries and ceramics. An excellent dessert choice is the *tres leches* (a rich cake of condensed and evaporated milk and sugar) with decaf coffee—a novelty in Costa Rica. ✉ *Off main road between Santa Elena and Monteverde, on turnoff to Jardín Mariposa,* ☎ *645–5337. AE, MC, V.*

$$–$$$ ✕ **Pizzeria de Johnny.** Everyone makes it to this stylish but informal place with candles and white tablecloths during a visit. The Monteverde pizza, with the works, is the most popular dish, and pastas, sandwiches, and a fine wine selection round out the menu. ✉ *1½ km (1 mi) from Santa Elena on road to reserve,* ☎ *645–5066. V.*

$–$$ ✕ **Jungle Groove Café.** This is nightlife, Monteverde-style—never raucous, but on the quiet side, with good food and soft music amid a lush garden setting. Miami native and owner Miriam Merino mixes Tico cuisine with mild Cuban spices. Try the fajita-like mixed *gallos,* warm tortillas with spicy meat and vegetable fillings. And Miriam sets a new standard for tapas with her seven-layer Cuban-style nachos. ✉ *50 yards northeast of CASEM,* ☎ *645–6270. MC, V.*

$$$–$$$$ ✕🏨 **Hotel El Sapo Dorado.** Having begun life as a nightclub, the Golden Toad became a popular restaurant and then graduated into a very pleasant hotel. Geovanny Arguedas's family arrived here to farm 10 years before the Quakers did, and he and his wife, Hannah Lowther, have built secluded hillside cabins with polished paneling, tables, fireplaces, and rocking chairs. The restaurant is renowned for its pasta, pizza, vegetarian dishes, and sailfish from Puntarenas. ✉ *6 km (4 mi) northwest of park entrance,* ☎ *645–5010,* FAX *645–5180,* WEB *www.cool.co.cr/usr/sapodorado (mailing address: Apdo. 9–5655, Monteverde). 30 rooms. Restaurant, bar, massage, laundry service. AE, MC, V.*

EYES AFLIGHT IN COSTA RICA

I F YOU VISIT A COSTA RICAN CLOUD forest, you'll probably have your eyes peeled for the emerald toucanet or the three-wattled bellbird, but if you're here between October and April, you'll actually be just as likely to see a Kentucky warbler. Experienced birders shouldn't be surprised to see that some of their feathered friends from home made similar vacation plans, but many people probably don't realize that when northern birds fly south for the winter, they don't all head to Miami.

Seasonal visitors are just part—about a quarter—of the amazing avian panorama in Costa Rica. Nearly 850 bird species have been identified here, more than the United States and Canada have between them—all in an area about half the size of Kentucky. The country is consequently a mecca for amateur ornithologists, who flock here by the thousands. Though the big attractions tend to be such spectacular species as the keel-billed toucan and resplendent quetzal, it is the diversity of shape, size, coloration, and behavior that makes bird-watching in Costa Rica so fascinating.

The country's avian inhabitants range in size from the scintillant hummingbird, standing a mere 2½ inches tall and weighing just over 2 grams, to the long-legged jabiru stork, which reaches a height of more than 1⅓ m (4 ft) and a weight of 14 pounds. The diversity of form and color varies from such striking creatures as the showy scarlet macaw and the quirky purple gallinule to the relatively inconspicuous, and seemingly ubiquitous, clay-color robin, which is, surprisingly enough, Costa Rica's national bird. These robins may look a bit plain, but their song is a melodious one, and since the males sing almost constantly toward the end of the dry season—the beginning of their mating season—local legend has it they call the rains, which play a vital role in a nation so dependent on agriculture.

Foreigners tend to ooh and aah at the sight of those birds associated with the tropics: parrots, parakeets, and macaws; toucans and toucanets; and the elusive but legendary quetzal. But there are many other, equally impressive species, flitting around, such as the motmots, with their distinctive racket tails; oropéndolas (golden orioles), which build remarkable hanging nests; and an amazing array of hawks, kites, and falcons.

On the color scale, the country's tanagers, euphonias, manakins, cotingas, and trogons are some of its loveliest plumed creatures, but none of them match the iridescence of the hummingbirds. Costa Rica hosts 51 members of the hummingbird family, compared to the just one species for all of the United States east of the Rocky Mountains. A bit of time spent near a hummingbird feeder will treat you to an unforgettable display of accelerated aerial antics and general pugnacity.

You just might find that the more you observe Costa Rica's birds, the more interesting they get. Bird-watching can be done everywhere in the country—all you need is a pair of binoculars and a copy of A Guide to the Birds of Costa Rica, the excellent field guide by Stiles and Skutch. Wake up early, get out into the woods or the garden, focus those binoculars, and you'll quickly be enchanted by the beauty on the wing. For more information about Costa Rican birds, see the Wildlife Glossary in Chapter 9.

$$$ ✕⊞ **Fonda Vela.** Owned by the Smith brothers, whose family was
★ among the first American arrivals in the 1950s, these steep-roof chalets
have large bedrooms with white-stucco walls, wood floors, and huge
windows. Some have markedly better views of the wooded grounds, so
specify when booking. The most innovatively designed of Monteverde's
hotels is also one of the closest to the reserve entrance. Local and in-
ternational recipes, prepared with flair, are served in the dining room
or on the veranda. ⊠ *1½ km (1 mi) northwest of park entrance,* ☎ *645–
5125,* FAX *645–5119,* WEB *www.fondavela.com (mailing address: Apdo.
70060–1000, San José,* ☎ *257–1413,* FAX *257–1416). 40 rooms. Restau-
rant, bar, refrigerator, horseback riding, meeting room; no air-condi-
tioning, no room phones, no room TVs. AE, MC, V.*

$$$ ✕⊞ **Hotel Belmar.** Built into the hillside, Hotel Belmar resembles two
tall Swiss chalets and commands extensive views of the Golfo de Nicoya
and the hilly peninsula. The amiable Chilean owners have designed both
elegant and rustic rooms, paneled with polished wood; duvets cover the
beds, and half the rooms have balconies. In the dining room, you can
count on adventurous and delicious *platos del día* (daily specials) of Costa
Rican and international fare. ⊠ *4 km (2½ mi) north of Monteverde,*
☎ *645–5201,* FAX *645–5135,* WEB *www.centralamerica.com/cr/hotel/
belmar.htm (mailing address: Apdo. 17–5655, Monteverde, Puntarenas).
34 rooms. Restaurant, bar, basketball, laundry service; no air-conditioning,
no room TVs. V.*

$$–$$$$ ⊞ **El Establo Mountain Resort.** Mixing old and new, The Stable began
life as just that, a stable near the road, remodeled and apportioned into
comfortable rooms with basic furnishings. A newer pink building
perches on the hill above with large suites with wood-and-stone walls.
Some contain lofts; all come with amenities rarely seen up here, such
as bathtubs, cable TV, in-room phones, and enormous windows with
views of the Golfo de Nicoya. ⊠ *3½ km (2 mi) northwest of Monteverde,*
☎ *645–5110,* FAX *645–5041,* WEB *www.hotelestablo.com. 50 rooms.
Restaurant, bar, cable TV, pool, hot tub. AE, MC, V.*

$$$ ⊞ **Trapp Family Lodge.** Take a whiff in this cozy lodge and you can imag-
ine yourself in a lumberyard. The enormous rooms, with wood panel-
ing and ceilings, have lovely furniture marvelously crafted from—you
guessed it—wood. The architectural style is appropriate, as the lodge
is surrounded by trees, just a 10-minute walk from the park entrance.
It's the closest to the reserve. The friendly Chilean owners are always
around to provide personalized service. ⊠ *On main road from park,*
☎ *645–5858,* FAX *645–5990,* WEB *www.trappfam.com (mailing address:
Apdo. 70–5655, Monteverde). 20 rooms. Restaurant, bar; no smoking,
no air-conditioning, no room phones, no room TVs. V.*

$$–$$$ ⊞ **Arco Iris Lodge.** You can't tell that you're in the center of town at
this tranquil spot, with its cozy cabins set among 4 acres of birding trails.
Cabin decor ranges from rustic to more plush, but all come with porches.
Start your day with a delicious breakfast buffet, including homemade
bread, granola, and marmalades. This is an "ecolodge," so many of the
kitchen's ingredients come from its own organic garden. The laid-back
German management can provide good advice about how to spend your
time in the area. ⊠ *75 yards south of Banco Nacional, Santa Elena,*
☎ *645–5067,* FAX *645–5022,* WEB *www.arcoirislodge.com. 10 cabins.
Horseback riding, laundry service; no air-conditioning, no room phones,
no room TVs. AE, MC, V.*

$$ ⊞ **El Bosque.** Convenient to the Bajo del Tigre nature trail and Meg's
Stables, El Bosque's quiet, simple rooms are grouped around a central
camping area with a volleyball court. A bridge crosses a stream and
leads to the hotel, which serves brick-oven pizzas on its a veranda.
⊠ *2½ km (1½ mi) from Santa Elena on road to reserve,* ☎ *645–5158,*
FAX *645–5129 (mailing address: Apdo. 5655, Santa Elena). 26 rooms.*

Restaurant, volleyball, laundry service; no air-conditioning, no room phones, no room TVs. AE, MC, V.

$$ 🏨 **La Colina.** This Colorado ranch-style place is a longtime Monteverde standby. Rust colors and earth tones prevail in the rooms, which are accentuated with the occasional wagon wheel and old western trunk. A hearty American-style breakfast is included in the rates, and it will keep you going until your evening dinner. The friendly management offers discounts for extended stays. ✉ *300 yards south of Cheese Factory,* ☎ *645–5009,* WEB *www.lacolina.com. 11 rooms, 6 with bath. Restaurant, hot tub; no air-conditioning, no room phones, no room TVs. V.*

$ 🏨 **Pensión Monteverde Inn.** The cheapest Monteverde inn is quite far from the park entrance, on a 28-acre private preserve. The bedrooms are basic, but they have stunning views of the Golfo de Nicoya and have hardwood floors, firm beds, and powerful, hot showers. Home cooking is served by the chatty David and María Savage and family. Their dog, Bambi, will warm up to you, too. ✉ *5 km (3 mi) past Butterfly Garden (on turnoff road), Monteverde,* ☎ *645–5156,* FAX *645–5945. 8 rooms. Dining room; no air-conditioning, no room phones, no room TVs. No credit cards.*

Outdoor Activities and Sports

CANOPY TOURS

One of the most unique ways to explore the rain forest canopy is on an exhilarating canopy tour. Be sure to ask questions about safety of all canopy tour companies and be prepared to walk away if the trip doesn't look professionally handled.

You can visit the Monteverde cloud forest treetops courtesy of the **Original Canopy Tour** (✉ 50 yards west of La Esperanza Supermarket, ☎ 645–5243; 257–5149 in San José, WEB www.canopytour.com), which has 11 platforms in the canopy—the company's longest tour—that you arrive at using a cable-and-harness traversing system and another that you climb 13 m (42 ft) inside a strangler fig tree to reach. This location also has a Tarzan Swing. Several knockoff tours, with uneven reputations, have sprung up around Costa Rica, also calling themselves "canopy tours." This one, which calls itself "the original," is top-notch. The tours last 2½ hours and are held at 7:30 AM, 10:30 AM, and 2:30 PM. The cost is $45.

Perhaps the idea of being in the tree canopy appeals to you, only you suspect the rock-climbing gear and zip line route are not for you? **Sky Walk** (✉ across from Banco Nacional, ☎ 645–5238, WEB www.sky-walk.co.cr), lets you walk between treetops, up to a height of 42 m (138 ft), by way of five hanging bridges connected from tree to tree. Imposing towers are also used as support although they somewhat mar the landscape. The hour-long walk can be done anytime between 7 and 4 daily and costs $12. Tours with an English-speaking guide leave at 8 and 1—be sure to make reservations. At the same facility is the more adventurous **Sky Trek,** which uses rock-climbing gear, zip lines, and has seven platforms and longer cables between them than the Original Canopy Tour. Tours cost $35 and leave at 7:30, 9:30, 11:30, 1:30, and 2. The company provides cheap transport to and from hotels when called a few hours in advance.

HIKING

The Monteverde Conservation League's **Bajo del Tigre trail** (follow signs along the highway to Monteverde, ☎ 645–5003, WEB www.acmonteverde.com), in the Bosque Eterno de los Niños, makes for a gentle, 1½-km (1-mi) hike through secondary forest. Admission to the trail is $5, and it's open daily 8–4:30.

HORSEBACK RIDING

Meg's Stables (✉ on main road, halfway between Santa Elena and Monteverde, ☎ 645–5029) offers horseback riding for everyone from toddlers to seasoned experts. Guided rides through the Monteverde area cost around $10 an hour, with prices dropping for longer rides. Reservations are a good idea in high season.

Shopping

In Monteverde, the **Comité de Artesanas de Santa Elena y Monteverde** (CASEM; ☎ 645–5190), an artisans' cooperative open next door to the El Bosque hotel-restaurant, sells locally made crafts, mostly by women, and English books. The **Hummingbird Gallery** (☎ 645–5030), just outside the reserve entrance, sells books, gifts, T-shirts, great Costa Rican coffee, prints, and slides by nature specialists Michael and Patricia Fogden, as well as watercolors by nature artist Sarah Dowell.

FAR NORTHERN GUANACASTE

This area encompasses the mountains, plains, and Pacific coastline north of Liberia up to the border of Nicaragua. The primary town in the area, Liberia (☞ Chapter 5), serves as the capital of Guanacaste and home to Costa Rica's second-largest airport. You'll most likely pass through it on your way to the beaches west of the city and on the Nicoya Peninsula (☞ Chapter 5) or up north to the national parks of Rincón de la Vieja, Guanacaste, or Santa Rosa. Volcán Rincón de la Vieja, an active volcano that last erupted in 1991, is pocked with eerie sites such as boiling creeks, bubbling mud pools, and vapor-emitting streams—look, but don't touch!

West of Rincón de la Vieja, on the coast, Santa Rosa National Park is a former cattle ranch where Costa Ricans defeated the invading mercenary army of American William Walker in 1857. Santa Rosa is also home to Playas Naranjo and Nancite, where hundreds of thousands of olive ridley turtles lay their eggs between August and November. Closer still to the Nicaraguan border are Guanacaste National Park and the town of La Cruz, overlooking the pristine beaches and a pair of resorts on the lovely Golfo de Santa Elena and Bahía Salinas.

En Route From Liberia, access to Rincón de la Vieja National Park is on 27 km (17 mi) of unpaved road. The road begins 6 km (4 mi) north of Liberia off the Pan-American Highway (follow signs for Albergue Guachipelín) or 25 km (15 mi) along the Colonia Blanca route northeast from Liberia, which follows the course of the Río Liberia to the Santa María park headquarters. A four-wheel-drive vehicle is recommended, though not essential, for either of these bone-rattling 1- to 1½-hour rides.

Rincón de la Vieja National Park

❾ *27 km (17 mi) northeast of Liberia.*

Parque Nacional Rincón de la Vieja is Costa Rica's Yellowstone, with volcanic hot springs and boiling, bubbling mud ponds. The Park protects more than 177 square km (54 square mi) of Volcán Rincón de la Vieja's upper slopes, much of which are covered by dry forest. The wildlife here is diverse: 200 species of birds, including keel-billed toucans and blue-crowned motmots, plus mammals such as brocket deer, tapirs, coatis, jaguars, sloths, and armadillos.

The mass of Volcán Rincón de la Vieja, often enveloped in a mixture of sulfurous gases and cloud, dominates the scenery to the right of the Pan-American Highway as you head north. The volcano has two peaks: **Santa María** (2,094 m [6,868 ft]) and **Rincón de la Vieja** (2,075 m [6,806 ft]). The latter, which is barren and has two craters, is thought unlikely to erupt violently due to the profusion of fumaroles through which it constantly lets off steam. (The last violent eruptions were between 1966 and 1970, but vulcanologists were alarmed by a temporary increase in activity in 1995.) **Las Hornillas** (The Kitchen Stoves), on the southern slope of the Rincón de la Vieja crater, is a 124-acre medley of mud cones, hot-water pools, bubbling mud pots, and vent holes most active during the rainy season. Don't get too close to the mud pots—their edges are brittle and several people have slipped in and been severely burned. To the east, **Los Azufrales** are hot sulfur springs in which you can bathe; be careful not to get sulfur in your eyes.

There are park entrances at Hacienda Santa María on the road leading northeast from Liberia, and Las Pailas, via the mostly unpaved road passing through Curubandé. Bosque Encantado, where the Río Zopilote cascades into the forest to form an enticing pool, is a 2-km (1-mi) hike from Santa María. Three kilometers (2 miles) farther are Los Azufrales, and 4 km (2½ mi) beyond that are the boiling mud pots and fumaroles of Las Hornillas, near the Las Pailas entrance to the park.

The trail to the summit heads into the forest above Las Pailas, but it's a trip for serious hikers, best done in dry season with preparation for cold weather at the top. A less strenuous option is the 3-km (2-mi) loop through the park, along which you'll see fumaroles, a *volcáncito* (baby volcano), Las Pailas, and many animals including semidomesticated, raccoonlike coatis, looking for handouts (a plea you should ignore: a cardinal rule of wildlife encounters is don't feed the animals).

Trail maps and hiking information are available at the park stations by both entrance gates. If you want to explore the slopes of the volcano, go with a guide; the abundant hot springs and geysers have given unsuspecting visitors some very nasty burns. In addition, the upper slopes often receive fierce and potentially dangerous winds—before your ascent, check at either ranger station for conditions. Alternatively, head to **Rincón de la Vieja Mountain Lodge** (☏ 661–8156), which has guides for hiking or horseback riding; call ahead to check availability. ✉ *Rincón de la Vieja National Park*, ☏ *661–8139.* ▤ *$6.* ☉ *Daily 7–4.*

Dining and Lodging

$$$–$$$$ ✕▥ **Posada El Encuentro.** A German–Costa Rican family runs this rambling, white stucco lodging near Curubandé, on the way to the volcano's southern slope. Deep blues and soft greens accentuate bright, clean white walls. The large-windowed dining room, with its stunning volcano views, has become a popular lunch place for businessmen from Liberia. Offerings, in particular the rich pastries, reflect the family's German origins. Horseback riding through the canyon behind the hotel and stargazing from the back terrace are popular activities, and the hotel will arrange customized tours complete with picnic lunch. Rates include a huge breakfast. ✉ *14 km (8 mi) northwest of Liberia on road to Curubandé,* ☏ FAX *382–0815,* WEB *www.arweb.com/encuentro. 2 cottages, 3 suites. Restaurant, pool, horseback riding, Ping-Pong, no room phones, no room TVs. AE, MC, V. Closed Apr.*

$$$ ▥ **Rincón de la Vieja Lodge.** On the slopes of Rincón de la Vieja are the lodge's paneled cabins, small doubles, and comfy dormitory-style rooms. The sitting room has a TV with a VCR and a few movies. Meat, fish, and vegetarian (made with homegrown produce) entrées are good, though on the pricey side. The affable staff can take you to explore the park and volcano on foot or on horseback through the woods. Trails lead to a hot-water, sulfur bathing pool and a blue lake and waterfall. The lodge provides transport up from Liberia for up to six people.

✉ *2 km (1 mi) northeast of park entrance,* ☎ FAX *661–8156,* WEB *www. rincondelaviejalodge.com (mailing address: Apdo. 114–5000, Liberia). 38 rooms. Bar, dining room, pool, horseback riding, no phone, no room TVs. AE, MC, V.*

Outdoor Activities and Sports

From the Rincón de la Vieja Mountain Lodge (☎ 661–8156), **Treetop Trails** runs four-hour canopy tours ($49.50) that include a forest-floor hike and canopy observation from 16 cable-linked treetop platforms. A more elaborate seven-hour tour ($79) also includes horseback riding to the park's blue lake and waterfall.

Santa Rosa National Park

❿ *48 km (30 mi) south of the Nicaraguan border, west of the Pan-American Hwy. at Km 269.*

Parque Nacional Santa Rosa is one of Costa Rica's most impressive parks with the largest swath of tropical dry forest in Central America. Because of its less luxuriant foliage, the park is a good one for viewing wildlife, especially if you station yourself next to water holes during the dry season. The park might also be the country's most beloved of protected areas because of its historic significance as the sight of the 1856 triumph over William Walker. Santa Rosa is also the country's first national park, so it has become a model for community involvement in preservation and conservation. As you approach Santa Rosa's entrance from the Pan-American Highway, you can see the forested slopes of Volcán Orosí, protected within Guanacaste National Park. A few miles after you enter Santa Rosa, a scenic overlook on the right grants your first good view of the park's dry forest.

Typical dry-forest vegetation includes oak, wild cherry, mahogany, calabash, bullhorn acacia, hibiscus, and gumbo-limbo, with its distinctive reddish-brown bark. Inhabitants include spider, white-faced, and howler monkeys, as well as deer, armadillos, coyotes, tapirs, coatis, and ocelots. Ocelots, commonly known as *manigordos* (fat hands) on account of their large feet, are wildcats that have been brought back from the brink of extinction by the park's conservation methods. These wildlands also define the southernmost distribution of many North American species such as the Virginia opossum and the *cantil* pit viper snake. From the ecology perspective, Santa Rosa is important because it protects and regenerates 520 square km (200 square mi) of forest land, both moist, basal-belt transition and deciduous, tropical dry forests.

Arsonists burned the park's centerpiece, the **Hacienda La Casona**, to the ground in 2001. The rambling colonial-style farmstead was the sight of a famous 1856 battle in which a ragged force of ill-equipped Costa Ricans routed the superior army of the notorious William Walker. Fund-raising is under way to rebuild the beloved monument, one of the few military historic sites in army-less Costa Rica.

From the entrance gate, 7 km (4½ mi) of paved road leads to the **park headquarters.** A small nature trail loops through the woods, and there's a large camping area nearby. Note that Santa Rosa's **campgrounds,** which can sleep 150 people, sometimes fill up during the dry season, especially in the first week of January and during Easter week. Throughout the park it's wise to carry your own water, since water holes are none too clean. ✉ ☎ *666–5020.* ☞ *$6.* ☉ *Daily 7–5.*

Thirteen kilometers (8 miles) west of the administrative area—a two- to three-hour hike or one hour by four-wheel-drive vehicle—is the white-sand **Playa Naranjo,** popular for beachcombing thanks to its abundance of shells and for surfing because of its near-perfect break. The campsite here has washing facilities, but bring your own drinking water. The lookout at the northern tip of the beach has views over the entire park.

Playa Nancite, a two-hour walk north from here (also accessible by four-wheel-drive vehicle), is a premier place to watch turtle *arribadas* (mass nestings). It is estimated that 200,000 turtles nest here each year. Backed by dense hibiscus and button mangroves, the gray-sand beach is penned in by steep, tawny, brush-covered hills. Previously a difficult point to get to, it's now the world's only totally protected **olive ridley turtle arribada.** Olive ridleys are the smallest of the sea turtles (average carapace, or hardback shell, is 21 inches–29 inches) and the least shy. The majority arrive at night, plowing the sand as they move up the beach and sniffing for the high-tide line, beyond which they use their hind flippers to dig the holes into which they lay their eggs. They spend an average of one hour on the beach before scurrying back to the sea. Hatching also takes place at night. The phototropic baby turtles naturally know to head for the sea, which is vital for their continued survival, since the brightest light is that of the shimmering ocean. Many of the nests are churned up during subsequent arribadas, and predators such as coatis, ghost crabs, raccoons, and coyotes lie in wait; hence just 0.2% of the eggs laid result in young turtles reaching the sea. Their nesting season is August to November, peaking in September and October. You need a permit to stay at Nancite; ask at the park's headquarters. ☎ 666–5020. ☞ $6. ☉ Daily 7–5.

Camping

$ ⚠ **La Casona.** Santa Rosa National Park has a rugged terrain and an isolated feel. The campsite, near the ruins of Hacienda La Casona, overhung by giant strangler figs, has no set sites—you choose where to set up—and provides washing facilities, rustic bathrooms, and picnic tables. Be careful of snakes. Between Playas Naranjo and Nancite, another campground at Estero Real is available with tables only. ✉ *Santa Rosa National Park,* ☎ 666–5051. *Picnic areas. No credit cards.*

Cuajiniquil

⑪ *10 km (6 mi) north of Santa Rosa National Park.*

North from Santa Rosa on the Pan-American Highway is the left turn to Cuajiniquil, famous for its waterfalls. If you have time and a four-wheel-drive vehicle, Cuajiniquil has lovely views. The Golfo de Santa Elena is renowned for its calm waters, which is why it's now threatened by tourist development. Playa Blanca in the extreme west has smooth white sand, as its name implies. The rough track here passes through a valley of uneven width caused, according to geologists, by the diverse granulation of the sediments formerly deposited here. To the south rise the rocky Santa Elena hills (777 m [2,548 ft]), bare except for a few chigua and nancite shrubs.

Guanacaste National Park

⑫ *32 km (20 mi) north of Liberia.*

To the east of the Pan-American Highway is the 325-square km (125-square mi) Parque Nacional Guanacaste (☎ 695–5598), created in 1989 to preserve rain forests around **Volcán Cacao** (1,814 m [5,950 ft]) and **Volcán Orosi** (1,625 m [5330 ft]), which are seasonally inhabited by migrant wildlife from Santa Rosa. The park is a mosaic of interdependent protected areas, parks and refuges; the goal is eventually to create a single Guanacaste megapark to accommodate the natural migratory patterns of myriad creatures, from jaguars to tapirs. Much of the park's territory is cattle pasture, which, it is hoped, will regenerate into forest. Currently, there are 300 different birds and more than 5,000 species of butterflies here.

The **Mengo Biological Station** (☎ no phone) lies on the slopes of Volcán Cacao at an altitude of 1,203 m (3,946 ft); accommodation is in rustic wood dormitories with bedding, but no towels, provided. From Mengo one trail leads up Volcán Cacao, and another heads north to the **Maritza Station** (☎ no phone), a three-hour hike away at the base of Orosí, with lodging. You can also reach Maritza by four-wheel-drive vehicle. From Maritza you can trek two hours to **Llano de los Indios,** a cattle pasture dotted with volcanic petroglyphs. Farther north and a little east is rustic **Pitilla Station** (☎ 661–8150) and, despite its lower elevation, it has views of the coast and Lago de Nicaragua across the border. Camping is possible at each of the biological stations. Call the **park headquarters** (☎ 666–5051) in advance to arrange accommodations.

Lodging

$$$$ 🏨 **Los Inocentes Lodge.** Built more than 100 years ago, this handsome, exquisitely maintained hardwood hacienda is in a private reserve along the northern border of Guanacaste National Park. A 14-km (8½-mi) drive on a smoothly paved road east from the Pan-American Highway to Santa Cecilia takes you to the entrance of the working ranch, with horses, cattle, and numerous birds. The hardwood-finished rooms are rustic but comfortable, with hot showers in bathrooms (some shared by two rooms) across the halls. Meals are included in most packages. Experienced ranch-hand guides, friendly horses, and miles of trails get you into the forests. ⊠ *15 km (9 mi) west of La Cruz,* ☎ *679–9190,* FAX *679–9224,* WEB *www.losinocenteslodge.com (mailing address: Apdo. 228–3000, Heredia,* ☎ *265–5484 in San José; 888/613–2532 in the U.S.,* FAX *265–4385). 11 rooms, 3 with bath; 3 cabins. Dining room, pool; no phone, no room TVs. AE, MC, V.*

La Cruz

❸ *56 km (35 mi) north of Liberia, 20 km (12 mi) south of the Nicaraguan border.*

Farther north on the west side of the highway is a turnoff to La Cruz, noteworthy for the stunning views of Bahía Salinas from the restaurants and hotels along the bluff. It also serves as a gateway to the resorts and beaches on the south shore of Bahía Salinas, the hamlet of Puerto Soley, and the Golfo de Santa Elena.

Dining and Lodging

$$ ✕ **El Mirador Ehecatl.** Don't pass up a chance to have a drink at this two-story restaurant-bar overlooking Bahía Salinas, Isla Bolaños, and the Nicaraguan coastline. Even better, the food is delicious: try anything with seafood—the ceviche is especially well prepared—or one of the many cheap, rice-based combination plates. Ehecatl means "god of the wind" in the old Chorotegan language, and the name suits these windy environs. *Turn left before main road from town square goes downhill toward the bay,* ☎ *679–9104. V.*

$$ ✕🏨 **Colinas del Norte.** On the Pan-American Highway halfway between La Cruz and the Nicaraguan border, 20 km (12 mi) north of Peñas Blancas, this rugged, two-story hardwood hotel bills itself as a touring base for the surrounding dry tropical forest, but its most appealing feature appears to be its large pool, surrounded by shady palms. At the outdoor disco you can dance till you drop, then hop into the pool. The

indoor-outdoor restaurant specializes in pizza and Italian food. Modest but comfortable upstairs rooms have private terraces. ✉ *Pan-American Hwy., about 6 km (4 mi) north of La Cruz,* ☎ FAX *679–9132 (mailing address: Apdo. 10493–1000, San José). 24 rooms. Restaurant, pool, miniature golf, dance club, laundry service. AE, MC, V.*

$$ 🏨 **Amalia's Inn.** The late U.S. artist Lester Bounds and his Costa Rican wife, Amalia, created this breezy little inn on the cliff overlooking Bahía Salinas. Amalia now runs the inn. Bounds is also survived by his art—colorful modern paintings and prints that decorate the place and rooms. On the left (south) side of the road as you head into town, the inn features spacious rooms with private baths and balconies. Amalia's is a fine budget alternative to the two pricier resorts on the bay's south shore. ✉ *East of central park,* ☎ FAX *679–9181. 8 rooms. Pool, laundry service; no air-conditioning, no phone, no room TVs. AE, MC, V.*

Bahía Salinas

⓮ *7 km (4½ mi) west of La Cruz.*

Several dirt and rock roads dead-end on different beaches along Bahía Salinas, the pretty little half-moon bay that lies at the very top of Costa Rica's Pacific coast—just turn right off the "main" road to the resorts. You'll probably end up on or near the beach, or in the hamlet of Puerto Soley, a tiny town tucked in off the bay—look for the salt flats to find the town, which is roughly 5–6 very slow-going km (3–4 mi) from La Cruz. There's public beach access along the bay.

The wind usually blows year-round, except in September and October, the height of the rainy season, so windsurfing here is supreme. Winds are generally not as powerful as those at Laguna de Arenal, but they're strong enough to make this a viable alternative (stay on the south side for stronger winds), or accompaniment, to the Arenal experience. Ranking among the most beautiful beaches in all of Costa Rica are a couple of secluded, wind-sheltered strands, including the gorgeous, pristine **Playa Rajada,** with fine swimming and snorkeling. Just offshore is **Isla Bolaños,** a bird refuge and nesting site for thousands of endangered frigate birds as well as brown pelicans. The Bolaños Bay Resort (☎ 679–9444) has a motor launch for Isla Bolaños tours, but don't try to land—it's against the law.

Lodging

$$$$ 🏨 **Bolaños Bay Resort.** The first thing you'll spot on your approach to this resort is the high double rancho (thatched roof) that shelters the reception area, bar, and restaurant. Closer up you'll see the modest rooms built into low-rise cabinas neatly arrayed across grassy lawns. Given the winds that rocket across the bay, the resort's emphasis on windsurfing comes as no surprise. For those left behind, a sheltered pool with a swim-up bar provides a diversion. Room rates include high-quality meals and especially hearty breakfasts. ✉ *Take dirt road 3 km (2 mi) down the steep hill from La Cruz and follow signs for about 15 km (9 mi),* ☎ *679–9444,* FAX *679–9654,* WEB *www.3cornersbolanosbay. com (mailing address: Apdo. 1680–1250, San José,* ☎ *289–5561,* FAX *228–4205). 72 rooms. Restaurant, 2 bars, pool, hot tub, beach, windsurfing, laundry service. AE, MC, V.*

$$$–$$$$ 🏨 **Ecoplaya Beach Resort.** Although it's on the same stretch of Bahía Salinas as the Bolaños Bay Resort, about 1 km (½ mi) to the west, Ecoplaya has plenty of luxury amenities unique to the area. Every room has a small but fully equipped kitchen, a phone, air-conditioning, hot water, and custom hardwood furniture. The nearly 1-km-long (½-mi-long) beach fronting the hotel is flanked by bird- and wildlife-filled estuaries. Be warned, nonsailors: the wind blows hard here much of the

time. ⊠ *La Coyotera Beach,* ☎ FAX 679–9380, WEB *www.ecoplaya.com (mailing address: Plaza Colonial, Escazú, No. 4, San José,* ☎ FAX 289– *8920,* FAX *289–4536). 36 suites. Restaurant, bar, kitchens, pool, beach, laundry service. AE, MC, V.*

Outdoor Activities and Sports

WATER SPORTS

The windsurfing **Pro Center** (☎ 679–9444) at Bolaños Bay Resort is run by friendly, knowledgeable Bjorn Voigt. Charlie at **Iyok Trips** (☎ 679– 9444) at Bolaños Bay Resort runs boat trips around Isla Bolaños and snorkeling, fishing, and waterskiing trips to Playa Cuajiniquil and other spots in the Golfo de Santa Elena. Charlie promises sightings of nurse sharks, manta rays, and lots of large fish. Iyok's guides also lead horseback and mountain-biking tours of the area and know where the monkeys hang out in the woods.

NORTHERN GUANACASTE AND ALAJUELA A TO Z

To research prices, get advice from other travelers, and book travel arrangements, visit www.fodors.com.

AIR TRAVEL

Central American airline Grupo TACA offers a few flights from abroad into Liberia's Daniel Oduber International Airport. Various charters serve the airport on changing schedules as well. If your destination lies in Guanacaste, make sure your travel agent investigates the possibility of flying into Liberia instead of San José—you'll save some serious hours on the road.

CARRIERS

SANSA, the domestic division of Grupo TACA, and Travelair fly to Liberia from San José daily. SANSA serves the small airstrip outside of La Fortuna from San José on a charter basis only.

➤ AIRLINES AND CONTACTS: **Grupo TACA/SANSA** (⊠ C. 42 and Avda. 3, San José, ☎ 296–0909). **Travelair** (⊠ Aeropuerto Internacional Tobías Bolaños, ☎ 220–3054).

➤ AIRPORTS: **Aeropuerto Internacional Daniel Oduber** (⊠ 5 km [3mi] west of Liberia, ☎ 296–0909).

BOAT TRAVEL

Desafío Expeditions in La Fortuna and Monteverde provides a fast, popular three-hour transfer between the communities. The taxi–boat– taxi service costs $25 one-way.

➤ BOAT INFORMATION: **Desafío Expeditions** (⊠ Central plaza, 50 m [164 ft] north of Banco Nacional, La Fortuna, ☎ 479–9464, WEB www. desafiocostarica.com).

BUS TRAVEL

Fantasy Bus's air-conditioned point-to-point shuttles connecting Arenal with San José and Tamarindo are preferable to buses, although buses cover most areas at a reasonable price. Buses in this region are typically large, clean, and comfortable, but often crowded Friday–Sunday. Don't expect air-conditioning, and even supposedly express buses marked *directo* often make some stops.

Auto Transportes San José–San Carlos buses leave San José for the threehour trip to San Carlos from Calle 12 between Avenidas 7 and 9, daily every hour 5 AM–7:30 PM. The company runs three buses daily from this same station in San José to La Fortuna, near Arenal, at 6:15, 8:40, and 11:30 AM. From San Carlos you can connect to Arenal and Tilarán. The company also has buses for Los Chiles (Caño Negro), which depart from Calle 12, Avenida 9, daily at 5:30 AM and 3:30 PM; the trip takes five hours.

Transportes La Cañera has service to Cañas, and the turnoff for Tilarán and Arenal, daily at 8:30 AM, 10:20 AM, 12:20 PM, 1:20 PM, and 2:30 PM from Calle 16, between Avenidas 3 and 5 in San José. The trip to Cañas takes 3½ hours. Transportes Tilarán sends buses on the four-hour trip to Tilarán daily from Calle 12, between Avenidas 7 and 9 in San José, at 7:30 AM, 9:30 AM, 12:45 PM, 3:45 PM, and 6:30 PM. From Tilarán you can continue to Nuevo Arenal and Volcán Arenal. Transmonteverde makes the five-hour trip to Monteverde, departing weekdays at 6:30 AM and 2:30 PM. This route is notorious for theft; watch your bags.

Pulmitan Liberia has four-hour buses to Liberia that leave San José daily from Calle 24, Avenidas 5 and 7, every hour between 6 AM and 8 PM, with direct buses at 3 and 5 PM. Friday buses leave every hour from 1 PM to 8 PM, and Saturday they leave at 6, 7, 9, 10, and 11:30 AM. Transportes Deldu goes to La Cruz and Peñas Blancas, normally a six-hour trip that passes through Liberia; daily departures are at 5 AM, 1:20 PM, and 4:10 PM. Express buses cut the trip to 4½ hours; they leave from Calle 20, Avenidas 1 in San José, at 4:30 AM and 7 AM. The slower buses pass the entrance to Santa Rosa National Park after about five hours.

Buses don't serve Rincón de la Vieja and Guanacaste national parks. ➤ BUS INFORMATION: **Auto Transportes San José-San Carlos** (☎ 256–8914 or 460–5032). **Interbus** (☎ 800/748–8853 in Costa Rica only).**Pulmitan Liberia** (☎ 256–9552). **Transmonteverde** (☎ 222–3854). **Transportes Deldu** (☎ 256–9072). **Transportes La Cañera** (☎ 222–3006). **Transportes Tilarán** (☎ 222–3854).

CAR RENTAL
A few of the high-end resorts on the beach will arrange car rentals. Otherwise, it's best to rent cars in San José or on the Nicoya Peninsula.

CAR TRAVEL
Road access to the northwest is by way of the paved two-lane Pan-American Highway (Carretera Interamericana, CA1), which starts from the west end of Paseo Colón in San José and runs northwest through Cañas and Liberia and to Peñas Blancas (Nicaraguan border). The drive to Liberia takes about three to four hours. Turnoffs to Monteverde, Arenal, and other destinations are often poorly marked—drivers must keep their eyes open. The Monteverde (Santa Elena) turnoff is at Río Lagarto, about 125 km (78 mi) northwest of San José. (From here, an unpaved 30-km [19-mi] track snakes dramatically up through hilly farming country; it takes 1½ to 2 hours to negotiate it, less by four-wheel-drive vehicle. At the junction for Santa Elena, bear right for the reserve.)

The turnoff for Tilarán and the northwestern end of Laguna de Arenal lies in the town of Cañas. At Liberia, Highway 21 west leads to the beaches of the northern Nicoya Peninsula. To reach San Carlos, La Fortuna, and Caño Negro from San José, a picturesque drive (Highway 35) takes you up through the coffee plantations and over the Cordillera Central by way of Sarchí and Zarcero.

On the Pan-American Highway (CA1) north of Liberia, the first turn for Rincón de la Vieja is easy to miss. Look for the Guardia Rural station on the right around 5 km (3 mi) north of town; turn inland and head for Curubandé. Turnoffs for Santa Rosa National Park and La Cruz on CA1 are well marked. Because of the nearness of the border, you need to stop at two police checkpoints on the Pan-American Highway south of La Cruz.

From the easterly zone of Arenal and the Cordillera de Tilarán (La Fortuna), you can head west by way of the road, badly potholed in sections, around Laguna de Arenal. For the paved road (Highway 4) that parallels the Nicaraguan border and loops west all the way to La Cruz, follow the signs out of Tanque (east of La Fortuna) northwest to San Rafael de Guatuso, Upala, and Santa Cecilia.

ROAD CONDITIONS

Four-wheel-drive vehicles are recommended, but not essential, for most roads. (If you don't rent a four-wheel-drive vehicle, at least rent a car with high clearance—you'll be glad you did.) The most important thing to know is that short drives can take a long time when the road is potholed or torn up. Plan accordingly. Most minor roads are unpaved and either muddy in rainy season or dusty in dry season— the pavement holds out only so far, and then dirt, dust, mud, potholes, and other impediments interfere with driving conditions and prolong hours spent behind the wheel.

The Pan-American Highway (CA1) and other paved roads run to the Nicaraguan border; paved roads run west to small towns like Filadelfia and La Cruz. The roads into Rincón de la Vieja are unpaved and very slow; figure on an hour from the highway, and be prepared to walk the last half mile to the Las Pailas entrance. The road into Santa Rosa National Park is smooth going as far as the ruins of La Casona. Beyond that, it gets dicey and very steep in places. The national park service encourages you to walk, rather than drive, to the beach. A couple of dirt roads lead into various sections of Guanacaste National Park.

EMERGENCIES

In case of any emergency, dial 911, or one of the specific numbers below.
➤ EMERGENCY SERVICES: **Fire** (☎ 118). **Police** (☎ 911). **Traffic Police** (☎ 227–8030).

ENGLISH-LANGUAGE MEDIA

Librería Chunches in Santa Elena maintains a good selection of books, magazines, and day-old U.S. newspapers in English.
➤ ENGLISH-SPEAKING BOOKSTORES: **Librería Chunches** (⊠ 50 yards south of Banco Nacional, Santa Elena).

LANGUAGE

Though isolated, Monteverde's large expatriate population makes it a good place to find English speakers. Elsewhere, those connected with large tourist establishments are likely to speak English.

MAIL, SHIPPING, AND INTERNET

Privatized Correos de Costa Rica provides reasonable postal service from this region, though you're better off waiting to post those cards and letters from San José. Public Internet access is not widespread in this part of the country. Expect to pay about $3–$4 per hour of access time.
➤ POST OFFICE: **Correos de Costa Rica** (⊠ 50 yards north of police station, La Fortuna; 50 yards downhill from La Esperanza Supermarket, Santa Elena [Monteverde]).
➤ INTERNET CAFÉS: **Desafío Expeditions** (⊠ Central plaza, La Fortuna, ☎ 479–9464, WEB www.desafiocostarica.com). **Tranquilo Comunica-**

ciones (✉ 150 yards downhill from La Esperanza Supermarket, Santa Elena [Monteverde], ☎ 645–5831).

MONEY MATTERS

Most larger tourist establishments are prepared to handle credit cards. Changing U.S. dollars or traveler's checks is possible at the few offices of Banco Nacional scattered throughout the region, but lines are long. Take care of getting local currency with your ATM card back in San José before venturing out here.

➤ BANKS: **Banco Nacional** (✉ Pan-American Highway, La Cruz, ☎ 679–9296; ✉ Central Plaza, La Fortuna, ☎ 479–9022; ✉ 50 yards north of bus station, Santa Elena (Monteverde), ☎ 645–5027; ✉ Central Plaza, Tilarán, ☎ 695–5255; ✉ 100 yards north of church, Zarcero, ☎ 463–3838).

SHUTTLE VANS

Alternatives to public buses exist. Fantasy Bus has daily service between San José and Arenal. Comfortable, air-conditioned vans leave variousSan José hotels at 8 AM and return at 2 PM. Tickets cost $21 and must be reserved a day in advance. Fantasy Bus also connects Arenal to Tamarindo on the Nicoya Peninsula.

➤ INFORMATION: **Fantasy Bus** (☎ 800/326–8279 in Costa Rica only).

TOURS

Tikal Tours runs highly informative weeklong eco-adventure tours in Santa Rosa, and Arenal. The excellent Horizontes specializes in more independent tours with as few as eight people, including transport by four-wheel-drive vehicle, naturalist guides, and guest lectures. Reputable, organized, and knowledgeable Sun Tours guides can customize trips or recommend some popular stops in the area and some that are off the map.

➤ TOUR COMPANIES: **Horizontes** (✉ 150 yards north of Pizza Hut, Paseo Colón, San José, ☎ 222–2022). **Sun Tours** (✉ Cerro Plano, next to Pizzeria de Johnny, Monteverde, ☎ 645–6328 or 296–7757 in San José). **Tikal Tours** (✉ Avda. 2 between Cs. 7 and 9, San José, ☎ 223–2811).

VISITOR INFORMATION

The ubiquitous TOURIST INFORMATION signs around La Fortuna and Monteverde are really storefront travel agencies hoping to sell you tours rather than provide unbiased sources of information.

The tourist office in San José has information covering the northwest, including maps, bus schedules, and brochures. It's next to the Museo de Oro, beneath the Plaza de la Cultura, and is open weekdays 9–12:30 and 1:30–5. In Liberia, the Casa de la Cultura is officially open weekdays 8–noon and 1:30–5 and Saturday 8–noon and 1:30–4, but it often doesn't adhere to this schedule.

➤ TOURIST INFORMATION: **Casa de la Cultura** (✉ 3 blocks from Central Plaza, Liberia, ☎ 666–4527). **Instituto Costarricense de Turismo** (ICT; ✉ C. 5 between Advas. Central and 2, Barrio del Catedral, San José, ☎ 222–1090).

5 THE NICOYA PENINSULA

On this sun-drenched Pacific protrusion,
expatriate California surfers wander endless
golden beaches, coatimundis caper, monkeys
howl in dry tropical forests, and turtles ride
in on nocturnal high tides to lay their eggs.
Combined with a burgeoning number of
high-end resorts, these natural wonders make
Nicoya a microcosm of Costa Rica.

Updated
by Dorothy
MacKinnon

WATCHING SURFERS MASTER THE PACIFIC'S WHITE-AND-BLUE waves, or getting a glimpse of turtles laying their eggs at Playa Grande on a midnight tour and you'll know why you're in Nicoya. Miles of palm-flanked beaches may characterize the peninsula, but limestone caverns, bird-filled river deltas, and tracts of wet and dry forest are also significant habitats, ecological parts of the landscape's complex whole. Separated from the mainland by the Gulf of Nicoya, the peninsula is a roughly thumb-shape spit of land comprising the southwestern section of the province of Guanacaste. Its southern end, including Playa Naranjo, Tambor, and Montezuma contains part of the Puntarenas province.

The Guanacastecos, descendants of the Chorotegan Indians and early Spanish settlers, started many of the traditions now referred to as typically Costa Rican, and a strong folkloric character is still evident here. As you travel down the peninsula, you might encounter traditional costumes, folk dancing, music, and meals made from recipes handed down from colonial times.

As a travel destination, Nicoya—especially the coastal areas—seems a bit confused at present: on one hand, earthy ecotourists and their younger, backpack- and surfboard-toting cousins still hang out in search of environmental enlightenment or good waves; on the other hand, sun- and golf-seekers, content to admire caged toucans in plush hotel lobbies, are lured by azure pools and manicured putting greens bathed in tropical sun. Because the area has received huge amounts of investment and it's been quickly developed—a new Four Seasons with two golf courses is being built here—the endless miles of untracked beaches and thousands of acres of wilderness are occasionally interspersed with sprawling, all-inclusive behemoths.

Pleasures and Pastimes

Beaches

Graceful palms and elegant tamarind trees line most Nicoya beaches, but the shrubby dry-forest vegetation of the northwestern Guanacaste coast contrasts sharply with the tropical beach backdrops you'll see farther south, in the Puntarenas province. The peninsula's great advantage is its climate, which in the rainy season (May–December) is far drier than that of the inland regions and the Caribbean coast. Swimmers, however, should be careful of riptides, which are most common at beaches with high waves, such as the surfing area at Playa Grande. As a general rule, where you see surfers, beware of riptides.

Two strands near Coco (which itself is rather dirty) are worth checking out: Playa Ocotal, in a cove with snorkeling potential and good views, and Playa Hermosa, a curving gray-sand beach hemmed in by rocky outcrops. Playa Pan de Azúcar is deserted and has good snorkeling, but it's rather stony in the rainy season. Despite burgeoning condominium developments and big hotels, Playa Flamingo is still relatively low-key, and the beach is white and handsome. Playa Brasilito gives you a feel for life in a Costa Rican fishing village. Playa Conchal is famous for its tiny shells. Playa Grande, a restricted-access (at night) turtle-nesting beach stretching north 5 km (3 mi) from Tamarindo, is safe for swimming except in the surfing area near the Hotel Las Tortugas. Tamarindo, a long, white strand interrupted by the occasional rock formation, shelters a fleet of fishing and sailing boats on the lee side of Isla Capitán, a few hundred yards offshore. There are several good local beachfront bars here.

Playa Langosta, adjoining a bird sanctuary, has good surfing waves, nesting turtles at night, and few people. Playa Avellanas offers 1 km (½ mi) of pristine sand, eight good surfing spots, and a river estuary and mangrove swamp close at hand for bird-watching. A mixture of short, sandy stretches and rocky outcrops, Playa Negra has some of the best surfing waves in Costa Rica. Playa Junquillal features an un-interrupted 3-km (2-mi) stretch of grayish-white sand with low, shore-break waves and very few buildings. Hemmed in by rocks on both sides, Playa Pelada is a perfect jewel of a beach and is great for snorkeling. Nosara has a long beach backed by dense jungle where you might see wildlife. The long, clean, smooth Playa Guiones has a good beach-break surfing wave and a coral reef suitable for snorkeling. Playa Sámara offers some lively stretches near the Sámara community and quieter stretches farther down the beach. Playa Carrillo sits on a highly picturesque half-moon bay. On the southwestern tip of the peninsula, Playa Cabo Blanco is a pristine gem reached only by hiking through the Reserva Natural Absoluta Cabo Blanco. In Malpaís you'll find action-packed surfing waves and miles of tidal pools to explore. Montezuma has several colorful, shell-strewn beaches, some long and some short. Tambor, in Bahía Ballena, edges calm swimming waters.

Dining

Seafood is plentiful here: *camarones* (shrimp), *langostinos* (a small variety of lobster), and a fine variety of fish are served in most restaurants at reasonable prices, though langostino dinners can get costly. Most places serve international as well as local dishes, the latter centering on the ubiquitous, moderately priced *casados* (plates of white rice, beans, fried plantains, salad, cheese, and meat, chicken, or fish).

CATEGORY	COST*
$$$$	over $20
$$$	$10–$20
$$	$5–$10
$	under $5

per person for main course at dinner.

Festivals

Santa Cruz celebrates its saint's day on January 15 with marimba music, folk dances, and bullfights. On July 16 Puntarenas honors its patron saint with a colorful regatta and carnival. The annexation of Guanacaste is celebrated July 17–25 in Liberia with folk dances, bullfights, and rodeos. Nicoya's festival of La Yeguita features a solemn procession, dancing, fireworks, and bullfights on December 12. Almost every small town in Guanacaste has a rodeo fiesta once a year, complete with carnival rides, gaming, and the Costa Rican rodeo version of bullfighting. It's wild! Guanacasteco cowboys ride the bulls, American-rodeo–style, while troupes of young men race around the ring distracting the bulls after they throw the riders, and cowboys with lariats stand by on horseback to lasso the beasts should they get too ornery. If you're in Guanacaste and aren't too squeamish, try to take in a rodeo; just be warned the men do torment the bulls to get them riled up and that riders get thrown violently and are occasionally stomped or gored. Ask around or read posters for details.

Lodging

Nicoya has a good mix of quality hotels, nature lodges, and more basic *cabinas* (cottages). Plenty act like B&Bs and include breakfast in the rate. It's wise to reserve ahead for the dry season (December–April), especially weekends, when Ticos can fill beach hotels to bursting. A number of luxury hotels line the coast, catering to an upscale clientele.

CATEGORY	COST*
$$$$	over $90
$$$	$50–$90
$$	$25–$50
$	under $25

for a double room, excluding service and tax (16.4%)

Spelunking

The caves in Barra Honda National Park beckon you toward a serious plunge into the underworld. Terciopelo Cave, in particular, contains a vast assortment of oddly shaped rock formations, and some stretches of the cave system are reputedly unexplored to this day.

Surfing

Costa Rica was "discovered" in the 1960s surf-film classic *The Endless Summer* and revisited in the sequel. But with its miles of coastline marked by innumerable points, rock reefs, river-mouth sandbars, and other wave-shaping geological configurations, the Nicoya Peninsula would have emerged as a surfer's paradise in any case. Warm water, beautiful beaches, cheap beer, and relatively uncrowded waves—what more can a surfer boy or girl ask for?

Boca Barranca near Puntarenas—a somewhat dingy mainland town you might check out while waiting for the ferry to the peninsula's south end—has one of the world's longest lefts, but the water is dangerously polluted with sewage runoff from the nearby river. Tamarindo is a good base for some decent sandbar and rock-reef breaks, a superb low-tide river-mouth break, and the consistently high-quality, if at times overcrowded, Playa Grande beach break, which lies 5 km (3 mi) up the coast. Playa Grande's best waves usually break just south of the Hotel Las Tortugas; inquire at Iguana Surf, the surfboard shop in Tamarindo. Sámara, Guiones, and Nosara have decent beach breaks. Avellanas has a total of eight different surf spots, ranging from beach breaks to rock-reef breaks to river-mouth sandbar breaks. Witches Rock, in Santa Rosa National Park, has a right river-mouth, and Ollie's Point, a bit farther north, offers excellent right point-break waves. (In the summer, Witches Rock is not accessible by public transportation. You can drive or take the 1½-hour boat ride, informally chartered at Playa del Coco or other beaches along the Guanacaste coast. Ollie's Point is accessible primarily by boat.) For well-heeled wave riders, there's a good break directly in front of the Tango Mar Resort. Playa Negra, about a 45-minute dirt-road drive south from Tamarindo, is also very good, and its excellent right rock-reef break was showcased in *The Endless Summer II*. Playa Langosta, just south of Tamarindo, has a good river-mouth wave. Malpaís, just above Cabo Blanco, is hit by some of the largest waves in Costa Rica. In all these places, be careful of riptides.

Turtle-Watching

The Nicoya Peninsula provides ace opportunities to watch the nesting rituals of several species of sea turtles. The olive ridley turtle nests year-round, but the peak nesting season runs July to October. Leatherbacks arrive between October and April, though nesting is largely over by mid-February. Occasionally you can see Pacific green turtles. Difficult to reach but worth the effort are Playa Nancite in Santa Rosa National Park and the Ostional National Wildlife Refuge near Nosara. (For more information, *see also* Close Up: Tico Turtles *in* Chapter 8.) Both are prime for watching the mass *arribadas,* or nestings, of thousands of olive ridley turtles. More accessible are Playas Langosta and Grande—bookends for the resort town of Tamarindo—which teem with enormous, ponderous, yet exquisitely dignified leatherback turtles, who arrive with high tide to dig holes and deposit their eggs. Leatherbacks also show up at Junquillal and other beaches. Alas, word of mouth has it that locals at Junquillal and possibly Langosta are still stealing turtle eggs as if there were an endless supply.

If you do want to watch the turtles, it's best to go with a legitimate guide and follow the rules. Playa Grande's turtle tours, now run by officially sanctioned guides drawn from the local populace, are very well organized.

Many people find the arrival and egg-laying ritual of the leatherback mothers a singularly moving event. (It can get crowded, but the guides at the Playa Grande park entrance take people out in groups, and rules limit the nightly numbers.) Others find the appearance of the babies, or hatchlings, even more charming, and you can see them during the day: just walk down Playa Grande at dawn two to three months after the onset of the egg-laying season, and the hatchlings just might be making their amazing emergence from the sand.

If you're like most ecotourists, you'll want to spend some time with these creatures, shepherding the tiny animals on their arduous, dangerous journey from the nest to the sea. If you don't perform this protective function, chances are you'll get to watch a less pleasant slice of life in the natural world, when a predatory frigate bird scoops your hatchling from the sand and eats it for breakfast. Don't pick them up though, because females will return to the beach where they were born to lay their eggs, and scientists believe it's this first journey from their nest to the ocean that imprints them. It may be a little frustrating to experience this natural phenomenon governed by such unnatural rules, but these rules are critical for the health of the turtles. Finally, you're better off *not* trying to watch the turtles the week between Christmas and New Year's Day, when the crowds get heavy indeed.

Exploring the Nicoya Peninsula

Bear in mind that aside from the Carretera Interamericana (Pan-American Highway, or CA1), many of the roads in this region are of the pitted, pocked, rock-and-dirt variety, with the occasional river rushing over the pavement. Covering seemingly short distances can require long hours behind the wheel, and four-wheel drive is often essential. If you can swing it, fly instead; some beach resorts, such as Tamarindo, Carrillo, and Tambor, have nearby airstrips. Many northern beach resorts are most easily reached from the international airport at Liberia.

Numbers in the text correspond to numbers in the margin and on the Nicoya Peninsula map.

Great Itineraries

The ideal Nicoya Peninsula trip can be comfortably divided between lazy days on the beach, swims in the surf, and hikes and leisurely exploration of natural sights—caverns, forests, rivers, and estuaries. The beach towns and resorts can be clustered into three loose geographical groups based partly on location and partly on the routes you take to reach them: those on the south end of the peninsula, accessible by ferry from Puntarenas or by plane to Tambor; areas in the central peninsula, accessible by plane to Punta Islita, Carrillo, and Nosara or by car via the new Río Tempisque bridge and the roads through Carmona, Curime, and Nicoya; and towns on the northern part of the peninsula, accessible by plane to Tamarindo or Liberia or by car through Liberia and Comunidad. If your time is limited, consider whether you want, for example, lively surf or calm waters; turtle-watching options at night; and an isolated resort or a more active beach town.

IF YOU HAVE 3–5 DAYS

Fly to ⊞ **Tamarindo** ⑦, ⊞ **Nosara** ⑪, **Tambor** ⑰, ⊞ **Punta Islita** ⑭, *or* **Playa Carrillo** ⑬ for a three-night stay at a beach resort. If you stay in Tambor or ⊞ **Montezuma** ⑱, a short drive takes you to Cabo Blanco, where you can hike through the **Cabo Blanco Strict Nature Reserve** to deserted Playa Cabo Blanco, diving and frolicking ground for hundreds of pelicans. You can also visit the ⊞ **Curú National Wildlife Refuge.** If you surf and are staying at the Tango Mar Resort, hit the waves here or at **Malpaís** ⑲, just north of Cabo Blanco, reputed home of the largest surfing waves in Costa Rica. If you have more time, book a three-day sea-kayaking adventure that leaves from **Curú National Wildlife Refuge,** or just settle into a hotel in **Tambor** ⑰ for a few days of R&R.

Or spend three to five nights at a beach between ⊞ **Playa Hermosa** ② and ⊞ **Tamarindo** ⑦. In season, you can also watch the leatherback turtles arrive by night at Las Baulas Marine National Park. For dedicated surfers, ⊞ **Playa Negra** ⑨ and Playa Avellanas offer great access to excellent waves and plenty of other recreational pastimes. You can also shop for pottery in the nearby artisan towns of Guaitil and Santa Cruz.

IF YOU HAVE 7 DAYS

Begin with some bird-watching in **Palo Verde National Park** ⑳ then continue on through **Nicoya** ㉒ and Santa Cruz and overnight in ⊞ **Tamarindo** ⑦ or at one of the beach resorts. Spend several days relaxing on the beach or exploring the Tamarindo and Río San Francisco estuaries north and south of Tamarindo, with nights watching turtles (in season) at Las Baulas Marine National Park. Fly to ⊞ **Tambor** ⑰, spending your nights here or in ⊞ **Montezuma** ⑱. Here you can hike, bird- and animal-watch, swim in the lazy, sheltered waters of the southern Nicoya Peninsula, and book a sea-kayaking tour that leaves from Curú National Wildlife Refuge. You can spend three days exploring the ruggedly beautiful islands in the gulf before flying back to San José.

When to Tour the Nicoya Peninsula

Averaging just 165 centimeters (65 inches) of rain per year, the Nicoya Peninsula and much of Guanacaste constitute Costa Rica's driest zone. The dry season, from December to April, is generally the best time to visit Costa Rica, but the northwest, especially the Nicoya Peninsula, is most appealing in the rainy season (barring only the *really* wet months of September and October). The Guanacastecos call the rainy season the "green" season, and that it is: the countryside—tending toward brown and arid the rest of the year—blooms lush and green from a few hours of rain each day. It's warm and sunny before and after the rain. The roads are muddy, but there are far fewer tourists in the rainy season, and prices are lower everywhere. If you're bent on turtle-watching, you have to come during the dry season, but for most other activities any time of year will do. A good bet would be to travel in November, April, or May, around the edges of the dry season.

THE NICOYA COAST

Strung along the coast of the Nicoya Peninsula are sparkling sand beaches lined with laid-back fishing communities along with hotels and resorts in every price category. Don't be in a rush to get anywhere; take things one hour at a time and you'll soon be as mellow as the locals. Liberia is a good gateway town to the coast with an international airport. However, there are airstrips from north to south at Tamarindo, Playa Nosara, Playa Carrillo, and Tambor—so flying in from San José is often the best way to start your vacation right away.

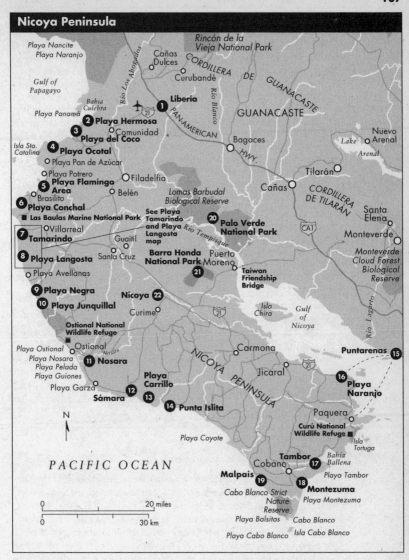

Nicoya Peninsula

Playa Nancite
Playa Naranjo

Rincón de la
Vieja National Park

Cañas
Dulces

CORDILLERA

Curubandé

DE

GUANACASTE

Gulf of
Papagayo

Río Los Ahogados

Río Blanco

① **Liberia**

GUANACASTE

Playa Panamá

Bahía
Culebra

PAN-AMERICAN

Bagaces

HWY.

Lake
Arenal

Nuevo
Arenal

② **Playa Hermosa**

③

Comunidad

④ **Playa Ocotal**

Playa del Coco

Isla Sta.
Catalina

Playa Pan de Azúcar

Filadelfia

Tilarán

Playa Potrero

⑤ **Playa Flamingo
Area**

Belén

Cañas

CORDILLERA
DE TILARÁN

Brasilito

⑥ **Playa Conchal**

Lomas Barbudal
Biological Reserve

Santa
Elena

■ **Las Baulas Marine National Park**

Villarreal

See Playa
Tamarindo
and Playa
Langosta
map

⑳ **Palo Verde
National Park**

CA1

Monteverde

⑦ **Tamarindo**

Guaitil

Río Tempisque

Monteverde
Cloud Forest
Biological
Reserve

⑧ **Playa Langosta**

Santa Cruz

**Barra Honda
National Park**

Puerto
Moreno

Playa Avellanas

㉑

Taiwan
Friendship
Bridge

⑨ **Playa Negra**

Nicoya ㉒

⑩ **Playa Junquillal**

Curime

Isla
Chira

Gulf
of
Nicoya

**Ostional National
Wildlife Refuge**

Ostional

Río Lagarto

Playa Ostional

Nosara

Carmona

Puntarenas ⑮

Playa Nosara
Playa Pelada
Playa Guiones

⑪ **Nosara**

NICOYA

CA1

⑯

Playa Garza

⑫

**Playa
Carrillo**

Jicaral

**Playa
Naranjo**

Sámara

⑬

PENINSULA

N

⑭ **Punta Islita**

Paquera

**Curú National
Wildlife Refuge** ■

Playa Coyote

Isla
Tortuga

PACIFIC OCEAN

Tambor

Bahía
Ballena

Malpaís

⑲

Cobano

⑰

Playa Tambor

⑱ **Montezuma**

	20 miles
0	
0	30 km

Cabo Blanco Strict
Nature
Reserve

Playa Montezuma

Playa Balsitas

Cabo Blanco

Playa Cabo Blanco

Isla Cabo Blanco

Liberia

① *234 km (145 mi) northwest of San José.*

North of San José on the Pan-American Highway, Liberia is a low-rise,
grid-plan cattle-market town with a huge central square dominated by
a not-so-pretty modern church. As the capital of Guanacaste province,
it's the gateway to Volcán Rincón de la Vieja, several spectacular and
biologically important national parks, and a turtle-nesting site on the
Pacific coast. More importantly, it is also a gateway for the coastal beaches.
The jet runway at Liberia's Daniel Oduber International Airport serves
both national and international flights, making it the arrival point of
choice for many travelers. Bus travelers also change buses here for on-
ward travel to Nicoya's Pacific beaches. Though pleasant and prosperous,
Liberia doesn't offer much to see or do beyond making a bank stop or
dropping in at the huge Burger King food court.

Museo del Sabanero , a small museum that chronicles the life of a cowboy in this cattle-ranching area, also has tourist information in the same building, **La Casa de la Cultura.** ✉ *3 blocks south of Parque Central,* ☏ *665–0135.* ☒ *Free.* ☉ *Weekdays 8–noon and 1:30–5, Sat. 8–noon and 1:30–4.*

Dining and Lodging

$ ✕ **Pizza Pronto.** This pizzeria in a white-adobe colonial house on a quiet side street offers 23 different pizzas and takes you a hundred years back in time. From the outdoor courtyard tables you can watch the pizza bakers push your pizza on long-handled wooden shovels into the stone ovens. Wooden booths are inside. It also serves pasta, roasted chicken, and sandwiches. ✉ *Avda. 4 and C. 1,* ☏ *666–2098. AE, MC, V.*

$$$ ⌂ **Best Western Hotel El Sitio.** If you're stopping for a night in Liberia, consider El Sitio for its spacious, modern rooms and extensive facilities: an Italian restaurant, a casino, two pools shaded by stately guanacaste trees, a car-rental agency, tour planning, and walking trails. It's basically a nondescript roadside motel, but the conveniences and free breakfast redeem it. ✉ *South of the Burger King complex,* ☏ *666–1211,* 🆇 *666–2059,* 🆆🅴🅱 *www.guanacaste.co.cr/elsitio (mailing address: Apdo. 134–5000, Liberia). 52 rooms. Restaurant, cable TV, 2 pools, spa, horseback riding, volleyball, casino, Internet, laundry service, meeting room, car rental. AE, MC, V.*

$$ ⌂ **Hotel La Siesta.** The advantage of this modern hotel is its quiet location. The rooms surround a landscaped patio presided over by a huge mango tree. Rooms are very simple, with narrow, firm beds, white walls, and functional bathrooms that are beginning to show signs of age. The upstairs rooms are slightly larger and even quieter. ✉ *3 blocks south of the central plaza, on main road, (☏ 666–0678,* 🆇 *666–2532 (mailing address: Apdo. 15–5000, Liberia). 24 rooms. Restaurant, bar, pool. AE, MC, V.*

Playa Hermosa

❷ *13 km (8 mi) east of Playa del Coco.*

Playa Hermosa, not to be confused with the mainland beach of the same name south of Jacó, has a relaxed village atmosphere that recalls a Mexican beach town. The full length of the village beach has long been occupied by hotels, restaurants, and homes, so the newer hotel behemoths and other developments have been forced to set up shop off the beach or on other beaches in the area. Playa Hermosa's crescent of grayish sand fronts a line of trees that provide a welcome respite from the heat of the sun. At the beach's north end, low tide creates wide, rock-lined tidal pools. Playa Panama, just to the north, is a dark-sand beach that is rapidly being developed with large all-inclusive resorts and luxury condominiums.

Dining and Lodging

$$ ✕ **Aqua Sport.** You can shop for a beach picnic in the minimarket and liquor store, buy souvenirs in the gift shop, and rent equipment or organize a trip here. Or you can just sit down and enjoy fresh seafood in the casual beachfront restaurant. For big appetites, there's a huge, grilled mixed-seafood platter, or try a fish fillet stuffed with shrimp or oysters. ✉ *Beach road (take the second entrance to Playa Hermosa and follow the signs), Playa Hermosa,* ☏ *672–0050. AE, MC, V.*

$$$ ⌂ **Playa Hermosa Inn.** Run by the family who owns Aqua Sport, this friendly B&B, with a pool and gardens, has spacious rooms in an attractive two-story stucco building. There are also two very cheap coldwater cabinas for rent and one large apartment. Breakfast is included

and the beach is at your doorstep. ✉ *Second entrance to Playa Hermosa, heading south*, ☎ 672–0063, FAX 672–0060, WEB *www.costarica-beach-hotel.com. 8 rooms, 2 cabins, 1 apartment. Pool; no air-conditioning in cabins. AE, MC, V.*

$$$ 🏨 **El Velero.** Spacious, attractive white rooms with arched doorways,
★ terra-cotta tiles, bamboo furniture, and large windows create an air of elegance at this two-story beachfront hotel elegant. A satellite TV room keeps you in touch with goings-on. The hotel runs daily snorkeling cruises on a handsome 13-m (43-ft) sailboat. In the restaurant, sample the jumbo shrimp with rice and vegetables, or anything with mashed potatoes—a rarity in Costa Rica. Or come for barbecue night with live music on Wednesday and Saturday. ✉ *110 yards north of Aqua Sport, Playa Hermosa*, ☎ 672–0036, FAX 672–0016, WEB *www.costaricahotel.net. 22 rooms. Restaurant, bar, pool, in-room safes, volleyball, snorkeling, boating, jet skiing, laundry service. AE, MC, V.*

$$ 🏨 **Hotel Cabinas Playa Hermosa.** Ocean breezes, the sound of waves lapping on the shore, and a garden shaded by immense trees are the main attractions at this budget hotel favored by backpackers. Rooms in the one-story, pink brick units are not all in tip-top shape; each has a curious hodgepodge of very cheap and very good furniture and art. The funky restaurant has an intriguing retro look, reminiscent of a 1960s writers' colony in a South Pacific backwater. ✉ *875 yards south of first entrance to Playa Hermosa, Playa Hermosa*, ☎ FAX 672–0046 *(mailing address: Apdo. 174, Playa del Coco). 22 cabinas. Restaurant, beach, laundry service; no air-conditioning, no room phones. V.*

Outdoor Activities and Sports

SCUBA DIVING

Just off the beach at Hotel Sol Playa Hermosa (at the north end of Playa Hermosa), **Bill Beard's Diving Safaris** (☎ 672–0012 or 800/779–0055 in the U.S., FAX 672–0231 or 954/351–9740 in the U.S., WEB www.costaricadiving.net) runs a complete range of scuba activities, from beginner training to open-water certification courses, and even multitank dives at more than 20 tantalizing sites off the Guanacaste coast. His guides and trainers know underwater Guanacaste—alive with rays, sharks, fish, and turtles. Prices range from $50 for a one-tank afternoon dive to $375 for a PADI (Professional Association of Diving Instructors) open-water certification course.

WATER SPORTS

At the general store–cum–restaurant **Aqua Sport** (☎ 672–0050), you can rent water-sports equipment or organize a fishing or surfing trip.

On the beach, below the dive shop, an independent **kiosk** rents Boogie boards, plastic kayaks, Jet Skis, and other water toys.

Playa del Coco

❸ *35 km (22 mi) southwest of Liberia.*

Playa del Coco is a slightly seedy beachfront town that should suit those inclined toward noise, dance clubs, and general commotion. As one of the most accessible beaches in Guanacaste, it serves as a playground for Costa Rica's college kids, who, like students the world over, cannot always be trusted to clean up after themselves. The beaches are often littered with garbage, and Christmas and Semana Santa in March is impossibly crowded. (The quieter part of the beach is north of town.) But Coco's scruffy pier, slightly down-at-the-heels appearance, and trinket and souvenir stands are appealing if you like your resorts with some color.

Dining and Lodging

$$
★
✕ **El Sol y La Luna.** Finding haute-Italian cuisine in a romantic alfresco restaurant in Playa del Coco is a welcome surprise. Host Alessandro Tolo has brought his design ideas and superb jazz CD collection from Rome, while his wife, Silvia Casu, has brought culinary skills from her native Sardinia. Both food and service are memorable, with homemade pasta and homegrown basil lending authentic Italian flavor. There are also home-baked desserts, a wide selection of Italian wines, and two other distinctively Italian tastes: sparkling San Pellegrino mineral water and aromatic sambuca. ⊠ *La Puerta del Sol Hotel, 200 yards left off main road to Playa del Coco,* ☎ *670–0195. AE, MC, V.*

$$ ✕ **Tequila Bar and Grill.** This popular gringo hangout with a concrete floor and old wooden tables is created in the image of a humble, almost grubby Mexican restaurant. The meals are also simple, but they're authentic and tasty, especially the fajitas, which come with chicken, beef, shrimp, or *pulpo* (octopus). Locally, this place is famous for its excellent margaritas. ⊠ *Main strip, 150 yards east or away from the beach.* ☎ *No phone. No credit cards. Closed Wed.*

$$$ ✕🏨 **La Puerta del Sol.** A tranquil enclosure of stylish suites overlooks a formal garden with sculpted shrubs and a lovely pool. An aqua-and-tangerine color scheme in the modern guest rooms shouldn't work, but it does. They have a cool, Mediterranean look and all the furniture and fabrics seem to float on a breeze. King-size beds roost atop adobe platforms and gleaming white bathrooms have high ceilings. El Sol y La Luna, the wonderful Italian restaurant in the garden, has wonderful homemade pasta, Italian wines, and Sardinian flare. ⊠ *200 yards left off main road to Playa del Coco,* ☎ *670–0195,* 𝔽𝔸𝕏 *670–0650,* 𝕎𝔼𝔹 *www. lapuertadelsol.com. 10 suites. Restaurant, cable TV, in-room safes, pool, gym, Ping-Pong. AE, MC, V.*

$$$ 🏨 **Villa Flores.** Weight-lifting, scuba-diving Italians run Villa Flores, a combination B&B and dive center, specializing in scuba trips and water sports. The beach is a minute away. Rooms on the lower level of the handsome hardwood building have fans; two rooms upstairs have air-conditioning. The more luxurious of these two, Room 9, also has a commodious bathtub. Italian dishes are served in the three-square-meal restaurant. ⊠ *200 yards east of the main road,* ☎ *670–0269,* 𝔽𝔸𝕏 *670– 0787 (mailing address: Apdo. 2, Playa del Coco). 9 rooms, 3 suites. Restaurant, fans, pool, gym, hot tub, laundry service. V.*

$$ 🏨 **Villa del Sol.** The French-Canadian owners of this B&B offer seven quiet, spacious, light-filled rooms in a contemporary building with a pool out front. There are also six open-plan studios, each with kitchen, a queen-size bed, and a pull-out trundle bed that sleeps two. Well away from Coco's main drag, Villa del Sol is just 100 m (109 yards) from the quiet part of the beach. Views of the lush tropical garden and the ocean are best from the upstairs balconies. ⊠ *200 yards north of Villa Flores,* ☎ 𝔽𝔸𝕏 *670–0085,* 𝕎𝔼𝔹 *www.villadelsol.com (mailing address: Apdo. 052–5019, Playa del Coco). 7 rooms, 5 with bath; 6 studios. Pool, laundry service. AE, MC, V.*

Playa Ocotal

❹ *3 km (2 mi) west of Playa del Coco.*

In spite of its proximity to student-thronged Coco, Playa Ocotal is a serene spot, with a lilliputian crescent of beach sheltered by rocks. Right at the entrance to the Gulf of Papagayo, it's a good place for sport-fishing enthusiasts to hole up between excursions. There's good diving at Las Corridas, just 1 km (½ mi) away.

Lodging

$$$$ 🏨 **El Ocotal Beach Resort.** This luxury hotel with a sportfishing fleet, dive shop, and day spa, is perched above secluded Ocotal Bay. The upper rooms look north to the Peninsula Santa Elena and northwest to Rincón de la Vieja. Inside, the rooms have tropical-patterned bedspreads, watercolors, and huge French windows. The freestanding, triangular bungalows down the hill are larger and have polished wood floors. ✉ *3 km (2 mi) south of Playa del Coco, down an unpaved road,* ☎ *670–0321,* FAX *670–0083,* WEB *www.ocotalresort.com (mailing address: Apdo. 1, Playa del Coco). 59 rooms, 5 suites, 12 bungalows. Restaurant, bar, fans, in-room safes, cable TV, 3 pools, spa, tennis court, horseback riding, dive shop, boating, Internet, laundry service. AE, MC, V.*

$$$
★ 🏨 **Villa Casa Blanca.** Secluded and romantic, and surely one of the finest B&Bs in Costa Rica, the Casa Blanca occupies a hillside Mediterranean-style building buried in a bower of tropical plantings. The intimate, junglelike setting attracts numerous colorful, talkative birds. Victorian-influenced rooms comfort you with pleasant wood details and artwork, canopy beds, and enormous bathrooms with wall-covering mirrors. The Casa Blanca also turns out Guanacaste's heartiest breakfasts. ✉ *Just inside the gated entrance to El Ocotal Beach Resort, on the same road,* ☎ *670–0518,* FAX *670–0448,* WEB *www.ticonet. co.cr/casablanca (mailing address: Apdo. 176–5019, Playa Ocotal). 10 rooms, 5 suites. Pool. AE, MC, V.*

Playa Flamingo Area

⑤ *39 km (24 mi) west of Filadelfia.*

Flamingo was one of the first of the northern Nicoya beaches to experience the wonders of overscale resort development, a fact immortalized in the huge Aurola Flamingo Marina Resort, which dominates the landscape. The beach, however, is still a welcome oasis. If you like the anonymity that large, character-free hotels offer, this is as good a place as any.

Playa Pan de Azúcar (Sugar Bread Beach), 8 km (5 mi) north of Playa Flamingo, at the end of a hilly dirt road, lends its only hotel one quality that can be hard to come by in this area—privacy. There are good islands for snorkeling just offshore. With more development than Azúcar, and less than Flamingo, **Playa Potrero,** between the two, is a wide, white-sand beach. There's excellent swimming at an island near Playa Potrero, and the **Isla Santa Catalina** bird refuge, home of the bridled tern (March to September), is 10 km (6 mi) offshore.

Dining and Lodging

$$
★ ✕ **Marie's Restaurant.** At the north end of Flamingo, look for a veranda furnished with sliced-tree-trunk tables painted with sea creatures and settle back for generous helpings of fresh seafood at very reasonable prices. Friendly Marie makes delightful ceviche and a delicious *plato de mariscos* (shrimp, lobster, and oysters served with garlic butter, potatoes, and salad). Save room for the darkly delicious banana-chocolate bread pudding. Drop in for happy hour between 4 and 6 PM and enjoy two-for-one drink prices and free *bocas* (snacks). ✉ *Main road, near north end of the beach,* ☎ *654–4136. V.*

$$$$
★ 🏨 **Colores del Pacífico.** Perched high on a cliff overlooking Potrero Bay, this small, exquisite hotel looks like a page out of *Architectural Digest*. The very modern, minimalist design incorporates terra-cotta walls, Mexican-tile floors, sculptural cactus plantings, and indirect lighting. Each room has a dramatic bed "treatment" by the Belgian interior-designer/owner. Fresh flowers, fruit, and cookies greet you in your room,

which has a private terrace with hammocks. Breakfast and lunch are served in a thatch-roof restaurant with a sweeping view of ocean and the fall-away infinity pool. Yoga is available. ⊠ *At intersection of roads leading out of Flamingo and to Playa Potrero,* ☎ 654–4769, 𝔽𝔸𝕏 654–4976, 𝔚𝔼𝔹 *www.coloresdelpacifico.com. 6 rooms. Restaurant, bar, fans, minibars, aerobics, snorkeling, waterskiing, fishing. AE, MC, V.*

$$$$ 🖭 **Flamingo Marina Resort.** These hillside pink buildings with orange, yellow, and maroon tile roofs have far more personality than the other, large area resorts. The fashionably decorated rooms, wash-painted in a mango hue, have terra-cotta lamps, hand-carved wooden furniture, and shell-shape sinks. The luxurious condos have full modern kitchens and spacious sitting areas with leather couches. Nearly all rooms and condos have large verandas with excellent views of the sea below. ⊠ *On the hill above Flamingo Bay,* ☎ 654–4141, 𝔽𝔸𝕏 654–4035, 𝔚𝔼𝔹 *www.flamingomarina.com (mailing address: Apdo. 321–1002, San José,* ☎ 290–1858, 𝔽𝔸𝕏 231–1858). 58 condos, 22 rooms, 18 suites. Restaurant, 2 bars, cable TV, some kitchenettes, minibars, 3 pools, wading pool, tennis court, dive shop, laundry service, meeting room. AE, DC, MC, V.*

$$$$ 🖭 **Hotel Sugar Beach.** A thin, curving white-sand beach is the view from this American-owned hotel. Most of the air-conditioned rooms have idyllic ocean views, and each room's wooden door has a hand-carved image of a local bird or animal. Bright yellow-and-blue fabrics along with watermelon, aqua, and yellow walls make the rooms feel fresh. The open-air rotunda restaurant serves good seafood dishes. The hotel offers surfing at Witches Rock, golf, and turtle-watching. ⊠ *8 km (5 mi) north of Playa Flamingo, Playa Pan de Azúcar,* ☎ 654–4242, 𝔽𝔸𝕏 654–4239, 𝔚𝔼𝔹 *www.sugar-beach.com (mailing address: Apdo. 90, Santa Cruz). 27 rooms, 2 suites, 1 house. Restaurant, bar, cable TV, minibars, pool, horseback riding, snorkeling, boating, laundry service; no air-conditioning in some rooms. AE, MC, V.*

$$$ 🖭 **Hotel Villaggio Flor de Pacifico.** Tuscany meets Costa Rica in an ambitious Italian-owned complex of red-roofed villas that will eventually include a shopping "village" and theater. Rooms have kitchenettes and wooden ceilings. You can opt for air-conditioning or open the big, screened windows to catch the breezes. The alfresco restaurant is elegant with crisp tablecloths and a bountiful breakfast buffet. The property is very flat and not right on the beach, but the gardens are lovely and the curvaceous pool is enticing. There's a scuba-diving school on-site. ⊠ *220 yards east of Playa Potrero, and 1 km (½ mi) north of Flamingo,* ☎ 654–4664, 𝔽𝔸𝕏 654–4663, 𝔚𝔼𝔹 *www.hotelflordepacifico. com. 65 villas. Restaurant, piano bar, pool; no air-conditioning in some rooms. AE, MC, V.*

$$$ 🖭 **Mariner Inn.** Near the marina, this two-story white building is the cheapest hotel in Flamingo. The tiny, compact rooms, with small TVs built into the dressers, feel like boat cabins; all have air-conditioning, ceiling fans, and firm beds. The upstairs bar is the main focus of the hotel with lots of sunburnt fishermen exchanging tall tales. The hotel happily arranges sportfishing trips. ⊠ *Near the Flamingo Marina,* ☎ 654–4081, 𝔽𝔸𝕏 654–4024. 11 rooms, 1 suite. Restaurant, bar, fans, cable TV, pool, laundry service. AE, MC, V.*

Playa Conchal

❻ *35 km (22 mi) west of Filadelfia; immediately south of Playa Brasilito.*

Playa Conchal, one of Guanacaste's finest and most secluded beaches, is aptly named—it's sprinkled with shells that offer themselves up for easy collecting. The sprawling Meliá Playa Conchal resort looms large here, and its presence is felt in the shops selling overpriced sunglasses, T-shirts, and water toys along the road leading to it. This tacky resort energy has begun to wear on the charm of nearby Brasilito, a small fishing village just north of Conchal. A ramshackle row of houses huddles around Brasilito's main square, which doubles as the soccer field. Before high tide, boats line up just off a white-sand beach that is the equal of Flamingo minus the megahotels.

Dining and Lodging

$$$ ✗ **El Camarón Dorado.** This bougainvillea-drenched bar-restaurant derives much of its appeal from its shaded setting on Brasilito's beautiful beach. Some tables are right on the beach, with the surf crashing just yards away, and a small-vessel fishing fleet anchored offshore assures you of the freshness of seafood on the menu. Thanks to its spectacular sunset views, this is a popular place for early evening drinks. A van will pick up diners from Flamingo Beach hotels. ⊠ *220 yards north of Brasilito Plaza, Brasilito,* ☎ *654–4028. AE, MC, V.*

$$$$ ⊞ **Meliá Playa Conchal Beach & Golf Resort.** Are you a golfing traveler who wants luxury in a remote locale? If so, Meliá caters to you in particular. From the enormous, open-air, marble-floored lobby, you can survey the massive grounds, encompassing almost 4 square km (1½ square mi) of manicured golf course, bungalows, tennis courts, the largest pool in Central America, and a distant beach. The suites, set in low-slung, colonial-style houses, are large and luxurious. The restaurants serve a range of international fare. ⊠ *Entrance less than 1 km (½ mi) south of Brasilito, Playa Conchal,* ☎ *654–4123; 800/336–3542 in the U.S.,* FAX *654–4181,* WEB *www.solmelia.com. 292 suites. 5 restaurants, 4 bars, in-room safes, cable TV, minibars, pool, hair salon, 18-hole golf course, 4 tennis courts, gym, beach, jet skiing, bicycles, casino, dance club, laundry service, meeting room. AE, MC, V.*

$$ ⊞ **Hotel Brasilito.** This simple establishment is just off the beach. Fronting the sea is the hotel's wooden, open-air restaurant, its tables and chairs arrayed beneath lazily turning ceiling fans. The sparely furnished but comfortable rooms occupy both floors of an old but freshly painted two-story wooden building behind the restaurant; ask for one of the two rooms with unobstructed sea views. There is no hot water. ⊠ *Next to square and soccer field, Brasilito,* ☎ *654–4237,* FAX *654–4247,* WEB *www.brasilito.com. 15 rooms. Restaurant, fans, horseback riding, snorkeling, laundry service, Internet; no air-conditioning; no phones. V.*

Tamarindo

❼ *37 km (23 mi) west of Filadelfia.*

Tamarindo is a lively town with a great variety of restaurants, cabins, bars, and hotels at all price levels. Surfing is the main attraction here—Tamarindo hosted the 2002 International Billabong Professional Surfing Tournament—for the young crowd that parties hard at beachfront bars after a day riding the waves. An older crowd is attracted by the upscale, beach-front hotels south of the bustling town center. Developmental hustle is everywhere, evidenced by the presence of condo projects and mini–strip malls. Still, Tamarindo remains appealing because it's virtually self-contained: its beaches are great for snorkeling, boating, kayaking, diving, surfing, and just plain swimming; there are estuaries north and south of town for bird- and animal-watching; and there are two turtle-nesting beaches nearby—Playa Langosta to the south, and Playa Grande to the north. With an airstrip just outside town, Tamarindo is also a convenient base for exploring all of Guanacaste.

114

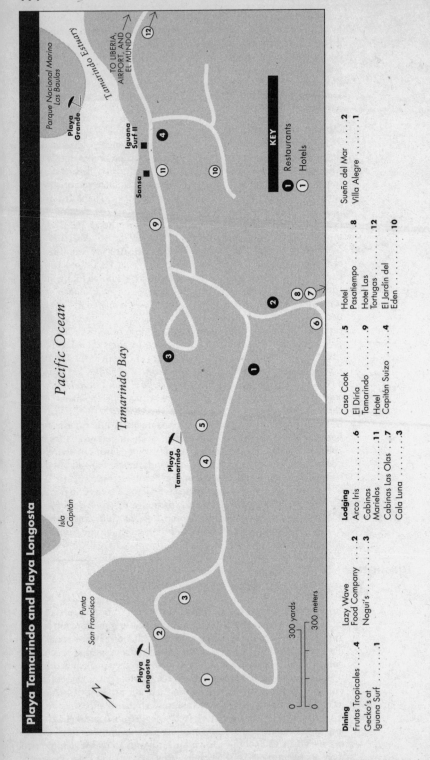

Playa Tamarindo and Playa Longosta

Parque Nacional Marino
Las Baulas

Playa Grande

Tamarindo Estuary

TO LIBERIA,
AIRPORT, AND
EL MUNDO

Pacific Ocean

Tamarindo Bay

Isla Capitán

Punta San Francisco

Playa Langosta

Playa Tamarindo

KEY

🚩 Restaurants
① Hotels

0 — 300 yards
0 — 300 meters

Dining
Frutas Tropicales **4**
Gecko's at
Iguana Surf **1**
Lazy Wave
Food Company **2**
Nogui's **3**

Lodging
Arco Iris **6**
Cabinas
Marielos **11**
Cabinas Las Olas . . . **7**
Cala Luna **3**

Casa Cook **5**
El Diriá
Tamarindo **9**
Hotel
Capitán Suizo **4**

Hotel
Pasatiempo **8**
Hotel Las
Tortugas **12**
El Jardín del
Eden **10**

Sueño del Mar **2**
Villa Alegre **1**

Except for some sections through the middle of town, the very dusty road is in dire need of repaving. The sickly sweet smell in the air is from the molasses mixture poured on the roads to keep down the dust in the dry season.

El Mundo de la Tortuga. To learn about the life cycle of the leatherbacks and the threats they face, visit this creative turtle museum in Playa Grande. Audio tours (in English, Spanish, German or French) are 30 minutes long and lead you through the interactive exhibits. The museum also conducts excellent turtle tours, which often occur late at night, sometimes till 3 AM, depending on turtle sightings. ⊠ *On road to Hotel Las Tortugas*, ☎ 653–0471. ☒ *$5.* ☉ *Late Oct.–end Mar., daily 4 PM–after midnight.*

Parque Nacional Marino Las Baulas. North of Tamarindo, across an estuary, this marine park and beach protects the long **Playa Grande**. This beach hosts the world's largest visitation of nesting leatherback turtles (nesting season is October through April). Playa Grande is also a great surf spot. Environmental activist Lewis Wilson, also the owner of the Hotel Las Tortugas, struggled for a decade to get Las Baulas established and has a true understanding of the importance of balancing the oft-conflicting needs of locals, turtles, and tourists. An evening spent discussing ecotourism and ecopolitics with him is a real education. The adjacent **Tamarindo Wildlife Refuge,** a mangrove estuary with some excellent bird-watching, has been under some developmental pressure of late. Just south of Tamarindo, accessible by dirt road, is the **Río San Francisco,** with an estuary system that's also rich in bird life. Unlike Tamarindo, it's free of motorboats. *3 km (2 mi) north of Tamarindo,* ☎ *653–0423,* ☎ FAX *653–0458,* WEB *www.cool.co.cr/usr/turtles.*

Dining

$$–$$$ ✕ **Gecko's at Iguana Surf.** This rustic, thatch-roof restaurant brimming with trickling fountains is attached to a surf shop and is very popular with local American families. Chef John Szilasi bakes his own bread and bread sticks studded with spicy seeds. His menu revolves around fresh local ingredients, such as tuna, calamari, and lobster. The chocolate cake here is famous and sells out quickly; a good backup dessert is the Brandy Freeze. ⊠ *Beside Iguana Surf, on the road to Playa Langosta,* ☎ *653–0334. No credit cards. Closed Mon.–Tues.*

$$–$$$ ✕ **Nogui's.** Also known as the Sunrise Café, Nogui's is considered by
★ local aficionados to have Tamarindo's freshest and most reasonably priced seafood—although even it is getting expensive. Only a dirt road separates Nogui's alfresco plastic tables and chairs from the beach. There are great salads and shrimp tacos for lunch; the full seafood menu is only available at dinner. The langostino is highly recommended, as is the swimsuit selection in the adjacent shop. ⊠ *South of Zullymar, on Tamarindo circle,* ☎ *653–0029. AE, MC, V.*

$$ ✕ **Lazy Wave Food Company.** For serious food at laughable prices, visit
★ this casual, open-air restaurant built around a giant dead tree. Chef Derek Furlani from Toronto entertains customers at the open-kitchen counter with his dry wit as he chops, swirls, and sautés fresh local ingredients. The eclectic menu changes daily. At lunch, there may be chunks of seared tuna with a heap of his signature crispy, hand-cut shoestring fries and blanched green beans swirled in sesame oil. For dinner, there may be a warm conch salad. Desserts are standouts, too. ⊠ *Beside Hotel Pasatiempo, behind the storefronts,* ☎ *no phone. No credit cards.*

$ ✕ **Frutas Tropicales.** Waiters hose down the road to dampen the dust that would otherwise smother this busy street-side eatery. The plastic tables and chairs stay full for a reason—the restaurant dishes out Costa Rican food at Costa Rican prices to travelers of every shape and description. The food is nothing fancy, but the casados and breakfasts are tasty and substantial. The menu includes U.S.-style hamburgers and fries, and great *frutas tropicales* (tropical fruit drinks). ⊠ *Main road, toward north end of town,* ☎ *653–0041. AE, MC, V.*

Lodging

$$$$ 🏠 **Casa Cook.** These one-bedroom, hardwood-detailed cabinas just off Tamarindo's beach are owned by a retired American couple, Chuck and Ruthann Cook. Each cabina has a full kitchen, its own water heater, a queen-size sofa bed in the living room, a queen bed in the bedroom, and screened doors and windows. The *casita* (literally, a small house)—a 550-square-ft, one-bedroom apartment—has a private bath, kitchen, living room, and outside eating area. Air-conditioning is $10 extra per night. ⊠ *On road to Playa Langosta, north of the Hotel Capitán Suizo,* ☎ *653–0125,* FAX *653–0753,* WEB *www.tamarindo.com/cook. 3 cabinas, 1 casita. Fans, in-room safes, cable TV, kitchenettes, pool, beach; no-smoking. AE, MC, V.*

$$$$ 🏠 **El Diriá Tamarindo.** A shady tropical garden right next to the beach eliminates the need to stray far from Tamarindo's first high-end hotel. Rooms in the contemporary three-story building with pre-Columbian design motifs have tile floors and modern furniture, and each has a spacious balcony. Try to avoid the rooms facing the noisy main road. The thatched rotunda bar and restaurant overlook a large rectangular pool. ⊠ *800 yards before Tamarindo center; next to the shopping center,* ☎ *653–0031,* FAX *653–0208,* WEB *www.tamarindodiria.co.cr (mailing address: Apdo. 476–1007, San José,* ☎ *258–4224). 123 rooms. Restaurant, bar, in-room safes, cable TV, minibars, 2 pools, casino, laundry service. AE, MC, V.*

$$$$ 🏠 **Hotel Capitán Suizo.** Steps from a relatively quiet stretch of Tamarindo's
 ★ gorgeous beach, these elegant, balconied bungalows (part of a small, upscale chain of inns) are set in a lushly landscaped garden, and surround a large, shady pool. The stunning, multilevel rooms have high, angled ceilings and amusing flourishes of color on the walls. A beautifully decorated and subtly lit restaurant serves contemporary cuisine and hosts beach barbecues. Monkeys and birds visit the Swiss Captain's place, so the price of your room includes some wildlife. Diving and kayaking trips can be arranged. ⊠ *Right side of road toward Playa Langosta (veer left before circle),* ☎ *653–0075 or 653-0353,* FAX *653–0292,* WEB *www. hotelcapitansuizo.com. 22 rooms, 8 bungalows. Restaurant, in-room safes, refrigerators, pool, horseback riding, boating, fishing, laundry service. AE, MC, V.*

$$$$ 🏠 **El Jardín del Eden.** The only drawback to the "Garden of Eden" (this one, anyway) is that it's not right on the beach. Instead, the two-tier, Mediterranean-style, pink building is among a lush hillside gardens. Rooms have carved hardwood furniture or oversize bamboo furniture, and elegantly styled bathrooms. All rooms have ocean views, and two beautiful pools provide the missing water element. The thatch-roof restaurant prepares a variety of fresh seafood dishes and outstanding steaks. ⊠ *From Hotel El Milagro on main road, turn left, go 200 yards, then right for 200 yards uphill, (mailing address: Apdo. 1094–2050, San Pedro),* ☎ *653–0137,* FAX *653–0111,* WEB *www.jardindeleden.com. 18 rooms, 2 apartments. Restaurant, 2 bars, fans, in-room safes, cable TV, refrigerators, 2 pools, hot tub, laundry service; no air-conditioning. AE, MC, V.*

$$$ 🏠 **Hotel Las Tortugas.** Who would have thought that architecture could be shaped by turtles? Indeed, the comfortable rooms here were built with them in mind. Guest room windows do not overlook the nesting beaches, since light interferes with the turtles' nighttime rituals. The rooms are otherwise quiet, with good beds, stone floors, and stucco walls. Owner Louis Wilson offers long-term rentals in apartments with kitchenettes or basic housing for turtle volunteers. The restaurant serves healthful, high-quality food. The surf is good but it sometimes has dangerous rip currents, at which times you can retreat to the turtle-shape pool. Local guides lead turtle tours at night, and the hotel also offers canoe trips in the nearby Tamarindo Wildlife Refuge. ⊠ *Las Baulas Marine National Park, 3 km (2 mi) north of Tamarindo,* ☎ *653–0423,* ☎ FAX *653–0458,* WEB *www.cool.co.cr/usr/turtles (mailing address: Apdo. 164, Santa Cruz de Guanacaste). 11 rooms, 7 apartments. Restaurant, pool, boating, laundry service; no room phones. V.*

$$$ 🛏 **Hotel Pasatiempo.** One of the better bargains in Tamarindo, the hotel's cabinas, each named after a Guanacaste beach, are scattered around the nicely landscaped grounds and the pool; each has a patio with a hammock, simple wooden furnishings, and a unique hand-painted mural. Sherbet-color suites have one bedroom and a pull-out sofa in the living room. The Yucca Bar frequently hires local musicians—a bonus if Costa Rica's otherwise slow nightlife leaves you restless—and a wide-screen satellite TV provides sports fans with their periodic fix. Water sports, a sailing cruise, and other activities are easily arranged. ⊠ *Off the dirt road to Playa Langosta, 200 yards from beach behind Tamarindo circle,* ☎ *653–0096,* FAX *653–0275,* WEB *www.hotelpasatiempo.com. 11 cabinas, 2 suites. Restaurant, bar, some cable TV, pool, laundry service. AE, MC, V.*

$$ 🛏 **Arco Iris.** This wonderful small hotel is on the hill behind the Tamarindo circle. The four cheery, wildly imaginative cabinas are painted in primary colors and decorated along distinct themes. One has two bedrooms and a kitchen. In the past aerobics, kick-boxing, or yoga sessions have been taught on-site, and in case it all gets to be too much, there's also a masseuse. At press time, however, it was unclear whether these unique services will be continued under a new owner. ⊠ *Follow signs past Hotel Pasatiempo and go up hill to the right,* ☎ *653–0330. 4 cabinas. Some kitchenettes; no air-conditioning, no phones. No credit cards.*

$$ 🛏 **Cabinas Marielos.** In high season Tamarindo presents few decent bargain rooms; among the best are the cabinas here, which have a slightly Alpine look. They're in two wings, flanking a colorful flower garden well back from the noise and dust of the road. Guests sometimes share their meals in the common kitchen. The atmosphere is surprisingly serene. Note that the water doesn't get terribly hot except in the three newest air-conditioned rooms. ⊠ *Across the main dirt road from the beach, north of the town center (follow signs),* ☎ FAX *653–0141. 20 rooms. Laundry service; no air-conditioning in some rooms, no room phones. AE, MC, V.*

Outdoor Activities and Sports

BOATING, SURFING, AND KAYAKING

Iguana Surf (⊠ on the road to Playa Langosta, ☎ FAX 653–0148) has information for surfers and visitors. Iguana Surf rents surfboards, Boogie boards, and snorkeling equipment at their second location, **Iguana Surf 2,** right on the beach. Naturalists lead tours into the bird-watching haven of the nearby San Francisco estuary, which might include an encounter with a troop of howler monkeys. Snorkeling tours by kayak or motorboat are also available.

SPORTFISHING

A number of fishing charters in Tamarindo cater to saltwater anglers. The best among them is probably **Tamarindo Sportfishing** (☎ 653–0090), run by Randy Wilson, who has led the way in developing catch-and-release techniques that are easy on the fish. Wilson has roamed and fished the Guanacaste waters for 25 years now, and he knows where the big ones lurk. His boat, the *Talking Fish,* is equipped with a marlin chair and a cabin with a shower. Full days run $975, half days $575.

Playa Langosta

8 *2 km (1 mi) south of Tamarindo.*

Playa Langosta, a leatherback-turtle nesting beach, is less protected than the beach at Tamarindo. As a result, informal viewings with private guides are a lot cheaper here than the more organized Playa Grande turtle tours. Big, well-shaped river-mouth waves near the north end of the beach make it popular with surfers. But with lots of expensive, private villas and refined B&Bs, Playa Langosta is fast becoming an upscale, gentrified extension of Tamarindo.

Quite separate, geographically and atmospherically from Langosta, **Playa Avellanas,** 32 km (20 mi) to the south, is a beautiful 1-km (½-mi) stretch of pale-gold sand with rocky outcroppings, a river mouth, and a mangrove swamp estuary. You have to drive inland to Villa Real to get from one to the other. Locals claim there are eight surf spots when the swell is strong.

Dining and Lodging

$$$$ ✕⌂ **Cala Luna.** A labyrinth of high hibiscus hedges leads to large, luxe, ocher-color rooms, with king-size beds and alcoves softly lit with signature moon sconces. Oversize bathrooms have dolphins cavorting on walls around curved bathtubs for two. The private villas each have their own small pool; two larger, and glorious pools are for shared use. Overlooking one is the pretty Cala Moresca restaurant. The chef leans toward Mediterranean cuisine: red snapper with a lime–caper butter accompanied by tabouli and hummus. The exotic fruit plate (part of the free Continental breakfast) is a work of art, and all the food is reasonably priced. ⊠ *Across from Sueño del Mar,* ☎ 653–0214, 𝔽𝔸𝕏 653–0213, 🆆🅴🅱 www.calaluna.com. 20 rooms, 21 villas. Restaurant, bar, in-room safes, cable TV, 2 pools, massage, snorkeling, fishing, bicycles. AE, MC, V.

$$$$ ⌂ **Sueño del Mar.** A garden gate opens onto a dreamy world of inti-
★   mate gardens and patios adorned with frescoes and antique tiles. Seashells are embedded in window frames and strung together in mobiles. The adobe-style house, which descends down a stepped passageway, contains three double rooms with high, queen-size beds and Balinese showers open to the sky. There's also a casita with its own kitchen and a breezy, book-filled honeymoon suite upstairs. A lavish breakfast is served on the patio looking onto a tiny garden pool. Or you can take your morning coffee a few steps down to the desert-island beach. Air-conditioning is $10 extra. ⊠ *150 yards south of Capitan Suizo, turn right for 50 yards, then right again for about 100 yards to entrance gate (across from back of Cala Luna Hotel),* ☎ 𝔽𝔸𝕏 653–0284, 🆆🅴🅱 www. tamarindo.com/sdmar. 3 rooms, 1 suite, 1 casita. Restaurant, pool, horse-back riding, snorkeling, boating, fishing, bicycles, laundry service; no room phones. V.

$$$$ ⌂ **Villa Alegre.** Owned by congenial and helpful Californians Barry and
★   Suzye Lawson, this homey but very sophisticated Spanish-style B&B has a lovely location, close to a stand of trees and a somewhat rocky but swimmable beach. Rooms are furnished with souvenirs from the Lawsons' travels to Japan, Russia, Guatemala, and other lands. Each room has a private patio. The lavish gourmet breakfast is included in the price. The hotel often plans and hosts weddings. ⊠ *Playa Langosta, south of Sueño del Mar,* ☎ 653–0270, 𝔽𝔸𝕏 653–0287, 🆆🅴🅱 www.tamarindo.

com/alegre. 7 rooms, 2 villas. Fans, no-smoking rooms, pool; no .
phones. AE, MC, V.

$$$ ⊞ **Cabinas Las Olas.** Frequented mainly by surfers, these spacious glass and stone cabinas in an airy forest behind Playa Avellanas should also appeal to bird-watchers, animal lovers, and naturalists. Monkeys and other critters lurk around this isolated spot, which has expansive grounds with trees galore. An elevated boardwalk leads from the cabinas to the beach through a protected mangrove estuary. The three-meal restaurant, complete with an adjacent outdoor video bar, serves reasonably priced food. ⊠ *20 km (12 mi) south of Tamarindo, in Playa Avellanas,* ☎ *233–4455 or 382–4366,* FAX *222–8685,* WEB *www.cabinaslasolas.co.cr (mailing address: Apdo. 1404–1250, Escazú). 10 cabinas. Restaurant, bar, dive shop, boating, bicycles, laundry service; no air-conditioning, no room phones. AE, MC, V.*

Playa Negra

❾ *44 km (27 mi) south of Playa Langosta.*

Americans—surfers at least—got their first look at Playa Negra in *The Endless Summer II,* which featured some dynamite sessions at this spectacular rock-reef point break. Surfing cognoscenti will dig the waves, which are almost all rights and often beautifully shaped. Surfer culture is also apparent in the wave of casual restaurants, health-food bakeries, Internet cafés, and bikini shops springing up along the road. A roadside tent bazaar sells sarongs and crafts.

Lodging

$$$ ⊞ **Hotel Playa Negra.** From sunny lawns strewn with lush plantings,
★ this collection of round, brilliantly colored, thatch-roof cabinas face the ocean. Inside, cooled by ceiling fans, the cabinas have built-in sofas and beautiful tile bathrooms. The ocean is good for swimming and snorkeling, with tidal pools, swimming holes, and rock reefs providing shelter. And for surfers, with a good swell running, this is paradise found. There is also a surfing school, as well as Boogie board classes. The restaurant serves deftly prepared Latin and European dishes. ⊠ *Go north on dirt road out of Paraiso and follow signs carefully at forks in the road,* ☎ *658–8034,* FAX *658–8035,* WEB *www.playanegra.com. 10 cabinas. Restaurant, bar, in-room safes, pool, horseback riding, volleyball, surfing, laundry service; no air-conditioning; no room phones. AE, MC, V.*

$$ ⊞ **Mono Congo Lodge.** Mono Congo translates as "howler monkey," and those noisy but endearing creatures have been plentiful here. But a new luxury-housing complex developed by the hotel owner is taking over this part of the beach and may scare away some of the wildlife. The shaded, three-story hardwood lodge has comfortable seating areas, a communal kitchen, and four guest rooms, with bathrooms down the hall. Decent waves, boards for rent, and rustic, comfortable accommodations still make this a good surfing holiday spot. ⊠ *50 yards north of La Plaza football field in Los Pargos,* ☎ FAX *382–6926 (mailing address: Apdo. 177–5150, Santa Cruz). 4 rooms share 2 baths, 1 house. Tennis court, horseback riding, surfing, laundry service. No credit cards.*

Playa Junquillal

❿ *2 km (1 mi) south of Paraiso*

Junquillal (pronounced hoon–key–*yall*), to the south of Playa Negra, is a long stretch of uninterrupted beach stretching about 3 km (2 mi), with calm surf and only one hotel on the beach side of the road. This one of the quieter beaches in Guanacaste and a real find for seekers f tranquillity.

Dining and Lodging

✗ **La Puesta del Sol.** Food aficionado Alessandro Zangari and his wife Silvana have created what he modestly calls "a little restaurant in my home." But regulars drive all the way from San José just to enjoy the haute-Italian menu at this dinner-only restaurant. Alessandro spares no expense or effort to secure the best ingredients: Every year he travels to Italy to buy truffles in season. The softly lit patio restaurant, tinted in tangerine and deep blue, evokes a Moroccan courtyard. All the pasta is made from scratch, of course; the ravioli *boscaiolo* contain a woodsy trio of cremini, porcini, and Portobello mushrooms. ⊠ *Just north of the beach, Playa Junquillal,* ☎ *658–8442. No credit cards. Closed May– June and Sept.–Oct.*

$$$ 🏨 **Guacamaya Lodge.** Secluded Guacamaya, on a breezy hill, has ex-
★ pansive views of surrounding rolling countryside and a river estuary below and is ideal for bird-watching. Swiss siblings Bernie and Alice Etene have a delightful compound, with flocks of visiting parrots in the morning and cranes rising up from the estuary. The landscaping around the pool is exceptional, with chenille plants trailing velvety pink tails and tall gingers blazing vibrant red torches. The three-meal restaurant serves excellent, reasonably priced food. In addition to spacious cabinas, with lovely fabric curtains and bedspreads and lots of windows to let in the cooling breezes, there's an airy, well-equipped modern house with a full kitchen. ⊠ *300 yards off Playa Junquillal,* ☎ FAX *653–0431 or 658– 8431,* WEB *www.guacamayalodge.com (mailing address: Apdo. 6, Santa Cruz). 6 cabinas, 1 house. Restaurant, bar, pool, volleyball, playground, laundry service; no air-conditioning, no room phones. AE, MC, V.*

$$$ 🏨 **Hotel Iguanazul.** This isolated beachfront resort on a bluff has a pool, a three-meal restaurant and bar, and 3 km (2 mi) of beach stretching south. Rooms (two per cabina) have wood-beam ceilings, tile floors, and are simply furnished, with two double beds. The hotel itself is looking a little tired, but the fabulous surf of Playa Negra is 10 minutes away, and there's often decent surfing in front of the hotel. Air-conditioned rooms cost more, but breakfast is free for all. Satellite TV is available in a recreation room. ⊠ *North end of Playa Junquillal,* ☎ *658–8124,* FAX *653–0123,* WEB *www.iguanazul.com (mailing address: Apdo. 130– 5150, Santa Cruz). 24 rooms. Restaurant, bar, fans, in-room safes, pool, volleyball, beach, recreation room, laundry service; no air-conditioning in some rooms, no room phones. AE, MC, V.*

$$$ 🏨 **Land Ho! at Hotel Villa Serena.** Cape Cod comes to Costa Rica—
★ American owners Olive and John Murphy have created a tropical version of New England, with shell-motif quilts and wall stencils, and hooked rugs with palm trees. Rooms are spacious and comfortable; for the ultimate in romance, ask for No. 10, a round room with an ocean view. There's a large pool in a lovely, landscaped garden and a full-service day spa. To reach the terrace restaurant overlooking the beach, you'll pass a collection of Costa Rican student art, some of it for sale. ⊠ *Across the dirt road from Playa Junquillal,* ☎ FAX *658–8430,* WEB *www.land-ho.com. 12 rooms. Restaurant, pool, spa, horseback riding, snorkeling, boating, fishing; no air-conditioning, no room phones. AE, MC, V. Closed Oct.*

Nosara

⓫ *10 km (6 mi) northeast of Garza.*

Set a bit inland, the minor and not very exciting town of Nosara is a good base of exploration for Playa Nosara and neighboring beaches of Playas Pelada and Guiones, as well as the nearby Ostional National Wildlife Refuge, a haven for nesting turtles.

This whole area of Guanacaste is currently being subdivided and settled by Europeans and Americans at a fairly rapid pace. Local hotel owners have joined forces to keep Nosara as free from large-scale development as possible and have placed wooden signs along the main road to help tourists find their way among the at-times confusing sideroads. To approach from the north, you'll need to ford the Río Nosara; from the south, you're coming from Garza and will already have accomplished the river crossings there.

Curú National Wildlife Refuge. Apart from sun and sand, the main reason to come to the central Nicoya is to visit the Refugio Nacional de Vida Silvestre Curú, with its top-notch turtle-watching. During the rainy season you'll probably need a four-wheel-drive vehicle to ford the river just north of Nosara; a track then leads through shrubs to the reserve, which protects one of Costa Rica's major breeding grounds for olive ridley turtles. Locals run the reserve on a cooperative basis, and during the first 36 hours of the arribadas they harvest the eggs, on the premise that eggs laid during this time would likely be destroyed by subsequent waves of mother turtles. These eggs, believed by some to be powerful aphrodisiacs, are sold to be eaten raw in bars. Members of the cooperative take turns guarding the beach from poachers, but they're happy to let you watch the turtles. Turtle arrivals at this and most other nesting sites depend on the moon and tides as well as the time of year; nesting peaks between October and April. Before you go, try to get a sense from the locals of when, if ever, the turtles will arrive. ⊠ *7 km (4½ mi) north of Nosara.*

Dining and Lodging

$$ ✕ **Café de Paris.** High-spirited French-Swiss owners set a friendly tone at this popular open-air café, where colorful Peruvian tablecloths adorn the tables. The pastries and desserts are the main draw, both in the restaurant and the bakery shop. Croissants, both sweet and savory, are excellent, as is the divine chocolate tart. You can also get pizza, nachos, casados, huge salads, and hearty sandwiches in the restaurant, where Spanish wines are available by the glass. ⊠ *Playa Guiones entrance and main road,* ☎ *682–0087. AE, MC, V.*

$$ ✕ **Pizzeria Giardino Tropical.** You can get good pastas and grilled chicken here, but the pizzas are particularly delicious—they're loaded with mozzarella cheese and have a crispy crust. Gardens surround the dining area and service is fast, a novelty in these parts. ⊠ *On main street, past entrance to Playa Guiones. No credit cards.*

$–$$ ✕ **La Mariposa Panadería Café-Bar.** Swiss bakers Karin Lang and Roland Locher started out selling their baked goods door to door. Now they sell their multigrain breads, baguettes, carrot cake, and brownies from a futuristic, terra-cotta building a stone's throw from Playa Pelada. You can get takeout, counter service, or sit down and enjoy a healthful meal at candlelit cedar tables under the sloping roof. They also serve savory empanadas, quiches, sandwiches, and daily hot specials. ⊠ *Across from Los Condominios las Flores, Playa Pelada,* ☎ *682–0545. No credit cards.*

$$$ ⚲ **Hotel Rancho Suizo Lodge.** The lodge is linked to tiny Playa Pelada, just 274 m (300 yards) away by a forest trail, so you can meander back and forth easily. Monkeys are partial to the property's shady environs, and a new aviary contains scarlet macaws imported from Switzerland; it's illegal to capture these birds in Costa Rica. The Swiss operators aren't superfriendly but are renowned for their hearty breakfasts, included in the room rate, and they also barbecue on the beach occa-

sionally. Turtle tours are run during the arribadas.⊠ *Follow the signs from the north end of Nosara, leading up a steep hill,* ☎ 682–0057, FAX *682–0055,* WEB *www.nosara.ch (mailing address: Apdo. 14, Bocas de Nosara 5233). 12 bungalows. Restaurant, 2 bars, laundry service, airport shuttle; no air-conditioning; no room phones. V.*

$$$ 🏨 **Lagarta Lodge.** This magnificent property on a promontory has the best views of Ostional National Wildlife Refuge. The private Nosara Biological Reserve is directly below, laced with trails running through mangroves. A 10-minute steep walk down takes you through a monkey-filled forest to beautiful Playa Guiones and surfing waves. The eagle's nest lobby/restaurant is famous for its views and Sunday barbecues. Seven comfortable rooms are in a separate building, each with a balcony and a view. At meals, served at a communal table, birders and naturalist share sightings with friendly Swiss host Marcel Schaerer. (There is an extra 6% charge for using credit cards.) ⊠ *At the top of the hill, north end of Nosara,* ☎ *682–0035,* FAX *682–0135,* WEB *www.lagarta.com (mailing address: Apdo. 18–5233, Nosara). 7 rooms. Restaurant, pool, hiking, boating, laundry service; no air-conditioning, no room phones. MC, V.*

$$–$$$ 🏨 **Hotel Villas Taype.** Bordering long, lovely Playa Guiones, the Villas Taype's 20 rooms are in a low-rise building that forms a U shape around a pair of garden swimming pools. Seven freestanding bungalows are more private. The breakfast buffet is complimentary. The German owners rent out surfboards, Boogie boards, and snorkeling gear as well as tennis rackets for the day-and-night tennis court; they can also arrange all local tours. ⊠ *Apdo. 8–5233, Nosara,* ☎ *682–0333,* FAX *682–0187,* WEB *www.villataype.com. 20 rooms, 9 bungalows, 1 suite. 2 bars, some refrigerators, 2 pools, tennis court, beach, dance club, laundry service. AE, MC, V.*

$$ 🏨 **Almost Paradise.** A five-minute walk from gorgeous Playa Pelada, this homey bed-and-breakfast is owned by a helpful German journalist. Perched high on a hill and surrounded by fruit trees, the hotel has original abstract art and landscapes on the walls and balconies with ocean views. Breakfast is complimentary. The hotel closes for a few weeks in the low season, so be sure to reserve ahead. ⊠ *2 km (1 mi) south of Nosara, on hill behind Playa Pelada,* ☎ *682–0173,* FAX *682–0173,* WEB *www.costarica/almostparadise.com. 6 rooms, 2 apartments with kitchens. Fans, pool, laundry service; no air-conditioning, no room phones. V.*

Sámara

⑫   *29 km (18 mi) south of Nicoya.*

When you reach Sámara you'll see a sign proclaiming it the BEST BEACH IN AMERICA. This may be an overstatement, but only a slight one. Two forest-covered hills jut out on either side of the clean, white beach, forming one giant cove that's ideal for swimming. A fantastic coral reef is 1½ km (1 mi) from the shore, and many area hotels can help arrange diving and snorkeling excursions. With a smooth road paved all the way from Nicoya, Sámara is flourishing these days, and the numerous hotels springing up around town have a distinctively Italian flavor and cater to both Ticos and foreigners. Happily, Tico spirit still predominates.

Dining and Lodging

$$ ✕ **El Dorado di Dolcetti.** After one visit to Costa Rica, Andrea Dolcetti
★   and his wife Luigina Sivieri sold their restaurant in Ferrara, Italy, and opened one here. Their open-air *palenque* (wood-and-thatch building) specializes in seafood, pasta, and, at dinner, wood-oven–baked pizzas.

Andrea brings home the fish and Luigina supervises the kitchen. Pasta is made from scratch and real Parmesan cheese and salami are imported to help create authentic Italian flavors. The spaghetti *al mare* is an inspired marriage of local shellfish and Italian cooking. For dessert, there are fruit *crostatas* (fruit-filled tarts) and chocolate "salami." ☒ *West off main road, just past the church in Sámara,* ☎ *656–0145. MC, V.*

$$$ ☷ **Casa del Mar.** Less than a block from the beach, on a small property, this well-tended hotel has simple, tidy rooms. Some rooms have private baths and air-conditioning. All have dark-wood furniture, white walls, and ceramic floors. Continental breakfast is included. The hotel has no swimming pool but it does have a giant cold-water whirlpool in a small garden. You'll pay extra for air-conditioning. ☒ *Main strip, 50 yards east of school,* ☎ *656–0264,* ℻ *656–0129,* ꊧꍏꍈ *www. casadelmarsamara.com. 17 rooms, 11 with bath. Restaurant, bar, fans, some refrigerators; no air-conditioning in some rooms, no room phones. AE, MC, V.*

$$$ ☷ **Hotel Villaggio La Guaria Morada.** Ocean breezes sweep through the thatch-roof white guest cottages that form an arc around a mature tropical garden. The good-size pool has a waterfall and a lurking stone crocodile. You can listen to the waves roll in at the open-air bar and drink in the spectacular view. This luxury complex is undergoing much-needed renovations but the location, on gorgeous (and private) Playa Garza, makes it well worth a visit. You'll reach the retreat via a drive down a dirt road. ☒ *16 km (10 mi) north of Sámara,* ☎ *661–8119 (mailing address: Apdo. 860–1007, San José,* ☎ *233–2476,* ℻ *222–4073). 30 rooms. Restaurant, bar, pool, beach, horseback riding, volleyball, snorkeling, fishing, laundry service; no air-conditioning, no room phones. AE, MC, V.*

$$$ ☷ **Villaggio Turistico Isla Chora.** It's a world unto itself, with a restaurant, Italian ice-cream parlor, a sophisticated amphitheater for bands, dancing on weekends, and direct beach access. Two-story white houses are arranged around a shimmering pool and manicured lawn planted with ficus trees, pruned to match the pagoda-like house roofs. Rooms are elegant with high-tech Italian bathroom fixtures in circular bathrooms decorated with pebble stonework. ☒ *West of main beach road, just past the church in Sámara,* ☎ *656–0174,* ℻ *656–0173. 15 rooms, 5 apartments with kitchens. Restaurant, cable TV, pool, dance club, laundry facilities; no room phones. AE, MC, V.*

$$$ ☷ **Villas Playa Sámara.** These white-stucco villas have a dreamy location on a long stretch of beach. The water here is shallow and safe enough for swimming, and there's also a large swimming pool. Families abound in this time-share tourist village, popular with a regular clientele of Europeans and North Americans. The one-, two- and three-bedroom fully equipped villas are comfortable and pretty. The restaurant food is not terrific; it's best to cook for yourself or dine in Sámara. ☒ *Off main road, south of Playa Sámara,* ☎ *656–0372 or 256–8228 in San José,* ℻ *656–0109 or 221–7222 in San José. 58 villas. Restaurant, bar, fans, kitchens, pool, outdoor hot tub, badminton, horseback riding, volleyball, beach, boating, fishing, mountain bikes, dance club; no room phones. AE, MC, V.*

$$
★ ☷ **Hotel Giada.** Giada, which means jade, is truly a gem of a hotel. The artistic Italian owners have used washes in watermelon, terra-cotta, and yellow to give the walls an antique Mediterranean look. In contrast, tropical thatch roofs overhang private terraces, which overlook a tropical garden and curvaceous blue pool. The large rooms have elegant bamboo furniture, and whimsical sea creatures are hand-painted on the bathroom tiles. Other arty and clever details make this hotel a delight to visit. ☒ *Main strip, 150 m from beach,* ☎ *656–0132,* ℻ *656–0131,*

WEB *www.hotelgiada.net (mailing address: Apdo. 5235–67, Sámara). 13 rooms. Pizzeria, pool, horseback riding, snorkeling, boating, fishing, laundry service; no air-conditioning, no room phones. AE, MC, V.*

Playa Carrillo

13 *6 km (4 mi) south of Sámara.*

With its long, reef-protected beach backed by an elegant line of swaying palms and sheltering cliffs, Carrillo is good for swimming, snorkeling, walking, and lounging. You can even camp here. This is one of the most beautiful and undeveloped beaches in Costa Rica—fly in and land at the airstrip, or head south on the dirt road from Sámara.

Dining and Lodging

$$ ✕ El Mirador. A fabulous view of yachts moored in Carrillo Bay makes the fresh seafood taste even better at this open-air restaurant perched on a cliff. Try the whole fried *pargo* (red snapper)—it's moist and crispy and comes with a salad and fries. Specialties include lobster (a good value here), jumbo shrimp, and mahimahi. ⌧ *Beachfront, at bend in main road,* ☎ *656–0307. AE, MC V.*

$$$$ ⌂ Hotel La Guanamar. The hotel used to be a private fishing club, and
★ it continues its tradition as a sportfishing mecca with two boats of its own for your fishing trips. With several levels connected by wooden terraces and steps beautifully positioned high above the southern end of Playa Carrillo, this luxury hotel brings to mind a luxury cruise liner. The large white bedrooms have blue nightstands, patterned bedcovers, olive-green carpets, and amazing views. ⌧ *On main road to beach, just before scenic overlook,* ☎ *656–0054 or 258–6015 in San José,* FAX *656–0001 or 258–6008 in San José,* WEB *www.guanamar.com. 41 rooms. Restaurant, bar, in-room safes, cable TV, pool, horseback riding, fishing, laundry service. AE, MC, V.*

$$$ ⌂ Hotel Esperanza. A young couple from Montreal designed this attractive bed-and-breakfast hotel, giving it an eclectic Mediterranean look, with columns seemingly from classical Greece and an arcade resembling one from Renaissance Italy. Rooms are stylishly simple with high ceilings, striking blue-and-yellow-tiled bathrooms, and handsome *pochote*-wood headboards and furniture, made locally. A huge breakfast is served in a small garden and fresh fish dinners can be ordered. ⌧ *100 yards west of Hotel Guanamar,* ☎ FAX *656–0564,* WEB *www.hotelesperanza.com. 7 rooms. Fans; no room phones. V.*

Punta Islita

14 *8 km (5 mi) south of Carrillo.*

Hidden in a slender cove, Islita beach is rather rocky, but there's some good snorkeling near the point. The only hotel in the area has a private dry-forest nature preserve threaded with well-made trails.

Lodging

$$$$ ⌂ Hotel Punta Islita. This secluded inn overlooking the Pacific has adobe-
★ style bungalows with barrel-tile roofs surrounding the main building, where a massive thatched dome covers the open-air restaurant. The French chef turns fresh seafood into inventive daily specials, and both the bar and restaurant open onto a blue-tile pool. Rustic bungalows have private porches with hammocks, big windows, terra-cotta floors, and beds with rough-hewn wooden bedposts. Suites have tiny private swimming pools; junior suites have outdoor hot tubs and interior gardens. Since the road to the hotel is passable only by a four-wheel-drive vehicle, most guests fly in and are picked up at the Playa Carillo

airstrip. ⊠ *Below Playa Camaronal, south of Playa Carrillo,* ☎ *656–0470,* FAX *656–0473,* WEB *www.hotelpuntaislita.com (mailing address: Apdo. 242–1225, San José,* ☎ *231–6122,* FAX *232–2183). 15 bungalows, 4 villas, 11 suites. Restaurant, bar, cable TV, minibars, 2 pools, spa, driving range, 2 tennis courts, gym, horseback riding, beach, snorkeling, boating, fishing, mountain bikes, Internet, laundry service; no room phones. AE, DC, MC, V.*

THE SOUTHERN TIP: PUNTARENAS TO MALPAÍS

Catch a ferry from Puntarenas to the southern tip of the Nicoya Peninsula and you'll be just a bus hop away from gorgeous beaches with waterfalls and tidal pools galore. Within the region are two quiet, well-preserved national parks where you can explore caves and pristine forests or travel by boat or sea kayak to remote islands and wildlife preserves for bird-watching, snorkeling, diving, and even camping. Not too remote, and thus at times overcrowded, is Isla Tortuga, ringed by some of Costa Rica's most beautiful beaches. If you like to mix nightlife with your outdoor adventures, the town of Montezuma and its nearby beaches are very often jammed with an international cast of surfers, ecotourists, and misfits of all sorts, from practitioners of alternative lifestyles to expatriate American massage therapists living out their dreams.

Puntarenas

⓯ *95 km (59 mi) west of San José.*

The main reason to visit Puntarenas is to catch one of the ferries to the eastern coast of the Nicoya Peninsula. Five kilometers (three miles) beyond Esparza, a popular truck stop about 90 km (56 mi) northwest of San José on the Pan-American Highway is the turnoff to Puntarenas. This bustling commercial fishing center and docking point for international cruise ships sits on a narrow spit of sand protruding into the Gulf of Nicoya, with splendid views, especially at sunset, across to the peninsula. Because the ocean is somewhat polluted, most travelers stop here only to catch ferries to Playa Naranjo, Paquera, and Montezuma (pedestrians only) on the Nicoya Peninsula. Both the locals—called *Porteños*—and tourist police scoot around on bicycles, enjoying what must be the smoothest stretch of paved road in Costa Rica, the Paseo de Los Turistas.

Sidewalk lamps, concrete benches, and a modern, cruise ship dock for smaller vessels have also spruced up this wide beachfront promenade. On days when cruise ships arrive, local artisans sell their wares at a market near the dock. The town's grid-plan streets are lined with restaurants and markets, and the palm-lined beach is popular with day-trippers from San José (though the Ministry of Health warns against swimming here). On Saturday night the massive influx of urban weekenders presents a golden opportunity to watch the Costa Rican middle class at play.

The **Casa de la Cultura** (⊠ *3 blocks from Parque Central,* ☎ *661–1394*) has art exhibitions in its grand entrance hall. The brand-new **Museo Regional-Histórico Marino** (☎ *257–1433*) shares the same august building, a former port headquarters. Exhibits focus on the history of Puntarenas as Costa Rica's main coffee-shipping port and on marine ecology. It's free and open Tuesday to Sunday, 9:45 to 12:15 and 1 to 5:15.

OFF THE
BEATEN PATH

ISLA TORTUGA – Soft, bleached sand and casually leaning palms fringe Isla Tortuga, an island of tropical dry forest that makes a perfect day trip from Puntarenas, Montezuma, and other beach towns. Though state-owned, the island is leased and inhabited by a Costa Rican family who funded efforts to reintroduce such species as deer and wild pig to the island some years ago. A 40-minute hiking trail wanders past monkey ladders, strangler figs, bromeliads, orchids, and the fruit-bearing *guanabana* (soursop) and *marañón* (cashew) trees and goes up to a lookout point with tantalizing vistas. You can take a short canopy tour on the beach. Calypso Tours (✉ Avda. 2 between Cs. 1 and 3, ☎ 256–2727, FAX 256–6767, WEB www.calypsotours.com) in San José arranges transportation and tours here. ☎ *Hike $5, canopy tour $10.*

Dining and Lodging

$–$$$ ✕ **La Caravelle.** Red tablecloths and dark-blue walls adorned with antique musical instruments are unexpectedly elegant touches—but then so is a French restaurant across the street from the ocean. True to the French manner, the service is somewhat insouciant and offhand. The cooking concentrates on sauces: try the corvina *ostendaise* (with a lemon and white-wine cream sauce smothered in tiny shrimp) or fillet *con salsa oporto y hongos* (with a port-and-mushroom sauce). Less expensive choices include delicious, crispy fried chicken. The decent wine selection ranges from inexpensive to pricey. ✉ *Paseo de los Turistas, between Calles 21 and 23,* ☎ *661–2262. AE, MC, V. Closed Mon. No lunch Tues.*

$$$ 🏨 **Complejo Turistico Yadran.** This Croatian-owned hotel may be overstating its claim as a tourist complex, but its location within walking distance of the Paquera and Naranjo ferry docks makes it a good choice if you've missed the last ferry or want to catch the one at 5 AM. The pool is big enough to swim laps in and has a great gulf view. Rooms are on the utilitarian side but comfortable; most can sleep a carload of four comfortably. ✉ *West end of Paseo Los Turistas,* ☎ *661–2662,* FAX *661–1944. 42 rooms. 2 restaurants, in-room safes, cable TV, 2 pools, bicycles, casino, dance club, meeting room. AE, MC, V.*

$$$ 🏨 **Hotel Las Brisas.** This white, two-story motel-style building wraps around its pool, where the views of the sun setting over the Nicoya Peninsula are terrific. The hotel is across the street from the beach and not far from the ferry docks. Three of the simple rooms have balconies with views of the ocean; all are air-conditioned. The restaurant serves decent, Greek-influenced seafood and meat, and some Mexican dishes: a full breakfast is included. ✉ *West end of Paseo de los Turistas,* ☎ *661–4040,* FAX *661–2120,* WEB *www.puntarenas.com/brisashotel. 19 rooms. Restaurant, pool, cable TV, Internet, laundry service; no room phones. AE, MC, V.*

$$$ 🏨 **Hotel Porto Bello.** Porto Bello's main asset is its thickly planted garden next to the wide estuary north of town. Guest rooms are in white stucco bungalows with tile floors, zany patterned bedspreads, and verandas. Breakfast is included. ✉ *2 km (1½ mi) from downtown, 1 block north of main road,* ☎ *661–1322,* FAX *661–0036 (mailing address: Apdo. 108, Puntarenas). 35 rooms. Restaurant, bar, pool; no air-conditioning in some rooms, no room phones. AE, MC, V.*

$$$ 🏨 **Hotel Tioga.** The pastel green-and-yellow courtyard in this central hotel has the look of an ocean liner. Your best bets are the seven guest rooms upstairs, overlooking the gulf—they're decorated with colorful, tropical bedspreads and heavy, varnished dark-wood furniture. Each has a balcony, tile floor, and air-conditioning. The courtyard centers on a tiny pool with a *guachepelín* tree growing from the islet in its center. ✉ *Paseo de los Turistas, Apdo. 96–5400, Puntarenas,* ☎ *661–0271,*

FAX 661–0127, WEB *www.hoteltioga.com. 52 rooms. Restaurant, bar, pool, casino, laundry service. AE, MC, V.*

Playa Naranjo

16 *1½–2 hrs by ferry southwest of Puntarenas.*

Its undeserved reputation as a kind of nowheresville en route from Puntarenas to Montezuma and points west belies the fact that Playa Naranjo is actually the best access point for the islands in the Gulf of Nicoya, and there's some excellent hiking, mountain biking, and sea kayaking nearby. Inquire at the Hotel Oasis del Pacifico for trips. The beach is sand mixed with shell, adequate for swimming but not spectacular.

Most folks arrive by ferry from Puntarenas or by car from Nicoya. Paquera, 45 minutes southeast of Playa Naranjo, is the closest town with shops and bars and is also linked to Puntarenas by ferry. Heading north toward Nicoya, the road from Playa Naranjo (Highway 21) is paved, but it's rather badly potholed almost all the way. If you're considering drive around the tip of the peninsula, be prepared to spend a lot of time in the car over partly paved roads.

The private **Curú National Wildlife Refuge** (Refugio Nacional de Vida Silvestre Curú), established by former farmer and logger turned conservationist Federico Schutt in 1933, was given the indigenous name for the pochote and guanacaste trees that flourish here. Trails lead through the forest and high-salinity mangroves, where you'll see hordes of phantom crabs on the beach, howler and white-faced monkeys in the trees, and plenty of hummingbirds, kingfishers, woodpeckers, trogons, and manakins (including the coveted long-tailed). The refuge is working to reintroduce spider monkeys and scarlet macaws into the wild. Some very basic accommodations, originally designed for students and researchers, are available by the beach ($25 per person, including three meals and park admission); call ahead to arrange for lodging, guides, and early morning bird-watching walks. The staff also leads boat excursions to Isla Tortuga. To get here take a passenger boat or ferry from Puntarenas to Paquera, where you can catch a bus to the refuge. ⌧ *7 km (4½ mi) south of Paquera; south of the Paquera ferry dock,* ☎ *641–0590,* FAX *641–0060 (mailing address: Schutt family, Box 206, Puntarenas 5400).* ☒ *$5.* ☉ *Daily 7–4.*

Lodging

$$$ ☒ **Hotel Oasis del Pacifico.** Former ship's captain Lucky Wilhelm and his Singapore-born wife, Aggie, run this waterfront hotel, where there's an enticing fishing pier. The 20-year-old hotel shows its age a bit, but you won't care once you're lazing in your hammock catching the afternoon breeze off the gulf, on a sea-kayaking trip, or basking around the two big pools. Simple but comfortable rooms are in a white stucco building, each with its own hammock in front. The indoor-outdoor restaurant-bar does a fine job with all three meals. There is an extra charge for in-room air-conditioning. ⌧ *Last cove on the left as you approach the Playa Naranjo ferry dock,* ☎ *641–8092,* FAX *641–8091* WEB *www.costaricareisen.com/oasis (mailing address: Apdo. 200–5400, Puntarenas; mailing address: P. L. Wilhelm 1552, Box 025216, Miami, FL 33102-5216). 36 rooms. Restaurant, bar, pool, beach, dock, boating, Internet, laundry service; no room phones. AE, MC, V.*

Sea-Kayaking

Ríos Tropicales (☎ 233–6455), a respected San José–based adventure tour operator, runs three- and four-day sea-kayaking trips, which start from Curú National Wildlife Refuge and take you along the coast and among the barely inhabited islands of the Gulf of Nicoya. The professionally run camping and kayaking trips give kayakers at every level the opportunity to explore wild islands, wildlife reserves, and more. Expert natural guides explain the natural history of the region and teach kayak surfing.

Tambor

🔟 *20 km (14 mi) south of Curú National Wildlife Refuge, 27 km (17 mi) south of Paquera.*

In the back of the large half-moon Bahía Ballena, Tambor is undergoing a land-sale frenzy similar to that at Tamarindo—you can see a golf course and housing development from the road, and signs of further development all around them. The area's luxe resort hotels have gotten a lot of press, thanks to *Temptation Island*, which filmed episodes here. The resorts arrange plenty of activities, but you could break out on your own. The hike from Tambor around the Piedra Amarilla point to Tango Mar Resort is about 8 km (5 mi) long, and the trees along the way resound with the throaty utterings of male howler monkeys. You can fly to Tambor from San José.

Along a dusty road are interesting souvenir shops, a supermarket, a SANSA office, and an adventure-tour office as well as restaurants and hotels. **Cóbano,** 12 km (7½ mi) to the west, is a bustling crossroads with supermarkets, a bank, restaurants, shops, a gas station, and even an ice-cream parlor.

Lodging

$$$$ 🏨 **Barceló Playa Tambor & Casino.** This Spanish-owned mega-complex was one of Costa Rica's first all-inclusive resorts; the price includes all food, alcoholic drinks (local brands), and the use of sports equipment, including kayaks and catamarans. You can partake of lots of activities around the resort's grassy grounds and an almost endless buffet beside the lovely beach. But be prepared to share with up to 1,200 other guests during high season. The airy although fairly standard rooms have spacious bathrooms, hair dryers, and some have coffeemakers. ⊠ *South of Tambor village, on the main road,* ☎ *683–0303,* 𝖥𝖠𝖷 *683–0304,* 𝖶𝖤𝖡 *www. barcelo.com. 402 rooms. 2 restaurants, 3 bars, snack bar, cable TV, pool, hair salon, massage, 3 tennis courts, aerobics, casino, dance club, Internet, laundry service, travel services. AE, MC, V.*

$$$$ 🏨 **Tambor Tropical.** Perhaps you've seen this collection of five cabinas,
★ which surround a pool in the palm trees off Playa Tambor in Bahía Ballena, when it was featured on the TV series *Temptation Island*? The remarkable buildings are made from strips of local hardwoods arranged in attractive diagonal patterns. Each comfortable and spacious 93-square-m (1,000-square-ft) cabina has a living room, bedroom, bathroom with hot water, and fully equipped kitchen. Friendly staff members go out of their way to be helpful. ⊠ *Follow main street of Tambor toward water (hotel fronts beach),* ☎ *683–0011,* 𝖥𝖠𝖷 *683–0013,* 𝖶𝖤𝖡 *www. tambortropical.com (reservations: 867 Liberty St. NE, Box 12945, Salem, OR 97301,* ☎ *503/365–2872,* 𝖥𝖠𝖷 *503/371–2471). 10 rooms. Restaurant, bar, kitchens, pool, hot tub, horseback riding, beach, Internet; no air-conditioning, no room phones. AE, MC, V.*

$$$$ 🏨 **Tango Mar Resort.** Chosen as an ideal tropical location for the
★ *Temptation Island* TV series, this alluring hotel is perfect for the part, with palm-thatch cabins on stilts. They look rustic on the outside but are pure luxury inside. Rooms in the main hotel are luxurious, too, with private balconies and sea views; some have whirlpool baths. The

breezy Cristobal restaurant serves international cuisine and has an ocean view. On the grounds are a lushly landscaped, spring-fed pool, a spectacular beachfront waterfall, and an immaculate golf course. The hotel is fronted by a good surfing wave. ✉ *2 km (1 mi) west of Tambor (mailing address: Apdo. 1–1260, Escazú,* ☎ *683–0001; 289–9328 in San José,* FAX *683–0003,* WEB *www.tangomar.com). 6 villas, 18 rooms, 12 suites. 2 restaurants, 2 bars, in-room safes, cable TV, some kitchenettes, refrigerators, pool, some in-room hot tubs, 9-hole golf course, 2 tennis courts, hiking, horseback riding, beach, boating, fishing, Internet. AE, DC, MC, V.*

Montezuma

⓲ *7 km (4½ mi) southeast of Cóbano, 45 km (28 mi) south of Paquera.*

Montezuma is beautifully positioned on a sandy bay, hemmed in by a precipitous wooded shoreline. At the bottom of the hill, the funky town center is a pastel cluster of new-age health-food cafés, trendy beachwear shops, and jaunty tour kiosks mixed in with older Tico *sodas* (casual eateries) and noisy open-air bars. Montezuma has been on the international vagabond circuit for years, attracting surfers and alternative-lifestyle types, and some unsavory characters as well. But now you are as likely to meet older, outdoorsy European tourists as dreadlocked surfers.

The main attraction for everybody is the beach that stretches across one national park and two nature preserves to the north, leading to a spectacular beachfront waterfall. Just over a bridge, 10 minutes south of town, a slippery path patrolled by howler monkeys leads upstream to two waterfalls, the second one an impressive 33 m (108 ft) high with a thrilling **swimming hole.** Do not jump or dive from the waterfalls. There are no signs posting the danger and some young people inadvertently jumped to their deaths in 2002.

Dining and Lodging

$$ ✕ **Playa Los Artistas.** This creative open-air Italian restaurant on the beach specializes in Mediterranean recipes for fresh seafood. Driftwood tables, lamps, and other rustic touches provide a romantic yet casual atmosphere. Try the carpaccio *de atun,* a raw tuna appetizer seasoned with oregano and garlic. ✉ *300 yards south of town, just past Los Mangos Hotel,* ☎ *no phone. No credit cards. Closed Sun. No lunch.*

$ ✕ **Cafe Iguana.** This funky café, subtitled *La Esquina Dulce* (The Sweet Corner), serves up real Italian espresso, fresh fruit juices, and baked goods from 6 AM on. Check out the impressive selection of huge muffins and dessert breads, including such exotic flavors as mango and pineapple. The overstuffed sandwiches, made on fresh, crusty homebaked bread, are big enough for two. Wooden stools on a terrace make perfect perches for watching the passing parade of *todo el mundo* Montezuma. ✉ *Town center, Montezuma,* ☎ *no phone. No credit cards.*

$$$ 🏠 **Cabinas El Sano Banano.** This colony of eight tropical igloo-like cab-
★ ins huddles in the woods north of town close to the beach. Each cozy, domed bungalow sleeps two and has a refrigerator. A two-story building has three air-conditioned suites, with kitchens above, and three double rooms below. Adding to the Smurf-world fantasy is the pool, with curvy mounds that form a series of waterfalls. There is no restaurant, but it's just a 10-minute walk into town with its many food options. ✉ *On the beach, north of Montezuma, main road,* ☎ *642–0638,* FAX *642–0068,* WEB *www.elbanano.com. 3 rooms, 3 suites, 8 bungalows. Some kitchenettes, refrigerators, pool, hiking, beach, laundry service; no air-conditioning in some rooms; no room phones. AE, MC, V.*

$$$ 🏨 **Hotel El Jardín.** Climbing the hill above town, this Italian-owned hotel has panoramic ocean views. True to its name, the cabins are scattered around a garden lush with flowering gingers and populated by indigenous stone-sculpture people. Teak paneling and furniture, stained-glass pictorial panels, and terraces with hammocks give this hotel style as well as comfort. ⊠ *Main road, entering Montezuma,* ☎ *642–0548,* FAX *642–0074,* WEB *www.hoteleljardin.com. 15 rooms, 2 houses with kitchens. Fans, refrigerators; no air-conditioning in some rooms, no room phones. No credit cards.*

$$$ 🏨 **Nature Lodge Finca Los Caballos.** A spirited Canadian woman runs
★ this charming, small hotel high on a hill. The open-air restaurant and reception area both have bird's-eye views of ocean and valley below. Designed with a southwestern U.S. motif, the rooms have pastel walls decorated with stencils of lizards and frogs. A two-bedroom bungalow, formerly the owner's house, is set apart from the hotel and accommodates up to four. The owner leads wonderful horseback tours and often invites guests to accompany her to rodeos. ⊠ *3 km (2 mi) north of Montezuma,* ☎ FAX *642–0124,* WEB *www.naturelodge.net (mailing address: Apdo. 22, Cóbano de Puntarenas). 7 rooms, 1 bungalow. Restaurant, fans, pool, horseback riding; no air-conditioning, no room phones. AE, MC, V.*

$$–$$$ 🏨 **Hotel Amor de Mar.** Take the time to walk 10 minutes south of town
★ to find this ruggedly handsome, two-story natural-wood hotel surrounded by trees and a grassy lawn stretching to the ocean. Great breakfasts and immediate access to the waterfall hike make this perhaps the finest little hotel in Montezuma. The rooms, with wood paneling, are comfortable and simply furnished. The dining room serves breakfast and lunch only. ⊠ *South of town on beach road,* ☎ FAX *642–0262,* WEB *www.amordemar.com. 11 rooms, 9 with bath. Dining room, beach, laundry service; no air-conditioning, no room phones. V.*

$$ ✕🏨 **El Sano Banano Restaurant and B&B.** Montezuma's original nat-
★ ural-food source has grown more sophisticated and now includes fish and chicken on its healthful but delicious menu. It's hard to believe that the sinfully rich-tasting chocolate mousse tart is made with tofu. A battalion of ceiling fans keeps the air moving in the renovated, spacious, adobe-style restaurant. It's open for breakfast from 7 AM but if you come for dinner around 7:30 PM, you can take in a nightly free movie. Attached to the restaurant is a new B&B annex, with air-conditioned rooms decorated in Mexican style with private baths for $50 a night. ⊠ *Main road, Montezuma,* ☎ *642–0638,* FAX *642–0068,* WEB *www.elbanano.com. 3 rooms, 3 suites, 8 bungalows. Restaurant, cable TV, pool, Internet. AE, MC, V.*

Malpaís

➒ *12 km (7½ mi) southwest of Cóbano, 52 km (33 mi) south of Paquera*

Until recently Malpaís was considered a remote preserve frequented by die-hard surfers in search of some of the country's largest waves and naturalists en route to the nearby Cabo Blanco Nature Preserve. Since the town and its miles of beach are accessible down a steep gravel road, it was likely that this reputation might remain the case. As in much of this coastal area, however, hotels and restaurants are now springing up at both ends of the populated part of the beach.

Surfing is best at Playa Santa Teresa, the sandy north end of this long stretch of beach. The more southerly Malpaís end of the beach is rockier but interesting for its tide pools and beachcombing. The crowd here is fairly young, with tanned-and-buff surfers walking or bicycling their boards to wherever the surf is up. But, increasingly, there's also an older, upscale visitor drawn to the tranquility of new luxury retreats.

Cabo Blanco Nature Preserve (Reserva Natural Absoluta Cabo Blanco). Conquistadors named this area Cabo Blanco on account of its white earth and cliffs, but it was a more benevolent pair of foreigners—Nils Olof Wessberg and his wife, Karen, who arrived here from Sweden in 1950—who made it a preserve. Appalled by the first clear-cut in the Cabo Blanco area in 1960, the couple launched a pioneering and international appeal to save the forest. In time, their efforts led not only to the creation of the 12-square-km (4½-square-mi) reserve but also to the founding of Costa Rica's national park service. Olof Wessberg was murdered on the Osa Peninsula in 1975 while researching the area's potential as a national park.

The tropical moist forest has a combination of evergreen species and lush greenery. Look for the sapodilla tress, which produce a white latex used to make gum; you'll often see V-shape scars where the trees have been cut to allow the latex to run into containers placed at the base. Olof Wessberg cataloged a full array of animals here: porcupine, hognosed skunk, spotted skunk, gray fox, anteater, cougar, and jaguar. Resident birds include coastal pelicans, white-throated magpies, toucans, cattle egrets, green herons, parrots, and turquoise-browed motmots. A fairly strenuous 4-km (2½-mi) hike, which takes about two hours in each direction, follows a trail from the reserve entrance to **Playa Cabo Blanco.** The beach is magnificent, with hundreds of pelicans flying in formation and paddling in the calm waters offshore—you can wade right in and join them. Off the tip of the cape is the 697 square-m (7,511-square-ft) **Isla Cabo Blanco**, with pelicans, frigate birds, brown boobies, and an abandoned lighthouse. As a strict reserve, Cabo Blanco has bathrooms and a visitor center but no other tourist facilities. Rangers and volunteers will act as guides. ⊠ *10 km (6 mi) southwest of Montezuma, about 7 km (4½ mi) south of Malpaís,* ☎ *642–0093.* 🖙 *$6.* ⊘ *Daily 8–4.*

Lodging

$$$$ 🏨 **Hotel Flor Blanco.** Named for the white flowers of the frangipani trees that shade the beachfront property, this luxurious collection of 10 villas is designed to minister to body and soul. Each villa has a fridge and a breakfast bar area, an outdoor Balinese bathroom, and a sunken tub. There's an open-air dojo for karate and yoga, a masseuse, and an art studio with a pottery wheel and kiln. Two landscaped pools flow into each other in front of the alfresco restaurant. Owners Susan Money and Greg Mullins, famous for creating the Sueño del Mar B&B in Playa Langosta, continue to serve their complementary lavish breakfasts here, as well as four-course dinners (not included). ⊠ *2 km (1 ¼ mi) north of Santa Teresa,* ☎ FAX *640–0232. 7 one-bedroom villas, 3 two-bedroom villas. Restaurant, refrigerators, 2 pools, massage, exercise equipment, hiking, beach, snorkeling, surfing, fishing, Internet. MC, V.*

$$$$ 🏨 **Milarepa.** Created by two Parisians searching for a tropical Shangri-
★ la, Milarepa is a perfect place for renewal, whether romantic or spiritual. The four bamboo houses are spaced apart to insure privacy and are furnished in ascetic but exquisite taste, with carved Indonesian wooden beds, draped with mosquito netting, and bamboo armoires. Bathrooms are open to the sky, with alcoves for Buddhist deities. Each cottage has a veranda looking out onto the carefully raked white beach, shaded by a grove of palms. The restaurant is *trés français*; try the salade niçoise. ⊠ *Turn right at the Malpaís crossroads to Playa Santa Teresa,* ☎ *640–0023,* FAX *640–0168 (mailing address: Apdo 49-5361 Cóbano, Puntare-*

nas). 4 cottages. Restaurant, fans, pool, hiking, horseback riding, snorkeling, surfing, fishing; no air-conditioning, no room phones. V.

$$$ 🔟 **Blue Jay Lodge.** Here's your chance to live in a tree house. The wooden cabins, with only screens for walls (on three sides), are built on stilts. Steep stairs lead up the recently reforested mountainside to these aeries with hot-water showers, which are open to nature on one side. Ceiling fans keep the air moving but warm blankets lay at hand for cool, breezy nights. Breakfast is included at the wooden-terrace restaurant back at ground level. From here it's a short walk to the beach, or you can climb the mountain to look for birds, howler monkeys, and armadillos. ⊠ *South at the main Malpaís crossroads,* ☎ *640–0089,* ℻ *640–0141,* 🕸 *www. bluejaylodgecostarica.com. 7 cabins. Restaurant, bar, laundry service; no air-conditioning, no room phones. V.*

NICOYA AND
THE TEMPISQUE RIVER PARKS

This northeastern section of the peninsula encompasses the parks in and around the Río Tempisque basin—prime places to watch birds and other wildlife—and Nicoya, the commercial and political hub of the northern Nicoya Peninsula. By road, Nicoya provides the best access to the central coastal beach towns, and is also linked by a smooth, well-paved road to the artisan communities of Santa Cruz and Guaitíl, to the northern Nicoya beach towns, and to Playa Naranjo and the southern peninsula by way of Carmona.

At press time, a $26.9–million bridge, built with funds from the Taiwanese government, was scheduled for completion in late 2002, crossing the Río Tempisque just above the present ferry crossing and Puerto Moreno. The Taiwan Friendship Bridge will eliminate the often-long wait for the ferry and speed travelers to points west and south. For the bridge, head north from San José on the Pan-American Highway, turn left about 48 km (30 mi) north of the Puntarenas turnoff, and drive about 25 km (16 mi) farther.

Palo Verde National Park and
Lomas Barbudal Biological Reserve

⓴ *Palo Verde is 28 km (17 mi) southwest of Bagaces; Lomas Barbudal is 20 km (12 mi) southwest of Bagaces.*

Bordered on the west by the Río Tempisque, these wildlife preserves protect a significant amount of deciduous dry forest. Verde extends over 95 square km (36½ square mi) of mainly flat terrain and its main attraction is bird-watching. Its swampland is a temporary home for thousands of migratory birds toward the end of the rainy season. From December through March a raised platform near the ranger station, about 8 km (5 mi) past the park entrance, helps you to see dozens of species of aquatic birds, including herons, ducks, wood storks, and elegant roseate spoonbills.

Camping, rustic dormitory facilities ($10), and meals ($5 for lunch or dinner) can be arranged through the park headquarters or through the **Organization for Tropical Studies** (☎ 240–6696, www.ots.ac.cr) in San José, although most visit on a tour.

If you're driving here, continue north of the Puntarenas turnoff on the Pan-American Highway for 42 km (26 mi) and turn left at the gas station in Bagaces, 15 km (9 mi) north of Cañas, which will lead you, on a fairly rough road, to the Lomas Barbudal Biological Reserve (after

15 km [9 mi]) and the adjacent Palo Verde National Park (after 35 km [22 mi]). ⊠ *Park headquarters, 8 km (5 mi) beyond the park entrance,* ☎ *671–1062.* 🎫 *$6.* ⊙ *Daily 8–4.*

From the Puerto Moreno area where the car ferry has traditionally crossed, you can hire a guided motorboat to take you north up the river into Palo Verde park for a closer look at **Isla Pajaros** (Bird Island), home to thousands of migratory and local birds from January to March. Boats are to the right of the ferry dock as you disembark. The trip takes roughly 45 to 60 minutes; the price is negotiable, but expect to pay around $50. The hefty price is worth it, since you might see alligators, howler monkeys, and other wildlife on the way to the birds themselves. Wear waterproof clothing—the river ride can be windy, bumpy, and wet.

Outdoor Activities and Sports

CATA Tours (☎ 674-0180) runs wildlife and bird-watching boating adventures down the Río Bebedero into Palo Verde from a starting point on the Pan-American Highway north of Cañas. The low-action adventure trips led by **Safaris Corobici** (☎ FAX 669–6191) on the Río Corobicí cover some of the same wildlife-rich territory not far from Palo Verde and Lomas Barbudal; follow signs from the highway to Km 193.

Barra Honda National Park

㉑ *6 km (4 mi) west of Puerto Moreno.*

The limestone ridge rising from the surrounding savanna was once thought to be a volcano but was later found to contain an intricate network of caves, formed as a result of erosion once the ridge had emerged from beneath the sea. Some caves on the almost 23 square km (9 square mi) park remain unexplored, and they're home to surprisingly abundant animal life, including bats, birds, blindfish, salamanders, and snails.

Every day in the dry season, from 8 AM to 1 PM, local guides will take you down a 20-m (67-ft) flexible aluminum ladder to the **Terciopelo Cave,** which shelters unusual formations shaped like fried eggs, popcorn, and shark's teeth, as well as sonorous columns collectively known as the organ. The guides will have you wear a harness and be attached to a rope for safety. The tour costs $25, in addition to the park admission. Travel companies no longer take tourists or speleologists deeper underground. Don't attempt to visit the caves unless accompanied by a guide authorized by the local community development association.

You can climb **Barra Honda peak**, 361 m (1,184 ft) high, from the northwest (the southern wall is almost vertical): follow the 3-km (2-mi) Los Laureles trail. From the summit you have fantastic views sweeping across the islet-filled Gulf of Nicoya. The surface is pocked with orifices and white rocks eroded into odd shapes, and some of the ground feels dangerously hollow. Surface wildlife includes howler monkeys, skunks, coatis, parakeets, and iguanas, and the relatively open, deciduous-forest vegetation makes viewing the fauna easy.

The two- to three-hour **Cascada Trail** begins near the ranger station, on the eastern side of the park, and makes a loop near the caves. Hikers must be accompanied by local guides. The park has camping facilities; a community tourism association provides guides and runs a simple, inexpensive restaurant and lodge, Las Delicias, by the park entrance. ☎ *686–6760.* 🎫 *$6.* ⊙ *Daily 8–4.*

Nicoya

㉒ *30 km (19 mi) west of Puerto Moreno.*

Though often referred to as Guanacaste's colonial capital, Nicoya is a typical provincial town, with a pleasant, shady central park where you can get a taste of everyday small-town life. The Chorotegan chief Nicoya greeted the Spanish conquistadors upon their arrival here in 1523, and many of his people were converted to Catholicism. Nicoya's only colonial landmark is the impressive, whitewashed 16th-century church of San Blas in the central park, inside of which a museum displays silver, bronze, and copper objects from pre-Columbian times. A Chinese population, descendants of 19th-century railroad workers, gives the place a certain cosmopolitan air, manifested in part by numerous Chinese restaurants. If you're heading to Tamarindo, consider a stop in Santa Cruz, a small town known for its arts festival, or in Guaitil for pottery shopping.

Dining and Lodging

$–$$ ✕ **Restaurant Nicoya.** There are many Chinese restaurants from which to choose in Nicoya. This one has an interesting room with hanging lanterns, a colorful collection of international flags, and a large menu with 85 Asian dishes, such as stir-fried beef with vegetables, and some international favorites, like fried chicken. The fresh sea bass sautéed with fresh pineapple, *chayote* squash, and red peppers is excellent. ✉ *Main road, 75 yards south of the Coopmani building,* ☎ *685–5113. No credit cards.*

$ ✕ **Café Daniela.** For baked goods and light lunches, including hamburgers and sandwiches, try this small, casual restaurant. The pizzas are Costa Rican style, with very little tomato sauce. The television in the dining room is usually tuned to a soccer game. ✉ *Main road, 75 yards south of the Coopmani building,* ☎ *686–6148. No credit cards.*

$$$ ▥ **Hotel Curime.** While the old hotel is undergoing many improvements (and new ownership by the Best Western chain) the tranquil, tree-shaded setting beside a stream can't be improved upon—well, at least not in the area. The large, comfortable rooms are in citrus-color, adobe-style buildings arranged around a mango-bordered soccer field, a great place for kids to let off steam. The huge swimming pool allows for serious laps. The open-air restaurant is a little spare, but the view of the pool and the mature gardens makes up for it. ✉ *On the road to Sámara, ½ km (¼ mi) south of town,* ☎ *685–5238,* ꜰᴀx *685–5530. 27 rooms. Restaurant, in-room safes, cable TV, some refrigerators, pool, horseback riding, volleyball, playground, meeting room; no room phones. AE, MC, V.*

$$ ▥ **Cabinas Río Tempisque de Lujo.** These rooms are luxurious by any
★ standards, but on the road to Santa Cruz they are a marvel. The owner is in the hardware business and the hotel teems with quality materials inside and out. Rooms have high wooden ceilings, big picture windows, and tasteful curtains and bedspreads. The huge, white-tiled bathrooms have mirrored closets and showers big enough for two. The gardens and pool area are beautifully landscaped. There is no restaurant but rooms have a coffeemaker and a fridge stocked with juice and soft drinks. ✉ *On the highway north to Santa Cruz, just outside Nicoya,* ☎ *686–6650. 30 rooms. Cable TV, refrigerators, pool; no room phones. MC, V.*

$ ▥ **Las Tinajas** This simple, clean hotel has a friendly staff and is the best of Nicoya's budget accommodations. The rooms, which have private bathrooms and cold water only, have white walls and wooden or tile floors. An outdoor café in back, from which you can watch strutting chickens in the neighbor's yard, is good for breakfast. ✉ *100 yards* *south of central park's southeast corner, 50 yards east of Banco Central,* ☎ FAX *685–5081. 28 rooms. Fans; no room phones. V.*

Shopping

In the country village of **Guaitil** (24 km [15 mi] north of Nicoya), artists—most of them women—have revived a vanishing tradition by producing clay pottery handmade in the manner of pre-Columbian Chorotegans. The town square is a soccer field, and almost every house facing it has a pottery shop out front and a round, wood-fired kiln in back. Pottery designs range from imitation Mexican to inspired Cubist abstractions. Every artisan's style is different, so take the time to wander from shop to shop. Prices are very reasonable, and although the pieces are rumored to crack rather too easily, they make wonderful keepsakes and gifts if you can get them home in one piece.

THE NICOYA PENINSULA A TO Z

To research prices, get advice from other travelers, and book travel arrangements, visit www.fodors.com.

AIR TRAVEL

Liberia has a tiny international airport, Aeropuerto Internacional Daniel Oduber. Small airstrips (and sometimes an adjacent building or shelter) are in Tamarindo, Playa Carrillo, Punta Islita, Nosara, and Tambor.

CARRIERS

SANSA flies daily from Juan Santamaría International Airport to Tamarindo, Tambor, Playa Carrillo, Punta Islita, and Nosara. Travelair leaves from Aeropuerto Internacional Tobías Bolaños in Tibás, a northern suburb of San José, to fly to Liberia, Tamarindo, Playa Carrillo, Punta Islita, and Tambor.

➤ AIRLINES AND CONTACTS: **Aeropuerto Internacional Daniel Oduber** (☎ 668–1032 or 296–0909, Liberia). **SANSA** (☎ 296–0909 Liberia airport, FAX 666–1017; 656–0131 in Sámara; 682–0168 in Nosara; ☎ 653–0012 in Tamarindo; 683–0015 in Tambor; WEB www.flysansa.com). **Travelair** (✉ Apdo. 8–4920, ☎ 220–3054, FAX 220–0413, WEB www.travelair-costarica.com).

BOAT AND FERRY TRAVEL

At press time it was unclear how the Taiwan Friendship Bridge will affect the river's passenger-and-car ferry routes at Puerto Moreno.

Car ferries run by Naviera Tambor and the Asociación de Desarrollo Integral Paquera (formerly Ferry Peninsula) connect Puntarenas with Paquera, with continuing bus service to Montezuma. The trip takes 1¼-hours and the car ferries leave six times daily, between 5 AM and 8:15 PM, with an equal number of return trips. The Puntarenas–Playa Naranjo car ferry, run by Cooantramar, takes 1½ hours, departing daily at 3:15, 7, and 10:50 AM and 2:50 and 7 PM.

A passenger-only *lancha* (launch), run by the Asociación de Desarrollo Integral de Paquera, leaves Puntarenas for Paquera three times daily, at 6 and 11 AM and 3:15 PM, from a hard-to-find small dock just west of the Banco Nacional near the market. On the Paquera side, launches leave for Puntarenas on the same schedule. Bus links and cabs are available at the Nicoya end of the ferry lines.

Note that these schedules are subject to change between the high and low seasons and during holidays. Expect long waits on all car ferries in high season and holiday weekends. To avoid a longer than necessary wait and to get up-to-the-minute schedules, always call ahead.

➤ BOAT AND FERRY INFORMATION: **Asociación de Desarrollo Integral de Paquera (formerly Ferry Peninsula)** [car ferry and passenger-only launch between Puntarenas and Paquera], ☎ 641–0118 or 641–0515. **Coonatramar** (car ferry to Playa Naranjo, ☎ 661–1069). **Naviera Tambor** (car ferry to Paquera, run by Barceló hotel company, ☎ 661–2084).

BUS TRAVEL TO AND FROM THE NICOYA PENINSULA

Bus service connects the larger cities to each other and to the more popular beaches, but forget about catching a bus from beach to beach; you'll generally have to backtrack to the inland hubs of Nicoya and Liberia unless you take a minibus, which may take just a long as a bus, although it should be more comfortable. Bus companies rarely answer their phones and the schedules are always changing, so if accurate information is important to you, it's best to ask at the stations in San José. Your hotel front desk should be able to confirm which station specific buses and lines depart from.

The buses here range from plush coaches to dirty old rattletraps, and there is no way of knowing which will be your fate until you get on the bus. During busy times, they add the worst buses. Only some have air-conditioning.

With the new bridge across the Río Tempisque, bus routes and schedules to some Nicoya beach destinations may change radically. Your best bet is to check with the main ICT tourist office beneath the Plaza de la Cultura in San José. They keep a list of bus schedules.

LIBERIA AND NORTHERN COAST ROUTES

From Calle 24 between Avenidas 5 and 7, Pulmitan buses leave San José daily hourly, 6 AM–8 PM for the 4-hour trip to Liberia, and leave twice daily at 8 AM and 2 PM for the 5-hour trip to Playa del Coco. Empresa Esquivel buses from Liberia leave daily for Playa Hermosa and Panamá at 4:45, 6:30, 7:30 and 11:30 AM and 1, 3:30, and 5:30 PM. Five-hour buses for Brasilito and Playa Flamingo run by Tralapa leave San José daily from Calle 20 between Avenidas 3 and 5 at 8 and 11 AM and 3 PM. For Tamarindo, a 5½-hour trip, buses run by Empresa Alfaro leave daily at 6 AM and 3:30 PM from Calle 14 at Avenida 5.

CENTRAL AND SOUTHERN COAST ROUTES

Empresa Alfaro buses run from San José (C. 14 between Avdas. 3 and 5) to Nicoya daily, via Liberia, at 6:30 AM, 10 AM, 1:30 PM, 3 PM, and 5 PM, a 5-hour trip; to Nosara daily at 6 AM, a 6-hour trip; and to Sámara daily at 12:30 PM, a 5-hour trip.

Tralapa runs a daily bus from San José to Junquillal at 2 PM from Calle 20, Avda. 3, taking 51//2 hours. There's also a daily bus from Santa Cruz to Junquillal.

Empresa Rojas buses leave Nicoya for Nosara, Garza, and Guiones daily at 10 AM and 2 PM; the same line runs from Nicoya to Samara, Monday–Friday at 6 and 10 AM, noon, 3 and 4:15 PM, and to Carrillo from Nicoya at 3 PM.

Empresarios Unidos buses leave for the 2 ½-hour trip from San José (C. 16 between Avdas. 10 and 12) to Puntarenas daily every half hour, 6 AM–7 PM. Buses currently run to Montezuma from Paquera, via Cóbano, six times daily between 6:15 AM and 6:15 PM, returning six times between 5:30 AM and 4:30 PM; but inquire about the latest schedule for this route before you set off. Buses to Malpaís run daily from Cóbano at 10:30 AM and 2:30 PM.

MINIBUS ROUTES

For $21, you can ride on the comfortable, air-conditioned Greyline Fantasy Tours minibuses that connect San Jose, Liberia, Playa Flamingo, Playa Hermosa, Tamarindo, and other destinations in Guanacaste. The Greyline bus from San José to Tamarindo and Liberia begins picking up passengers from hotels daily around 6 AM. The return bus leaves Tamarindo around 2 PM and passes through Liberia around 3:30 PM.

➤ Bus Information: **Empresa Alfaro** (☎ 222–2666 or 685–5032 in Nicoya). **Empresa Esquivel** (☎ 666–0042). **Empresarios Unidos** (☎ 222–1867). **Empresa Rojas** (☎ 685–5352). **Greyline Fantasy Tours** (☎ 223–4650). **Pulmitan** (☎ 222–1650). **Tralapa** (☎ 223–5859 or 680–0392).

CAR RENTAL

It's best to stick with the main rental offices in San José because they have more cars available and you're more likely to reach an English-speaking agent on the phone; some have local satellite offices. There are also a few local rental agencies. Alamo offers pickup and car delivery in Liberia. Budget has branches in San José and also 6 km (4 mi) west of Liberia's airport. Economy and Alamo now offers cars in Tamarindo. Elegante also offers cars in Tamarindo. Sol Rentacar is in front of Hotel El Bramadero in Liberia.

➤ International Agencies: **Alamo** (✉ 2 km [1.2 mi]) north of the Liberia airport, Liberia, ☎ 668–1111 or 800/462–5266; Hotel Diría, Tamarindo, ☎ 653–0727 or 653–0357). **Budget** (✉ 6 km [4 mi]) southwest of Liberia airport, Liberia, ☎ 668–1024 or 668–1126; Tamarindo Vista Villas Hotel, Tamarindo, ☎ 653–0829). **Economy** (✉ 5 km [3 mi] south of Liberia on road to airport, Liberia, ☎ 666–2816 or 666–7560; on the main road entering Tamarindo, across from Restaurant Coconut, Tamarindo, ☎ 653–0728).

➤ Local Agencies: **Elegante** (✉ C. 10 between Avdas. 13 and 15, San José, ☎ 257–0026). **Sol Rentacar** (✉ Liberia, ☎ 666–2222).

CAR TRAVEL

The northwest is accessed via the paved two-lane Pan-American Highway (CA1), which begins at the top of Paseo Colón in San José. The new bridge across the Río Tempisque, scheduled to open in late 2002 or early 2003, should cut down travel time considerably to the Pacific beaches south of Liberia. Ferries will continue to run from Puntarenas to Paquera and Playa Naranjo for access to destinations on the Gulf of Nicoya side of the peninsula.

Paved roads run down the spine of the Nicoya Peninsula all the way to Playa Naranjo, with just a few unpaved and potholed stretches. Once you get off the main highway, the pavement holds out only so far, and then dirt, dust, mud, potholes, and other factors come into play. The roads to Playa Sámara and Playa del Coco are paved all the way; every other destination requires some dirt-road maneuvering. If you're headed down to the coast via unpaved roads, be sure to get advance information on road conditions. Take a four-wheel-drive vehicle if possible.

If you want to drive be prepared to spend some serious time in the car. The road to Nicoya's southern tip is partly paved and partly just gravel, and it winds up and down and around various bays. Some roads leading from Liberia to the coast are intermittently paved. As you work your way toward the coast, pay close attention to the assorted hotel signs at intersections—they may be the only indicators of which roads to take to your lodging.

EMERGENCIES
In case of any emergency, dial 911, or one of the specific numbers below.
➤ EMERGENCY SERVICES: **Fire** (☎ 118). **Police** (☎ 118). **Red Cross Ambulance** (☎ 128).

TOURS
In addition to the following major agencies, most hotels can organize guided tours for you.

Ríos Tropicales, a high-quality adventure tour company, runs excellent multiday sea-kayaking trips that leave from Curú National Wildlife Refuge and meander among the islands of the Gulf of Nicoya. The company also leads river-rafting trips throughout the country and a float trip for bird-watchers down Guanacaste's Río Corobicí. Day trips to the idyllic Isla Tortuga in the Gulf of Nicoya are very popular, and Calypso Tours has been leading them longer than anyone else. The excellent Horizontes specializes in more independent tours with as few as eight people, including four-wheel-drive transport, naturalist guides, and guest lecturers.
➤ TOUR COMPANIES: **Calypso Tours** (✉ Avda. 2 between Cs. 1 and 3, San José, ☎ 256–2727, FAX 256–6767, WEB www.calypsotours.com). **Horizontes** (✉ 150 yards north of Pizza Hut Paseo Colón, San José, ☎ 222–2022, FAX 255–4513, WEB www.horizontes.com). **Ríos Tropicales** (✉ 50 yards south of the Centro Colón on Calle 38 in San José, ☎ FAX 233–6455, WEB www.riostropicales.com).

VISITOR INFORMATION
The tourist office in San José has information on Guanacaste and the peninsula. As a cruise ship and ferry port, Puntarenas has two tourist offices. In Liberia, three blocks south of Parque Central, the Casa de la Cultura also has local tourist information.
➤ TOURIST INFORMATION: **La Camera de Turismo** (✉ Plaza de las Artesanias, in front of the Muelle de Cruceros, Puntarenas, ☎ 661–2980) is open weekdays 8–noon and 2–5, and weekends when cruise ships are in port. **La Casa de la Cultura** (✉ 3 blocks south of the central park, Liberia, ☎ 665–0135) is open weekdays 8–noon and 1:30–5, and Saturday 8–noon and 1:30–4. **La Oficina de Información Turistica** (☎ 661–9011), near the car ferry terminal, also provides information daily 8–7:30.

6 THE CENTRAL PACIFIC COAST

It doesn't cover much ground, but Costa Rica's central Pacific coast has disproportionate natural assets. Playas Jacó, Hermosa, and Manuel Antonio promise sparkling surf and sunbaked sand, while rare and beautiful wildlife species reside in the Carara Biological Reserve and Manuel Antonio National Park. And since it's so close to San José, this region lets you get quickly down to the business of rest and relaxation.

WITH THE ATTRACTIONS THAT PROBABLY DREW YOU to Costa Rica—lush tropical forests, palm-lined beaches, and hospitable terrain for an array of outdoor activities—

Updated by
Gregory
Benchwick

there's really no need to explain why this coastal area has become so popular. The area's verdant hills, crashing surf, and soft sand beaches combine to provide a veritable cornucopia of vacation opportunities. The region—and the Carara Biological Reserve in particular—is a transition zone between the tropical dry forests of the northwest and the wet forests of the Pacific coast farther south. Since most of its woodlands were cut years ago, however, the central Pacific landscape is dominated by steep coffee farms, vast oil-palm plantations, and rolling green pastures ideal for horseback riding. Manuel Antonio National Park protects an indented stretch of coastal rain forest and idyllic white-sand beaches. Despite the fact that the region's protected areas are among the smallest in the country, they are vibrant habitats with an amazing variety of flora and fauna, including such endangered species as the scarlet macaw and the Central American squirrel monkey. Decent snorkeling and world-class sportfishing are paramount in Playas Jacó and Manuel Antonio, thanks to abundant marine life. Ideal conditions for surfing, sea-kayaking, horseback riding, rafting, hiking, and bird-watching also abound—all within just 160 km (100 mi) of San José.

Pleasures and Pastimes

Dining

Restaurants in Manuel Antonio and Jacó serve some of Costa Rica's best meals, from upscale Pacific Rim flavors to traditional Continental fare. They haven't cornered the dining market, however; a number of isolated lodges also serve delicious local food. Thanks to world-class fishing, seafood—from fresh-caught dorado and yellowfin tuna to crustaceans—is the forte of the area's best chefs.

CATEGORY	COST*
$$$$	over $20
$$$	$10–$20
$$	$5–$10
$	under $5

*per person for main course at dinner.

Lodging

Manuel Antonio has some of the priciest lodgings in the country, charging more than $150 for a double during high season, but places in nearby Quepos rent rooms at backpackers' rates, and plenty of the area's inns fall between the two extremes. As a rule, prices drop 20%–30% during low season.

CATEGORY	COST*
$$$$	over $90
$$$	$50–$90
$$	$25–$50
$	under $25

*for a double room, excluding service and tax (16.4%)

Nightlife

Jacó has the region's most lively nightlife, with slews of *Josefinos* (residents of San José) rolling into town every weekend. Around Quepos and Manuel Antonio you'll also find a fairly lively nightlife scene, the latter tending toward the upscale with Quepos offering Hemingway-esque, islands-in-the-stream type of dives.

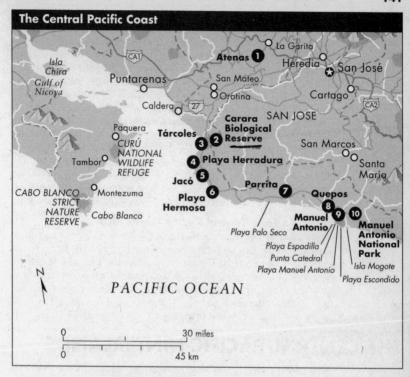

The Central Pacific Coast

PACIFIC OCEAN

0 — 30 miles
0 — 45 km

Outdoor Adventures

Several white-water rivers —Ríos Parrita, Naranjo, and the less accessible Savegre—flow northeast from the Cordillera de Talamanca chain, allowing for great Class III and IV rafting during and just after the rainy season. Want to stay on land? You can ride horseback just about everywhere. Skin-diving is good in the Manuel Antonio area, and the offshore sportfishing is among the best in the world. Other options include surfing and sea-kayaking. Local ocean excursions range from waverunner tours to dolphin-watching sunset cruises.

Exploring Central Pacific Costa Rica

Attractions lie conveniently close to each other, making it easy to combine beach time with forest exploration or country living with marine diversions. Every destination in this chapter is between two and four hours from San José by road. A winding mountain road passes through Atenas on the way to Orotina, from where the coastal highway, or Costanera, heads southeast to Tárcoles, Jacó, Playa Hermosa, and Quepos. The flight from San José to Quepos is speedy, a mere half hour.

Numbers in the text correspond to numbers in the margin and on the Central Pacific Costa Rica map.

Great Itineraries

IF YOU HAVE 3 DAYS

Fly directly to ⊡ **Quepos** ⑧ and hit the beach at ⊡ **Manuel Antonio** ⑨. If you're driving from San José, be sure to stop at **Carara Biological Reserve** ② on your way to Manuel Antonio. Rise early the next day to spend the morning exploring **Manuel Antonio National Park** ⑩, and spend the afternoon horseback riding or relaxing on the beach. Dedicate the third morning to white-water rafting, skin-diving, or taking another tour; then catch an afternoon flight back to San José.

IF YOU HAVE 6 DAYS

Spend your first night at one of the lodges near the ⊞ **Carara Biological Reserve** ②, enjoying horseback riding, rafting, and bird-watching from the beautiful trails. On the second morning, head to either ⊞ **Tárcoles** ③, ⊞ **Jacó** ⑤, or ⊞ **Playa Hermosa** ⑥ to get your beach or surfing fix. You'll want to spend another night here to get into the smooth rhythm of relaxation. On day four, go south to ⊞ **Manuel Antonio** ⑨ and spend the day fishing, skin-diving, rafting, horseback riding, or lounging on the beach. Visit **Manuel Antonio National Park** ⑩ early on day five; then drive back into the mountains to spend your last night in **Atenas** ①, just 40 minutes from the international airport. Alternately, since Quepos and Manuel Antonio have so much to offer, fly straight there and stay put. If you want more remote conditions, spend two days in the Manuel Antonio area and head south to the Osa Peninsula for the last three days, catching a flight from Golfito back to San José.

When to Tour Central Pacific Costa Rica

The weather in the central Pacific region follows the same dry- and rainy-season weather patterns common to the rest of the Pacific slope, which means lots of sun from December to May and frequent rain from September to November. Since you'll have to share the area with other travelers in the dry season, consider touring the region at another time. The weather tends to be perfect in July and August, with lots of sunny days and occasional light rain.

THE CENTRAL PACIFIC HINTERLANDS

Beaches may be this region's biggest draw, but the countryside hides vast haciendas interspersed with patches of tropical wilderness where you might encounter any critter from the capuchin monkey to the collared aracarito crocodiles lurking amid the estuaries' mangroves. Because it's an ecological transition zone, the region is extremely diverse biologically, making it a boon for bird-watchers and other wildlife enthusiasts.

Atenas

❶ *42 km (26 mi) west of San José.*

National Geographic once listed Atenas as having one of the 12 best climates in the world, and that's pretty much this little town's only claim to fame. In addition to having spectacular weather, Atenas is a pleasantly quiet, traditional community that few foreigners visit, despite the fact that it's en route to the central Pacific beaches. Some well-kept wooden and adobe houses are scattered around a small church and central plaza, and surrounding the town are coffee farms, cattle ranches, and patches of forest. Just west of Atenas, the road to Orotina winds its way down the mountains past breathtaking views.

Dining and Lodging

$ ✕ **C@fé K–puchinos.** A popular meeting place among North Americans living in Atenas, this Internet café offers six hearty breakfast specials, good pastries, and delicious sandwiches across the street from the town's palm-shaded central park. A perfect pit stop on the way to Jacó, a good hour away, the café affords the chance to glimpse the heart of an old-time Costa Rican town. The Spanish owners are proudest of their ice-cream desserts and savory Catalonian dishes. ⊠ *Across from northwestern corner of Central Park,* ☎ *446–4184. Reservations not accepted. No credit cards. Closed Mon.*

$$$–$$$$ ⊞ **El Cafetal Inn.** The friendly owners of this bed-and-breakfast, a Salvadorean-Colombian couple, go out of their way to make you comfortable and help with your travel plans. Set on a hill amid a coffee

farm, their two-story cement lodge
The tower rooms are larger and have
views. Complimentary breakfast—i
usually served on the patio out back
of Grecia, turn left just before brid
FAX *446–7028,* WEB *www.cafetal.cor*
nas). 10 rooms. Restaurant, bar, f

$$–$$$ ☐ **Villas de la Colina.** A colorful
to rustic quarters at this mountain re
dant countryside and an ample pool—also with a
best assets, making it an ideal overnight stop on the way to the
The wood cabins are simple, but each has a private balcony with a comfortable hammock. The lodge is one of the few in the country to offer motorcycle tours. ⊠ *6 km (4 mi) from Coopeatenas on road to Orotina,* ☎ *446–5015,* FAX *446–6635,* WEB *www.motoscostarica.com (mailing address: Apdo. 165, Atenas). 6 cabinas. Kitchenettes, pool, horseback riding. No credit cards.*

Carara Biological Reserve ✗

❷ *21 km (13 mi) southwest of Orotina, 83 km (51 mi) southwest of San José.*

On the road between Puntarenas and Playa Jacó, the Reserva Biológica Carara protects one of the last remnants of an ecological transition zone between Costa Rica's drier northwest and the more humid south. This means that it packs a tremendous variety of plants and animals. Much of the 47-square-km (18-square-mi) reserve is covered with primary forest on steep slopes, the massive trees laden with vines and epiphytes. The sparse undergrowth makes wildlife easier to see here than in many other parks, but nothing is guaranteed; if you're lucky, you'll glimpse armadillos, basilisk lizards, blue-crowned motmots, iguanas, coatis, and any number of monkey species. Carara is also one of the two places in Costa Rica where you can see scarlet macaws.

Look for the first trail on the left shortly after the bridge that spans the Río Tárcoles (which is a good place to spot crocodiles). This leads to a horseshoe lagoon, which is almost entirely covered with water hyacinths and is home to river turtles as well as such waterbirds as the northern jacana and the boat-billed heron. The main ranger station is several miles farther south; from there another trail takes you on a one-hour loop through the forest. (Although the longer trail north of the station provides the best animal-watching, cars parked at that trailhead have been broken into.) Carara's proximity to San José and Jacó means that tour buses arrive regularly in high season, scaring the animals into the depths of the forest by midday, so come very early or late in the day. Camping is not permitted in Carara. ⊠ *Turn left off CA1 for Atenas and follow signs for Jacó; reserve is on left after you cross the Río Tárcoles,* ☎ *383–9953.* ⊡ *$6.* ☉ *Daily 8–4.*

Tárcoles

❸ *90 km (56 mi) southwest of San José.*

The town of Tárcoles doesn't warrant a stop, but it's the departure point for a crocodile-watching boat tour up the Río Tárcoles. Two exceptional hotels are nearby, as is a spectacular waterfall in a private nature reserve. If you pull over just after crossing the Río Tárcoles bridge, you can often spot such elegant birds as roseate spoonbills, great egrets, and baby-blue herons strutting through the shallows, as well as massive crocodiles lounging along the banks (bring binoculars). The

ce to Tárcoles is on the west side of the road, just south of the
ara Biological Reserve; across the highway is a dirt road that leads
the Hotel Villa Lapas and the waterfall reserve.

Manantial de Agua Viva. A 200-m (656-ft) waterfall, on a private reserve across from Tárcoles, flows into 10 natural pools, any of them
perfect for a refreshing dip after the hike into the reserve. The forest
surrounding the waterfall is home to parrots, monkeys, scarlet macaws,
and most of the other animals found in the adjacent Carara Biological Reserve. A tough 2½-km (1½-mi) trail makes a loop through the
woods, passing the waterfall and pools; it takes between 40 minutes
and two hours to hike, depending on how much bird-watching you
do. The entrance is 5 km (3 mi) from the coastal highway, up the same
dirt road that leads to the Hotel Villa Lapas. ☎ *$10.* ⊙ *Daily 8–5.*

Lodging

$$$$ ☒ **Hotel Villa Lapas.** A trail on the grounds of this hotel leads to a series of suspension bridges that wend through the canopy of the hotel's
patch of protected forest. The tall trees and stream flowing by make
Villa Lapas a great place from which to bird-watch. White bungalows
with barrel-tile roofs and small porches have rustically furnished
rooms; those nearest the restaurant have views of the stream and forest. All meals are included in the room price. ☒ *Off the coastal highway, 1½ km (1 mi) after the bridge over the Tárcoles river,* ☎ *637–
0232,* FAX *663–0227 (mailing address: Apdo. 185–4021, Orotina). 46
rooms. Restaurant, bar, pool, 2 hot tubs, recreation room, meeting room.
AE, MC, V.*

$$$$ ☒ **Villa Caletas.** Set on a promontory of lush slopes in the rain forest,
★ this elegant collection of villas may seem remote, but it's only minutes
from Jacó and Carara. The architecture recalls Southeast Asia, but guest
rooms are decorated in a French and Caribbean style, with fine antiques and art, black furniture, and sweeping drapes. France is also the
predominant influence in the cuisine, which is served in an attractive
open-air restaurant with spectacular views. Enter on the west side of
the road between Tárcoles and Jacó. ☒ *Off the coastal highway, 8 km
(5 mi) south of Hotel Villa Lapas,* ☎ *637–0606,* FAX *637–0404,* WEB *www.
hotelvillacaletas.com (mailing address: Apdo. 12358–1000, San José).
15 rooms, 12 suites, 7 villas. Restaurant, bar, pool. AE, MC, V.*

Outdoor Activities and Sports

BOAT TRIPS
After hiking the trails of Carara, the most popular activity in the area
is the river trip up the muddy Río Tárcoles to see ferocious crocodiles
and colorful birds. **Jacó Adventures** (☎ 643–1049) runs a boat tour
that guarantees close encounters of the crocodilian kind. Jacó's **Fantasy Tours** (☒ Best Western lobby, ☎ 777–0082 or 643–1000) leads
its own boat trip on the Río Tárcoles.

THE COAST NEAR SAN JOSÉ

Along this short stretch are some of Costa Rica's most accessible
beaches and the popular Manuel Antonio National Park. Convenient
to the capital city, this region is great for a quick overview of Costa
Rica's rich natural splendor.

Playa Herradura

❹ *16 km (10 mi) south of Tárcoles.*

Large-scale development has put this once-secluded rocky beach on the
map for both travelers and investors, who can opt for North Ameri-

can amenities in a tropical setting. The new, multimillion-dollar Los Sueños Resort arrived hand in hand with an 18-hole, Ted Robinson–designed ecological golf course and luxury condos.

Dining and Lodging

$$$$ ✕⊞ **Marriott Los Sueños Beach and Golf Resort.** This palatial Spanish colonial–style masterpiece was built to resemble a Latin American village. The design mixes modern elegance with such authentic touches as Nicaraguan terra-cotta tile roofing, painted Costa Rican floor tiles, Guatemalan textiles, and antique furniture. The enormous horizon pool has landscaped islands of its own, and several bars and restaurants ensure that companions of different tastes can relax together. ⊠ *Playa Herradura,* ☎ *630–9000 or 800/831–4004 in the U.S.,* FAX *630–9090,* WEB *www.costarica-marriott.com. 191 rooms, 10 suites. 3 restaurants, 2 bars, café, pool, 18-hole golf course, gym, travel services. AE, DC, MC, V.*

Jacó

⑤ *2 km (1 mi) south of Playa Herradura, 108 km (67 mi) southwest of San José.*

Relative proximity to San José coupled with the attractiveness of its wide, sandy bay and a various lodging options has made Jacó a popular and affordable beach getaway. More than 50 hotels and cabinas back its long gray-sand beach, and the cluttered appearance of the town's main drag makes it look distinctly overdeveloped; from the water, though, the development is mostly hidden behind the palms. The beach itself is large enough to allow you to escape from the package tours and surfer dudes, except during major holidays. Aside from sunbathing and surfing, you can rent bicycles, ride horseback, or tour the nearby Carara Biological Reserve or Río Tárcoles.

The gray sand of Jacó's long, palm-lined Playa Jacó can burn the soles of your feet on a sunny afternoon. It's popular with surfers for the consistency of its waves, but riptides make the sea hazardous for swimmers when the waves are robust. If you're traveling with children, you might appreciate the **miniature golf** course on the town's main drag. Kids might also enjoy the **butterfly garden** across from the Best Western hotel.

Dining and Lodging

$$–$$$ ✕ **Marisquería El Recreo.** If it swims in the sea, they probably serve it here, with the possible exception of surfers and tourists, of course. Sure, there are few meat and vegetable dishes, but the menu is dominated by tuna, lobster, shrimp, and mahimahi, each prepared in a variety of ways. You dine beneath a thatched roof overlooking Jacó's main street; a colorful marine mural covers the only wall. ⊠ *Across from Mas X Menos supermarket,* ☎ *643–1172. AE, MC, V.*

$$ ✕ **Rioasis.** The menu at this colorful, open-air restaurant is eclectic—burritos and other Tex-Mex treats, a few pastas, and salads—but the big draw is the pizza, with more than two dozen different pies baked in a wood-burning oven. You eat on the front patio or under a high roof hung with ceiling fans, and there's a long bar in back. This is also a good place to shoot pool or play darts during happy hour (6 to 7). ⊠ *North of Banco Nacional, 20 ft off main street,* ☎ *643–3354. V.*

$–$$ ✕ **Chatty Cathy's.** This small, second-floor restaurant is *the* place to go for breakfast. The friendly Canadian owners serve fast-breaking favorites—banana pancakes, bacon, hash browns, cinnamon buns—as well as some tasty inventions of their own and a small lunch menu. The name's no joke; Cathy will happily talk your ear off if you let her.

Note that Cathy and her husband take a break and close up shop for a week or so from time to time. ⊠ *Across from Mas X Menos supermarket,* ☎ *643–1039. No credit cards. Closed Fri.–Sun. and Apr. No dinner.*

$$$$ ✕⊞ **Hotel Amapola.** This all-inclusive Mediterranean-style hotel is a few blocks from the beach, but is the only place in town with a casino and dance club. Rooms are modern, with white-tile floors, pastel bedding and curtains, and large sliding glass doors that open to private patios or balconies. Three one-story villas have plenty of windows that look out to the lovely gardens and ornamental trees. Buffet meals are served in the spacious, open-sided dining room and include international fare with tropical touches and plenty of seafood. ⊠ *150 yards east of municipality (government building) de Garabito,* ☎ *643–2255,* FAX *643–3668,* WEB *www.barcelo.com (mailing address: Apdo. 133, Jacó). 44 rooms, 6 suites, 3 villas. Restaurant, bar, some kitchenettes, pool, casino, dance club. AE, MC, V.*

$$$ ✕⊞ **Hotel Poseidon.** Beautiful hardwoods run throughout the lobby
★ of this quaint little bed-and-breakfast run by Colorado transplants Tim and Chrissy. The hotel's rooms are simple and brilliantly clean; some have balconies and large blue-tiled half-moon-shape baths. There is a plunge pool in the center garden. The small restaurant with its alfresco seating serves up Jacó's most innovative dinners, focusing on Pacific Rim flavors. ⊠ *Calle Bohío, 30 yards west of Main St.,* ☎ *643–1642 or 888/643–1242 in the U.S.,* FAX *643–3558,* WEB *www.hotel-poseidon. com. 15 rooms. Restaurant, pool; no air-conditioning in some rooms. AE, MC, V.*

$$$ ⊞ **Aparthotel Flamboyant.** This quiet oceanfront hotel is a good deal, especially if you take advantage of the cooking facilities. The rooms, though lacking in charm, have kitchenettes, breakfast bars, and a double and single bed. Tiny terraces with chairs overlook the verdant pool area, where there's a grill for your use. It's all just a few steps from the beach and Jacó's busy main strip. ⊠ *Behind Wishbone Restaurant,* ☎ *643–3146,* FAX *643–1068 (mailing address: Apdo. 018–4023, Puntarenas). 13 rooms. Fans, kitchenettes, pool. AE, MC, V.*

$$$ ⊞ **Mar de Luz.** It may be a few blocks away from the beach, and it doesn't look like much from the street, but Mar de Luz is a surprisingly pleasant place. The Dutch owners are dedicated to cleanliness and providing often overlooked amenities, such as the poolside grill and well-stocked kitchenettes. The older rooms, colored in pastels, have two queen-size beds and small porches; the newer, split-level rooms are a bit larger, with attractive stone walls, white tile floors, and windows overlooking the gardens. ⊠ *50 yards east of main road, across from Tangerí Chalets,* ☎ FAX *643–3259,* WEB *www.mardeluz.com. 27 rooms. Kitchenettes, pool. No credit cards.*

$$$ ⊞ **Tangerí Chalets.** Six of the rooms in these two-story cement building have ocean views, while the remaining eight overlook the hotel's lawn and two pools. Every room has a tile floor, high ceiling, two double beds, and a balcony or porch. As an alternative, each eccentrically designed bungalow has a kitchen, covered patio, and eight beds—perfect for a family or group of friends. ⊠ *On main street between Jacó center and Best Western,* ☎ *643–3001,* FAX *643–3636 (mailing address: Apdo. 622–4050, Alajuela). 14 rooms, 9 bungalows. 2 restaurants, pool, basketball. AE, MC, V.*

$–$$ ⊞ **La Cometa.** If you want clean, convenient rooms without expensive frills, this place delivers. Across the street from Jacó's strip of souvenir shops and restaurants, La Cometa fills with budget travelers, who can usually be found reading or lazing on the long patio that overlooks a parking lot camouflaged by a simple tropical garden. Ceiling fans in the rooms lend a bit of a breeze. ⊠ *Across from Restaurante Colonial,* ☎ FAX *643–3615 (mailing address: Apdo. 116–4023, Jacó). 10 rooms, 6 with bath. Fans; no air-conditioning. No credit cards.*

Nightlife and the Arts

In high season, Jacó gets lively when the sun goes down. **Beatles Bar** (☎ 643–2211), 200 yards north of Tangerí Chalets, has a large-screen TV and that oh-so-precious wasting-away-in-Margaritaville feel. Cut loose at the popular disco **La Central** (☎ 643–3076), on the beach opposite Tienda La Flor. Next door to La Central, you can dance at the smaller **Los Tucanes** (☎ 643–3226), when there is not enough people to fill the vast hall of La Central. Cater-corner from the Beatles Bar **La Hacienda** (☎ 643–3191) caters to a younger crowd.

Outdoor Activities and Sports

HORSEBACK RIDING

Jacó Beach Equestrian Center (☎ 643–1569) leads three- to four-hour horseback rides with English or Western equipment. To get there, follow the signs at the bridge.

KAYAKING

Kayak Jacó (☎ 643–1233) runs river- and sea-kayaking tours for both novices and seasoned adventurers. Owner Neil Kahn also arranges half-day outrigger canoe trips to secluded Jacó area beaches.

SURFING

Jacó has several excellent beach breaks, all of which are best around high tide, and its reputation has spread far and wide. Surfboard-toting tourists abound here. Surfboard rentals are easy to arrange; one good outfitter is **Surf Shop Walter** (⊠ main street, south of the bridge, ☎ 643–1056), which buys and sells boards. They also offer ding repair. If you plan to spend more than a week surfing, it might be cheapest to buy a used board and sell it before you leave—**Mother of Fear** (⊠ main street, south of Tangerí Chalets, ☎ 643–2001) has the best selection of used surfboards in the country.

Playa Hermosa

6 *5 km (3 mi) south of Jacó, 113 km (70 mi) southwest of San José.*

Just over the rocky ridge that forms the southern edge of Jacó is Playa Hermosa, a swath of gray sand stretching southeast as far as the eye can see. Unlike its *tranquilo* northern neighbor of the same name, this Southern Belle has jaw–dropping surf breaks and caters to a much younger crowd. The beach's northern end is popular with surfers: because of its angle, it often has waves when Jacó and other spots are flat. But you don't have to be a surfer to enjoy Hermosa, a quiet alternative to Jacó; just keep mind, if you want to swim, that dangerous rip currents are common when the surf is up.

Dining and Lodging

$$$$ ✕🏠 **Terraza del Pacifico.** This surfer dream spot has charms for non-surfers as well, with its Mediterranean look and secluded beach location. The hotel lights up the shore in the evening so that surfers can take advantage of the stellar waves long after dark. You can enjoy the show from the oceanfront restaurant, which specializes in Italian food. The white-walled rooms are simple, comfortable, and clean, with ocean views and tubs. The attractive pool area has a swim-up bar. ⊠ *Off the coastal highway, before the entrance to Playa Hermosa,* ☎ *643–3222,* FAX *643–3424,* WEB *www.terraza-del-pacifico.com (mailing address: Apdo 168–4023, Jacó). 43 rooms. Restaurant, bar, pool, beach. AE, MC, V.*

$$ ⊞ **Ola Bonita.** Just steps from the surf break, this two-story building with a barrel-tile roof is a nicer alternative to Hermosa's other budget hotels. Rooms have red-tile floors, white stucco walls, simple kitchenettes, and one bunk and double bed each. There's a tiny pool out back for quick post-ocean dips. ⊠ *On the Costanera, Playa Hermosa,* ☎ FAX *643–3990. 6 rooms. Fans, kitchenettes, pool. AE, MC, V.*

Outdoor Activities and Sports

HORSEBACK RIDING

In case you tire of surf and sand, **Diana Trail Rides** (☎ 643–3808) runs a nice horseback tour through the countryside, taking in some waterfalls on the way.

SURFING

Most people who bed down at Playa Hermosa are here for the same reason. The surf is best at high tide. You can rent, repair, and purchase boards in nearby Jacó.

Parrita

❼ *45 km (28 mi) south of Jacó, 150 km (93 mi) southwest of San José.*

Set in the heart of an African-palm plantation, Parrita is a dusty town of painted wooden bungalows. First planted in 1945 by the United Fruit Company after its banana plantations were decimated by Panama Disease, the palms are cultivated for their fruit, from which oil is extracted for margarine, cooking oil, scent, and soap. The town has little to offer travelers, but a dirt road heading west from the Costanera just south of town leads to **Playa Palo Seco,** a seemingly endless beach backed by palms and mangrove swamps.

Quepos

❽ *23 km (14 mi) south of Parrita, 174 km (108 mi) southwest of San José.*

With a population of around 12,000, Quepos is the largest and most important town in this corner of Costa Rica. It owes its name to the tribe that inhabited the area when the first visiting Spaniard, Juan Vásquez de Coronado, rode through the region in 1563. It's not certain whether those Indians were called Quepos or Quepoa, but we do know that they lived by a combination of farming, hunting, and fishing until the violence and disease that accompanied the Spanish conquest wiped them out.

For centuries following the Spanish conquest, the town of Quepos barely existed, but in the 1930s the United Fruit Company put it on the map, building a banana port and populating the area with workers from other parts of Central America. The town thrived for a decade, until Panama disease decimated the banana plantations around 1945. The fruit company then switched to (less lucrative) oil palms, and the area slipped into a prolonged depression. Only in the last decade have tourism revenues lifted the town out of its slump—a renaissance owed to natural causes, the beauty of the nearby beach and Manuel Antonio National Park. The town today, though still a bit seedy and down-at-the-heels owing to the vestiges of its Banana Port past, draws a number of expats for the world-class sportfishing. The nightlife moves along at a good clip and some of the bars pace themselves just as well during the day. As Hemingway said of drinking in the morning, it must be noon somewhere in the world.

If you're traveling with children and/or have a keen interest in flora, you may want to visit the **Jardín Gaia** (☎ 777–0535), an orchid garden and butterfly farm. Call in advance to set up a tour of the botanical project, which houses more than 1,000 orchid species. Admission is free for kids under 12. ⊠ *Left side of road to Manuel Antonio, 2½ km (1½ mi) east of Quepos,* ☎ 777–0535. ⊠ *$5.* ☉ *Daily 9–4.*

Dining and Lodging

$$–$$$ ✕ **El Banco Bar.** It's a cozy spot that specializes in Mexican food, but you can also get good steaks and seafood. Wide-open windows overlooking the street and a funky, relaxed atmosphere, make this an easy place to sit and watch the world go by for the entire afternoon. This is also a popular nightspot for the expat crowd. ⊠ *In town, in front of Hotel Ramos,* ☎ 777–0478. *AE, MC, V.*

$$–$$$ ✕ **El Gran Escape.** A favorite with sportfishermen—"You hook 'em, ★ we cook 'em"—The Great Escape menu ranges from broiled shrimp with a tropical sauce to the catch of the day prepared in any of a half dozen ways. Seating is scattered between an old wooden building, patio, and second-floor bar. In the back is the popular Epicentro Bar, which draws young crowds late into the night. ⊠ *Southwest corner of Quepos waterfront,* ☎ 777–0395. *V. Closed 2 wks in June.*

$–$$ ▥ **Hotel Malinche.** One block west of the Quepos bus station, this small hotel has two kinds of rooms, both of which are a bargain. Newer, air-conditioned rooms are carpeted and have large tile baths with hot-water showers. The older rooms, cooled by ceiling fans, cost about half as much; those on the ground floor are nicer, with white tile floors and baths, while those on the second floor have wooden floors and are slightly smaller. ⊠ *Avda. Central, ½ block west of bus station,* ☎ 777–1833, FAX 777–0093. *29 rooms. No air-conditioning in some rooms, some fans. AE, MC, V.*

Nightlife

The popular disco **El Arco Iris** (☎ 777–0449), built over the estuary just north of the bridge, gets packed on weekends and holidays. American expats gather beneath the ceiling fans of **El Banco Bar** (☎ 777–0478), on Avenida Central, to watch U.S. sports on TV or listen to live rock and roll. **Byblos** (☎ 777–0411), on the way to Manuel Antonio, has a small casino. The **Epicentro Bar** in El Gran Escape restaurant (☎ 777–0395) draws a young crowd looking for good music. There is a small casino on the ground floor of the **Hotel Kamuk** (☎ 777–0811) in Quepos. A popular watering hole with younger travelers is **Tiburón** (☎ 777–3337), upstairs behind the bus station, where wild murals cover the walls and reggae is usually blasting on the stereo.

Outdoor Activities and Sports

HORSEBACK RIDING

Lynch Travel (⊠ Behind the bus station, Quepos, ☎ 777–1170) can arrange two horseback tours: a three-hour ride to a scenic overlook and an all-day trip to the Catarata de Nara, a waterfall that pours into a natural swimming pool. **Rain Maker** (⊠ Hotel Sí Como No, Manuel Antonio, ☎ 777–3565) leads an exclusive horseback excursion through the pristine rain forest of a private reserve in the mountains, as well as a fascinating walk through suspended bridges over the forest canopy. Other guided tours of the 1,500-acre reserve include hikes to waterfalls and natural pools.

SPORTFISHING

The southwest has some of Costa Rica's finest deep-sea fishing, and Quepos is one of the best points of departure. Fewer boats troll these waters than troll off Guanacaste, and they usually catch plenty of sailfish, marlin, wahoo, mahimahi, roosterfish, and yellowfin tuna. **Garobo Tours** (☎ 777–3566) offers full- and half-day fishing trips out of Quepos. **Bluefin Tours** (☎ 777–2222) can customize fishing trips from

Quepos. **Lynch Travel** (✉ Behind the bus station, Quepos, ☎ 777–1170) arranges sportfishing excursions from the Quepos area.

WHITE-WATER RAFTING

There are three white-water rivers near Quepos, but they have rather limited seasons. The Parrita is a mellow route (Class II–III), perfect for a first rafting trip; it's navigable in rafts from May to January, after which it drops so low that you can only float in two-person inflatable "duckies." The Naranjo (Class III–IV) requires some experience and can only be run from June to December. The Savegre (Class II–III) is fun: it flows past plenty of rain forest and wildlife and is passable from June to March, but landslides sometimes limit access. **Iguana Tours** (✉ next to the soccer field, ☎ FAX 777–1262) is the oldest rafting outfitter in Quepos and also runs sea-kayaking tours. **Amigos del Río** (✉ about 2 km on the road to Manuel Antonio from Quepos, ☎ 777–0082) leads trips down all the Quepos area's rivers.

Manuel Antonio

❾ *3 km (2 mi) south of Quepos, 179 km (111 mi) southwest of San José.*

Once you're here, it's not hard to see why Manuel Antonio has become one of Costa Rica's most famous destinations: you need only contemplate one of its views of beach, jungle, and the shimmering Pacific dotted with rocky islets. Spread over the hill that separates Quepos from Manuel Antonio National Park, the town of Manuel Antonio is surrounded by dozens of hotels and restaurants, scattered along the road between Quepos and the park. The best hotels are near the top of the hill, as the views are most spectacular; and since there is nearly as much rain forest around these hotels as in the nearby national park, most of the wildlife in the park can also be spotted near the hotels.

As the road approaches the national park, it skirts the lovely, palm-lined strand of **Playa Espadilla,** which stretches north from the rocky outcropping that borders the park. The beach is popular with sunbathers, surfers, volleyball players, and vacationing Ticos; just beware of deadly rip currents when the waves are large.

Dining

$$$–$$$$ ✗ **Gato Negro.** Though seafood reigns here (as it does all over town), this open-air restaurant at the top of the hill stands out thanks to its Italian chef, who has a flair for international cooking. The extensive menu combines classic Italian preparations with innovative dishes like spaghetti *a lo scoglio* (mixed seafood pasta) and penne *con salmone e gamberi* (pasta with salmon and shrimp). Breakfast and lunch are also served in the Mediterranean-style dining room, with a terra-cotta tile floor. ✉ *Next to Hotel Casitas Eclipse,* ☎ 777–1728. *AE, MC, V.*

$$$ ✗ **Karolas.** In the forest just below Barba Roja, with tables on two simple patios surrounded by greenery, Karolas is easily Manuel Antonio's most attractive, intimate restaurant at night. At any time of day, it compensates its lack of ocean view with quality cuisine, particularly fresh fish and shrimp dishes. The homemade desserts are top-notch—leave room for a piece of macadamia pie. Reservations are recommended. ✉ *Main road, at the top of the hill,* ☎ 777–1557. *AE, MC, V.*

$$ ✗ **Barba Roja.** Perched near the top of the hill, with sweeping views of the Manuel Antonio shoreline, Barba Roja is one of this town's oldest and most popular restaurants. The dining room is furnished with dark hardwoods and decorated with colorful prints. Food takes a close second to atmosphere; try the daily fish specials or, at lunchtime, the excellent sandwiches. Desserts are delicious as well. Breakfast is

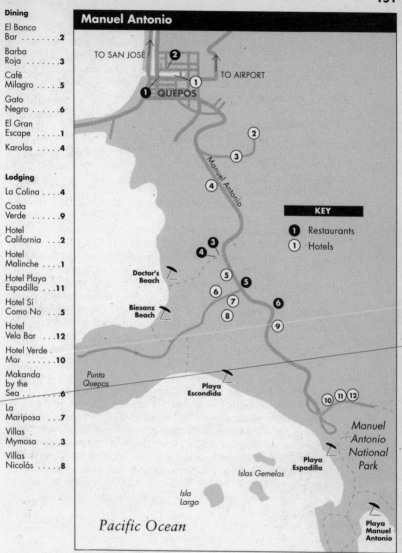

popular, but the view is most impressive at sunset. ⊠ *Main road, just before the top of the hill,* ☎ *777–0331. AE, MC, V. No lunch Mon.*

$ ✕ **Café Milagro.** The only place in town serving banana bread and home-roasted coffee, Café Milagro doubles as a souvenir shop and meeting place right off the road to the national park and Playa Espadilla. The atmosphere is decidedly North American, and the consistently good breakfast food—available all day—keep locals and travelers coming back for seconds. The café also sells local and international newspapers here and at its sister locale in Quepos. ⊠ *Main road at top of the hill, in front of Hotel Casa Blanca,* ☎ *777–0794. AE, MC, V.*

Lodging

$$$$ ✕⊡ **Hotel Sí Como No.** Designed to damage as little of the forest as possible, this modern, eco-friendly place was built to use solar power, energy-efficient air-conditioning systems, and very little hardwood. The hotel has its own nature reserve. The rooms are a good size and bright—some have ocean views—and have stained-glass windows in the bathrooms. The blue-tile pool has an artificial cascade, water slide, and swim-up bar; there's also a poolside grill, a formal Costa Rican restaurant, and a small movie theater. ⊠ *Top of the hill, opposite Café Milagro,* ☎ *777–0777; 800/282–0488 Ext. 300 in the U.S.,* FAX *777–1093,* WEB *www.sicomono.com. 58 rooms. 2 restaurants, 2 bars, grill, some kitchenettes, minibars, 3 pools, hot tub, cinema. AE, MC, V.*

$$$$ ✕☲ **Makanda by the Sea.** If you've got an occasion coming up, give
★   yourself the gift of a stay at Makanda, a secluded luxury retreat on a rain-forested hill, with its own infinity pool and ocean views through the trees. Tropical fruit trees, which regularly attract troops of monkeys and colorful birds, conceal the handful of villas from each other. All villas have high roofs, hammocks, couches, modern kitchenettes, phones, and modem lines. The poolside restaurant serves some of the best food in town. ⊠ *1 km (½ mi) west of La Mariposa,* ☎ *777–0442,* FAX *777–1032,* WEB *www.makanda.com. 5 villas, 4 studios. Restaurant, fans, kitchenettes, minibars, pool, beach. AE, MC, V.*

$$$$ ✕☲ **La Mariposa.** Set high on a promontory, Manuel Antonio's classi-
★   est hotel has the best view in town, perhaps in Costa Rica: a sweeping panorama of verdant hills, pale beaches, rocky islands, and the shimmering Pacific. The main building is a white, Spanish-style villa over an open-air dining room and pool area, with swim-up bar. The older, secluded, split-level units are perched on the edge of the ridge and have sitting rooms, balcony bedrooms, and conservatory bathrooms alive with plants. ⊠ *Top of the hill, west of the main road at the Café Milagro,* WEB *www.lamariposa.com,* ☎ *777–0355; 800/416–2747 in the U.S.,* FAX *777–0050. 14 rooms, 22 suites, 4 villas. Restaurant, bar, pool, some in-room hot tubs. AE, MC, V.*

$$$$ ☲ **Costa Verde.** You might well spot squirrel monkeys, sloths, and iguanas right outside your room, since the builders of this place were careful to damage the forest as little as possible—although it may be surprising to see the imported train car, which serves as the hotel's reception area. The spacious studios have tile floors, large beds, tables, chairs, air-conditioning, and kitchenettes. All rooms have ceiling fans, lots of screened windows, and large balconies. The open-air restaurant serves good seafood and killer tropical drinks. ⊠ *Southern slope of hill, near park,* ☎ *777–0584,* FAX *777–0560,* WEB *www.hotelcostaverde. com. 44 rooms. 2 restaurants, fans, bar, kitchenettes, 2 pools; no a-c in some rooms. AE, MC, V.*

$$$$ ☲ **Hotel California.** Just uphill from the Villas Mymosa, this lovely place has stylish, modern rooms with attractive wood furnishings and balconies that overlook the large pool area, surrounding jungle, or the coast. The hotel is painted a pleasant cream color with wooden doors and Mediterranean-blue accents. The poolside bar and restaurant are run by a Tico chef who makes fresh bread every morning for breakfast. A gift shop shows the work of local artists. ⊠ *Left from the main road about, about 2 km from Quepos,* ☎ *777–1234,* FAX *777–1062,* WEB *www. hotel-california.com (mailing address: Apdo. 159, Quepos). 22 rooms. Restaurant, bar, pool, hot tub. AE, MC, V.*

$$$–$$$$ ☲ **Hotel Playa Espadilla.** It's a short walk from the beach and national park entrance to Espadilla, a hotel and preserve. (The owners' land was declared part of the park decades ago, but they were never paid for it, so they petitioned the government to create a private preserve.) Two cement buildings hold simple but spacious rooms with tile floors and kitchenettes. A blue-tile pool and bar are covered by a barrel-tile roof in back. You can also opt for one of the smaller, cheaper cabinas across the street. ⊠ *1 block east of beach,* ☎ FAX *777–0903,* WEB *www.espadilla. com (mailing address: Apdo. 195, Quepos). 16 rooms, 16 cabins. Restaurant, bar, kitchenettes, pool. AE, MC, V.*

$$$–$$$$ 🏨 **Villas Mymosa.** These tasteful, incredibly spacious condos are simple, clean, inviting, and well worth the not-excessive price. Second-floor rooms have the best views of mountains and estuaries to the north. High barrel-tile ceilings, clever irregular architectural details, and oversize private balconies with tables and hammocks make the already commodious quarters feel even larger. All rooms have kitchenettes and futons or daybeds. Outside, the grounds are less charming, though there are a few intimate spaces. ⊠ *Up side road from Mimo's Aparthotel,* ☎ *777–1254,* FAX *777–2454 (mailing address: Apdo. 271–6350, Quepos). 8 rooms, 2 suites. Restaurant, bar, kitchenettes, pool. AE, MC, V.*

$$$–$$$$ 🏨 **Villas Nicolás.** There's a certain serenity to the rooms in these
★ Mediterranean-style villas that sets them apart from other options in this price range. Narrow walkways between whitewashed, garden-lined villas lead to attractive split-level rooms built on a cliff, the higher of which have wonderful Pacific views. Half the units have well-equipped kitchens; all have terra-cotta floors and oversize balconies furnished with a dining table, chairs, and hammocks. Waterfalls unite two small pools. ⊠ *Top of the hill, near La Mariposa,* ☎ *777–0481,* FAX *777–0451,* WEB *www.villasnicolas.com. 18 rooms. Restaurant, kitchenettes, pool. AE, MC, V.*

$$$ 🏨 **Hotel Verde Mar.** Also known as La Casa del Sol, this whimsical hotel just off the main road borders the rain forest and offers direct access to the beach. The rooms, all in one long cement building, have colorfully artistic interiors and windows on each end overlooking surrounding gardens and wild foliage. There's a pool in back, from which a wooden catwalk leads through the woods and out to the shore. ⊠ *½ km (¼ mi) north of park,* ☎ *777–1805,* FAX *777–1311,* WEB *www.verdemar.com (mailing address: Apdo. 348, Quepos). 20 rooms. Kitchenettes, pool, library, travel services. AE, MC, V.*

$$–$$$ 🏨 **La Colina.** The cement tower of this B&B on the Quepos side of Manuel Antonio's hill has the nicest rooms, with tile floors, big windows, and balconies. Smaller rooms without views are less expensive; there are also two cozy apartments. Next to the split-level pool is the thatched-roof, open-air restaurant, where complimentary breakfast, a light lunch menu, and nightly dinner specials are served. The friendly American owners are happy to book tours and help you with travel arrangements. ⊠ *North side of hill,* ☎ *777–0231,* FAX *777–1553,* WEB *www.lacolina.com. 11 rooms, 2 apartments. Restaurant, bar, fans, pool. AE, MC, V.*

$$–$$$ 🏨 **Hotel Vela Bar.** Set just a hundred yards back from Playa Espadilla on a paved road, this low-key hotel has rooms of varying size and with various views; all have white stucco walls decorated with framed tapestries, terra-cotta floors, and ceiling fans. A casita sleeps four and is a good value for a group. The open-air restaurant set beneath a high, circular roof is popular with nonguests for its selection of fresh seafood, vegetarian, and meat entrées. ⊠ *Next to Hotel Playa Espadilla,* ☎ *777–0413,* FAX *777–1071,* WEB *www.velabar.com. 8 rooms, 1 casita, 1 studio apartment. Restaurant, bar. AE, MC, V.*

Nightlife and the Arts

Costa Verde's owner just opened **El Avión** (☎ 777–0548), a great sunset place on the top of the hill. The bar's centerpiece is a 1954, C-123 Fairchild Provider airplane used by Ollie North and his compatriots in Nicaragua's Contra War. **Barba Roja** (⊠ main road, just before the top of the hill, ☎ 777–0331) has a bit of a bar scene to complement the dining and is a favorite among Manuel Antonio's older crowd. **Billfish Bar** (⊠ Byblos Hotel, across from Villas Nicolás, ☎ 777–0411), is another relaxed place to have a nightcap in Manuel Antonio. **Byblos Hotel** (⊠ Top of the hill, ☎ 777–0041) is also home to the only casino in Manuel Antonio. The **Costa Verde** (☏ 777–0548) hosts live jazz and reggae in a bar-and-Internet café off the road to Manuel Antonio National Park. **Mar y Sombra** (✉ across from Villas Nicolás, ☏ 777–0510), a restaurant on the beach, becomes an open-air disco on weekend evenings and is the most popular place for late-night lounging in Manuel Antonio. **Torumoco** (✉ 2 km [1 mi] from Quepos on the road to Manuel Antonio, ☏ no phone) has a spectacular sunset view and is a perfect place to escape the crowds of travelers that pack Manuel Antonio's other bars in high season.

Outdoor Activities and Sports

HORSEBACK RIDING

Malboro Stables (☏ 777–1108) rents horses and leads customized guided tours through the forest around Manuel Antonio. **Equus** (☏ 777–0001) provides mounts and leads you through Manuel Antonio's forest and beach.

SEA-KAYAKING

Iguana Tours (☏ 777–1262) runs sea-kayaking adventures to the islands of Manuel Antonio National Park, which requires some experience when the seas are high, and a mellower paddle to the mangrove estuary of Isla Damas, where you might see monkeys, crocodiles, and plenty of birds.

SKIN-DIVING

Playa Manuel Antonio, inside the national park, is a good snorkeling spot, as is Playa Biesanz, near the **Hotel Parador** (600 yards south of Makanda by the Sea). During high season, **Lynch Travel** (☏ 777–1170) in Quepos offers scuba diving for experienced divers only, around the islands in the national park.

SWIMMING

Manuel Antonio's safest swimming area is the sheltered second beach in the national park, Playa Manuel Antonio, which is also great for snorkeling. When the surf is up, rip currents are a dangerous problem on Playa Espadilla, the long beach north of the park. Riptides are characterized by a strong current running out to sea; the important thing to remember if you get caught in one of these currents is not to struggle against it but instead to swim parallel to shore. If you can't swim out of it, the current will simply take you out just past the breakers, where its power dissipates. If you conserve your strength, you can then swim parallel to shore a bit, then back into the beach. Needless to say, the best general policy is not to go in deeper than your waist when the waves loom large.

Shopping

There's no shortage of shopping in this town, between the T-shirt vendors near the national park and the boutiques in major hotels. You'll find little in the way of local handicrafts, however; goods here are similar to those in San José, at slightly elevated prices. **La Buena Nota** (☏ 777–1002), to the right on the southern slope of the hill, is one of the oldest and largest souvenir shops in town; it also sells used books and international newspapers and magazines.

Manuel Antonio National Park

⑩ *5 km (3 mi) south of Quepos, 181 km (112 mi) southwest of San José.*

Parque Nacional Manuel Antonio, though small (6½ square km [2½ square mi]), is one of the most popular protected areas in Costa Rica. A tropical storm that hit Manuel Antonio several years ago toppled many of the park's largest trees, but there's still plenty to see here, including three beaches; rain forest with massive ficus, cow kapok, and gumbo-limbo trees; mangrove swamps; marshland; and coves that hold submerged rocks and an abundance of marine life, such as coral formations. Manuel Antonio is home to two- and three-toed sloths, green and black iguanas, capuchin monkeys, agoutis (large jungle rodents), and nearly 200 species of birds. It is also one of the two places in Costa Rica where you can see squirrel monkeys.

The park entrance is at the end of the road to the Hotel Playa Espadilla. Here you will find the ranger station and maps for the trails that take you through the rain forest. The first beach after the ranger station, **Playa Espadilla Sur**, is the longest and least crowded, since the water can be rough. At its southern end is a tombolo (isthmus formed from sedimentation and accumulated debris) leading to a steep, forested path that makes a loop over **Punta Catedral**, offering a good look back at the rain forest. The path also passes a lookout from which you can gaze over the blue Pacific at some of the park's 12 islands; among them, **Isla Mogote** was the site of pre-Columbian Quepos Indian burials. The lovely strand of white sand east of the tombolo is **Playa Manuel Antonio,** a small, safe swimming beach tucked into a deep cove. At low tide you can see the remains of a Quepos Indian turtle trap on the right—the Quepos stuck poles in the semicircular rock formation, which trapped turtles as the tide receded. The bay is good for snorkeling, with nearby coral formations. Walk even farther east and you'll come to the rockier, more secluded **Playa Escondido.**

Be careful of *manzanillo* trees (indicated by warning signs)—their leaves, bark, and applelike fruit secrete a gooey substance that irritates the skin. And don't feed or touch the monkeys, who have seen so many tourists that they sometimes walk right up to them and have been known to bite overfriendly visitors. Because Manuel Antonio is so popular (the road between the park and the town of Quepos is lined with hotels), the number of people allowed entrance on any given day is limited to 600; come as early as possible, especially during the dry season. Plans are in the works to add some 10 km (6 mi) of beach at the southern end of the park. ☎ 777–0654. ✉ $6. ☉ Tues.–Sun. 7–4.

CENTRAL PACIFIC COAST A TO Z

To research prices, get advice from other travelers, and book travel arrangements, visit www.fodors.com.

AIR TRAVEL
Most travelers find the 30-minute flight between San José and Quepos preferable to the 3-hour drive or 3½-hour bus trip.

CARRIERS
SANSA flies eight times daily between San José and Quepos in the high season, four in the low season. Travelair also has eight daily flights between San José and Quepos in the high season, four in the low season, and Travelair flies once daily between Quepos and Palmar Sur.
➤ AIRLINES AND CONTACTS: **SANSA** (☎ 777–0683 in Quepos; 221–9414 in San José). **Travelair** (☎ 777–1170 in Quepos; 220–3054 in San José).

BUS TRAVEL
From San José, Coopetransatenas buses leave for Atenas from the Coca-Cola bus station, Calle 16 between Avenidas 1 and 3, daily at 3:30 and every 30 minutes until 7. All buses heading *toward* San José can drop you off at the airport, but you need to ask the driver ahead

of time. Buses to Jacó and Quepos from San José can drop you off at the Carara Biological Reserve.

Transporte Jacó buses to Jacó leave from San José's Coca-Cola station daily at 7:30 AM, 10:30 AM, and 3:30 PM (2½-hr trip), returning at 5 AM, 11 AM, and 3 PM. There are direct, more-frequent buses on weekends, and buses to Quepos and Manuel Antonio National Park can also drop you off at Jacó or Playa Hermosa. Fantasy Tours runs a comfortable, if expensive, two-hour daily shuttle to Jacó from San José's Best Western Irazú at 9:30 AM, returning at 2 PM. Express buses piloted by Transportes Delio Morales depart from San José's Coca-Cola bus station daily for the 3½-hour trip to Quepos and Manuel Antonio National Park at 6 AM, noon, and 6 PM, returning at 6 AM, noon, and 5 PM. If you're moving on to the southern Pacific region, buses leave Quepos for Dominical daily at 9 AM and 1:30, 4:30, and 6:30 PM, returning at 6 AM, 2 PM, and 2:45 PM (2½ hrs).

Buses make the short trip from Quepos to Manuel Antonio every half hour daily from dawn till dusk, with a few more runs after dark. Buses leave Puntarenas for the three-hour trip to Quepos daily at 5 AM and 2:30 PM, returning at 10:30 AM and 3 PM; these stop at Hermosa and on the outskirts of Jacó.

➤ BUS INFORMATION: **Coopetransatenas** (✉ Coca-Cola bus station, C. 16 between Avdas. 1 and 3, ☎ 446–5767). **Fantasy Tours** (☎ 777–0263 in Quepos; 220–2126 in San José). **Transporte Jacó** (✉ Coca-Cola bus station, ☎ 223–1109).

CAR RENTAL
There are two car-rental agencies in Jacó and one in Quepos.
➤ MAJOR AGENCY: **Economy** (☎ 643–1719 in Jacó).
➤ LOCAL AGENCY: **Elegante** (☎ 643–3224 in Jacó; 777–0115 in Quepos).

CAR TRAVEL
The quickest way to get to this region from San José is to take the Carretera Inter-Americana (Pan-American Highway, CA1) west past the airport to the turnoff for Atenas, turn left (south), and drive through Atenas to Orotina. The coastal highway, or Costanera, heads southeast from Orotina to Tárcoles, Jacó, Hermosa, and Quepos and is well marked. A paved road winds up the hill from Quepos to Manuel Antonio National Park.

The well-marked, newly paved Costanera connects Orotina with Carara Biological Reserve, Tárcoles, Jacó, Playa Hermosa, and Quepos. The drive from Quepos to Manuel Antonio National Park takes about 15 minutes.

EMERGENCIES
In case of an emergency, dial 911 or one of the specific numbers below.
➤ EMERGENCY SERVICES: **Ambulance** (☎ 777–0116). **Fire** (☎ 118). **Police** (☎ 117 in towns; 127 in rural areas). **Traffic Police** (☎ 222–9245).

TOURS
The *Okeanos Aggressor* makes all-inclusive 9- and 10-day guided dive trips to Cocos Island, one of the best dive spots in the world. Transfers to and from San José are provided from Puntarenas. Cruceros del Sur offers a seven-day natural-history cruise through Costa Rica's central and south Pacific regions and some islands off Panama aboard the *Temptress*, a 63-passenger ship. The *Undersea Hunter* also leads 10-day dive trips to Cocos Island.

Any number of agencies can help you arrange land-bound tours. Camino Travel can help you plan tours to Jacó and Manuel Antonio. Cosmos Tours can also help plan a stay in Costa Rica's central Pacific region. Costa Rica Expeditions specializes in rafting and nature tours to Carara Reserve and other points of interest in the central Pacific region. Horizontes also specializes in nature tours to Carara Reserve as well as Manuel Antonio National Park and has expert guides.

Fantasy Tours leads an array of tours from Jacó, among them hikes in Carara Biological Reserve, boat trips on the Río Tárcoles, horseback rides, kayak outings, and cruises to Isla Tortuga. Jacó Adventures offers an unforgettable crocodile- and bird-watching tour.

In Quepos, Lynch Travel offers a wildlife-watching boat trip to the Isla Damas Estuary, guided tours of the national park, several horseback trips, river rafting, kayaking, sportfishing, and more. Iguana Tours specializes in sea-kayaking and white-water rafting. The Eco-Era Foundation runs an invigorating jungle hike to a waterfall in its private reserve and a less strenuous bird-watching and conservation tour. Rain Maker leads horseback rides, hikes, and canopy tours in its private reserve.

➤ TOUR COMPANIES: **Camino Travel** (✉ between Avdas. Central and 1, at C. 1, San José, ☎ 257–0107, FAX 257–0243). **Cosmos Tours** (✉ 50 yards north and 50 yards east of Centro Cultural Norteamericano Coastarricense, ☎ 234–0607, FAX 253–4707). **Costa Rica Expeditions** (✉ Avda. 3 and C. Central, San José, ☎ 222–0333, FAX 257–1665). **Cruceros del Sur** (✉ across from Colegio Los Angeles, Sabana Norte, San José, ☎ 232–6672, FAX 220–2103). **Eco-Era Foundation** (✉ Manuel Antonio, ☎ 777–1661). **Fantasy Tours** (✉ Best Western Jacó Beach Hotel, ☎ 643–3032). **Horizontes** (✉ 150 yards north of Pizza Hut Paseo Colón, ☎ 222–2022, FAX 255–4513). **Iguana Tours** (✉ across from soccer field, Quepos, ☎ 777–1262). **Jacó Adventures** (☎ 643–1049). **Lynch Travel** (✉ behind bus station, Quepos, ☎ 777–1170). *Okeanos Aggressor* (✉ 1–17 Plaza Colonial, Escazú, ☎ 556–8317 or 877/506–9738 in the U.S., FAX 556–2825). **Rain Maker** (✉ Hotel Sí Como No, Manuel Antonio, ☎ 777–0850). *Undersea Hunter* (✉ San Rafael de Escazú, 600 yards north and 50 yards west of Rosti Pollos, ☎ 228–6535, FAX 289–7334).

VISITOR INFORMATION

The tourist office in San José has information on the central Pacific region. It's located beneath the Plaza de la Cultura, next to the Museo de Oro, and is open 9–12:30 and 1:30–5. Lynch Travel in Quepos can also give general advice.

➤ VISITOR INFORMATION: **Instituto Costarricense de Turismo** (ICT; ✉ C. 5 between Advas. Central and 2, Barrio del Catedral, ☎ 222–1090). **Lynch Travel** (behind bus station, Quepos, ☎ 777–1170).

7 THE SOUTHERN PACIFIC COAST

The wild southern Pacific zone is marked by the cloud forests of the Cordillera de Talamanca and remote Osa Peninsula beaches. With isolated national parks, sybaritic lodges, one of Latin America's finest botanical gardens, and sublime surfing, fishing, hiking, bird-watching, skin diving, and horseback riding, this terrain is perfect for those who like their settings heavy on outdoor beauty, hold the civilization.

OME TO SOME OF COSTA RICA'S WILDEST COUNTRY, the south-ern pacific coast, though remote, well merits the visit. A trip here reveals what most of the country looked like decades, or even centuries, ago. Because it was the last part of the country to be settled—a road into the region from San José wasn't completed until the 1950s—the southern Pacific zone retains a disproportionate percentage of its wilderness. Much of that nature lies within several of Costa Rica's largest national parks, and other patches are protected as private reserves. From the surprising highland scenery of the Cordillera de Talamanca, Costa Rica's highest mountain range, to the pristine beaches and coastal rain forest of the Osa Peninsula, the southern Pacific has some of the country's most dramatic scenery and wildlife.

Updated by Gregory Benchwick

In Chirripó National Park you can climb Costa Rica's highest mountain, Cerro Chirripó, and wander lands ranging from rugged forest to glacial lakes. On the Osa Peninsula, the creation of Corcovado National Park put something of a halt to the furious logging and gold mining that was destroying the rain forest; the park now contains a wide range of habitats, including large areas of swamp, deserted beach, cloud forest, and luxuriant lowland rain forest, and houses most of the country's endangered species.

Conditions for a variety of outdoor sports are excellent here, including some of Costa Rica's best surfing breaks and the country's second-best diving area. Anglers can fish the renowned Pacific waters. Rafters can take on the rambunctious Río General. Trekkers can climb Cerro Chirripó. Bird-watchers who go to the right places are almost guaranteed glimpses of the country's two most spectacular birds: the resplendent quetzal and scarlet macaw. Botany lovers, too, will find their jaws dropping here, especially at the Wilson Botanical Garden near San Vito, with its spectacular displays of plant life.

Pleasures and Pastimes

Dining

Thanks to prime fishing off the coast, seafood is a staple. Apples, peaches, and plums are grown in profusion in the upper reaches of the Cordillera de Talamanca, and the lowlands are the source of those thirst-quenching pineapples. If you're here between June and August, try rambutans, locally called *mamones chinos,* their red spiky shells protecting a succulent white fruit very similar to a litchi.

CATEGORY	COST*
$$$$	over $20
$$$	$10–$20
$$	$5–$10
$	under $5

*per person for main course at dinner.

Lodging

Accommodations here range from budget ocean-side *cabinas* (cottages) to tranquil mountain retreats and luxury rain forest hotels. Remember that nature lodges may be less expensive than they initially appear, as the price of a room usually includes three hearty meals a day.

CATEGORY	COST*
$$$$	over $90
$$$	$50–$90
$$	$25–$50
$	under $25

for a double room, excluding service and tax (16.4%)

Outdoor Adventures

Outdoors enthusiasts may never want to leave these parts. This is hiking territory, with treks ranging from one-day jaunts through private reserves to more demanding multiday treks up Chirripó or into the Corcovado jungles. Simple horseback rides take you along spectacular beaches and forest trails. The lively habitat of the water surrounding Isla del Caño offers some of Costa Rica's best skin-diving, and there's prime sportfishing off the entire southern Pacific coast. The surf whips up into a half dozen breaks, and you can navigate in the quieter waters of Golfo Dulce in a sea kayak.

Private Nature Preserves

In addition to celebrated national parks, this region has a growing number of private nature preserves, some of which run their own lodges. Dominical's Hacienda Barú, a 700-acre reserve, offers a number of ways to experience the rain forest, as does Lapa Ríos, on the southern tip of the Osa Peninsula, with its extensive protected rain forest. Cabinas Chacón, in San Gerardo de Dota, has a large cloud-forest reserve crisscrossed by footpaths.

Exploring the Southern Pacific Coast

This coastal area includes the western slope of the Cordillera de Talamanca, the Valle de El General, and the Osa Peninsula. Costa Rica's two domestic airlines offer regular flights from San José to Golfito, Palmar Sur, Puerto Jiménez, and Coto 47 and charter flights to more-isolated spots. Because the drive from San José to this region takes six to eight hours, a one-hour flight is that much more attractive.

If you're traveling by car, there are two routes into the region: the paved, heavily traveled Carretera Interamericana (Pan-American Highway, CA2) and the Costanera (Route 34), or coastal highway, which is not paved between Quepos and Dominical. From Dominical south the road offers relatively smooth sailing, but is nevertheless riddled with potholes. To reach the Southern Zone from the Central Valley via the Pan-American Highway, drive east out of San José and turn south outside Cartago. Be sure to leave in the morning, because dense clouds and fog often reduce the visibility to zero in the afternoons during both dry and wet seasons. The two-lane highway heads up through the perennial fog at the top of the Cordillera de Talamanca, then descends to cross the rolling hills of the Valle de El General all the way to Panama. The Costanera runs into the Interamericana highway at Palmar Norte, south of which is the turnoff for Puerto Jiménez. Though a faithful translation of the Spanish, "highway" is really a misnomer for these neglected two-lane roads.

Numbers in the text correspond to numbers in the margin and on the Southern Pacific Coast map.

Great Itineraries

IF YOU HAVE 3 DAYS

Fly straight to the Golfo Dulce–Osa Peninsula area, where you can stay in a comfortable nature lodge in or near any of three pristine wilderness areas. You can fly direct to ⊞ **Playa Pavones** ⑩ on a charter ar-

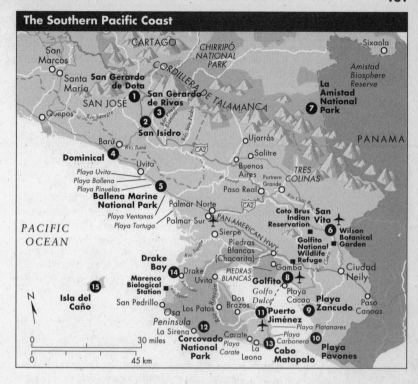

The Southern Pacific Coast

ranged by the Tiskita Jungle Lodge, *or* fly to 🏨 **Puerto Jiménez** ⑪, a short drive from the lodges of 🏨 **Cabo Matapalo** ⑬ and the Tent Camp at the edge of 🏨 **Corcovado National Park** ⑫. The third option is to fly to Palmar Sur, where the taxi and boat trip to 🏨 **Drake Bay** ⑭ begins.

IF YOU HAVE 5 DAYS

In five days you can stretch out the three-day itinerary above or concentrate on inland areas. Drive south on the Pan-American Highway (CA2) into the cool mountain air and cloud forests of 🏨 **San Gerardo de Dota** ①, a perfect place to hike and bird-watch. The next day explore the Dota Valley. On day three, head down out of the mountains to the coastal enclave of 🏨 **Dominical** ④ or the nearby 🏨 **Ballena Marine National Park** ⑤. Spend day four and the morning of day five enjoying the area's waterfalls, nature reserves, and beaches.

When to Tour the Southern Pacific Coast

In the rainy season, it rains considerably more here than in the northwest, but in July and August you may catch a week without any serious precipitation. The Osa Peninsula and Talamanca highlands are especially susceptible to downpours, making this region the last place you want to visit during the October–November deluge.

THE GENERAL VALLEY

The Valle de El General is bounded to the north by the massive Cordillera de Talamanca and to the south by the Golfo Dulce, or Sweet Gulf (the name connotes tranquil waters). This area includes vast expanses of highland wilderness, on the upper slopes of the Cordillera de Talamanca and the high-altitude *páramo* (shrubby ecosystem) of Chirripó National Park, as well as the isolated beaches and lowland rain forest of the Dominical and Golfito areas.

San Gerardo de Dota

❶ *80 km (50 mi) southeast of San José.*

Cloud forests, cool mountain air, pastoral imagery, and excellent bird-watching make San Gerardo de Dota one of Costa Rica's best-kept secrets. You'll find it in a narrow valley of the Río Savegre, 9 km (5½ mi) down a twisting track that descends abruptly to the west from the Pan-American Highway. The town's peaceful surroundings look more like the Rocky Mountains than like typical Central America, but hike down the waterfall trail and the vegetation quickly turns tropical again. Beyond hiking, activities include horseback riding and trout fishing, but you might well be content just to wander around the pastures and forests, marveling at the valley's avian inhabitants.

The damp, epiphyte-laden forest of giant oak trees, now broken up by logged, bare patches strewn with stumps, is renowned for its high count of quetzals, for many the most beautiful bird in the Western world. Male quetzals are more spectacular than females, with metallic green feathers, bright crimson stomachs, helmetlike crests, and long tail streamers that look especially dramatic in flight. Quetzals commonly feed on *aguacatillos* (avocado-like fruits) in the tall trees scattered around the valley's forests and pastures. The staff in your hotel can usually point you in the direction of some quetzal hangouts; early morning is the best time to spot them. They are most easily seen here in their nesting season, March through May.

Lodging

$$$ ⊞ **Cabinas Chacón.** Nearly 40 years ago, Efrain Chacón and his brother bushwhacked their way through the mountains to homestead in San Gerardo. Through hard work and business acumen, they built a successful dairy farm. Now a hotelier and staunch conservationist, Efrain aids researchers and leads quetzal-spotting tours on his extensive farm. Chacón's hotel consists of clean, comfortable cabinas with electric heaters and a main building with a fireplace, veranda, restaurant, and bar. All meals are included, and the staff will pick you up from the turnoff on the Pan-American Highway. ⊠ *Turn right at the sign to San Gerardo de Dota on the Pan-American Hwy., around 80 km (50 mi) from San José,* WEB *www.costaricaexpeditions.com/lodging/savegre (mailing address: Apdo. 482, Cartago,* ☎ FAX *771–1732). 31 cabinas. Restaurant, hiking, horseback riding, fishing, bar; no air-conditioning, no room phones, no room TVs. AE, MC, V.*

$$$ ⊞ **Trogon Lodge.** A collection of green cabins nestled in a secluded part
★   of an enchanting valley, the Trogon Lodge overlooks the cloud forest and boulder-strewn Río Savegre. Each cabin has two rooms with hardwood floors, colorful quilts, big windows, white-tile baths with hot showers, and electric heaters for chilly mountain nights. Meals are served in a small dining hall and can be taken separately or as part of a package. Quetzal-watching, horseback riding, and waterfall tours are offered. ⊠ *Turn right at the sign to San Gerardo de Dota on the Pan-American Hwy., around 80 km (50 mi) from San José, and follow signs; the lodge is 7½ km (4½ mi) down a decent dirt road,* ☎ *740–1051,* WEB *www.grupomawamba.com (mailing address: Apdo. 10980–1000, San José,* ☎ *223–2421,* FAX *222–5463). 16 rooms. Restaurant; no air-conditioning, no room phones, no room TVs. AE, DC, MC, V.*

Outdoor Activities and Sports

HIKING

The network of trails and country roads around San Gerardo de Dota can keep you happily hiking for days. Above the Trogon Lodge, a short trail heads through the forest and ends in a pasture, and miles of trails wind through the forest reserve belonging to Cabinas Chacón. The best trail in the General Valley is the one that follows the Río Savegre down to a waterfall. Follow the main road past Cabinas Chacón to a fork, where you veer left, cross a bridge, and head over the hill to a pasture that narrows to a footpath. The hike is steep and vigorous, especially near the bottom, and takes about three hours each way; it's well worth the effort if you're in shape. A long, guided hike is led by Cabinas Chacón: they drive you up to the páramo (high altitude, shrubby ecosystem) near **Cerro de la Muerte,** and you spend the day hiking from there back down through the forest into the valley.

San Isidro

② *54 km (34 mi) south of San Gerardo de Dota, 205 km (127 mi) northwest of Golfito.*

San Isidro has no attractions of its own, but it's not a bad place to get stuck spending a night, as it has friendly inhabitants and a fairly agreeable climate. The second-largest town in the province of San José, San Isidro has a bustling market and grid-plan streets of colorfully painted houses. The large central plaza is the town's hub, with a modern church towering to the east. A few blocks south is the market, where buses depart for San Gerardo de Rivas, the starting point of the trail into Chirripó National Park. The regional office of the **National Parks Service** (⊠ across from Camara de Cañeros, ☎ 771–3155) can provide information about Chirripó and help you reserve lodging in the park's cabins. Buses to the nearby beach town of Dominical leave from a point near the fire station.

OFF THE BEATEN PATH

LAS QUEBRADAS BIOLOGICAL CENTER – In a lush valley 7 km (4 mi) north of San Isidro, a community-managed nature reserve (*centro biológico*) protects 1,853 acres of dense forest in which elegant tree ferns grow in the shadows of massive trees and where colorful tanagers and euphonias flit about the foliage. A 3-km (2-mi) trail winds through the forest and along the Río Quebradas, which supplies water to San Isidro and surrounding communities. To get here you'll have to drive or take a taxi from San Isidro. ⊠ *2 km (1 mi) north of the town of Las Quebradas,* ☎ *771–3038 (mailing address: Apdo. 73–8257, Perez Zeledon, San Isidro).* 🖼 *$5.* ☉ *Tues.–Sun. 8–2.*

Lodging

$$–$$$ 🏨 **Hotel del Sur.** The extensive grounds of this rambling complex include a pool, a tennis court, and well-tended gardens. The hotel doubles as a local country club, with casino, which makes for lively weekends and more tranquil weekday stays. The rooms are spacious and have large windows and tile floors. Bungalows in back are good for families and offer an escape from the drone of the highway; these have kitchenettes, bunks, and separate bedrooms. ⊠ *6 km (4 mi) south of town on the Pan-American Hwy.,* ☎ *771–3033,* 𝖥𝖠𝖷 *771–0527,* 𝖂𝖤𝖡 *www.hoteldelsur.com (mailing address: Apdo. 4–8000, Perez Zeledon, San Isidro). 48 rooms, 12 bungalows. Restaurant, bar, some in-room safes, some kitchenettes, pool, tennis court, basketball, casino. AE, MC, V.*

$$ 🏨 **Talari.** A 10-minute drive northeast from San Isidro on the road to San Gerardo de Rivas takes you to this family-run lodge on a small farm, where the gurgling of the Río General lulls you to sleep and dozens of bird songs awaken you. Simple rooms with big windows, tile floors, and porches are set in two cement buildings, with a pool nearby. The surrounding fruit trees and forest patches make for good bird-watching. The hotel is closed from September 15 to October 31. ⊠ *Turn left*

off of the Pan-American Hwy. after the second bridge south of San Isidro,
☎ *771–4582,* FAX *771–8841 (mailing address: Apdo. 517–8000, Perez
Zeledon, San Isidro). 8 rooms. Restaurant, pool; no air-conditioning,
no room phones, no room TVs. AE, MC, V.*

Outdoor Activities and Sports

WHITE-WATER RAFTING

With the country's longest white-water run, the Río General makes for
a rousing raft or kayak trip. The white water begins south of San Isidro,
flowing through predominantly agricultural land before winding its way
through a rocky canyon. Three-day camping expeditions on the Río
General, a Class III–IV river, are offered by San José's major rafting
companies in the wettest months (September to November). In San Isidro,
Brunca Tours (⊠ 4 km [2½ mi] west of San Isidro in Barrio Hoyon, ☎
771–3100, WEB www.ecotourism.co.cr/docs/rafting/main.htm) runs
one- to three-day rafting trips on the Río General and nearby Río Coto
Brus from May to January. Brunca Tours also leads snorkeling excursions to Isla del Caño and guided trips to Chirripó National Park, La
Amistad Biosphere Reserve, the hot springs near San Gerardo de Rivas,
and Wilson Botanical Garden.

San Gerardo de Rivas

❸ *20 km (12 mi) northeast of San Isidro.*

The trail up to **Parque Nacional Chirripó,** home of the highest mountain in Costa Rica, begins above this scenic agricultural community.
Because it's so remote, there is no easy way in; hikers usually spend
one night in San Gerardo de Rivas, which has several inexpensive
lodges. From San Gerardo it's a tough climb to the park—6 to 10 hours,
depending on your physical condition—so try to head out of San Gerardo with the first light of day. You'll hike through pastures, then forests,
and then the burnt remains of forest fires. There is a modern but un-
heated (and chilly) hostel near the top. This will be your base for a night
or two, if you want to continue your hike up to the peaks, glacier lakes,
and páramo—a highland ecosystem common to the Andes with flora
that includes shrubs and herbaceous plants. Trails lead to the top of
Chirripó—the highest point in Costa Rica—and the nearby peak of Terbi.
The hostel consists of small rooms with four bunks each, cold-water
bathrooms with extremely cold showers, and a cooking area; the hostel rents camp stoves and blankets, but you'll need to bring food,
water for the hike, a good sleeping bag, and plenty of warm clothes.
There are plans to build a cafeteria in the park—which will make for
lighter backpack loads; inquire when you call to reserve space.

If you aren't up for this adventure, San Gerardo de Rivas is still a great
place to spend a day or two. Spread over steep terrain at the end of
the narrow valley of the boulder-strewn Río Chirripó, the town offers
a cool climate, good bird-watching, spectacular views, and an outdoor
menu that includes hiking and horseback riding to waterfalls. A favorite
stop is the **Aguas Termales,** hot springs on a farm above the road to
Herradura, about 1½ km (1 mi) after the ranger station.

Lodging

$ 🍴 **El Pelicano.** Perched on a ridge south of town, this wooden lodge
has an odd name for a mountain hotel—it refers to a chunk of wood
that resembles a pelican—and that's not its only oddity. The restaurant, which has a gorgeous view of the valley below San Gerardo, is
decorated with dozens of idiosyncratic wooden statues carved by
owner Rafael Elizondo. Many are made out of tree roots. All the
rooms upstairs have lots of wood and share several clean, tiled bath-

rooms. ⊠ *182 m (200 yards) south of the National Parks Office,* ☎ *382–3000,* FAX *771–0781 (mailing address: Apdo. 942–8000, San Gerardo de Rivas). 10 rooms. Restaurant, horseback riding; no air-conditioning, no room phones, no room TVs. No credit cards.*

Dominical

④ *22 km (14 mi) southwest of San Isidro.*

Fifty minutes southwest of San Isidro, Dominical, once a sleepy fishing village, is slowly being "discovered." It still has a mere fraction of the tourists that cover beaches like Tamarindo and Manuel Antonio, but not for want of natural attractions. Dominical's magic lies in its combination of terrestrial and marine wonders: the rain forest grows right up to the beach in some places, and the sea offers world-class surfing. The beaches here are long, practically empty, and perfect for strolling and shell collecting (just beware of rip currents when the waves are large).

There's also plenty to see and do inland as well. The local steep hillsides are covered with lush forest, much of it protected within private nature reserves. By leading hikes and horseback tours, several of these reserves are trying to finance preservation of the rain forest through ecotourism. Two reserves border the spectacular **Cataratas de Nauyaca** (Nauyaca Waterfalls), a massive double cascade that is one of the most spectacular sights in Costa Rica. The **Pozo Azul** is a considerably smaller waterfall in the jungle about 5 km (3 mi) south of town. Both are accessible on foot or on horseback.

Dining and Lodging

$–$$ ✕ **San Clemente Restaurant.** Signs you're in the local surfer hangout: Dozens of broken surfboards ply the ceiling, and photos of the sport's early years adorn the walls. Fresh seafood (grilled outdoors for dinner), sandwiches, and Tex-Mex standards like burritos and nachos make up the menu. The local post office, surf shop, Internet café and Laundromat (rolled into one) are right next door. Owner Mike McGinnis is famous for his hot sauces and is a great source of information about the area. ⊠ *Next to soccer field,* ☎ FAX *787–0055. AE, MC, V.*

$$$ ✕🏠 **Roca Verde.** A festive atmosphere pervades the thatched-roof open-air restaurant, and it's a good choice for drinks or a meal, even if you aren't staying here. If you are, the sunny rooms of the beachfront hotel are decorated in warm yellows, greens, and whites and have tropical murals, tile floors, and private balconies. Look for the large concrete replicas of pre-Columbian statues on the grounds. The owners, who are from Miami, hold Saturday-night dances that draw people from surrounding towns. ⊠ *1 km (½ mi) south of Dominical,* ☎ *787–0036,* FAX *787–0013,* WEB *www.doshermanos.com. 10 rooms. Restaurant, pool, beach, laundry service; no room phones, no TV in some rooms. AE, MC, V.*

$$$ 🏠 **Hacienda Barú.** These bungalows are part of a large private reserve, making them an ideal base for exploring the rain forest. The bungalows are basic, with red cement floors, bare white walls, small kitchens, sitting rooms, and two or three bedrooms (perfect for three or four people). You can linger for an hour or two at a lofty bird observation platform in the hotel's rain forest canopy or stay overnight at a shelter in the heart of the forest. Breakfast is included. ⊠ *2 km (1 mi) north of bridge into Dominical,* ☎ *787–0003,* FAX *787–0004,* WEB *www.haciendabaru.com (mailing address: Apdo. 215–8000, Perez Zeledon, San Isidro; mailing address: AAA Express Mail, 1641 N.W. 79th Ave., Miami, FL 33126–1105). 6 bungalows. Restaurant, fans, kitchenettes, hiking, horseback riding; no air-conditioning, no room phones, no room TVs. AE, MC, V.*

$$$ 🏨 **Pacific Edge.** The forest grows right up to this lodge, set on a moun-
★ tain ridge south of town. The four rustic but comfortable bungalows
are surrounded by screened windows and have large, hammock-strung
porches, and the lodge's thatched-roof dining room serves great break-
fasts and dinners, including some Thai dishes. The road leaves the coastal
highway 4 km (2½ mi) south of Dominical and requires a four-wheel-
drive vehicle, but the hotel will pick you up in town with advance no-
tice. Note that the reception desk closes at 6 PM. ☒ *Turn inland 4 km
(2 ½ mi) south of Dominical on a rough road, follow the road for 2
km (1¼ mi),* ☎ *381–4369 or 771–4582,* FAX *771–8841 (mailing address:
Apdo. 531–8000, Dominical). 4 bungalows. Restaurant; no air-con-
ditioning, no room phones, no room TVs. AE, MC, V.*

$$$ 🏨 **Villas Río Mar.** Upriver from the beach on landscaped grounds, this
hotel is the fanciest in town. The adobe-style bungalows have thatched
roofs, white-tile floors, and cane ceilings. Rooms and bathrooms are
on the small side, but each room has a porch with a hammock, wet
bar with refrigerator, and mosquito-net curtains. The restaurant, with
lots of plants and elegant table settings, is covered by a giant thatched
roof. ☒ *1 km west of Dominical on the riverfront road,* ☎ *787–0052,*
FAX *787–0054,* WEB *www.villasriomar.com (mailing address: Apdo.
1645–2050, San José,* ☎ *866/850–5260 in the U.S.) 40 rooms. Restaurant, bar, pool, massage, tennis court, gym; no air-conditioning, no room
phones, no room TVs. AE, MC, V.*

$–$$ 🏨 **Cabinas San Clemente.** With a great location (just across the road
from the beach) and a wide selection of accommodations, San Clemente
has something for just about everyone. A two-story building has the
best rooms, which are spacious, bright, nicely decorated, and equipped
with screened windows. Rooms in the building next door are smaller,
darker, and warmer, but they're much cheaper. ☒ *Across from beach,*
☎ *787–0026,* FAX *787–0158. 16 rooms. Fans, travel services; no air-
conditioning in some rooms, no room phones, no room TVs. AE,
MC, V.*

$ 🏨 **Posada del Sol.** Going no frills? Here you'll find simple, clean ac-
commodations in a tranquil atmosphere. Rooms are on the ground floor
of a cement building, opening onto a narrow porch with chairs and
tables. In back is a little garden with a cement table and an area for
washing clothes (by hand). The Costa Rican owners are friendly and
helpful. ☒ *Main road, just south of the San Clemente Restaurant,* ☎
FAX *787–0085 or 787–0082. 5 rooms. Fans; no air-conditioning, no room
phones, no room TVs. No credit cards.*

Outdoor Activities and Sports

ECOTOURISM

Hacienda Barú (☎ 787–0003) is the best-organized ecotourism operation in Dominical, offering such unusual tours as a trip into the rain
forest canopy—which entails being hoisted up to a platform in the crown
of a giant tree—and a night in a shelter in the woods.

INNER TUBING

Longtime Dominical resident Kayak Joe will take you paddling through
a series of limestone arches and caves with his **Kayak Joe's Sea Kayaking Adventure.** The half-day tour leaves from Playa Piñuelas, 30 minutes south of Dominical. Arrange a trip through your hotel or at the
San Clemente Restaurant (☎ 787–0055).

SPORTFISHING

Angling options range from expensive sportfishing charters to a trip
in a small boat with a local fisherman to catch red snapper and snook.
The Roca Verde hotel and the San Clemente Restaurant (☎ 787–
0055) can arrange trips.

SURFING

Surfers have long flocked to Dominical for its consistent beach breaks. The surf shop next to the San Clemente Restaurant rents, sells, and repairs surfboards.

WATERFALLS

The easiest way to get to Nauyaca Waterfalls is with **Don Lulo** (✉ 12 km [8 mi] north of town, ☎ 787–0198). Lulo's horseback trips to the falls include swimming in the natural pools below the cascades, a light breakfast, and a hearty Costa Rican lunch. Reserve through your hotel, or the **San Clemente Restaurant** (☎ 787–0055). You can travel to the falls via the private reserve of the **Bella Vista Lodge** (☎ 771–1903), which entails a long horseback ride but takes you through much more rain forest than the Don Lulo trip. To hike to **Pozo Azul,** head up the road toward the Bella Vista lodges, and when it begins to climb the hill, look for a trail down to the river on your right.

Ballena Marine National Park

⑤ *20 km (12 mi) southeast of Dominical.*

One of Costa Rica's few marine parks, the Parque Nacional Marino Ballena (literally, Whale Marine National Park) protects several beaches, a mangrove estuary, an important coral reef, and a vast swath of ocean with rocky isles and islets. There's some great snorkeling here. Humpback whales can be seen with their young from December to April, and frigate birds and brown boobies, a tropical seabird, nest on the park's rocky islands. At the park's northern end, **Playa Uvita** stretches out into Punta Uvita, a long swath of sand, or *tombolo,* connecting a former island to the coast. **Playa Ballena,** to the southeast, is an even lovelier strand, backed by lush vegetation. Tiny **Playa Piñtuelas** is in a deep cove that serves as the local port. **Playa Ventanas,** south of the park, is another beautiful beach that's popular for sea-kayaking. The mountains that rise behind these beaches hold rain forests, waterfalls, and wildlife. This is one of the only parks in the country that doesn't charge an admission fee; there are too many places to enter it.

Lodging

$$$ ▦ **Villas Gaia.** Far from the beaten track, this tasteful lodge gives you
★ access to beaches and wilderness that few foreigners see. The hotel has a collection of colorful villas spread around the jungle on a ridge behind Playa Tortuga, south of Playa Ventanas. Decorated with pastel colors and local hardwoods, the villas have balconies overlooking forested ravines. The restaurant serves some of the region's best food; and the Dutch owners can arrange horseback, mangrove, and sea-kayaking tours. ✉ *15 km south of Uvita on the Coastal Highway, Playa Tortuga,* ☎ *382–8240,* ☎ FAX *256–9996,* WEB *www.villasgaia.com. 12 cabinas. Restaurant, bar, pool, laundry service; no air-conditioning, no room phones, no room TVs. AE, MC, V.*

San Vito

⑥ *139 km (86 mi) southeast of San Isidro, 93 km (58 mi) northeast of Golfito.*

The little town of San Vito owes its 1952 founding to a government scheme whereby 200 Italian families were awarded grants to convert the rain forest into coffee, fruit, and cattle farms. It's now a busy, modern agricultural center near the Panama border, with little to offer travelers beyond the nearby botanical garden. Because of its proximity to the Coto Brus Indian Reservation, San Vito is one of the few towns in Costa Rica where you might see Ngwobe, or Guaymí, Indians, who are easy to recognize by the colorful dresses worn by the women.

Six kilometers (4 miles) south of San Vito is the extensive and enchanting **Wilson Botanical Garden,** 25 hillside acres converted from a coffee plantation in 1961 by U.S. landscapers Robert and Catherine Wilson. The Wilsons planted a huge collection of tropical species, including palms (an amazing 700 species), orchids, aroids, ferns, bromeliads, heliconias, and marantas, all linked by a series of neat grass paths; the gardens now hold around 3,000 native and 4,000 exotic species. The property was transferred to the Organization for Tropical Studies (OTS) in 1973, and in 1983 it became part of **Amistad Biosphere Reserve.** Wilson functions mainly as a research and educational center, but visitors and overnight guests are welcome; a night in the garden is a pleasure, if considerably pricier than sleeping in San Vito. ⊠ *6 km south of San Vito on the road to Ciudad Neily,* ☎ *773–4004,* ᴘᴀx *773– 3665,* ᴡᴇʙ *www.ots.duke.edu (mailing address: Apdo. 73–8257, San Vito).* 🖃 *$6.* ☉ *Daily 8–4.*

OFF THE BEATEN PATH   **CIUDAD NEILY –** The 33-km (21-mi) road between San Vito and Ciudad Neily is twisting and spectacular, with views over the Coto Colorado plain to the Golfo Dulce and Osa Peninsula beyond. Much of this steep terrain is covered with tropical forest, making it an ideal route for bird-watching and picture-taking.

Dining and Lodging

$$ ✕ **Pizzeria Liliana.** It's good lucky when you find a simple, small-town restaurant, like this one, with wooden tables and a bar at one end, with good food. Here it's the pastas and pizzas that are delicious, and the portions are large. If you don't feel like Italian food, go for the baked chicken or the steak with mushroom sauce. ⊠ *1½ blocks west of central square,* ☎ *773–3080. V.*

$$$ 🏨 **Wilson Botanical Garden.** A row of 12 rooms with hardwood floors, ★   high ceilings, and large balconies lines a ridge in the heart of this pretty garden. Room rates include three hearty, home-style meals (at fixed times) and 24-hour access to the garden. Staying overnight is the easiest way to see the garden at dusk and dawn, a highly recommended experience. ⊠ *6 km south of San Vito on the road to Ciudad Neily,* ☎ *773–4004,* ᴘᴀx *773–3665,* ᴡᴇʙ *www.ots.ac.cr (mailing address: OTS, Apdo. 676–2050, San Pedro,* ☎ *240–6696,* ᴘᴀx *240–6783). 16 cabinas. Restaurant; no air-conditioning, no room phones, no room TVs. AE, MC, V.*

$ 🏨 **Hotel El Ceibo.** Having arrived here from Italy at age two, owner Antonio Papili has some interesting stories about his early days in San Vito. He's arranged pleasantly modern and clean guest rooms, with firm mattresses. Rooms at the back of the two-story buildings overlook a forested ravine. The airy restaurant, with its sloping wood ceiling, arched windows, and wine trolley, serves a solidly good mix of Italian and Costa Rican fare. All in all, it's quite a deal. ⊠ *137 m (150 yards) east of San Vito's central park, behind Municipalidad,* ☎ *773– 3025,* ᴘᴀx *773–5025. 40 rooms. Restaurant, bar; no air-conditioning, no room phones, no room TVs. MC.*

Shopping

In an old farmhouse on the east side of the road between San Vito and the botanical garden, **Finca Cántaros** (⊠ 3 km [2 mi] south of San Vito, ☎ 773–3760) is a shop that sells crafts by local indigenous artisans as well as ceramics from San José artists. Profits help support the adjacent children's library. There is also a private park here.

La Amistad National Park

❼ *40 km (25 mi) northwest of San Vito.*

Covering more than 1,980 square km (765 square mi), Parque Nacional La Amistad is by far the largest park in Costa Rica, yet it's actually a mere portion of the vast **Amistad Biosphere Reserve** (Reserve La Biósfera La Amistad)—a collection of protected areas stretching from southern Costa Rica into western Panama. The national park covers altitudes ranging from 700 ft to 11,600 ft and has an array of ecosystems that hold two-thirds of the country's vertebrate species. Unfortunately, the park is practically inaccessible, but it's a worthwhile excursion for the adventurous. The easiest part to visit is **Tres Colinas,** 23 km (14 mi) north of Potrero Grande, a small town just north of Paso Real. There's a ranger station in Potrero Grande, and from here a road suitable only for four-wheel-drive vehicles winds its bumpy way up into the mountains. Camping is allowed here; reserve space at the regional office in San Isidro (☎ 771–3155).

Golfito

❽ *339 km (211 mi) southeast of San José.*

Beautifully situated overlooking a small gulf (hence its name) and hemmed in by a steep bank of forest, Golfito has a great location and little else—that is, unless you're an angler. Sport and fly-fishing has taken off in this area, and many lodgings here exclusively run these trips. Otherwise, the town consists of a pleasant older section and a long, ugly strip of newer buildings, dilapidated former workers' quarters, and abundant seedy bars. Golfito was a thriving banana port for several decades—United Fruit arrived in 1938—and a center of activity, with a dock that could handle 4,000 boxes of bananas per hour and elegant housing for its plantation managers. The northwestern end of town is the so-called **American Zone,** full of stilted wooden houses where the expatriate managers lived courtesy of United Fruit; these were purchased by Costa Ricans when the company departed. With several swimming pools and a golf course nearby, life here must have been more than bearable for the privileged few.

United Fruit pulled out in 1985 in response to labor disputes and rising export taxes, and Golfito promptly slipped into a state of poverty and neglect from which it has yet to recover completely. In an effort to inject some life into the town, the government declared it a duty-free port—the handful of shops called the **Depósito Libre** (Duty-Free Zone) is in a fenced compound in the former American Zone. It does much of its business the month before Christmas, at which time Costa Ricans come in droves, and it can be very difficult to find a room in Golfito.

Golfito doesn't have a beach of its own, but **Playa Cacao** is a mere five-minute boat ride across the bay. The beach has several restaurants and lodges, making it a convenient all-around option when the hotels in Golfito are full.

The hills behind Golfito are covered with the lush forest of the **Golfito National Wildlife Refuge** (Refugio Nacional de Vida Silvestre Golfito). Adjacent is **Piedras Blancas National Park** (Parque Nacional Piedras Blancas; literally, White Stones National Park), which lends the Golfito area some great birding. Piedras Blancas is covered in verdant forest

CRUISING THE PACIFIC COAST

"**A** WOODPECKER," WHISPERED MAX, binoculars trained on a tree wrapped with strangler figs and bromeliads. Cicadas chanted a hypnotic mantra, broken by the throaty call of the three-wattled bellbird and the crashing of waves. A morpho butterfly floated by, winking atomic blue. "No, it's a branch," Max sighed sheepishly, inspiring a collective chuckle.

Led by a naturalist guide, this group of 12 had sped to the beach in a dinghy at 6 AM for a hike through Caña Blanca, a privately owned patch of lush tropical jungle. They were part of an eco-adventure tour aboard the 185-ft *Temptress Explorer,* which nudges right up to the pristine islands, funky towns, and rain forests of the Pacific coast, some too remote for roads. From the shore, excellent rain forest hikes, horseback riding, bird-watching, snorkeling, sea-kayaking, and a visit to a luxuriant botanical garden are easily accessible.

On the trails, friendly Tico guides point out fascinating organisms in the forest—a cavalcade of leaf-cutter ants, the coveted treasure of a cacao tree—and such critters as the scarlet macaw and white-faced capuchin monkey. The day ends with drinks at sunset shared by tanned travelers and their guides, who tell stories as the ship glides to its next destination. For more information, *see* Boat Tours *in* The Southern Pacific Coast A to Z, *below,* and Cruise Travel *in* Smart Travel Tips A to Z.

and is home to many species of unique, local plants and animals. It's an important wildlife corridor because it connects to Corcovado National Park and it's one of the few places in Costa Rica where jaguars still live. Follow the main road northwest through the old American Zone, past the airstrip and a housing project: the place where a dirt road heads into the rain forest is ground zero for bird-watchers. If you have four-wheel drive, you can follow that dirt track through the heart of Piedras Blancas National Park to the community of La Gamba and the comfortable **Esquinas Rain Forest Lodge** (☎ 775–0901 or 888/504–2910 in the U.S., WEB www.regenwald.at). This back route can cut miles off a trip to or from the north, and it passes through some gorgeous wilderness.

Farther into the Golfo Dulce, accessible by boat, is **Casa Orquideas** (✉ North of Golfito on the Golfo Dulce, ☎ 775–1614), a mass of ornamental plants, palms, bromeliads, heliconias, cycads, orchids, and flowering gingers tended with care by American owners Ron and Trudy MacAllister. A two-hour tour (Saturday through Thursday at 8:30 AM) includes touching, tasting, and smelling, plus spotting toucans and hummingbirds. A cabin on the grounds rents expensive ($$$$) rooms; the price includes transport from Golfito.

Dining and Lodging

$ ✕ **Restaurant Coconut.** You can find all your favorite greasy spoon dishes here splashed with a little local flavor. The diner touts the best breakfast in town, but the lunch and dinner aren't bad either. Try the ceviche for a refreshing palate cleanser after scarfing down a BLT or tuna melt. You can use the Internet here and the friendly owners will help you make travel arrangements to local attractions. ✉ *Main road, fac-*

ing the boxing gym and harbor, Golfito, ☎ *775–0518 or 775–1742. No credit cards.*

$$$$ 🏨 **Golfito Sailfish Rancho.** With all-inclusive fishing packages for the die-hard angler and a lodge in a beautiful setting, Sailfish Ranch is a vacation and a hotel all in one. The lodge is based near a waterfall and has its own beach. Simple rooms are intended mostly for resting after your day in the sun. The Rancho's fleet includes 10 new fishing boats, upon which you'll spend the majority of your days, fishing for the big boys. ⊠ *10-minute boat ride from Golfito,* ☎ *813/249–9908 or 800/ 450–9908 in the U.S.,* FAX *813/889–9189,* WEB *www.golfitosailfish.com (mailing address: 5700 Memorial Hwy., Tampa, FL, 33615). 10 rooms. Restaurant, fans, pool, beach, bar; no kids under 12, no air-conditioning, no room phones, no room TVs. AE, DC, MC, V.*

$$–$$$ 🏨 **Hotel Las Gaviotas.** Just south of town on the water's edge, this hotel has wonderful views over the inner gulf. Rooms have terra-cotta floors, teak furniture, and outside each one is a veranda with two chairs overlooking the well-tended tropical gardens and the shimmering ocean beyond. An open-air restaurant looks onto the pool, whose terrace is barely divided from the sea. The hotel can book sportfishing trips for guests and nonguests alike. ⊠ *Playa Tortuga, just south of Golifito,,* ☎ *775– 0062,* FAX *775–0544 (mailing address: Apdo. 12–8201, Golfito). 18 rooms, 3 suites. Restaurant, bar, fans, pool; no room phones, no room TVs. AE, DC, MC, V.*

Outdoor Activities and Sports

SPORTFISHING

Fishing is great in the waters off Golfito, either in the Golfo Dulce or out in the open ocean. The open ocean holds plenty of sailfish, marlin, and roosterfish during the dry months, as well as dolphin, tuna, and wahoo during the rainy season; there's excellent bottom fishing any time of year. **Hotel Las Gaviotas** (☎ 775–0062) runs well-known sportfishing trips. **Golfito Sailfish Rancho** (☎ 800/450–9908 in the U.S.) runs a fishing lodge and offers charters. **Roy Ventura** (☎ 776–0008) personally runs fishing trips out of Golfito.

Shopping

Most travelers in Golfito are drawn by duty-free bargains on such imported items as TV sets, stereos, linens, and tires. You can shop in the **Depósito Libre,** but you won't find things too much cheaper than they are back home. To buy anything in the Depósito you have to spend the night, which means you register in the afternoon with your passport and shop the next morning. Shopping is sheer madness in December.

Playa Zancudo

❾ *32 km (20 mi) south of Golfito.*

Playa Zancudo, a long, palm-lined beach fronting the tiny fishing village of Zancudo, is accessible by car or by boat, the latter of which you can hire at the municipal dock in Golfito. Zancudo has a good surf break, but it's nothing compared with Playa Pavones. There are also some good swimming areas, and if you get tired of playing in the surf and sand you can arrange a boat trip to the nearby mangrove estuary to see birds and crocodiles. Zancudo is also home to the area's best sportfishing operation, headquartered at Roy's Zancudo Lodge.

Lodging

$$ 🏨 **Cabinas Sol y Mar.** This group of beachside cabins is a 20-minute walk south of where you disembark from the Golfito boat. The simple, tidy cabinas have elegant charcoal-clay tiles, wooden beds, and white canvas sofas. Guests love the large stone-and-tile bathrooms with sky-

lights. The staff can arrange transportation from the dock or from Golfito if you call ahead. ⊠ *Main road, at the entrance to Playa Zancudo,* ☎ *776–0014,* FAX *776–0015,* WEB *www.zancudo.com (mailing address: Apdo. 87, Golfito). 5 cabinas, 1 house. Restaurant, bar, fans, beach; no air-conditioning, no room phones no room TVs. V.*

$$ 🏨 **Roy's Zancudo Lodge.** Most people who stay at Roy's are anglers on all-inclusive sportfishing packages, but the hotel is a good choice even if you've never caught anything more exciting than a cold. It's right on the beach—its ample, verdant grounds surround a pool and an open-air restaurant serves buffet meals. Guest rooms have hardwood floors, firm beds, air-conditioning, and ocean views. You can rent lodgings on their own, or with three meals and open bar included. ⊠ *Main road, 1 km west of Cabinas Sol y Mar, Playa Zancudo,* ☎ *776–0008 or 877/529–6980,* FAX *776–0011,* WEB *www.royszancudolodge.com (mailing address: Apdo. 41, Zancudo). 18 rooms, 4 cabins. Restaurant, bar, fans, kitchenettes, pool, hot tub, beach; no room TVs. V.*

Outdoor Activities and Sports

SPORTFISHING

If you've got your own gear, you can do some good shore fishing from the beach or the mouth of the mangrove estuary, or hire one of the local boats to take you out into the gulf. **Roy Ventura** ☎ 776–0008 runs the best charter operation in the area, with 10 boats ranging in length from 22 ft to 32 ft. Packages include room, food, and drink, and you can arrange to be picked up in Golfito or Puerto Jiménez.

Playa Pavones

⑩   *45 km (28 mi) south of Golfito.*

On the southern edge of the mouth of Golfo Dulce stands Pavones, a windswept beach town at the end of a dirt road. Famous among surfers for having one of the longest waves in the world, the town also has pristine black-sand beaches and virgin rain forest in its favor. It's not close to anything in particular—although there's a bar across from the beach—it's the seclusion that makes it a worthwhile destination for adventurous types.

Lodging

$$$$ 🏨 **Tiskita Jungle Lodge.** Peter Aspinall has planted 100 different fruit trees from all over the world and will give you a thorough tour of his garden. He has also built wooden cabins on stilts, surrounded by screens and lush vegetation, and equipped them with rustic furniture and open bathrooms from which you can look right out at the fauna. Trails invite you to explore the jungle, a waterfall and freshwater pools, and there's a wide variety of wildlife lured by the fruit trees' fine pickings. Although the lodge is very remote you should ask for privacy when booking through its San José office or you may have an immediate neighbor. ⊠ *4 km (2½ mi) south of Pavones(reserve through: Apdo. 13411–1000, San José,* ☎ *296–8125,* ☎ FAX *296–8133,* WEB *www.tiskita-lodge.co.cr). 16 rooms. Dining room, fans, pool, hiking, horseback riding, beach, private airstrip; no air-conditioning, no room TVs, no room phones. MC, V. Closed Oct.*

THE OSA PENINSULA

Some of Costa Rica's most breathtaking scenery and wildlife thrives on the Osa Peninsula, one-third of which is covered by Corcovado National Park. A paradise for backpackers and upscale vacationers alike, who can hike into the park on any of three routes, Corcovado also works for day trips from nearby luxurious nature lodges, most of which lie within private preserves that are home for much of the same wildlife you might see in the park. And to complement the peninsula's lush forests and pristine beaches, the sea around it offers great sportfishing and skindiving.

Most fly to Puerto Jiménez, but there's also a 90-minute water-taxi ride from Golfito. A rickety-looking launch leaves at 11:20 AM every day from the *muellecito* (small municipal dock) in Golfito. It returns the next morning from Puerto Jiménez.

Puerto Jiménez

⑪ *127 km (79 mi) west of Golfito, 364 km (226 mi) southeast of San José.*

There isn't much to write home about in Puerto Jiménez—the nature lodges are a boat ride away—but it's the largest town on the Osa Peninsula and can make a convenient base for exploring some of the nearby wilderness. You won't be dodging any pigeons in this urban center, but you are likely to see scarlet macaws flying noisily over the rooftops or perching in the Indian almond trees. Most people spend a night here before or after visiting Corcovado National Park, as Puerto Jiménez has the best access to the park's two main trailheads. The town also lies just 40 minutes by car from spectacular Cabo Matapalo, where virgin rain forest meets the sea at a rocky point.

The headquarters of the **National Parks Service** (☎ 735–5036, FAX 735–5276) is next to the airport. Check in here to enter Corcovado or just to inquire about hiking routes and trail conditions. The parks service takes reservations for camping space, meals, or accommodations at the **Sirena ranger station** in Corcovado National Park. During the dry season, it takes reservations for each month on the first day of the preceding month. You may be asked to deposit money into the Environment Ministry's account in the Banco Nacional to reserve space. Be sure to reconfirm your reservation a few days before you enter the park.

Dining and Lodging

$ ✕⊡ **Restaurante Carolina.** It doesn't look like much, but this simple
★ restaurant in the heart of Puerto Jiménez serves what is widely considered the best food in town, especially fresh seafood. The five small guest rooms in back make this a good rest stop for backpackers entering or leaving Corcovado; rooms are your basic cement boxes, with private bathrooms and cold running water, but they're clean and convenient. The truck to Carate leaves daily from the market next door. ⊠ *Center of town, 2 blocks south of soccer field,* ☎ *735–5185,* FAX *735–5210. 5 rooms. V.*

$$$$ ⊡ **Caña Blanca Beach and Rain Forest Lodge.** Spread out on a truly
★ idyllic beach on a cove in the lush, private Caña Blanca reserve are three open-air cabins and a lodge run by Bay Area natives Earl and Carol Crews. The cabins are made entirely of fine wood and have double or single beds, built-in benches, and lights covered with wicker and the occasional shell. The package includes transport from Puerto Jiménez or Golfito, all drinks, three delicious meals, and a daily tour through the reserve, which is a verdant primary and secondary forest. Reservations are best since the hotel closes periodically. ⊠ *30 minutes by boat from Golfito or Puerto Jiménez,* ☎ *735–5062 or 383–5707,* FAX *735–5043. 3 cabins. Restaurant, bar, hiking, beach, boating; no airconditioning, no room phones, no room TVs. MC, V.*

$$ ⚏ **Cabinas Los Manglares.** Though it's fairly basic, it's also the most comfortable accommodations in Puerto Jiménez proper, and you can see an amazing amount of wildlife in the surrounding mangrove forest. Cabins have tile floors, pastel-color walls, and simple wooden furniture. Five stand by the parking lot, and five are scattered around a lawn on the other side of the mangroves, which are crossed by a catwalk. The restaurant serves an unexciting selection of meat and seafood. ⊠ *Puerto Jiménez, 91 m (100 yards) west of airport,* ☎ *735–5605,* FAX *735–5002. 10 cabins. Restaurant, bar, fans; no air-conditioning, no room phones, no room TVs. No credit cards.*

Outdoor Activities and Sports

HIKING
A truck carries hikers to **Carate** and its nearby beach from the Mini Mercado El Tigre every morning at 6 AM. If you have four-wheel drive, it's just a 30-minute ride to **Dos Brazos** and the Tigre sector of the park, which few hikers explore.

RAFTING AND SEA-KAYAKING
Puerto Jiménez is a good base for boat or sea-kayaking trips on the Golfo Dulce and the nearby mangrove rivers and estuaries. **Escondido Trex** (⊠ Restaurant Carolina, ☎ 735–5210) arranges sea-kayaking, charter fishing, and small-boat outings for watching wildlife (in addition to a number of land-based outings).

Corcovado National Park

⑫ *From Puerto Jiménez: 1-hr four-wheel drive to Carate plus 20-min walk to La Leona; 20-min drive to Río Rincón plus 2- to 3-hr hike to Los Patos.*

Comprising 435 square km (168 square mi) and covering one third of the Osa Peninsula, the Parque Nacional Corcovado is one of the largest and wildest protected areas in Costa Rica. Much of the park is covered with virgin rain forest, where massive *espavel* and *nazareno* trees tower over the trails, thick lianas hang from the branches, and animals such as toucans, spider monkeys, scarlet macaws, and poison dart frogs abound. Corcovado is also home to seldom-seen boa constrictors, jaguars, anteaters, and tapirs. In and around the park you will find some of Costa Rica's swankiest jungle lodges and retreats.

The easiest way to visit remote Corcovado is on a day trip from one of the lodges in the nearby Drake Bay area, or from the Corcovado Tent Camp; but if you have a backpack and strong legs, you can spend days deep in its wilds. There are three entrances: La Leona (to the south), San Pedrillo (to the north), and Los Patos (to the east). The park has no roads, however, and the roads that approach it are dirt tracks that require four-wheel drive most of the year. A very limited number of bunks are available at the La Leona and (more remote) Sirena ranger stations—you'll need sheets and a good mosquito net—and meals can be arranged at any one of the stations if you reserve in advance. Camping is allowed at the Sirena, La Leona, Los Patos, and San Pedrillo stations, but only 35 people are allowed to camp at any given station, so reservations with the **National Park Service** (☎ 735–5036, FAX 735–5276) are essential in high season.

Lodging

$$$$ ⚏ **Corcovado Lodge Tent Camp.** This rustic yet elegant lodge and the ★ surrounding 400-acre forest reserve are owned by Costa Rica Expeditions. The 20 tents, each with two single beds, are pitched on wooden platforms just off the beach. Bathrooms are communal, and a bar-restau-

rant serves family-style meals. Resident naturalist guides will lead you through the jungle and hoist you into the forest canopy via a platform 100 ft high. Bring a flashlight (there's electricity only a few hours each day) and insect repellent. Charter planes leave San José for Carate, a 20-minute walk from here, several times a week, but it's cheaper to fly to Puerto Jiménez and take a cab to Carate. Breakfast is included. ✉ *On the beach, near the La Leona entrance to Corcovado National Park,* ☎ *222–0333,* FAX *257–1665,* WEB *www.costaricaexpeditions.com (mailing address:* ✉ *Apdo. 6941–1000, San José). 20 tents, with 2 baths (8 showers). Restaurant, bar, beach; no air-conditioning, no room phones, no room TVs. AE, MC, V.*

Outdoor Activities and Sports

HIKING

There are three hiking routes to Corcovado, two beginning near Puerto Jiménez and the other in Drake Bay, which follows the coast down to the San Pedrillo entrance. You can hire a boat in Sierpe to take you to San Pedrillo or Drake Bay (from Drake it's a four-hour hike to San Pedrillo). Alternately, hire a taxi in Puerto Jiménez for the inland Los Patos trailhead, or at least to the first crossing of the Río Rincón (from which you hike a few miles upriver to the trailhead). The beach route, via La Leona, starts in Carate, about 37 km (23 mi) southwest of Puerto Jiménez. A four-wheel-drive truck carries hikers to Carate every day from Puerto Jiménez, departing at 6 AM and returning at 10:30 AM; for information call the **Mini Mercado El Tigre** (☎ 735–5075) in Puerto Jiménez.

Hiking is always tough in the tropical heat, but the forest route (from Los Patos) is easier than the two beach hikes (from La Leona and San Pedrillo), and the latter are accessible only at low tide. The hike between any two stations takes all day, and the longest hike is between San Pedrillo and Sirena. (Note that this trail is only passable in the dry season, as the rivers get too high to cross in the rainy months.) The Sirena ranger station has great trails around it. There is potable water at every station; don't drink stream water. Be sure to bring insect repellent, sun hat and sunblock, and good boots.

Cabo Matapalo

⑬ *16 km (10 mi) south of Puerto Jiménez.*

The southern tip of the Osa Peninsula retains the kind of natural beauty that people travel halfway across the country to experience. From its ridges you can look out on the blue Pacific Ocean, sometimes spotting schools of dolphin and whales in the distance. The forest is tall and dense, its giant trees draped with thick lianas and its branches covered with aerial gardens of bromeliads and orchids. The name Cabo Matapalo means "Cape Strangler Fig," a reference to the fig trees that germinate in the branches of other trees and eventually grow to smother them with their roots and branches. Strangler figs are common in this area, as they are nearly everywhere else in the country, but Matapalo's greatest attractions are its rarer species, such as the *gallinazo* tree, which bursts into yellow blossom as the rainy season draws to a close (and the brilliant scarlet macaw).

A forested ridge extends east from Corcovado down to Matapalo, where the foliage clings to almost-vertical slopes and waves crash against the black rocks below. This continuous forest corridor is protected within a series of private preserves, which means that Cabo Matapalo has most of the same wildlife as the national park—even the big cats. Most of the point itself lies within the private reserves of the area's two main hotels, and that forest is crisscrossed by footpaths, some of which head to tranquil beaches or to waterfalls that pour into pools.

Lodging

$$$$ 🏨 **Bosque del Cabo.** More than half of the lodge's 300 acres are cov-
★ ered with primary forest, which is home to all kinds of wild critters. And the lodge, whose name means "Forest of the Cape," encompasses the tip of Cabo Matapalo. Comfortably rustic bungalows are scattered along the edge of a wide lawn, affording breathtaking views of the ocean through the foliage. Each bungalow is slightly different, but all have wood floors, private baths, and porches with hammocks. Trails wind down through the forest to two secluded beaches and a waterfall with a natural swimming pool. ✉ *16 km south of Puerto Jiménez on the rough dirt road to Carate,* ☎ FAX *735–5206,* WEB *www.bosquedelcabo. com (Apdo. 15, Puerto Jiménez). 9 bungalows. Restaurant, pool, horseback riding, boating, fishing; no air-conditioning, no room phones, no room TV. V.*

$$$$ 🏨 **Lapa Ríos.** Spread along a ridge in the jungle, within its own nature
★ reserve, Lapa Ríos is more than just one of Costa Rica's finest hotels— it's part of an innovative conservation project engineered by owners Karen and John Lewis to preserve endangered wildlife. You can ex- plore the pristine wilderness on foot or on horseback, accompanied by one of several resident naturalist guides. The spacious, airy villas, built of local hardwood and embellished with thatched roofs, four-poster beds draped with mosquito nets, and large balconies, suggest how Tarzan might live on Bill Gates's budget. ✉ *20 km (12½ mi) south of Puerto Jiménez, on Playa Carbonera,* ☎ *735–5130,* FAX *735–5179,* WEB *www. laparios.com (mailing address: Apdo. 100, Puerto Jiménez; mailing ad- dress: Box 025216, SJO 706, Miami, FL 33102-5216). 14 bungalows. Restaurant, bar, pool, hiking, horseback riding, laundry service; no air- conditioning, no room phones, no room TV. AE, MC, V.*

$$$$ 🏨 **Luna Lodge.** Decidedly the most remote of the Cape's accommo- dations, the Luna Lodge's charm lies not in high-end, frilly luxury, but in the atavistic charms of simplicity and isolation. Perched on a moun- tain overlooking the Pacific and the rain forest, this retreat hails of a time before laptops and cell phones. The local hardwood and white cane cabins are spaced apart for privacy. All have decks for bird- watching and thatched roofs. The lodge also hosts yoga retreats and leads guided tours. ✉ *2 km (1 mi) up the rough track from Carate,* ☎ *380–5036 or 888/409–8448,* WEB *www.lunalodge.com (mailing ad- dress: Box 025216, Miami, FL 33102-5216). 7 cabinas. Restaurant, hiking, horseback riding, boating; no air-conditioning, no room phones, no room TV. V.*

$$$ 🏨 **Playa PreciOsa Nature Lodge.** Less luxurious than the other ac- commodations in this area, this nature lodge consists of modest, cylin- drical cabins set near the beach amid palm trees, well-tended gardens, and forest. The comfortable, two-story cabins are clean with simple wooden furnishings and balconies; they have no hot water. The wooden main building's second-floor dining area has a great view of the ocean. A popular night excursion takes you into the jungle to hear and see tiny, endangered red and green frogs. ✉ *5 km (3 mi) south of Puerto Jiménez, on Playa Platanares,* ☎ *735–5062,* FAX *735–5043,* WEB *www. playa-preciosa-lodge.de. 4 cabinas. Restaurant, fans; no air-condi- tioning, no room phones, no room TV. MC, V.*

Outdoor Activities and Sports

WATER SPORTS

On the eastern side of the point, waves break over a platform that cre- ates a perfect right, drawing surfers from far and wide. This area also has excellent sea-kayaking, and both Lapa Ríos and Bosque del Cabo can arrange horseback excursions, guided tours to Corcovado, or deep-sea fishing trips.

Drake Bay

⓮ *10 km (6 mi) north of Corcovado, 40 km (25 mi) southwest of Palmar Sur.*

Bahía Drake was named after Sir Francis Drake (1540–96), the British explorer who is supposed to have anchored here more than four centuries ago. The rugged coast that stretches south from the mouth of the Río Sierpe to Corcovado probably doesn't look much different than it did in Drake's day: small beaches backed by thick jungle, cropped by rocky points, and overlooking dark, igneous islets. The tiny villages and nature lodges scattered along the coast are hemmed in by the rain forest, which is home to troops of monkeys, inconspicuous sloths, striking scarlet macaws, and hundreds of other bird species.

A trip here is a real tropical adventure, with plenty of hiking and some rough boat rides. Most people reach this isolated area by boat via the sometimes treacherous Río Sierpe, but direct charter flights are now available. At the height of the dry season you can reach the town via a treacherous four-by-four-required road. Before heading out, ask about road conditions in Puerto Jimenez at Escondido Trex. Backpackers occasionally hike north out of Corcovado (two hours from Marenco, four from Drake Bay). You can also reach the area via **Temptress Adventure Cruises,** whose 185-ft Costa Rican ship runs three-, four-, and seven-night nature trips to Drake Bay, Corcovado, and Isla del Caño; a four-day cruise sails from Golfito.

The town of **Drake,** scattered along the bay, has the cheapest accommodations, and there are several nature lodges—Drake Bay Wilderness Camp, Aguila de Osa Inn, and La Paloma Lodge—near the Río Agujitas on the bay's southern end, all of which offer comprehensive packages including trips to Corcovado and Isla del Caño as well as horseback tours, scuba dives, and deep-sea fishing trips. Lodges farther south, such as the Marenco Beach and Rainforest Lodge and Casa Corcovado, run the same excursions from even wilder settings.

Lodging

Some of the lodges in this area sell package tours including round-trip air transportation from San José and tours, while others include just land and boat transportation or no transportation at all when they quote you the price of a room. All can arrange transportation from San Jose, Palmar Sur, and other points. All packages and room rates include breakfast, lunch, and dinner. Only a handful of the hotels have hot water, but in the sultry weather of the Osa Peninsula, it isn't something you'll really miss.

$$$$ ⊞ **Aguila de Osa Inn.** Just because you're out in the woods doesn't mean you have to rough it. The inn has a three-boat fleet for sportfishing, its specialty, and scuba diving, snorkeling, and other excursions are easily arranged. The spacious rooms with their gorgeous hardwood interiors are in a series of cement buildings spread along a ridge, with views of Drake Bay through the bamboo and unusual details like hand-carved doors and large tile baths. ⊠ *4 km south of Drake Bay,* ☎ *296– 2190, 291–0318, or 291–0319;* FAX *232–7722,* WEB *www.aguiladeosa.com (reserve through: Apdo. 10486–1000, San José). 13 rooms. Restaurant, bar, fans, horseback riding, fishing, laundry service; no air-conditioning, no room phones, no room TV. AE, MC, V. Closed Oct.*

$$$$ 🏠 **Casa Corcovado.** The advantage to this place is its park-side location: since a trail leads right into Corcovado National Park from here, you can explore its forests hours before anyone else arrives if you get moving early enough. Guest rooms are spread around a garden surrounded by the rain forest, into which trails lead, and there's a sunset bar down the hill. The modern cement rooms have bright tile floors, large bathrooms, screened walls. The package tours include air and ground transportation, all meals, and a tour to Isla de Caño or Corcovado National Park. ✉ *Northern border of Corcovado(mailing address: Apdo. 1482-1250, Escazú,* ☎ *256–3181 or 888/896–6097,* FAX *256–7409,* WEB *www.casacorcovado.com). 10 rooms. 2 bars, dining room, fans, pool, hiking, horseback riding, beach, snorkeling, boating; no air-conditioning, no room phones, no room TV. AE, MC, V. Closed Sept.–mid-Nov.*

$$$$ 🏠 **Drake Bay Wilderness Camp.** Spread over a grassy point between the Río Agujitas and the ocean, at the southern end of the bay, the camp has spectacular views and comfortable rooms. The rooms are in cement buildings scattered around manicured grounds; inside, each has a porch and hardwood furniture. Most guests come here to see the rain forest, but you can also opt for scuba diving, sportfishing, horseback riding, canoeing, and sea-kayaking. Charter flights direct to Drake Bay make this lodge the quickest, easiest place to reach. ✉ *On the peninsula just south of Río Agujitas, on the southern end of the bay,* ☎ FAX *770–8012,* WEB *www.drakebay.com (Apdo. 98–8150, Palmar Norte,* ☎ *561/371–3437 in the U.S.). 20 rooms. Restaurant, bar, fans, pool, horseback riding, boating, fishing; no air-conditioning, no room phones, no room TV. MC, V.*

$$$$ 🏠 **Marenco Beach and Rainforest Lodge.** Bordering a wildlife refuge
★ that protects almost 52 square km (20 square mi) of rain forest along the coast between Drake Bay and Corcovado National Park, Marenco was one of Costa Rica's first ecotourism enterprises. Resident biologist guides interpret the wonders of tropical nature on a series of well-marked trails through the forest. Overlooking the forest and ocean from a high ridge are breezy, wooden bungalows with large balconies; some less desirable smaller rooms; and an open-air dining hall. ✉ *11 km (7 mi) southwest of Drake Bay(mailing address: Apdo. 4025–1000, San José,* ☎ *258–1919 in San José; 800/278–6223 in the U.S.,* FAX *255–1346 in San José,* WEB *www.marencolodge.com). 17 bungalows, 8 rooms. Restaurant, fans, hiking, horseback riding, beach, snorkeling; no air-conditioning, no room phones, no room TVs. MC, V.*

$$$$ 🏠 **La Paloma Lodge.** Sweeping views and a feeling of jungle seclusion
★ make these deluxe bungalows the area's best. Scattered on a forested hill south of Drake Bay, the airy wooden villas have bedroom lofts and large porches with hammocks. The smaller standard rooms, not nearly as nice, are farther up the hill. The tiled pool, overlooking forest and ocean, is an important plus, and the hotel runs skin-diving, river kayaking, and trips to Corcovado and Isla del Caño. The restaurant serves guests only. ✉ *Apdo. 97–4005, San Antonio de Belen, Heredia,* ☎ *239–2801,* FAX *239–0954,* WEB *www.lapalomalodge.com. 4 rooms, 5 bungalows. Restaurant, pool, horseback riding, fishing; no air-conditioning, no room phones, no room TV. MC, V.*

Isla del Caño

❶⑤ *19 km (12 mi) off Osa Peninsula, due west of Drake Bay.*

Most of this uninhabited isle (2½ square km [1 square mi]) and its biological reserve are covered in evergreen forest that includes fig, locust, and rubber trees. Coastal Indians used it as a burial ground, and the numerous bits and pieces unearthed here have prompted archae-ologists to speculate about pre-Columbian long-distance maritime trade. Occasionally, mysterious stones that have been carved into per-fect spheres of varying sizes are still found on the island. The uninhabited island's main attraction now is the ocean around it, which offers su-perb scuba diving and snorkeling. The snorkeling is excellent around the rocky points flanking the island's main beach; if you're a certified diver, you'll want to explore Bajo del Diablo and Paraiso, where you're guaranteed to encounter thousands of good-size fish. Lodges in Drake Bay run day trips here.

THE SOUTHERN PACIFIC COAST A TO Z

To research prices, get advice from other travelers, and book travel ar-rangements, visit www.fodors.com.

AIR TRAVEL
The quickest way to move between the central and southern Pacific coasts is from Quepos to Palmar Sur.

CARRIERS
SANSA has several flights daily from San José to Golfito and some daily flights to Palmar Sur (for Drake Bay) and Puerto Jiménez. Travelair has daily flights to Golfito, Palmar Sur, and Puerto Jiménez. Both air-lines also have daily flights from Quepos to Palmar Sur. Costa Rica Expeditions runs several charter flights weekly to Carate, a 40-minute hike from the company's Corcovado Tent Camp. Drake Bay Wilder-ness Camp runs its own daily charter flights from Drake Bay and will fly in passengers going to neighboring lodges, if room allows.

Aerotaxi Alfa Romeo offers charter flights to Carate, Drake Bay, Puerto Jiménez, the Sirena ranger station in Corcovado National Park, the Tiskita Jungle Lodge in Playa Pavones, and anywhere else you want to go. You have to charter the whole plane, which is expensive, so it's best to fill it with the maximum capacity of five.

➤ AIRLINES AND CONTACTS: **Aerotaxi Alfa Romeo** (☏ FAX 735–5178). **Costa Rica Expeditions** (☏ 222–0333, FAX 257–1665). **Drake Bay Wilderness Camp** (☏ FAX 770–8012). **SANSA** (✉ in front of Restau-rant Uno, Golfito, ☏ 775–0303, FAX 775-0021; 150 m south and 100 m east of the Caja Costarricense del Seguro Social offices, Palmar Sur, ☏ 786–6353; 75 m west of the Catholic church, Puerto Jimenez, ☏ 735–5017, FAX 735–5495). **Travelair** (✉ Aeropuerto Tobias Bolaños, Pavas, ☏ 220–4844, FAX 220–0413).

BOAT AND FERRY TRAVEL
Drake Bay is usually connected by boat to Sierpe, south of Palmar Norte. Many local boatmen use open dinghies, so bring a sun hat. The mouth of the river can have dangerous waves at low tide or during storms; make sure your boat has life jackets. The crossing takes about an hour and a half. Travel between the Drake Bay lodges, Corcovado, and Isla del Caño is most commonly accomplished in small boats owned by the major lodges.

A ferry crosses the Golfo Dulce, leaving Puerto Jiménez daily at 6 AM and returning from Golfito at 11:30 AM. Boat transportation to Zan-cudo or the more distant Pavones can be arranged through the Coconut Restaurant, which doubles as a general information center and Inter-net café.

➤ BOAT AND FERRY INFORMATION: **Coconut Restaurant** (✉ Golfito, ☏ 775–1742).

BUS TRAVEL

Musoc buses from San José to San Isidro, a three-hour trip, depart almost every hour between 5:30 AM and 5 PM from Calle 16 and Avenidas 1 and 3, returning at the same times. Transportes Blanco buses from San Isidro to Dominical leave from a point 114 m (125 yards) east of the church at 7 AM, 9 AM, 1:30 PM, and 4 PM.

Tracopa-Alfaro buses leave San José (Calle 14) for the eight-hour trip to Golfito daily at 7 AM and 3 PM, returning at 5 AM and 1 PM. Tracopa-Alfaro buses from San José (also Calle 14 between Avenidas 3 and 5) to San Vito, a seven-hour trip, leave daily at 5:45 AM, 8:15 AM, 11:30 AM, and 2:45 PM.

Transportes Blanco-Lobo buses from San José to Puerto Jiménez, an eight-hour trip, leave Calle 14 between Avenidas 9 and 11 at noon and return at 5 AM and 11 AM. Tracopa Alfaro buses from San José to Palmar Norte, a six-hour trip, depart from Calle 14 and Avenida 5 daily at 5, 7, 8:30, 10 AM and 1, 2:30, and 6 PM; buses to Golfito, Puerto Jiménez, and San Vito also stop here. In Palmar Norte, you can hire a taxi to Sierpe, the port for boats to Drake Bay.

Buses run by Transportes Blanco leave San Isidro for the one-hour trip to Dominical daily at 5:30 and 7 AM and 1:30 and 3 PM from 125 m south of the church. Take a bus from San Isidro to San Gerardo de Rivas, the starting point of the trail into Chirripó National Park, at the terminal near the central market at 5 AM and 2 PM.

From San Isidro, Transportes Blancos buses make the five-hour trip to Puerto Jiménez at 6 AM, noon, and 3 PM from the Transportes Blancos terminal, 114 m (125 yards) south of the church. A truck for hikers leaves Puerto Jiménez daily at 6 AM for Carate, returning at 10:30 AM.

➤ BUS INFORMATION: **Musoc** (✉ C. 16 and Avdas. 1 and 3, ☎ 222–2422). **Tracopa-Alfaro** (☎ 222–2666). **Transportes Blanco** (☎ 771–4744 or 771–2550). **Transportes Blanco-Lobo** (☎ 257–4121).

CAR RENTAL

There are no area car-rental agencies, which is quite appropriate given the roads or lack of them. You may rent in San José, but having a car is not an economical way to get around in this region.

CAR TRAVEL

The quickest way to reach the Costanera, or coastal highway, which leads past Jacó and Quepos to Dominical and the rest of the southern Pacific zone, is to take the Carretera Interamericana (Pan-American Highway or CA2) west past the airport to the turnoff for Atenas, turn left, and drive through Atenas to Orotina, where you head south on the half-paved coastal highway. You can also get to this region by taking the Pan-American Highway south past Cartago and over the Cerro de la Muerte—where you'll pass the turnoff for San Gerardo de Dota—to San Isidro, Valle de El General, and the Osa Peninsula. Foggy conditions atop Cerro de la Muerte make it best to cross the mountains as early in the day as possible.

EMERGENCIES

In case of any emergency, dial 911, or one of the specific numbers below.
➤ EMERGENCY SERVICES: **Ambulance** (☎ 128). **Fire** (☎ 118). **Police** (☎ 911). **Traffic Police** (☎ 227–8030).

TOURS

Horizontes designs customized tours led by naturalist guides to many remote jungle lodges. Costa Rica Expeditions, one of Costa Rica's old-

A REMOTE DIVE ADVENTURE

THE HAMMERHEAD SHARKS that sometimes swim alongside divers at Isla del Coco are more interested in the hawksbill sea turtles and other sea life gliding by than in the human visitors exploring the waters. Rated one of the top diving destinations in the world, Isla del Coco is uninhabited and remote, and its waters are teeming with marine life. Divers here enjoy 100-ft visibility, and what they usually get to see is the underwater equivalent of a big game park. Scalloped hammerheads, white-tipped reef sharks, whale sharks, Galápagos sharks, bottlenose dolphins, billfish, and manta rays mix with huge schools of brilliantly colored fish. Despite the profusion of sharks, divers shouldn't fear them. Most species that live around Isla del Coco aren't aggressive toward humans.

Geologists aren't certain about the island's origins but believe it to be a volcanic hot spot in the center of the Cocos tectonic plates. It's thought that European sailors first made landfall here in the 1500s. The island's subsequent history has swirled with stories of outlaws, rebels, and treasures. Pirates sought refuge here in the 17th and 18th centuries—and left their names carved into rocks on the island. Legend has it that buccaneer Benito Bonito buried a fantastic treasure on these shores in the early 19th century. During Peru's 19th-century wars of independence from Spain, Captain William Thompson is believed to have absconded with gold and jewels belonging to the Peruvian aristocracy and to have hidden them on the island. Neither treasure has been found, despite the efforts of many treasure hunters over the last 200 years.

Because of Isla del Coco's distance from shore and craggy topography, few visitors to Costa Rica—and even fewer Costa Ricans—have stepped foot on the island. Costa Rica annexed Coco in 1869, and it became a national park in 1978. Today, only specialty-cruise ships,

park rangers, scientists, and yachts carrying scuba divers visit the place Jacques Cousteau called "the most beautiful island in the world." Encompassing about 22½ square km (14 square mi), it is the largest uninhabited island on earth. The dramatically rocky topography is draped in rain forest and cloud forest and includes more than 200 waterfalls—some of which cascade from high cliffs into the ocean. The climate is extremely rainy. Coco's isolation has led to the evolution of dozens of endemic plant and animal species. Wildlife includes deer and wild pigs—descendents of domestic animals released by sailors centuries ago—and several species of native lizards and freshwater fish.

Most dive cruises to Isla del Coco are about 10 days long, including three days on the open ocean traveling to and from the island. Several San José–based companies use dive boats with cabins to run trips year-round; these include the *Okeanos Agressor* (☎ 556–8317 or 877/506–9738 www.intladventures.com/coco) and the *Undersea Hunter* (☎ 228–6535, www.underseahunter.com). Trips cost roughly $3,000. The boats anchor offshore at Coco, and several day excursions to the island are included. A few trails are maintained by the local rangers, and your dive master may act as your nature guide on a hike.

The dry season, from November to May, has calmer seas and a more comfortable crossing. It is also the best time to see silky sharks. During the rainy season, large schools of hammerheads can be seen, but the ocean is rougher, making for a less pleasant ocean journey.

The Isla del Coco is no place for beginners, but for serious divers it provides some of the best diving the world has to offer and the likely opportunity to swim with large, breathtaking sea animals.

est and best tour companies, runs guided tours to its Corcovado Tent Camp.

➤ Tour Operator Recommendations: **Costa Rica Expeditions** (✉ Avda. 3 at C. Central, San José, ☎ 222–0333, ℻ 257–1665). **Horizontes** (✉ 137 m [150 yards] north of Pizza Hut on Paseo Colón, San José, ☎ 222–2022, ℻ 255–4513).

BOAT TOURS

Temptress Adventure Cruises runs three-, four-, and seven-day adventure cruises on the *Temptress Explorer* that visit Corcovado National Park, Drake Bay, Isla del Caño, and Manuel Antonio National Park. Guests catered to are generally those drawn to "soft adventure trips" and senior citizens; activities include hiking through national parks and refuges, bird-watching, nature walks, snorkeling, horseback riding, fishing, and diving accompanied by excellent naturalist guides. The ship sails from Puntarenas (three- or seven-day cruises) and Golfito (four-day cruises), with transport to and from the airport in San José. Contact Temptress directly or reserve through Cruceros del Sur. For serious scuba divers in search of a thrill, there are 10-day skin-diving expeditions to distant Coco Island on the *Okeanos Agressor.* A smaller vessel, the *Undersea Hunter,* makes similar dive trips to Coco Island.

From a sunset paddle to a one-week trip around the entire Golfo Dulce, Escondido Trex, in Puerto Jiménez, can arrange any type of sea-kayaking adventure. Other adventures include rappelling down waterfalls.

➤ Fees and Schedules: **Cruceros del Sur** (✉ across from Colegio Los Angeles, Sabana Norte, San José, ☎ 232–6672, ℻ 220–2103). **Escondido Trex** (✉ Restaurante Carolina, Apdo. 9, Puerto Jiménez, ☎ 735–5210). *Okeanos Agressor* (✉ Box 025216, Miami, FL 33102–5216, ☎ 556–8317 or 877/506–9738, ℻ 556–2825, WEB www.intladventures.com/coco). **Temptress Adventure Cruises** (✉ 2401 4th Ave., Suite 700, Seattle, WA 98121, ☎ 800/366–8423 in the U.S., ☎ ℻ 220–2103 in San José). *Undersea Hunter* (☎ 228–6535, ℻ 289–7334, WEB www.underseahunter.com).

HIKING TOURS

Brunca Tours leads hikes and nature tours to Chirripó and other areas. In Dominical, Hacienda Barú offers a number of guided hikes through the rain forest. Ecole Travel runs inexpensive guided hikes into Chirripó and Corcovado national parks.

➤ Fees and Schedules: **Brunca Tours** (☎ 771–3100). **Ecole Travel** (✉ C. 7 between Avdas. Central and 1, San José, ☎ 223–2240, ℻ 223–4128). **Hacienda Barú** (✉ 1 km [½ mi] north of Dominical, ☎ 787–0003).

TRAVEL AGENCIES

In Puerto Jiménez, Osa Tropical sells domestic airline tickets, offers varied tours, and makes reservations at the lodges on the Osa Peninsula. Selva Mar, in San Isidro, can make hotel reservations throughout the country but specializes in working with remote jungle lodges and tour operators in the Southern Zone.

➤ Local Agent Referrals: **Osa Tropical** (✉ 46 m [50 yards] south of the Catholic church, Puerto Jiménez, ☎ 735–5062, ℻ 735–5043), open Monday–Saturday 8–5. **Selva Mar** (✉ 46 m [50 yards] south of central park, San Isidro, ☎ 771–4582, WEB www.exploringcostarica.com).

VISITOR INFORMATION

The tourist office in San José has information on the southern Pacific coast. In San Isidro, CIPROTUR is a helpful visitor information center, with an Internet café. Also in San Isidro, the travel agency Selva

Mar doubles as a visitor information center. In Dominical, the San Clemente Restaurant provides visitor's information and books tours. In Golfito, Land Sea Services offers traveler information. In Puerto Jiménez, the Osa Tropical travel agency is also a visitor center.

➤ TOURIST INFORMATION: **CIPROTUR** (✉ 69 m [75 yards] south of the Instituto Costarricense de Electricidad, San Isidro, ☎ 771–6096). **Land Sea Services** (✉ next to Banana Bay Marina on left as you enter Golfito, Golfito, ☎ 775–1614). **Osa Tropical** (✉ 46 m [50 yards] south of the Catholic church, Puerto Jiménez, ☎ 735–5062, FAX 735–5043), open Monday–Saturday 8–5. **San Clemente Restaurant** (✉ next to soccer field, Dominical, ☎ FAX 787–0055). **Selva Mar** (✉ 46 m [50 yards] south of central park, San Isidro, ☎ 771–4582, WEB www.exploringcostarica.com).

8 THE ATLANTIC LOWLANDS AND CARIBBEAN COAST

Inhabited by African-Caribbean, Spanish, and indigenous peoples, the Atlantic lowlands mix wild outposts, banana and cacao plantations, and dense primary jungle. Too hot and humid to be anything but laid-back, the lowlands are a world unto themselves. Along the Caribbean coast, it's turbulent rivers, verdant national parks, easy-going villages, and coral-fringed beaches, on which you can spot turtles.

Updated by
Jeffrey Van
Fleet

C LOUD FORESTS, SPRAWLING BANANA PLANTATIONS, and thick tropical jungle, characterize the Atlantic lowlands, in the provinces of Heredia and Limón on the Caribbean Sea. This expansive, largely untamed region stretches from the eastern slope of the Cordillera Central up to the Sarapiquí area northeast of San José (home to the private Rara Avis and La Selva reserves), east through banana-growing country, and down to the pristine beaches at Cahuita and Puerto Viejo de Talamanca on the southern Caribbean coast. The region also stretches north to the Nicaraguan border, encompassing the coastal jungles and canals of Tortuguero National Park and Barra del Colorado Wildlife Refuge, on whose beaches turtles arrive by the thousands to lay their eggs. The occasional caiman can be spotted here, sunning on a bank or drifting like a log down a jungle waterway; and farther north still, sportfishing fans will find tarpon and snook to detain them off the shores of Barra del Colorado.

Roughly a third of the people in Limón province are Afro-Caribbeans, descendants of early 19th-century turtle fishermen and the West Indians who arrived in the late 19th century to build the Atlantic Railroad and remained to work on banana and cacao plantations. Some 4,000 Jamaicans are reputed to have died of yellow fever, malaria, and snakebites during construction of the first 40 km (25 mi) of railroad to San José. They were paid relatively well, however, and gradually their lot improved: by the 1930s many had obtained their own small plots of land, and when the price of cacao rose in the 1950s they emerged as comfortable landowners employing landless, migrant Hispanics. Until the Civil War of 1948, Afro-Caribbeans were forbidden from crossing into the Central Valley lest they upset the country's racial balance, and they were thus prevented from following work when United Fruit abandoned many of its northern Caribbean blight-ridden plantations in the 1930s for green-field sites on the Pacific plain. Although Jamaicans brought some aspects of British colonial culture with them, such as cricket and the maypole dance, these habits have long since given way to reggae, salsa, and soccer, much to the chagrin of the older generation. Many Atlantic-coast Ticos are bilingual, speaking fluent Caribbean-accented English and Spanish, and around Puerto Viejo de Talamanca you may even hear some phrases derived from the language of the indigenous peoples, among them the Kekoldi, the Bribri, and the Cabecar.

With some justification, Caribbean residents bemoan the lack of attention their region gets from the government in San José and the tourism industry. Development has been slower to reach this part of the country. (Telephones and electricity are still newfangled inventions in some smaller communities here.) The Instituto Costarricense de Turismo, anxious to tout Costa Rica to northerners as a fun-in-the-sun destination, devotes less space to the rainier Atlantic coast in its glossy tourist literature. The attention the region does get usually comes in the form of crime stories splashed across the front pages of San José newspapers. In the 1990s, some of the cocaine flowing from Latin America into the United States spilled into the area near Puerto Viejo de Talamanca and Cahuita, resulting in a drug-related crime problem. Many Ticos will advise you to avoid Limón province, but few have ever visited the area themselves. Communities are working hard to combat the problem with visibly beefed up security, and crime is really no worse here than elsewhere in Costa Rica. If you stick to well-trodden tourist routes, you ought to be fine.

You will receive a warm welcome when you visit this "other" Costa Rica, a section of the country long ago discovered by European visitors, but little known in North American circles. Venture here and you'll be pleasantly surprised to discover the personalized attention and quality you get for your colones. The flashy resorts so common on the Pacific are no where to be found here. Though they sometimes look with envy at their west-coast counterparts, most folks here on the Caribbean remain perfectly content to keep their tourism offerings smaller scale.

Pleasures and Pastimes

Dining

Upscale hotels and restaurants have brought a varied international cuisine to this region. Still, much of the cooking along the Caribbean has its roots in old Jamaican recipes. *Rondón,* for example, is a traditional Jamaican vegetable-and-beef stew that requires hours of preparation. Equally labor-intensive, rice and beans, not at all the *gallo pinto* you've been eating elsewhere in Costa Rica, is flavored with coconut; meat is fried with hot spices to make *paties* (pies); and fish or meat are boiled in coconut milk along with yams, plantains, breadfruit, peppers, and spices. Johnnycakes and *panbón* (a heavy, spicy dried-fruit bread) are popular baked goods. Seafood is, of course, readily available, as is a wide variety of fresh fruit.

CATEGORY	COST*
$$$$	over $20
$$$	$10–$20
$$	$5–$10
$	under $5

per person for main course at dinner.

Fishing

World-class tarpon and snook attract serious sportfishing to the northern Caribbean shore in and off the Tortuguero and Barra del Colorado national parks. The months between January and May are best for tarpon, August through November for snook.

Hiking and Jungle Boating

From the beach hikes of Cahuita National Park to the more leisurely jungle-boat cruises arranged by the lodges near Tortuguero National Park, opportunities for plunging into tropical jungle and rain forest abound in the Atlantic lowlands. Farther inland, on the eastern slope of the mountains, Braulio Carrillo's cloud- and rain-forested mountains have scenic trails, and the private lowland reserves of La Selva and Rara Avis beckon with excellent jungle terrain. To the southeast, the remote and little-visited Hitoy Cerere Biological Reserve lays out both easy and difficult hiking trails as the jungle climbs into the hills of the Talamanca range; look for waterfalls, swimming holes, and an encyclopedic variety of Costa Rican flora and fauna.

Lodging

The Atlantic lowlands have little in the way of luxury hotels, though a number of relatively upscale, self-proclaimed ecotourist lodges and some other, pricier accommodations exist along the highway south of Puerto Limón and (especially) on the beach road south of Puerto Viejo de Talamanca. The region's lower number of visitors compared to the Pacific coast means you'll usually find vacancies at reasonable prices. Most lodgings along the north Caribbean coast are rustic *cabinas* (cottages) or nature lodges. Often isolated in the jungle—accessible only by boat or strenuous hike—the lodges can be rough, no-frills places or can verge on the luxurious. Because it's hard to haul supplies to these places, you'll pay a hefty price if you insist on hot showers and cold beers in the middle of the jungle.

CATEGORY	COST*
$$$$	over $90
$$$	$50–$90
$$	$25–$50
$	under $25

for a double room, excluding service and tax (16.4%)

Snorkeling and Scuba Diving

Costa Rica's largest coral reef is off the coast of Cahuita National Park, and although it has been severely damaged by pollution, there's plenty still to admire. Other dive spots include the coral reef at Uvita Island (Isla Uvita) off Puerto Limón, the many reefs off the beaches of the Gandoca-Manzanillo Wildlife Refuge, and the sea caverns off Puerto Viejo de Talamanca. The water is clearest during the dry season (September–October and March–April).

Surfing

Some point breaks were badly affected by coastal uplift during the 1991 earthquake, but others were created—a left at Punta Cocles and a right at Punta Uva. You can still ride Puerto Viejo de Talamanca's famous and formidable Salsa Brava, but its spectacular waves are really only for the experienced and fearless surfer. Less hairy spots include Playa Negra, Cahuita, the beach break just south of Puerto Viejo, Playa Bonita north of Puerto Limón, and Uvita Island, 20 minutes from Puerto Limón by boat. You must always beware of riptides. This coast is best surfed from December to March and June to August.

Turtle-Watching

Costa Rica's northern Caribbean shore is one of the few places in the world where the green sea turtle nests: great groups of them descend on Tortuguero National Park from July to October each year. Three other turtle species—the hawksbill, loggerhead, and giant leatherback—also nest here (☞ Close-Up: Tico Turtles, *below*).

Exploring the Atlantic Lowlands and Caribbean Coast

Below the cloud- and rain-forested mountains and foothills of the Central and Talamanca ranges lie fertile plains and dense tracts of primary tropical jungle. Much of this land has been cleared and given over to farming and ranching, but vast expanses are still inaccessible by car. No roads lead to Barra del Colorado or Tortuguero; you have to fly from San José, take a jungle boat from Moín, or via one of the many organized tours from San José, an alluring prospect if it's solitude you crave. Coastal Talamanca, the region to the south, however, is accessible by car via the Carretera Guápiles.

Keep in mind that there are two towns called Puerto Viejo in this region. One, Puerto Viejo de Sarapiquí, is a former river port in the northern, inland section of the lowlands; the other, Puerto Viejo de Talamanca, is on the southern coast not far from the Panamanian border. Keeping the two straight can be confusing, as locals often call both of them Puerto Viejo. To compound the problem, plain old Puerto Limón (usually called Limón) is north along the coast from Puerto Viejo de Talamanca (which is sometimes called Puerto Viejo de Limón).

Numbers in the text correspond to numbers in the margin and on the Atlantic Lowlands and Caribbean Coast map.

Great Itineraries

You need at least a week to cover this territory, but three days are enough to sample its charms if you plan your time judiciously. In addition to keeping in mind the difficulties of getting around, remember that the

The Atlantic Lowlands and the Caribbean Coast

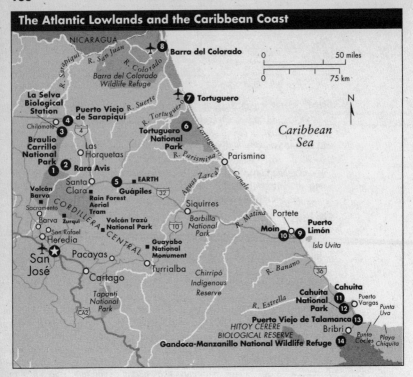

Atlantic lowlands offer various activities requiring different levels of physical endurance and commitment, ranging from seaside lounging to rain forest trekking. If your time, energy, and stomach for discomfort—mud, mosquitoes, and rain, for starters—are limited, you'll have to make choices. Another consideration is travel time. The Rara Avis preserve, for example, is a great place to visit, but because it's so hard to reach—via two- to four-hour tractor haul into the park—the lodge obliges you to stay for at least two nights. Note that many lodges require reservations.

IF YOU HAVE 3 OR 4 DAYS: THE BEACH

Hop on an early flight from San José to ▦ **Tortuguero** ⑦ or ▦ **Barra del Colorado** ⑧ for a jungle-boat tour, turtle-watching session, or fishing trip. The next morning take the boat down to **Moín** ⑩ and then head to ▦ **Puerto Limón** ⑨. Drive or take a bus south to ▦ **Cahuita** ⑪ and/or ▦ **Puerto Viejo de Talamanca** ⑬, where you can relax on the beach, play in the surf, snorkel, or hike in Cahuita National Park. Camp at Puerto Vargas or stay a couple of nights in Cahuita, Puerto Viejo de Talamanca, Punta Uva, or farther south along the beach road that terminates at the bird-filled jungles and deserted beaches of the **Gandoca-Manzanillo National Wildlife Refuge** ⑭.

IF YOU HAVE 3 OR 4 DAYS: THE BEACH AND THE RAINFOREST

Set out early from San José and drive or take a bus over the Guápiles Highway to hike in **Braulio Carrillo National Park** ① or ride the Rain Forest Aerial Tram. Drive to ▦ **La Selva Biological Station** ③ and hike its trails in the afternoon. Spend a night here or in one of the lodges in the ▦ **Puerto Viejo de Sarapiquí** ④ area. Drive south to ▦ **Cahuita** ⑪ and/or ▦ **Puerto Viejo de Talamanca** ⑬, where you can relax on the beach, play in the surf, snorkel, or hike in Cahuita National Park. Stay a night or two in Cahuita, Puerto Viejo de Talamanca, Punta Uva, or farther south along the beach road that terminates at the bird-filled jungles and deserted beaches of the **Gandoca-Manzanillo National Wildlife Refuge** ⑭. Head back to San José, about a four-hour drive.

IF YOU HAVE 7 DAYS
Throw in some variations on the above two themes: add an overnight rafting trip down the Río Pacuare, near Turrialba, or take a multiday fishing trip out of **Tortuguero** ⑦ or **Barra del Colorado** ⑧. Arrange to visit the Bribri, Cabecar, or Kekoldi indigenous reservations in the hills west of **Puerto Viejo de Talamanca** ⑬; hike into the remote Hitoy Cerere Biological Reserve.

When to Tour the Atlantic Lowlands and Caribbean Coast

In three words: when it's dry. This coastal area absorbs 5 m (200 inches) or more of annual rainfall, so unless you want to watch turtles lay their eggs on the beach (each species has its own schedule), you'll want to avoid the worst of it. Chances are you'll be rained on no matter when you go, but your best bets for good weather are the Atlantic coast's two short "dry" seasons—September and October and March and April—which unfortunately do not correspond to the dry season in the rest of the country. If you don't mind rain, come in the rainy season: in exchange for being waterlogged, you'll pay lower prices and see few tourists.

BRAULIO CARRILLO NATIONAL PARK AND THE NORTHERN LOWLANDS

The immense Braulio Carrillo National Park, looming northeast of San José, protects virgin rain forest on either side of the highway to Guápiles. You can get a feel for it as you pass through on the highway, but inside it's another world: everywhere you look green things sprout, twist, and bloom. Bromeliads and orchids cling to arching trees while white-faced monkeys climb and swing and blue morpho butterflies dance and flutter. Adjacent to the park is a private reserve where you can explore the flora and fauna of the rain forest canopy from a Rain Forest Aerial Tram gondola.

After threading through Braulio Carrillo, the Guápiles Highway branches at Santa Clara, having completed its descent onto the Caribbean plain, and continues southeast to Puerto Limón and the Caribbean coast. If you turn left and head north, the smoothly paved road (Highway 4) leads through flat, deforested pasture and pockets of old-growth forest toward two preserves, Rara Avis and La Selva. Just north are the old river-port town of Puerto Viejo de Sarapiquí and the forest-clad hills of the eastern slope of the Cordillera Central.

Continuing due east from Santa Clara, the well-maintained highway takes you through sultry lowlands to the growing community of Guápiles and the tropical agriculture research institution EARTH, and farther on, to Puerto Limón, the region's largest city.

Braulio Carrillo National Park

❶ *30 km (19 mi) north of San José.*

In a country where deforestation is still rife, Parque Nacional Braulio Carrillo provides a rare opportunity to witness dense, primary tropical cloud forest. The park owes its foundation to the public outcry provoked by the construction of the Guápiles Highway through this region in the late 1970s—the government bowed to pressure from environmentalists, and, somewhat ironically, the park is the most accessible one for travelers from the capital thanks to the highway. Covering 443 square km (171 square mi), Braulio Carrillo's extremely diverse terrain ranges from 33 m (108 ft) to more than 3,166 m (10,384 ft) above sea level and extends from the central volcanic range down the Atlantic slope to La Selva research station near Puerto Viejo de Sarapiquí. The park protects a series of ecosystems ranging from the cloud forests on the upper slopes to the tropical wet forest of the Magsasay sector; it is home to 6,000 tree species, 500 bird species, and 135 mammal species.

The **Zurquí ranger station** is to the right of the highway, ½ km (¼ mi) before the Zurquí Tunnel. Here a short trail loops through the cloud forest. Hikes are steep; wear hiking boots to protect yourself from mud, slippage, and snakes. The main trail through primary forest, 1½ km (1 mi) long, culminates in a *mirador* (lookout point), but alas, the highway mars the view. Monkeys, tapirs, jaguars, kinkajous, sloths, raccoons, margays, and porcupines all live in this forest, and resident birds include the quetzal and the eagle. Orchids, bromeliads, heliconias, fungi, and mushrooms live closer to the floor. Another trail leads into the forest to the right, beginning about 17 km (11 mi) after the tunnel, where it follows the Quebrada González, a stream with a cascade and swimming hole. There are no campsites in this part of the park.

The **Carrillo ranger station,** 22 km (14 mi) northeast along the highway from Zurquí, marks the beginning of trails that are less steep. For access to the 3,166-m (10,384-ft) **Volcán Barva,** start from Sacramento, north of Heredia. The walk through the cloud forest to the crater's two lakes takes two to three hours, but your efforts should be rewarded by great views (as long as you start early, preferably before 8 AM, to avoid the mist). You can camp at the Barva ranger station, which is far from any traffic. Stay on the trail when hiking anywhere in Braulio; it's easy to get lost in the cloud forest, and the rugged terrain makes wandering through the woods very dangerous. In addition, muggings of hikers have been reported in the park. Go with a ranger if possible. ☎ 283–8004 (*Sistemas de Areas de Conservación in San José*) or 192 *national parks toll-free hot line.* ✉ $6. ☉ *Daily 7–4.*

Rain Forest Aerial Tram

★ Adjacent to Braulio Carrillo, a 4-square-km (2½-square-mi) preserve houses a privately owned and operated engineering marvel: a series of gondolas strung together in a modified ski-lift pulley system. (To lessen the impact on the jungle, the support pylons were lowered into place by helicopter.) The tram gives students, researchers, and travelers a way of seeing the rain forest canopy and its spectacular array of epiphyte plant life and birds from just above, a feat you could otherwise accomplish only by climbing the trees yourself. The founder, Dr. Donald Perry, also developed a less elaborate system of canopy touring at nearby Rara Avis; of the two, this is more user-friendly. Though purists might complain that it treats the rain forest like an amusement park, it's an entertaining way to learn the value and beauty of rain forest ecology.

The 21 gondolas hold five people each, plus a bilingual biologist-guide equipped with a walkie-talkie to request brief stops for gaping or snapping pictures. The ride covers 2½ km (1½ mi) in 1½ hours. The price includes a biologist-guided walk through the area for ground-level orientation before or after the tram ride; the tour starts at 7 AM (after 9 on Monday). You can arrange a personal pickup in San José for a fee; alternately, there are public buses (on the Guápiles line) every half hour. Drivers know the tram as the *teleférico*. Ten rustic (no AC or TV) but cozy cabinas in the $$$ range are available on-site, as well as a breakfast and lunch café, if you wish to stay in the area. Cabin rates include meals and tram tours. ☎ 257–5961, FAX 257–6053 *reservations*, WEB *www.rainforesttram.com.* ⚐ *Guided walk and tram $49.50. AE, MC, V.* ☺ *Mon. 9–4, Tues.–Sun. 6:30–4. Call for reservations 6* AM– *9* PM.

Rara Avis

❷ *Las Horquetas: 17 km (11 mi) north of Santa Clara, 100 km (62 mi) north of San José.*

Toucans, sloths, green macaws, howler and spider monkeys, vested anteaters, and tapirs may be on hand to greet you when you arrive at Rara Avis, one of Costa Rica's most popular private reserves and open only to overnight guests. Ecologist Amos Bien founded Rara Avis with the intent of combining research, tourism, and the sustainable extraction of forest products. Bilingual guides take you along the muddy trails and canopy observation platforms and help point out wildlife. Or go on your own to the orchid house and butterfly garden. Bring a camera: the reserve's lacy double waterfall is one of Costa Rica's most photogenic sights.

The town of **Las Horquetas** is the jumping-off point for the 13-square-km (8-square-mi) private reserve. The 16-km (10-mi) trip from Las Horquetas to the reserve can be accomplished in three hours on horseback, two to three hours by tractor (leaves daily at 8:30 AM), or one hour by four-wheel-drive vehicle, plus a rough 3-km (2-mi) hike up to the lodge proper. The trails are steep and rugged, but the flora and fauna en route are remarkable. Note: some readers have complained that, although the reserve itself is lovely, they found the guides and services considerably less impressive. From Braulio Carrillo, turn left at signs for Puerto Viejo de Sarapiquí and go 17 km (11 mi) to Las Horquetas.

Lodging

$$$$ 🏨 **Rara Avis.** There are three lodging options here. The Waterfall Lodge, near a 60-m (197-ft) waterfall, has hardwood-paneled rooms with chairs, firm beds, balconies, and hammocks. Despite the prices, this accommodation is rustic, with minimal amenities and no electricity. The more basic Las Casitas are four two-room cabins with shared bath. On the high end, ideal for a rustic honeymoon, is the River Edge Cabin. The cabin is a 10-minute walk through the forest (it's dark at night, but you're given a flashlight), has private bath and balcony, and uses solar panel–generated electricity. Rates include transport from Las Horquetas, guides, and all meals. Minimum stay is two nights. ✉ *Las Horquetas*, ☎ *710–6872 or 764–3214,* FAX *764–4187,* WEB *www.rara-avis. com. 18 rooms, 10 with bath. Restaurant. AE, MC, V.*

La Selva Biological Station

❸ *14 km (9 mi) north of Rara Avis, 79 km (49 mi) northeast of San José.*

Sitting at the confluence of the Puerto Viejo and Sarapiquí rivers, La Selva is a biologist's paradise, its 15 square km (6 square mi) packing about 420 bird species, 460 tree species, and 500 butterfly species. Spottings might include the spider monkey, poison dart frog, agouti, collared peccary, and dozens of other rare creatures. If you want to see wildlife without having to rough it, La Selva is much more agreeable than Rara Avis. Run by the **OTS (Organization for Tropical Studies)**, a consortium of 58 Costa Rican and North American universities, the research station is designed for scientists but welcomes visitors in the daytime and offers basic lodging. Extensive, well-marked trails and swing bridges connect habitats as varied as tropical wet forest, swamps, creeks, rivers, secondary regenerating forest, and pasture. To see the place, take an informative 3½-hour nature walk with one of La Selva's guides, who are some of the country's best. Reserve a walk and lunch ($5 additional) in advance. To get here, take a public bus or use the OTS van, which leaves San José on Monday at 7 AM and returns on Monday at 3 PM. The cost is $10. ⊠ *6 km (3½ mi) south of Puerto Viejo de Sarapiquí; look for sign on west side of road,* ☎ *766–6565,* FAX *766–6535,* WEB *www.ots.ac.cr (mailing address: OTS, Apdo. 676– 2050, San Pedro,* ☎ *240–6696).* 🎫 *Nature walk $25, lunch $5.* ☉ *Walks at 8 AM and 1:30 PM.*

Lodging

$$$ 🏨 **La Selva.** Other lodges provide more comfort for the money, but none can match La Selva's tropical nature experience. The dorm-style rooms have large bunk beds, ceiling fans, tile floors, and lots of screened windows. The restaurant, something like a school cafeteria, serves decent food but has a very limited schedule (reserve ahead). For $66 per person ($79 per person in single room), you get three meals and a guided nature walk. Priority is given to researchers, so advance reservations are essential. ⊠ *6 km (3½ mi) south of Puerto Viejo de Sarapiquí,* ☎ *766–6565 (mailing address: OTS, Apdo. 676–2050, San Pedro,* ☎ *240– 6696,* FAX *240–6783). 60 bunk beds share 12 baths, 3 cabins. Restaurant, hiking, laundry facilities; no air-conditioning, no room phone, no room TVs. AE, MC, V.*

Puerto Viejo de Sarapiquí

❹ *6½ km (4 mi) north of La Selva.*

In the 19th century, Puerto Viejo de Sarapiquí was a thriving river port and the only link with the coastal lands straight east, now Barra del Colorado National Wildlife Refuge and Tortuguero National Park. Fortunes nose-dived with the construction of the coastal canal from the town of Moín, and today Puerto Viejo has a slightly run-down air. The activities of the Nicaraguan Contras made this an actual danger zone in the 1980s, but now that the political situation has improved, boats once again ply the old route up the Río Sarapiquí to the Río San Juan on the Nicaraguan frontier, from where you can travel downstream to Barra del Colorado or Tortuguero. There's not much here to grab your attention, except for Gavilán Sarapiquí River Lodge, but a few tour companies, such as **Costa Rica Expeditions** (☎ 222–0333), offer river tours with up to Class III rapids and there's plenty of wildlife around.

Curious about the life and times of Costa Rica's most famous yellow fruit? The Standard Fruit Company, known as Dole in North America, has daily **Banana Tours** (☎ 768–8683 or 383–4596) to guide you through the process from plantation to processing to packing. The two-hour visit costs $10 and is best arranged through several San José travel agencies. Options include a plantation here in Sarapiquí or sites in Siquirres or south of Puerto Limón.

If you don't have much time to spend in this region, **Ecoscape Nature Tours** (☎ 297–0664, WEB www.ecoscapetours.com) has a daylong Highlights Tour of the Sarapiquí loop for $79. In addition to a boat ride on the river, and a stop at a banana processing plant, the day includes a visit to a coffee plantation and the Poás volcano.

Dining and Lodging

$ ✕📶 **Rancho Leona.** Built by owners Ken Upcraft and Leona Welling-
ton largely to accommodate kayaking tours, this roadside ranch has
rustic dormitories with shared bath facilities. The restaurant, which is
open to the public, serves tasty, reasonably priced food including numerous vegetarian dishes and such Italian classics as eggplant parmi-
giana and chicken cacciatore. Dazzling works of stained glass, all Ken
and Leona's creations, are crafted in the adjacent studio. Activities include kayaking on the Sarapiquí, hiking to a 10-m (33-ft) waterfall,
and swimming in the river. ✉ *La Virgen de Sarapiquí, 17 km (11 mi)
southwest of Puerto Viejo,* ☎ FAX *761–1019,* WEB *www.rancholeona.com.
5 rooms without bath. Restaurant, sauna, hiking, boating, library; no
air-conditioning, no room phone, no room TVs. MC, V.*

$$$ 📶 **Hotel Bambú.** Unlike the many isolated properties in this region,
Bambú is in the heart of Puerto Viejo de Sarapiquí. The rooms are sim-
ple but comfortable; all have air-conditioning. A dense cluster of tall bam-
boo stalks climbs like Jack's bean stalk out of the garden, lending shade
for the bar and restaurant, the latter of which serves Costa Rican–influ-
enced Chinese food at reasonable prices. ✉ *Main street across from
town square/soccer field,* ☎ *766–6359,* FAX *766–6132,* WEB *www.elbambu.
com (mailing address: Apdo. 151–A–2100, Guadelupe). 11 rooms.
Restaurant, bar, pool, laundry service; no room phone, no room TVs. AE,
MC, V.*

$$$ 📶 **Selva Verde Lodge.** Built on stilts over the Río Sarapiquí, this ex-
pansive complex stands on the edge of a 2-square-km (1-square-mi)
private reserve of tropical rain forest and caters primarily to natural-
history tours. The buildings have wide verandas strung with hammocks, and the rooms come with polished wood paneling, fans, and
mosquito blinds. Activities include guided walks, boat trips, canoeing,
rafting, and mountain biking. Room prices include all meals and a bird-
watching tour. ✉ *7 km (4 mi) west of Puerto Viejo de Sarapiquí (mailing address: Apdo. 55, Chilamate,* ☎ *766–6800,* FAX *766–6011,* WEB *www.
selvaverde.com). 40 rooms, 5 bungalows. Restaurant, hiking, horseback riding, boating, fishing, library, laundry service; no air-conditioning,
no room phone, no room TVs. AE, MC, V.*

$$ 📶 **Gavilán Sarapiquí River Lodge.** Beautiful gardens run down to the
★ river, and colorful tanagers and three types of toucan feast in the cit-
rus trees. Not bad for an erstwhile hub of a fruit and cattle farm. The
two-story lodge has comfortable rooms with white walls, terra-cotta
floors, and decorative crafts. The food, Costa Rican *comida típica* (typ-
ical fare), has earned its good reputation. Most guests are with tours,
having been picked up in San José; prime activities are horseback jun-
gle treks and boat trips up the Río Sarapiquí. ✉ *1 km (½ mi) south-
east of Comando Atlántico (naval command),* WEB *www.gavilanlodge.
com (mailing address: Apdo. 445–2010, San José,* ☎ *766–6743,* FAX
*253–6556). 13 rooms. Restaurant, hot tub, horseback riding, fishing;
no air-conditioning, no room phone, no room TVs. AE, MC, V.*

Guápiles

❺ *60 km (38 mi) northeast of San José.*

You may not see any reason to stop in the Guápiles area—the town
itself is off the main road—other than weariness or the need for a fuel
fix, automotive or gastronomic. This farm and forest area is a cross-
roads of a sort: more or less equidistant are the palm beaches of the
Caribbean shore, the jungles to the north, and the rain-forested moun-
tains looming in the west. For this reason it's not a bad place to linger

for a day or two, day-tripping in any of three directions. Guápiles is home to several major biological-research facilities as well as commercial producers of tropical plants.

Lodging

$$ ☷ **Hotel Río Palmas.** Think of it as a hacienda motel. Proximate to EARTH, near the town of Guácimo, the Río Palmas' red-tile roof, open-air restaurant grabs your eye as you're speeding by on the Guápiles Highway. Behind an arched, whitewashed entry gate, one-story, tile-roof whitewashed cabinas wrap around a central courtyard with a fountain and plants. The guest rooms inside have ceiling fans. Exotic plantings abound (the hotel is actually on an ornamental-plant farm), and the staff can arrange hikes, farm and jungle tours, and horseback rides to private waterfalls. ⊠ *Guápiles Hwy.,* ☎ *760–0330,* ☒ *760–0296. 32 rooms, 24 with bath. Restaurant, pool, hiking, horseback riding, laundry service; no air-conditioning, no room phone, no room TVs. AE, MC, V.*

EARTH

15 km (9 mi) east of Guápiles on Guápiles Hwy.

Agriculture and ecology buffs will want to check out **EARTH** (Escuela de Agricultura de la Región Tropical Húmeda; ☎ 713–0000, ☒ 713–0001, ☷ www.earth.ac.cr), a nonprofit organization researching the production of less pesticide-dependent bananas and other forms of sustainable agriculture, as well as medicinal plants. (You'll see EARTH's elegant stationery and other paper products made from banana stems in many tourist shops.) The property encompasses a banana plantation and a forest reserve with nature trails. Though priority is given to researchers and conference groups, you're welcome to stay in the school's 50-person lodging facility, replete with private bathrooms, hot water, and ceiling fans, for $55 a night, which includes the use of a swimming pool and exercise equipment. Advance reservations are required.

En Route If you're bypassing Puerto Limón entirely en route south to Cahuita and Puerto Viejo de Talamanca, a right turn via Moín 3 km (2 mi) shy of Puerto Limón will give you an alternate route—a smooth road that weaves through the hills. Look for the green road sign indicating a right turn to Sixaola (the Panamanian border) and other points south.

TORTUGUERO AND BARRA DEL COLORADO

Tortuguero means "turtle region," and, indeed, this northeastern sector remains one of the world's prime places to watch the life cycle of sea turtles. The stretch of beach between the Colorado and Matina rivers was first mentioned as a nesting ground for sea turtles in a 1592 Dutch chronicle, and because the area is so isolated—there's no road here to this day—the turtles nested undisturbed for centuries. By the mid-1900s, however, the harvesting of eggs and catching of turtles had reached such a level that these creatures faced extinction. In 1963 an executive decree regulated the hunting of turtles and the gathering of eggs, and in 1970 the government established Tortuguero National Park. You can continue up the canals that begin in Moín and run parallel to the coast, to the less-visited Barra del Colorado Wildlife Refuge, an immense protected area that's connected to the park.

TICO TURTLES

COSTA RICA'S TURTLE visitations are renowned among devoted ecotourists. An array of species makes predictable yet astonishing annual visits to beaches on both the Pacific and the Atlantic-Caribbean coasts, many set aside to protect them. Nesting turtles come ashore at night, plowing an uneven furrow with their flippers to propel themselves past the high-tide line, then using their hind flippers to scoop out a hole in which to lay their eggs. A few months later, hatchlings struggle out of the nests and make their perilous journey back, in effect, to the sea.

In spite of this protection, their "endangered" classifications, and the earnest ecologists and well-meaning animal lovers looking after them, turtle populations remain seriously threatened. Poachers have for generations harvested the eggs—a rumored aphrodisiac—and the meat and shells. Beachfront development, with its bright lights, can disorient the turtles; and long-line fishermen's hooks and lines entangle and drown them.

On Costa Rica's east coast, four species of turtles nest at Tortuguero National Park: the green turtle, hawksbill, loggerhead, and giant leatherback. Green turtles reproduce in large groups from July to October. A green turtle lays eggs on average every two to three years and produces two or three clutches each time; between those times, the turtles feed as far afield as Florida and Venezuela. Small in comparison with their peers, hawksbills are threatened by hunters because of their shells, a transparent brown hide much sought-after for jewelry making in, among other countries, Japan. Loggerheads, as their name implies, have outsize heads and shorter fins and make rare appearances at Tortuguero. Giant leatherbacks are the largest of all turtles—

they grow up to 2 m (6½ ft) long and can weigh in at up to 1,000 pounds— and have a tough outer skin rather than a shell, hence the name. From mid-February through April, leatherbacks nest mainly in Tortuguero's southern sector.

Olive ridleys are the smallest sea turtles— the average carapace, or hardback shell, is 53 cm to 74 cm (21 inches to 29 inches) long—and the least shy. During mass nestings, or *arribadas,* thousands of olive ridley turtles take to the Pacific shores at night, plowing the sand as they move up the beach sniffing for the high-tide line. An estimated 200,000 of the 500,000 turtles that nest in Costa Rica each year choose Playa Nancite, a gray-sand beach in Guanacaste's Santa Rosa National Park, backed by dense hibiscus and button mangroves. This is the world's only totally protected olive ridley arribada.

Easier to reach is the Ostional National Wildlife Refuge, near Nosara on the Nicoya Peninsula. Locals harvest the eggs in the early stages of the arribada—turtle visits run from August to December and peak in September and October—because later waves of mother turtles invariably destroy the earlier nests. Another more accessible spot is Playa Grande, also on Nicoya, stomping ground of the mammoth, ponderous, exquisitely dignified leatherback turtles from November to April. Marino Las Baulas National Park was created specifically to protect the leatherbacks, who also show up in smaller numbers at Playas Langosta and Junquillal.

To help save these gentle giants, you can volunteer with turtle research and protection at such organizations as ATEC, the Asociación Talamanqueña de Ecoturismo y Conservación.

Tortuguero National Park

★ **⑥** *50 km (31 mi) northwest (3 hrs by boat) of Puerto Limón.*

The palm-lined beaches of Parque Nacional Tortuguero stretch off as far as the eye can see, and its additional ecosystems include lowland rain forest, estuaries, and swampy areas covered with *jolillo* palms. You can wander the beach independently, but riptides make swimming dangerous, and shark rumors persist. At various times of the year, green, hawksbill, loggerhead, and giant leatherback turtles lumber up the beaches and deposit their eggs for safekeeping—a fascinating natural ritual. If you want to watch the turtles nest, contact your hotel or the parks office to hire a certified local guide. You won't be allowed to use a camera on the beach and must cover your flashlight with red plastic, as lights can deter the turtles from nesting.

Freshwater turtles inhabit Tortuguero's rivers, as do crocodiles—most populous in the Río Agua Frío—and the endangered *vacas marinas*, or manatees. Manatees consume huge quantities of aquatic plants and are endangered mainly because their lack of speed makes them easy prey. You might also glimpse tapirs (watch for these in jolillo groves), jaguars, anteaters, ocelots, howler monkeys, collared and white-lipped peccaries, raccoons, otters, skunks, and coatis. Some 350 species of birds and countless butterflies, including the iridescent blue morpho, also call this area home. At a station deep in the Tortuguero jungle, volunteers from the Canadian Organization for Tropical Education and Rainforest Conservation manage a butterfly farm, catalog plants and animals, and explore sustainable forest practices.

Tortuguero

⑦ *There are officially no roads to Tortuguero, though illegal attempts have been made to cut one through the jungle. Travel time is 30 mins by plane from San José, 3 hrs by boat from Moín.*

North of the national park, the hamlet of Tortuguero is a pleasant little place to spend an hour or two, with its 600 inhabitants, two churches, three bars, and two souvenir shops. Pick up information on the park, turtles, and other wildlife at the kiosk in the town center. You can also take a stroll on the 32-km (20-mi) beach, but swimming is not recommended due to strong riptides and the presence (not threatening, say the locals) of large numbers of bull sharks and barracuda. Visitors who have more than a week's time in Costa Rica typically spend a couple of nights here.

The **Caribbean Conservation Corporation** (CCC) runs a visitor center and museum, with excellent animal photos, a video in which actor Cliff Robertson narrates local history, and detailed discussions of the latest ecological goings-on and what you can do to help. There's a souvenir shop next door. ✉ *From beach, walk north along path and watch for sign,* ☎ *710–0547; 224–9215 in San José,* WEB *www.cccturtle.org (mailing address: Apdo. 246–2050, San Pedro).* 🖼 *Donations accepted.* ◷ *Mon.–Sat. 10–noon and 2–5, Sun. 2–5.*

For the committed ecotourist, the **John H. Phipps Biological Field Station** (✉ *near airport, across canal from Tortuga Lodge,* ☎ *352/373–6441 in the U.S.*) has camping areas as well as dorm-style quarters with a communal kitchen. If you want to get involved in the life of the turtles or help catalog the population of neotropical migrant birds, arrange a stay in advance through the CCC.

OFF THE
BEATEN PATH

COASTAL CANALS – The jungle life that you'll see on a three-hour boat trip through the combination of natural and man-made canals between Tortuguero and Moín is awesome, providing a kind of real-life Indiana Jones adventure. Running parallel to the coast a couple of miles inland, the waterway provides a safer alternative to making the journey up the coast via the ocean. Most San José tour operators will not take you all the way to Moín to board canal boats but instead access them via the Parismina or Aguas Zarcas rivers. As you swoop through the sinuous turns of the natural waterways, your captain-guide may spot monkeys, snakes, caimans, mud turtles, sloths, and dozens of bird species, including flocks of bright and noisy parrots, kingfishers, aracaris, and assorted herons. The densely layered greenery is highlighted by brilliantly colored flowers, and the visual impact is doubled by the jungle's reflection in the mirror-smooth surface of the water. Consider hiring a dugout canoe and a guide to explore some of the rivers flowing into the canal; these waterways bear less boat traffic and, often, have more wildlife.

Tortuguero is one of those "everybody's a guide" places; quality varies, but most are quite knowledgeable. The **Caribbean Conservation Corporation** (☎ 710–0547) can recommend good local guides. If you stay at one of the lodges, guided tours are included in your package price.

Dining and Lodging

$–$$ ✕ **Miss Junie.** Most Tortuguero travelers take meals at their lodges, but Miss Junie, the village's most well-known cook, serves cheap, filling, tasty food from her combination restaurant–hotel and is worth a detour. Selection is limited, and it's best to call ahead, but you can usually count on a chicken, beef, or fish platter with rice and beans simmered in coconut milk, which includes a beverage and dessert. ⊠ *Tortuguero Village*, ☎ *710–0523. No credit cards.*

$$$$ 🛏 **Jungle Tarpon Lodge.** On 100 acres at the Parsimina River lagoon, this intimate lodge specializes in sportfishing packages—it has a sister program in Alaska—and also arranges eco-adventure activities, turtle-watching, and custom tours. (There's plenty to do here if you don't fish.) Though small, the lodge is a deluxe affair, crafted in fine wood with large rooms, modern tiled bathrooms, and beamed ceilings. Savory local cuisine—heavy on fish, of course—is served in the dining room; some meals are enjoyed riverside. Transfers to San José, meals, and charters are included in the four- to eight-day packages. ⊠ *May–mid-Oct.: mailing address: Great Alaska, 33881 Sterling Hwy., Sterling, AK 99672,* ☎ *800/544–2261 or 907/262–4515,* Ⓕ𝔸𝕏 *907/262–8797; mid-Oct.–Apr.: mailing address: Great Alaska Box 2670, Poulsbo, WA 98370,* ☎ *360/697–6454,* Ⓕ𝔸𝕏 *360/697–7850),* 🕸 *www.jungletarpon. com. 4 rooms. Restaurant, hiking, boating, fishing; no air-conditioning, no room phone, no room TVs. AE, MC, V.*

$$$$ 🛏 **Mawamba Lodge.** Nestled between the river and the ocean,
★ Mawamba is the perfect place to kick back and relax. Once you're whisked from Moín in a 2½-hr launch ride, you stay in comfortable rustic cabinas with hot water, garden views, and fans, taking meals in the spacious dining room, all on a 15-acre site. Packages include all meals, transfers, and guided tours of the jungle and canals; trips to turtle-heavy beaches cost $10 extra. ⊠ *500 yards north of Tortuguero on ocean side of canal,* ☎ *710–7282,* 🕸 *www.grupomawamba.com (mailing address: Apdo. 10980–1000, San José,* ☎ *223–2421,* Ⓕ𝔸𝕏 *222–5463). 54 cabinas. Restaurant, bar, pool, hot tub, volleyball, beach, laundry service, meeting room; no air-conditioning, no room phone, no room TVs. AE, MC, V.*

$$$$ ★ ⊞ **Pachira Lodge.** This is the prettiest and most luxurious of Tortuguero's lodges—although not the costliest. Each almond-wood cabina set amid lush, well-manicured gardens contains four guest rooms, each of which has high ceilings, an overhead fan, king-size beds, and bamboo furniture. The stunning pool is shaped like a giant sea turtle: the head is a hot tub, the left paw is a wading pool, and the right paw is equipped for swimmers with disabilities. The only drawback is that you have few options at night, as there is no cross-river transportation into town. Package deals include transport from San José, a jungle tour, and all meals. ⊠ *Across river from Mawamba Lodge,* ☎ *382–2239,* WEB *www.pachiralodge.com (mailing address: Apdo. 1818–1002, San José,* ☎ *256–7080,* FAX *223–1119). 34 rooms. Restaurant, bar, pool, wading pool, laundry service; no air-conditioning, no room phone, no room TVs. AE, MC, V.*

$$$$ ⊞ **Tortuga Lodge.** Owned by Costa Rica Expeditions, this thatched riverside lodge is surrounded by lush lawns, orchids, and tropical trees and renowned for its tarpon- and snook-fishing packages. The second-largest tarpon ever caught in Costa Rica, weighing 182 pounds, was reeled in here in 1987. Guest rooms are comfortable, with fans and mosquito blinds—much needed, as the mosquitoes can be voracious. Considering that most of the restaurant ingredients are flown in, the chefs do an excellent job preparing hearty food. The lodge is across the river from the airstrip, 2 km (1 mi) from Tortuguero. ⊠ *20 mins north by boat from Tortuguero National Park or 35 mins by plane from San José,* ☎ *710–8016,* WEB *www.costaricaexpeditions.com (mailing address: Apdo. 6941–1000, San José,* ☎ *222–0333 or 257–0766,* FAX *257–1665). 24 rooms. Dining room, bar, pool, hiking, fishing; no air-conditioning, no room phone, no room TVs. AE, MC, V.*

$$ ⊞ **El Manatí.** Simple and reasonably priced, El Manatí is popular with budget travelers and researchers, some of whom study the lodge's namesake—the endangered manatee. The comfortable but slightly run-down rooms have firm beds and mosquito screens. The contiguous terraces look across a narrow lawn to the river, where you can kayak and canoe. Chestnut-beaked toucans, poison dart frogs, and three types of monkey hang out in the surrounding jungle. The price of a stay includes breakfast. ⊠ *Across river, about 1 km (½ mi) north of Tortuguero,* ☎ FAX *383–0330. 8 rooms. Restaurant, fans, Ping-Pong, boating; no air-conditioning, no room phone, no room TVs. No credit cards.*

Barra del Colorado

❽ *25 km (16 mi) northwest of Tortuguero.*

Farther up the coast from Tortuguero is the ramshackle hamlet of Barra del Colorado, a popular sportfishing hub characterized by plain stilted wooden houses, dirt paths, and a complete absence of motorized land vehicles (though some locals have added outboard motors to their handhewn canoes). Bordered to the north by the Río San Juan and the frontier with Nicaragua is the vast, 905-square-km (350-square-mi) **Barra del Colorado Wildlife Refuge** (Refugio Nacional de Fauna Silvestre Barra del Colorado), really the only local attraction for nonanglers. Most people approach by air or boat (via the canals) from San José or Tortuguero; you can also come from Puerto Viejo de Sarapiquí up the Sarapiquí and San Juan rivers. Transportation once you get here is almost exclusively waterborne, as there are virtually no paths in this swampy terrain. The list of species that you're likely to see from your boat is almost the same as that for Tortuguero; the main difference here is the feeling of being farther off the beaten track.

Lodging

$$$$ ⊡ **Río Colorado Lodge.** This jungle lodge caters almost exclusively to sportfishing folk and tours, complete with a modern fleet of 3- and 8-m (10- and 26-ft) sportfishing vessels. Guest rooms have twin beds with patterned bedspreads, paneled ceilings, white curtains, and basket lamp shades. The pricey, all-inclusive tours include airport pickup, all meals, and fishing trips; alternately, some fly-in, boat-out nature-tour packages include Tortuguero National Park at lower prices. ⊠ *35-min flight from San José via Travelair,* ☎ *710–6879,* ℻ *231–5987,* ™ *www. riocoloradolodge.com (mailing address: Apdo. 5094–1000, San José,* ☎ *232–4063; 800/243–9777 in the U.S.). 18 rooms. Restaurant, bar, fishing, laundry service; no room phone, no room TVs. AE, MC, V.*

COASTAL TALAMANCA

The quickest route from San José to the Atlantic coast runs through the magnificent cloud forest of Braulio Carrillo National Park on its way to the Caribbean Sea and the lively and sometimes dangerous port town of Puerto Limón. The 160-km (100-mi) trip along the Guápiles Highway to the coast takes about 2½ hours if all goes well; the highway is carved out of mountainous jungle and is susceptible to landslides. Make sure it's not blocked before you set off. (The alternate route is a long, painfully slow journey via Turrialba and Siquirres—it's doable, but best avoided.) As the highway descends and straightens toward Guápiles, you'll enter the province of Limón, where cloud forest gives way to banana plantations and partially deforested pastureland. (Note well that the highway gives way to potholes, some big enough to swallow an entire wheel and ruin your car's suspension.) Local farms produce cocoa, exotic export plants, and macadamia nuts. After passing through villages with names like Bristol, Stratford, and Liverpool, you'll arrive in the provincial capital, Puerto Limón.

Puerto Limón

❾ *130 km (81 mi) southeast of Braulio Carrillo National Park, 100 km (62 mi) southeast of Guápiles.*

Puerto Limón inherited its promontory setting, overlooking the Caribbean, from the ancient Indian village of Cariari, which lay close to Uvita Island, where Christopher Columbus dropped anchor on his final voyage in 1502. The colorful Afro-Caribbean flavor of Costa Rica's most important port (population 50,000) is the first sign of life for seafaring visitors to Costa Rica's east coast. Puerto Limón is a lively, if shabby, town with a 24-hour street life. The wooden houses are brightly painted, but the grid-plan streets look rather worn, due largely to the damage caused by the 1991 earthquake. Street crime, including pickpocketing and nighttime mugging, is not uncommon here. But *"Limón cambia,"* (Limón is changing) say residents. Long charged with neglecting the city, the national government has turned attention to Puerto Limón. New businesses are coming in, providing hopeful signs of urban renewal, and the town has beefed up security with a more visible police presence. Staying overnight in center city may still be somewhat dicey, but there are several appealing hotels at Portete, just north of Límon town, with easy access to the docks at Moín.

On the left side of the highway as you enter Puerto Limón is a large **Chinese cemetery,** Chinese workers having made up a large part of the 1880s railroad-construction team that worked here. Thousands died of malaria and yellow fever. Follow the railroad as far as the palm-lined promenade that runs around the **Parque Vargas.** From the promenade you can see the raised dead coral left stranded by the quake. Nine or so Hoffman's two-toed sloths live in the trees of Parque Vargas; ask a passerby to point them out, as spotting them requires a trained eye. From the park, find the lively enclosed market on Avenida 2—a pedestrian mall—between Calles 3 and 4, where you can buy fruit for the road ahead.

Dining and Lodging

$–$$ ✕ **Springfield.** Protected from the street by a leafy conservatory, this Caribbean kitchen whips up tasty rice-and-bean dishes. Decor consists of wood paneling, red tablecloths, and a white-tile floor. Bring your dancing shoes: the huge dance floor out back creaks to the beat of soca, salsa, and reggae on weekends. ⊠ *On road north from Puerto Limón to Portete, left opposite hospital,* ☎ *758–1203. AE, MC, V.*

$$$$ ⬚ **Hotel Maribú Caribe.** Perched on a cliff overlooking the Caribbean
★ Sea between Puerto Limón and Portete, these white conical thatched huts have great views and hot water, and most are air-conditioned. The lovely grounds have green lawns, shrubs, palm trees, and a large, kidney-shape pool. The poolside bar discourages exertion. Breakfast is included. ⊠ *2 km (1 mi) north on road to Portete, Apdo. 623–7300, Puerto Limón,* ☎ *758–4543,* FAX *758–3541,* WEB *www.costaricabureau.com/maribu.htm. 52 rooms. Restaurant, bar, snack bar, pool, laundry service; no air-conditioning in some rooms, no room phone, no room TVs. AE, MC, V.*

$$$ ⬚ **Hotel Matama.** If you're coming from San José and planning to catch an early boat north out of Moín, this is a great place to get your first taste of the Caribbean. Across the street from the beach, the property has a pool and bar in close proximity, and the grounds are gorgeously landscaped with botanical trails exhibiting 50 tropical plant species. The open-air restaurant has lovely garden views. ⊠ *4 km (2½ mi) from Puerto Limón on road to Portete, Apdo. 606–7300, Puerto Limón,* ☎ *758–1123 or 758–4409,* FAX *758–4499,* WEB *www.matama.com. 16 rooms. Restaurant, bar, pool, dance club, laundry service, meeting room; no room phone, no room TVs. AE, MC, V.*

Moín

🔟 *5 km (3 mi) north of Puerto Limón.*

The docks at Moín are a logical next stop after visiting neighboring Puerto Limón, especially if you want to take a boat north to explore the Caribbean coast. You'll probably be able to negotiate a waterway and national-park tour with a local guide, and if you call in advance, you'll find the man considered the best guide on the Caribbean coast: Modesto Watson, a local Miskito Indian guide, legendary for his bird- and animal-spotting skills as well as his howler-monkey imitations (☎ 226–0986).

Cahuita

⓫ *44 km (27 mi) southeast of Puerto Limón.*

The Caribbean character of the Atlantic lowlands becomes powerfully evident in the surf rolling shoreward, as you head south from Puerto Limón to Cahuita; the hot, humid stir of the Caribbean trade winds; and the laid-back pace of the people you meet. This is tropical Central America, and it feels like another country, its slow, somewhat sultry atmosphere far removed from the business and bustle of San José.

Dusty Cahuita, its main dirt street flanked by wooden-slat cabins, is a backpackers' vacation town with something of a seedy reputation— a hippie hangout with a dash of Afro-Caribbean spice tossed in. The town's image as a drug center is only partially deserved; like Puerto Viejo de Talamanca, Cahuita has a few junkies, but the locals don't see them as a threat. And after years of negative crime-related publicity, Cahuita has beefed up security and is making a small but well-deserved comeback on the tourist circuit. Tucked in among the backpackers' digs are a few surprisingly nice get-away-from-it-all lodgings, yours to have at surprisingly decent prices.

Lively reggae, soca, and samba blast from the turquoise **Coco's Bar,** on the main road, weekend evenings, and the assemblage of dogs dozing on its veranda illustrates the rhythm of local life. Go 200 yards north of the bus stop for **Cahuita Tours** information center (☎ 755–0232), where the friendly folks can set you up with any of a variety of adventures including tours of the canals, indigenous reservations, and mountains; river rafting and kayaking; and bike and snorkeling-equipment rentals. They can also reconfirm flights and make lodging reservations. At the southern end of Cahuita's main street is the start of **Cahuita National Park.**

Dining and Lodging

$$ ✕ **Cha Cha Cha.** You can order anything from Thai shrimp salad to Tex-Mex fajitas at this "world cuisine" restaurant. A delectable specialty is *langosta cha cha cha,* lobster in a white-wine garlic sauce with fresh basil. Paintings by local artists hang on the light-blue walls of the candlelit outdoor dining area, separated from the street by miniature palm trees. ⊠ *1 block north of bus stop on main strip,* ☎ *394–4153. MC, V. Closed Mon. No lunch.*

$$ ✕ **Miss Edith.** Miss Edith is revered for her flavorful Caribbean cook-★ ing, vegetarian meals, and herbal teas for whatever ails you. You won't be fed in a hurry—most dishes are made to order—but the rondón and spicy jerk chicken are worth the wait. Back in the day, Miss Edith used to serve on her own front porch; she's since moved to more ample surroundings on an easy-to-miss side street at the north end of town. ⊠ *From bus stop, follow main road north and turn right at police station,* ☎ *755–0248. No credit cards. Closed Sun.*

$–$$ ✕ **Spaghetteria Relax.** You'll first notice the skewers of shrimp and chicken turning on the grill at this open-air restaurant in the center of town, but the Italian-Mexican owners also toss in pastas and fajitas to give their native cuisines sufficient representation, too. There are just four tables here. If they're full, take a seat at the bar and engage in some lively conversation with your fellow diners. ⊠ *50 yards south of bus stop,* ☎ *755–0322. No credit cards. Closed Tues.*

$$$ ✕🏠 **Magellan Inn.** This group of bungalows is arguably Cahuita's ★ most elegant lodging. Graced with tile-floored terraces facing a pool and gardens growing on an ancient coral reef, the Magellan has carpeted rooms with original paintings, custom-made wooden furniture, and ceiling fans. Feast on intensely flavored French and Creole seafood specialties in the Casa Creole, a freestanding coral-pink structure with an outdoor dining room, and don't miss the house pâté or the homemade ice cream. The hotel's enticing open-air bar rocks to great blues and jazz recordings in the evenings and mellows with classical music at breakfast. ⊠ *2 km (1 mi) north of Cahuita at far end of Playa Negra (Apdo. 1132–7300, Puerto Limón),* ☎ FAX *755–0035,* WEB *www.costaricabureau.com/magellan.htm. 6 rooms. Restaurant, bar, pool; no room phones, no room TVs. AE, MC, V.*

$$$ 🏨 **Atlántida Lodge.** Atlántida's main assets are its attractively landscaped grounds, the beach across the road, and the large pool. You're welcomed to your room with a lovely assortment of fresh and dried flowers; the rooms themselves have tile floors and pretty terraces. Enjoy complimentary breakfast in the pleasant thatch-roof restaurant. ⊠ *Next to soccer field at Playa Negra,* ☎ *755–0115,* FAX *755–0213,* WEB *www.atlantida.co.cr. 30 rooms. Restaurant, pool, hot tub, massage, laundry service, meeting room; no air-conditioning, no room phones, no room TVs. AE, MC, V.*

$$$ 🏨 **Aviarios del Caribe.** It's a lodge, sloth rescue center, and bird-watch-
★   ing sanctuary all rolled into one. More than 285 bird species have been spotted here, many with the help of the telescope on the wide second-floor deck. Buttercup, the resident three-toed sloth, oversees the proceedings in the upstairs open-air dining room. The spacious guest rooms have white walls, blue-tile floors, and fresh flowers. For $3 you can hike the adjoining wildlife refuge, and $30 will get you an unforgettable 3½-hour riverboat tour guided by the owner, Luis, himself. ⊠ *9 km (5 mi) north of Cahuita, follow hotel signs on Río Estrella delta, (mailing address: Apdo. 569–7300, Puerto Limón),* ☎ FAX *382–1335. 6 rooms. Hiking, laundry service; no room phones, no room TVs. AE, MC, V.*

$$–$$$ 🏨 **El Encanto Bed & Breakfast.** Zen Buddhists Pierre-Léon Tetreault
★   and Patricia Kim Chiaw have cultivated a serene and beautiful environment here, ideal for physical and spiritual relaxation. Lodgings are in an enchanting garden, with an extensive bromeliad collection and Buddha figures. There's a choice of minimalist yet comfortable rooms or bungalows, decorated with art from all over the globe. Amenities include queen-size beds, hot water, and secure parking—and breakfast is included, of course. The beach is across the street and massage and yoga classes are available weekends. ⊠ *West of the police station,* ☎ FAX *755–0113,* WEB *www.2000.co.cr/elencanto (Apdo. 7-7302, Cahuita). 3 rooms, 3 bungalows. Breakfast room, fans; no air-conditioning in some rooms, no room phones, no TV in some rooms. AE, MC, V.*

$$ 🏨 **Kelly Creek Hotel-Restaurante.** Owners Andrés and Marie-Claude de Alcalá of Madrid have created a wonderful budget option in this handsome wooden hotel, on the creek bank across a short pedestrian bridge from the park entrance. Each of the four hardwood-finished guest rooms is big enough to sleep a small army, and has two double beds. Señor de Alcalá barbecues meat and fresh fish on an open-air grill and also cooks paella and other Spanish specialties. Caiman come to the creek bank in search of snacks, and the monkeys, parrots, jungles, and beaches of the national park are just yards away, as is the lively center of Cahuita. ⊠ *Next to park entrance,* ☎ *755–0007,* WEB *www.2000. co.cr/hotelkellycreek. 4 rooms. Restaurant, fans, beach; no air-conditioning, no room phones, no room TVs. AE, MC, V.*

Cahuita National Park

⑫ *Puerto Vargas is 5 km (3 mi) south of Cahuita.*

The only Costa Rican park jointly administered by the National Parks Service and a community, Parque Nacional Cahuita starts at the southern edge of the town of Cahuita. The park's rain forest extends right to the edge of its curving, 3-km (2-mi) utterly undeveloped white-sand beach. Roughly parallel to the coastline, a 7-km (4-mi) trail passes through the forest to Cahuita Point, encircled by a 2½-square-km (1½-square-mi) coral reef. The hike takes only a few hours, but you have to ford several rivers on the way—check conditions beforehand, as they can be prohibitive in the rainy season.

You'll find good snorkeling off Cahuita Point—watch for blue parrot fish and angelfish as they weave their way among equally colorful species of coral, sponges, and seaweeds. Sadly, the coral reef is slowly being killed by sediment, intensified by deforestation and the erosive effects of the 1991 earthquake. Use a local guide to find the best reefs (or to snorkel independently, swim out from the beach on the Puerto Vargas side), and don't snorkel for a few days after it rains, as the water is sure to be murky. You can also take a ride in a glass-bottom boat from Cahuita (visibility is best in September and October). The road to the park headquarters at Puerto Vargas is 5 km (3 mi) south of Cahuita on the left. Here you'll find the ranger station as well as campsites that have been carved out of the jungle, scattered along the beachfront. ☎ 755–0302. ✉ *Donation requested at Cahuita entrance, $6 at Puerto Vargas entrance.* ☉ *Weekdays 8–4, weekends 7–5.*

Outdoor Activities and Sports

BICYCLING

You can bike through Cahuita National Park, but the trail gets pretty muddy at times, and you'll run into logs, river estuaries, and other obstacles. Nevertheless, mountain bikes are a good way to get around on the dirt roads and trails surrounding Cahuita and Puerto Viejo de Talamanca. Cycling is easiest in the dry season, of course, though you'll see many hardy souls cycling during the long rainy season. There are several area bike rental outlets. **Caribbean Flavor** (☎ 755–0017), in the center of town, charges a mere $2 an hour for a mountain bike.

HIKING

A serious hiking trail extends as far as Puerto Vargas. If you're staying in Cahuita, you can take a bus or catch a ride into Puerto Vargas and hike back around the point in the course of a day. If you camp at Puerto Vargas, you can also hike south along the beach to Puerto Viejo de Limón and bus or cab it back to the park. Be sure to bring plenty of water, food, and sunscreen. Along the trail you might spot howler and white-faced monkeys, coatis, armadillos, and raccoons. Swimming is prohibited here because of the extremely strong current.

SNORKELING AND SURFING

Cahuita's reefs are just one of several high-quality snorkeling spots around here. You can rent snorkeling gear in Cahuita or Puerto Viejo de Talamanca or through your hotel; most hotels will also organize trips. It's wise to work with a guide, as the number of good snorkeling spots is limited and they're not always easily accessible.

The staff at the friendly storefront **Cahuita Tours,** 200 yards north of the bus stop, can assist with tourist information, travel arrangements, snorkeling and surfing-equipment rental, horseback-riding, and other tours. Although it's not in town, **ATEC** (☎ 750–0398), an ecotourism organization in nearby Puerto Viejo de Talamanca, has tourism information and can help with travel arrangements, equipment rentals, and much more.

Puerto Viejo de Talamanca

⑬ *16 km (10 mi) south of Cahuita.*

Puerto Viejo de Talamanca was once quieter than Cahuita, but no more—it's one of the hottest spots on the international surfpunk circuit. This muddy, colorful little town swarms with surfers, new-age hippies, beaded and spangled punks, would-be Rastafarians of all colors and descriptions, and wheelers and dealers both pleasant and otherwise.

Time was when most kids came here with only one thing on their mind: surfing. Today, many seem to be looking only for a party, with or without surf. (Nevertheless, the waves are at their best between December and April and again in June and July.)

But if alternative lifestyles aren't your bag, there are plenty of more "grown-up" offerings on the road heading southeast out of town. Some locals bemoan the loss of their town's innocence, as the ravages of crack cocaine and other evils have surfaced, but only in small doses: this is still a fun town to visit, with a great variety of hotels, cabinas, and restaurants in every price range.

You do have access to the beach right in town, and the Salsa Brava, famed in surfers' circles for its pounding waves, is here off the coast as well. But you'll find the best strands of Caribbean sand outside the village. Play Negra, a black-sand beach, extends northwest from Puerto Viejo for about a kilometer. Heading southeast from town, Playa Cocles begins about 2 km (1 ¼ mi) from Puerto Viejo. A series of small beaches, collectively referred to as Playa Chiquita, runs from 4 to 7 km (2 ½ to 4 mi) out of town. Farther-flung Punta Uva extends for the next 2 km (1 ¼ mi) beyond Playa Chiquita. In these beach areas, you'll see some of the region's first luxury, though still quite small-scale, tourist developments and some interesting ecolodges. This is the place for those preferring creature comforts who also wish to see this less-frequented part of the country.

A few services exist in town. Comisario Manuel León (southeast of bus stop), a local general store often called **El Chino** (☎ no phone), will change cash or traveler's checks daily 9 to 8 if there is enough cash on hand. Although during the December–May high season, most hotels will also change money. You can check e-mail at **Ciber Café** (☎ 750–0456), across from Stanford's Disco. Rent snorkeling equipment and buy your official Puerto Viejo T-shirt at **Color Caribe** (100 yards south of bus stop, ☎ 750–0284).

In the middle of town, **ATEC**—the Talamancan Association for Ecotourism and Conservation—plays an important role in the south coast's ecotourism movement. The agency's small office also serves as a fax and phone center, a post office, and a general travel-information center for the town and the region. You can arrange walks focusing on Afro-Caribbean or indigenous culture; rain forest hikes; coral-reef snorkeling or fishing trips; bird-watching; night walks; and adventure treks. ATEC is also an excellent source for information on volunteer vacations. Of the money collected for tours booked through the agency, 15%–20% goes to local organizations and wildlife refuges. ⊠ *Across from Restaurant Tamara, Puerto Viejo de Talamanca,* ☎ *750–0398,* FAX *750–0191,* WEB *www.greencoast.com/atec.htm.* ☉ *Mon.–Tues. and Thurs.–Fri. 8 AM–9 PM; Wed. 8–12 and 2–9; Sat. 8–12 and 1–9; Sun. 8–12 and 4–8.*

Dining

$$–$$$ ✕ **The Garden.** Though this is one of the country's best restaurants,
★   The Garden can be unpredictably closed—even in peak season and despite its posted open hours. So, if you find it open when you're in town, thank your lucky stars and be sure to eat here. Chef-owner Vera Maron, transplanted to Costa Rica from Trinidad by way of Toronto, incorporates her Indian heritage into her beautifully prepared and presented Asian-Caribbean food. You'll find a colorful room with candlelight, linen, and flowers in the round, wood- and thatch-roof open-air building, which is enveloped in a flowering garden. The Cab-

inas Jacaranda, on the same property, also belongs to Vera Maron. ⊠ *Follow signs near beach,* ☎ 750–0069. *AE, MC, V. Closed Mon. and Mar.–Nov.*

$$–$$$ **✕ La Pecora Nera.** Though the name means "black sheep" in Italian,
★ there's nothing shameful about this thatch-roof roadside restaurant. There's always a lot more to choose from than what appears on the sparse-looking menu; the owners come out of the kitchen and triumphantly announce which additional light Tuscan entrées, appetizers, and desserts they've decided to concoct that day. Be prepared for a pleasantly long, leisurely dining experience with all the attentive, fussed-over service. ⊠ *3 km (2 mi) south of Puerto Viejo on road to Manzanillo,* ☎ 750–0490. *No credit cards. Closed Mon. Apr.–Nov..*

$$–$$$ **✕ Salsa Brava.** The restaurant at Salsa Brava—with sublime surf vistas—has taken the name of this famed surfing locale. Opt for casual counter service or grab a seat at one of the colorful roadside tables. Lunch and dinner center on grilled fish and meat. ⊠ *100 yards south of Stanford's Disco,* ☎ 750–0241. *No credit cards. Closed Mon.*

$–$$ **✕ Café Coral.** It's a quaint but true tale that Café Coral shocked Puerto Viejo with the introduction of pizza in 1989; those were pre-telephone days here after all. These folks still do a bang-up job out of their open-air, thatch-roof restaurant. The "Smoky," with everything on it, is the most requested dish, but other pizzas and pasta round out the offerings. Mornings, Coral transforms itself into the town's quintessential American-style breakfast joint. Feast on pancakes before heading out for the day. ⊠ *50 yards south of Adventist church,* ☎ 750–0051. *No credit cards. Closed Mon. No lunch.*

$–$$ **✕ Restaurant Tamara.** In the nondescript indoor seating area you'll be cooled by a fan and entertained by TV; the outdoor seating area—with a large image of Bob Marley on red, yellow, and green walls—has a palpable Jamaican motif. The Caribbean food at this two-story unpretentious place is tasty and authentic: You can't lose with the chicken in Caribbean sauce or virtually any of the fresh fish dishes. And it's near the beach. ⊠ *Across from ATEC,* ☎ 750–0148. *AE, MC, V.*

Lodging

$$$$ **⊡ Shawandha Lodge.** Remote and refined, Shawandha's spacious, beau-
★ tifully designed bungalows are well back from the road at Playa Chiquita. The individually furnished bungalows have elegant hardwoods, custom-made furniture, such as four-poster beds, and large verandas with hammocks—and their bathrooms, with gorgeous tile work, were designed by French ceramicist Filou Pascal. Well-known local chef Madame Oui Oui lovingly crafts her distinctive French-Caribbean cuisine in the open-air restaurant; a hearty breakfast is complimentary. A white-sand beach protected by a coral reef lies 200 yards away. ⊠ *6 km (4 mi) from Puerto Viejo on road to Manzanillo, at Playa Chiquita,* ☎ 750–0018, ℻ 750–0037, ⓦⓔⓑ *www.shawandhalodge.com. 11 bungalows. Restaurant, hiking, horseback riding, snorkeling, boating, laundry service; no room phones, no room TVs. AE, MC, V.*

$$$ **⊡ Cariblue Bungalows.** Cariblue's finely crafted all-wooden bunga-
★ lows are spaciously arrayed on the edge of the jungle, across the road from the splendid black- and white-sand beaches of Punta Cocles. Cabinas are linked to the main ranch-style building by paths that meander through a gently sloping lawn shaded with enormous trees. Expansive verandas and beautiful bathroom-tile mosaics add an air of refinement; hammocks add an air of relaxation. The youthful Italian owners serve a huge complimentary breakfast. ⊠ *2 km (1 mi) south of Puerto Viejo on road to Manzanillo, across road from Playa Cocles,* ☎ 750–0035, ℻ 750–0057, ⓦⓔⓑ *www.cariblue.com. 15 bunga-*

lows. Restaurant, fans, laundry service; no room phones, no room TVs. AE, MC, V.

$$$ 🏨 **Casa Camarona.** Though half the rooms have air-conditioning at this secluded lodging, you'll hardly need it. The abundant shade and sea breezes of the Gandoca-Manzanillo Wildlife Refuge, where the Casa is set, keep the rooms delightfully cool. All the spacious, wooden, rustic rooms front the ocean and have two double beds. Rates include breakfast. Camarona offers packages including all meals in its seaside Caribbean restaurant, as well as bicycle and kayak rental. ⊠ *Playa Cocles, 3 km (2 mi) south of Puerto Viejo,* ☎ *750–0151,* FAX *750–0210 or 222–6184,* WEB *www.casacamarona.com. 17 rooms. Restaurant, bar, bicycles, laundry facilities; no air-conditioning in some rooms, no room phones, no room TVs. AE, MC, V.*

$$$ 🏨 **Hotel La Perla Negra.** The owners' previous experience as designers is evident in the fine construction of this handsome, two-story wooden structure across a tiny dirt road from Playa Negra. All rooms have balconies, half with ocean views, half with jungle views. The three-meal restaurant features grilled meats and fish. Between the building and the beach is a spacious, inviting pool. ⊠ *1 km [1/2 mi] north of Puerto Viejo on Playa Negra,* ☎ *750–0111 or 800/221–4713 in North America,* FAX *750–0114,* WEB *www.laperlanegra.com. 24 rooms. Restaurant, pool, tennis court, laundry service. No credit cards.*

$$$ 🏨 **El Pizote Lodge.** El Pizote observes local architectural mores while offering more than most in the way of amenities. All standard rooms have polished wood paneling, reading lamps, mirrors, and firm beds, and the four deluxe rooms are air-conditioned. Each of the two-room bungalows sleeps six. The restaurant serves breakfast, dinner, and drinks all day. Guanábana and papaya grow on the grounds, and hiking trails lead off into the jungle. ⊠ *Right side of road into Puerto Viejo, 500 yards before town,* ☎ *750–0088,* FAX *750–0226. 8 rooms, 4 with bath; 6 bungalows; 1 cabin. Restaurant, bar, fans, pool, volleyball, laundry service; no air-conditioning in some rooms, no room phones, no room TVs. V.*

$$$ 🏨 **Villas del Caribe.** Right on the beach north of Punta Uva, Del Caribe's multiroom villas are commodious and comfortable, if somewhat pedestrian in design. Each has a blue-tile kitchen with stove and refrigerator, a small sitting room with low-slung couches, a plant-filled bathroom, and a patio with excellent views of the beach. Upstairs are one or two spacious bedrooms with a wooden deck. Though coffee is served at the reception counter, the nearest restaurant is several hundred yards away. If you bring your own edibles, you're set, as the hotel rents all kinds of water-sports equipment and will arrange any kind of diversion. ⊠ *4 km (2½ mi) southeast of Puerto Viejo de Talamanca,* ☎ *750–0202 or 233–2200 in San José,* FAX *750–0203 or 221–2801 in San José,* WEB *www.villascaribe.net. 12 villas. Kitchens, beach; no room phones, no room TVs. AE, MC, V.*

$$–$$$ 🏨 **Yaré Hotel.** The sound of the jungle is overpowering, especially at night, as you relax in your brightly painted Yaré cabina. All rooms have fans, hot water, and verandas with hammocks. The restaurant is open for breakfast, lunch, and dinner, and the owner organizes all kinds of tours. ⊠ *4 km (2½ mi) southeast of Puerto Viejo,* ☎ FAX *750–0106 or 256–2353,* WEB *www.hotelyare.com. 21 rooms. Restaurant, some kitchenettes, laundry service; no room phones, no room TVs. AE, MC, V.*

$$ 🏨 **Playa Chiquita Lodge.** Elevated a few feet above the damp jungle floor and set 100 yards back from the beautiful, secluded Chiquita beach near Punta Uva, these wooden cabinas and three small *casitas* (houses) across the road are tastefully furnished with sunken bathrooms and wooden furniture and have spacious verandas. The property is run by

German-born Wolf Bissinger and his artistically talented Talamancan-born wife, Wanda Patterson-Bissinger. The lodge sponsors the annual Southern Caribbean Music Festival on-site each year, February–April. ⊠ *6 km (4 mi) southeast of Puerto Viejo,* ☎ *750–0408,* FAX *750–0062,* WEB *www.playachiquitalodge.com. 11 cabinas, 3 casitas. Restaurant, beach, bar, laundry service; no air-conditioning, no room phones, no room TVs. MC, V.*

$–$$ ⊡ **Cabinas Casa Verde.** Set back a few blocks from the waterfront hustle, the comfortable cabinas at this Swiss-run hotel in town are decorated with an interesting variety of items such as shell mobiles, watercolor frescoes, and indigenous tapestries. And yet, overall, rooms have a neat-as-a-pin quality. Exotic birds flutter constantly through the lush plantings that screen the cabinas from the street. The place is immensely popular, since the price is low and it's clean and well-run; reserve ahead. ⊠ *200 m south and 200 m east of bus stop,* ☎ *750–0015,* FAX *750–0047,* WEB *www.cabinascasaverde.com (mailing address: Apdo. 1115, Puerto Limón). 17 rooms, 9 with bath. Restaurant, fans, some refrigerators, laundry service. AE, MC, V.*

Outdoor Activities and Sports

SURFING

Surfing is the name of the game in Puerto Viejo. There are a number of breaks here, most famously Salsa Brava, which breaks rather far offshore and requires maneuvering past some tricky currents and a shallow reef. Hollow and primarily right-breaking, Salsa Brava is one gnarly wave when it gets big. If it gets *too* big, or not big enough, check out the breaks at Punta Uva, Punta Cocles, or Playa Chiquita. Boogieboarders and bodysurfers will also dig the beach-break waves at various points along this tantalizingly beautiful coast. But a surfer's paradise makes for dangerous swimming here. Undertows can carry you far from shore before you realize what's happening; exercise extreme caution.

NIGHTLIFE

Reggae bars pretty much constitute Puerto Viejo's nightlife. Enjoy the seductive reggae sounds at the appropriately named **Sunset Reggae Bar** (⊠ 50 yards south of the bus stop). **Stanford's Disco** (⊠ 100 m from the town center on the road to Manzanillo) is the place to dance the weekend night away.

Gandoca-Manzanillo National Wildlife Refuge

⑭ *15 km (9 mi) south of Puerto Viejo de Limón.*

The Refugio Nacional de Vida Silvestre Gandoca-Manzanillo stretches along the southeastern coast from the town of Manzanillo to the Panamanian border. Because of weak laws governing the conservation of refuges and the value of coastal land in this area, Gandoca-Manzanillo is less pristine than Cahuita National Park and continues to be developed. However, the refuge still bears plenty of rain forest, orey and jolillo swamps, 10 km (6 mi) of beach where four species of turtles lay their eggs, and almost 3 square km (2 square mi) of cativo forest and coral reef. The Gandoca estuary is a nursery for tarpon and a wallowing spot for crocodiles and caimans.

The easiest way to explore the refuge is to hike along the coast south of Manzanillo. You can hike back out the way you came in, or arrange (in Puerto Viejo de Talamanca) to have a boat pick you up at Monkey Point (a three- to four-hour walk from Manzanillo) or Gandoca (six to eight hours). The park administrators, Benson and Florentino

Grenald, can tell you more and recommend a local guide; inquire when you enter Manzanillo village and the locals will point you toward them. You can also arrange boat trips to dive spots and beaches in the refuge in Puerto Viejo de Talamanca and Manzanillo. Phones are still a rarity this far down the coast. ATEC in Puerto Viejo de Talamanca can get you the number for any place in these parts. *10 km (6 mi) southeast of Puerto Viejo,* ☎ *ATEC 750–0398.* ☉ *Daily 7–4.*

Dining and Lodging

$–$$$ ✕ **Restaurant Maxi's.** Cooled by sea breezes and shaded by tall, stately palms, this two-story, brightly painted wooden building offers weary travelers cold beer, potent cocktails, and great seafood at unbeatable prices after a day's hike in the refuge. Locals and expatriates alike—and even chefs from Puerto Viejo's fancier restaurants—come here for their lobster fix, and the fresh fish is wonderful, too. Locals tend to congregate in the rowdy but pleasant downstairs bar, where reggae beats throb into the wee hours. ✉ *Main town road, Manzanillo,* ☎ *no phone. No credit cards.*

$$$ 🏕 **Almonds & Corals Tent Lodge Camp.** Buried in a dark, densely atmospheric beachfront jungle within the Gandoca-Manzanillo Wildlife Refuge, Almonds & Corals takes tent camping to a new level. The "campsites" are freestanding platforms raised on stilts and linked by boardwalks lit by kerosene lamps. Each safari-style tent is protected by a peaked roof, enclosed in mosquito netting, and, in addition to beds, is equipped with electric lamps, hammocks, and a hot-water bath. A fine, three-meal restaurant is tucked into the greenery halfway down to the property's exquisite, secluded beach, although it's not cheap. Your wake-up call is provided by howler monkeys and gossiping parrots. ✉ *Near end of road south from Puerto Viejo to Manzanillo,* ☎ *759–0656 or 272–2024,* ℻ *272–2220,* ᴡᴇʙ *www.almondsandcorals.com (mailing address: Apdo. 681–2300, San José). 24 tent cabins. Restaurant, fans, hot tub, beach, snorkeling, laundry service, airport shuttle (fee). AE, MC, V.*

OFF THE BEATEN PATH

HITOY CERERE NATIONAL PARK – The remote, 90-square-km (56-square-mi) Reserve Biológica Hitoy Cerere occupies the head of Valle de la Estrella (Star Valley). The park's limited infrastructure was badly damaged by the 1991 quake, since the epicenter was precisely here. Paths that do exist are very much overgrown due to limited use—travelers scarcely come here. Jaguars, tapirs, peccaries, porcupines, anteaters, and armadillos all carry on, however, along with more than 115 species of birds. Watch for the so-called Jesus Christ lizards, which walk on water. The moss-flanked rivers have clear bathing pools and spectacular waterfalls. To get here, catch a bus in Puerto Limón for Valle de la Estrella and get off at Finca Seis; then rent a four-wheel-drive vehicle and you'll come within 1 km (½ mi) of the reserve. Check with the park service in San José if you want to stay overnight. ☎ *283–8004.*

THE ATLANTIC LOWLANDS AND CARIBBEAN COAST A TO Z

To research prices, get advice from other travelers, and book travel arrangements, visit www.fodors.com.

AIR TRAVEL

You can fly from San José to the airstrips in either Tortuguero or Barra del Colorado. Though Puerto Limón has an airport, no airline flies here on a regular basis.

Travelair flies from San José to Tortuguero daily at 6:45 AM. SANSA flies to Barra del Colorado daily at 6 AM. Several tour companies, such as Costa Rica Eco Adventure Services, offer regular or charter flights into Tortuguero and Barra del Colorado in conjunction with stays in their lodges.

➤ AIRLINES AND CONTACTS: **Costa Rica Eco Adventure Services** (☎ 222–0333, FAX 257–0766). **SANSA** (✉ C. 42 at Avda. 3, San José, ☎ 296–0909, FAX 255–2176). **Travelair** (✉ Aeropuerto Internacional Tobías Bolaños, Pavas, ☎ 220–3054 or 232–7883, FAX 220–0413).

BIKE TRAVEL

Bicycles are a popular means of utilitarian transport in Puerto Viejo de Talamanca and Cahuita. Seemingly everyone rents basic touring bikes for $2–$4 per hour, but quality varies widely.

➤ BIKE RENTALS: **Atlántico Tours** (✉ Puerto Viejo de Talamanca, ☎ 750–0004).**Caribbean Flavor** (✉ Cahuita, ☎ 755–0017).

BOAT AND FERRY TRAVEL

From Puerto Viejo de Sarapiquí, boats ply the old route up the Río Sarapiquí to the Río San Juan on the Nicaraguan border. From here you can travel downstream to Barra del Colorado or Tortuguero, but departure times vary—contact Gavilán Sarapiquí River Lodge or negotiate your own deal dockside. Many private operators will take you from the docks at Moín, just outside of Puerto Limón, up the canals to Tortuguero, but there is no scheduled public transportation. Show up to the docks early and expect to pay around $100 round-trip for up to four people. Modesto Watson, an eagle-eyed Miskito Indian guide, will take you upstream if he has room on his boat. You can also hire boats to travel between Tortuguero and Barra del Colorado, but prices are quite high.

➤ CONTACTS: **Gavilán Sarapiquí River Lodge** (✉ 1 km [1//2] mi) southeast of Comando Atlántico (naval command), ☎ 766–6743, FAX 253–6556, WEB www.gavilanlodge.com). **Fran and Modesto Watson** (☎ FAX 226–0986, WEB www.tortuguerocanals.com).

BUS TRAVEL

If you prefer a more private form of travel, consider taking a shuttle.

Empresarios Guapileños buses from San José to Guápiles can drop you off in Braulio Carrillo National Park or at the Rainforest Aerial Tram, a one-hour trip; they leave every half hour between 5 AM and 9 PM daily from the Gran Terminal del Caribe on Calle Central and Avenida 13. Autotransportes Sarapiquí buses also go to Río Agua Frío and Puerto Viejo de Sarapiquí (a two-hour trip, with stops at Las Horquetas and La Selva en route) via Braulio Carrillo from the Gran Terminal del Caribe on Calle Central; they depart daily at 6:30, 8, 10, and 11:30 AM and 1:30, 2:30, 3:30, 4:30, and 6 PM. Buses travel from San José to Puerto Viejo de Sarapiquí via Vara Blanca—a four-hour trip that does *not* pass through Braulio Carrillo—daily at 6:30 AM, noon, and 3 PM.

Autotransportes Caribeños offers daily direct service from San José to Puerto Limón, a 2½-hour trip, departing the Gran Terminal del Caribe on Calle Central hourly from 5:30 AM to 7 PM.

Transportes Mepe runs daily service to Cahuita and Puerto Viejo de Talamanca, about a four-hour trip, from the Gran Terminal del Caribe at 6 and 10 AM and 1:30 and 3:30 PM.

There are also Transportes Mepe buses, which leave from in front of Radio Casino in Puerto Limón for Cahuita (1 hour), Puerto Vargas, and Puerto Viejo de Talamanca (1½ hours), daily at 5, 8, and 10 AM and 1, 4, and 6 PM.

➤ BUS INFORMATION: **Autotransportes Caribeños** (☏ 221–2596). **Autotransportes Sarapiquí** (☏ 257–6859). **Empresarios Guapileños** (☏ 222–0610). **Transportes Mepe** (☏ 257–8129).

CAR RENTAL

There are no rental agencies in the area. Rent in San José.

CAR TRAVEL

The Carretera Guápiles (Guápiles Highway) passes the Zurquí and Quebrada González sectors of Braulio Carrillo National Park, whereas the Barva sector lies to the north of Heredia. The roads in the Sarapiquí part of the Atlantic lowlands are mostly paved, with the usual rained-out dirt and rock sections; road quality depends on the time of year, the length of time since the last visit by a road crew, and/or the amount of rain dumped by the latest tropical storm.

The paved two-lane Guápiles Highway runs from Calle 3 in San José to Puerto Limón, a distance of about 160 km (100 mi).

You cannot drive to Tortuguero or Barra del Colorado. To get here, you must fly or take a boat.

South of Puerto Limón, a paved road covers the roughly 40 km (25 mi) to Cahuita, then passes the Cahuita turnoff and proceeds for roughly 16 km (10 mi) toward Puerto Viejo de Talamanca. It is paved as far as Punta Uva (and, until paving is completed, navigable as far as Manzanillo in the dry season). Four-wheel drive is always preferable, but the major roads in this region are generally passable by any car. Just watch for potholes and unpaved sections—they can appear on any road at any time, without marking or warning.

EMERGENCIES

In case of any emergency, dial 911, or one of the specific numbers below.
➤ EMERGENCY SERVICES: **Ambulance** (☏ 128). **Fire** (☏ 118). **Police** (☏ 911). **Traffic Police** (☏ 227–8030).

LANGUAGE

The Atlantic coast's long African-Caribbean heritage makes it the most likely place to find English speakers, though residents will speak a Caribbean-accented English that may sound unfamiliar to you. With Spanish now the language of instruction in all schools, young people here are less likely to speak English than their elders.

MAIL AND SHIPPING

The privatized Correos de Costa Rica provides reasonable postal service from this part of the country, though you're best bet is to wait and post letters and cards from San José.

Cíber Café offers Internet access in Puerto Viejo de Talamanca. Check e-mail at Edutec in Puerto Limón. Expect to pay about $4 per hour.
➤ POST OFFICE: **Correos de Costa Rica** (✉ east of police station, Cahuita; Avda. 2 and C. 4, Puerto Limón; 50 yards north of soccer field, Puerto Viejo de Sarapiquí; 50 yards west of ATEC, Puerto Viejo de Talamanca).
➤ INTERNET CAFÉS: **Cíber Café** (✉ across from Stanford's Disco, Puerto Viejo de Talamanca, ☏ 750–0456). **Edutec** (✉ Avda. 3 and C. 4, Puerto Limón, ☏ 798–0101).

MONEY MATTERS

Most larger tourist establishments are prepared to handle credit cards. Banks are sparse in this region. Changing U.S. dollars or traveler's checks is possible at the few offices of Banco Nacional, but lines are long. The Scotiabank in downtown Puerto Limón has an ATM machine that accepts Plus- and Cirrus-affiliated cards. You're best off taking care of getting cash with your ATM card back in San José before venturing here.

Banco Nacional (⊠ 50 yards north of Central Plaza, Puerto Viejo de Sarapiquí, ☎ 766–6263; ⊠ Av. 2, Calles 3 and 4, Puerto Limón, ☎ 758–0094). **Scotiabank** (⊠ Av. 3 and Calle 2, Puerto Limón, ☎ 798–0009).

SHUTTLE VAN TRAVEL

Alternatives to public buses exist. Fantasy Bus stops in Cahuita on its daily service between San José and Puerto Viejo de Talamanca; these comfortable, air-conditioned vans leave San José from many hotels at 8 AM and return at 2 PM. Tickets cost $21 and must be reserved a day in advance.

➤ SHUTTLE VAN INFORMATION: **Fantasy Bus** (☎ 800/326–8279 in Costa Rica only).

TOURS

Tortuguero tours are usually packaged with one- or two-night stays in local lodges. Cotur's offers three-day, two-night tours, including bus and boat transport from San José to the Jungle Lodge in Tortuguero, for about $230. Mawamba leads a slightly more expensive version of the same tour, with nights at the Mawamba Lodge, or a less expensive version with nights in Cabinas Sabina. Costa Rica Expeditions flies you straight to its rustically charming Tortuga Lodge for three days and two nights, for about $380 a head. Fran and Modesto Watson are experts on the history and ecology of the area; among other tours, they offer a two-day tour on their *Riverboat Francesca,* with the overnight at a nature lodge. The cost is about $190 per person, including meals and transfers. The Watsons can put together made-to-order packages for fishing as well.

ATEC conducts such special-interest tours as "Sustainable Logging," "Yorkin Indigenous Tour," and assorted bird-watching, turtle-watching, indigenous culture, and ecologically oriented excursions on the southern coast. Atlántico Tours leads you around Tortuguero and Gandoca-Manzanillo Wildlife Refuge as well as renting the best-quality surfboards, bicycles, Boogie boards, and snorkeling gear.

The excellent Horizontes specializes in more independent tours with as few as eight people, including transport by four-wheel-drive vehicle, naturalist guides, and guest lectures. The Caribbean Conservation Corporation can also recommend good local guides.

➤ TOUR OPERATOR RECOMMENDATIONS: **ATEC** (⊠ across from Soda Tamara, Puerto Viejo de Talamanca, ☎ 750–0191, WEB www.greencoast. com/atec.htm). **Atlántico Tours** (⊠ Waterfront, Puerto Viejo de Limón, ☎ 750–0004). **Caribbean Conservation Corporation** (☎ 710–0547 in Tortuguero or 224–9215 in San José, WEB www.cccturtle.org). **Costa Rica Expeditions** (⊠ C. Central and Avda. 3, Barrio Amon, San José, ☎ 222–0333, FAX 257–1665). **Cotur's** (⊠ Paseo Colón and C. 38, Paseo Colón, San José, ☎ 233–0133). **Fran and Modesto Watson** (☎ FAX 226–0986, WEB www.tortuguerocanals.com). **Horizontes** (⊠ 150 yards north of Pizza Hut, Paseo Colón, San José, ☎ 222–2022). **Mawamba** (☎ 710–7280 in Tortuguero or 223–2421 in San José).

VISITOR INFORMATION

The tourist office in San José has information on the Atlantic lowlands. The ATEC office in Puerto Viejo de Talamanca is a great source of information on local tours, guides, and interesting activities for Puerto Viejo, Cahuita, and Manzanillo.

➤ TOURIST INFORMATION: **ATEC** (⊠ across from Soda Tamara, Puerto Viejo de Talamanca, ☎ 750–0191, WEB www.greencoast.com/atec.htm). **Instituto Costarricense de Turismo** (ICT; ⊠ C. 5 between Advas. Central and 2, Barrio del Catedral, San José, ☎ 222–1090).

9 BACKGROUND AND ESSENTIALS

A Biological Superpower

Wildlife Glossary

Books and Videos

Spanish Vocabulary

A BIOLOGICAL SUPERPOWER

Costa Rica may lack oil fields and coal deposits, but it's not without natural assets. The country's ecological wealth includes fertile volcanic soil, sun-swathed beaches, massive trees whose thick branches support elevated gardens of orchids and bromeliads, and hundreds of colorful bird species—the kind of priceless commodities that economists have long ignored. Bankers may wonder how this tiny nation ended up with so pretentious a name as "Rich Coast," but many a grizzled biologist and binocular-toting traveler understands where the republic's wealth lies hidden.

Costa Rica's forests hold an array of flora and fauna so vast and diverse that scientists haven't even named many of the plant and insect species therein; and of the species that have been identified, few have been thoroughly studied. These forests are among the most diverse and productive ecosystems in the world: although tropical forests cover a mere 7% of the earth's surface area, they hold more than half the planet's plant and animal species, and few countries offer better exposure to tropical biological treasures than Costa Rica.

About half the size of the U.S. state of Kentucky, Costa Rica covers less than .03% of the earth's surface, yet it contains nearly 5% of the planet's plant and animal species. The variety of native flora and fauna is astonishing even if you're not professionally acquainted with the norms: Costa Rica contains at least 9,000 plant species, more than 1,200 varieties of orchid, in excess of 2,000 different butterflies, and at least 850 bird species (more birds than the United States and Canada combined). But such numbers don't begin to convey the awe you can feel when you're staring up the convoluted trunk of a centennial strangler fig, listening to the roar of a howler monkey reverberate through the foliage, or watching a delicate hummingbird drink nectar from a multicolored heliconia flower.

All these plants and animals are as beautiful as they are intriguing, and their habitats as complex as they are fascinating. It may be hard to apprehend the richness of a Costa Rican forest at first glance—the overwhelming verdure of the rain forest, for instance, can give the false impression of uniformity—but look closely and you'll come to understand why scientists have dubbed Costa Rica a "biological superpower."

Costa Rica's biological diversity is the result of its tropical location (on a slip of land connecting North and South America), its varied topography, and the many microclimates resulting from the combination of mountains, valleys, and lowlands. But to understand why Costa Rica is so biologically important today, we need to look back to prehistoric times, to a world that human eyes never saw but that scientists have at least partially reconstructed.

Just a Few Dozen Millennia Ago

In geological terms, Costa Rica is relatively young, which explains why there are precious few valuable minerals beneath its soil. Five million years ago, this patch of land didn't even exist: North and South America were separated by a canal the likes of which Teddy Roosevelt—father of the Panama Canal—couldn't have conjured up in his wildest dreams. In the area now occupied by Panama and Costa Rica, the waters of the Pacific and Atlantic oceans flowed freely together. Geologists have named that former canal the Straits of Bolívar, after the Venezuelan revolutionary who wrested much of South America from Spain.

Far beneath the Straits of Bolívar, the incremental movement of tectonic plates slowly created the Central American isthmus. Geologists speculate that a chain of volcanic islands appeared in the gap around 30 million years ago; a combination of volcanic activity and plate movement caused the islands to grow and rise from the water, eventually forming a connected ridge. The land bridge was completed around 3 million years ago, closing the interoceanic canal and forming a corridor, biological and otherwise, between the Americas.

Because several tectonic plates meet beneath Central America, the region has long been geologically unstable, experiencing occasional earthquakes, frequent tremors, and regular volcanic eruptions. While it seems a curse to be hit by one of these natural disasters, there actually wouldn't be a Costa Rica were it not for such frightening phenomena. What is now the country's best soil was once spewed from the bowels of the volcanoes that dominate its landscape, and the jarring adjustments of adjacent tectonic plates actually pushed most of today's Costa Rica up out of the sea. A recent example of this movement was the earthquake of 1991—7.2 on the Richter scale—which thrust Costa Rica's southern Caribbean coastline up several feet, leaving portions of some coral reefs literally high and dry. When the shallow coral platforms around the points of Limón and Cahuita were thrust from the water, as many as 27 m (30 yards) of land were added to some oceanfront property. For humans, that quake was a devastating natural disaster, damaging or destroying almost half the homes along the Caribbean coast, yet it was but a tiny adjustment in the incremental tectonic process that created the country in the first place.

The intercontinental connection completed 3 million years ago had profound biological consequences: it separated the marine life of the Pacific and Atlantic oceans, and it created a pathway for interchange between North and South America. Though hardly the kind of lapse that excites a geologist, 3 million years is a long time by biological standards, and the region's plants and animals have changed considerably since the inter-American gap was stopped up. Whereas evolution took different paths in the waters that flank the isthmus, organisms that had evolved on separate continents were able to make their way into the opposite hemisphere, and the resulting interaction determined what lives in the Americas today.

Mind-Boggling Biodiversity

Costa Rica's outdoor menagerie is in many ways the result of the intercontinental exchange, but the country's flora and fauna actually add up to more than what has passed between the continents. Although it is a biological corridor, the isthmus also acts as a filter, a hospitable haven to many species that couldn't complete the journey from one hemisphere to the other. The rain forests of Costa Rica's Atlantic and southwestern lowlands, for example, are the most northerly home of such southern species as the crab-eating raccoon and a dreaded jungle viper known as the bushmaster. The tropical dry forests of the northern Pacific slope, on the other hand, are the southern limit for such North American species as the white-throated magpie jay and the Virginia opossum. In addition to species whose range extends only as far as Costa Rica in one direction, and those whose range extends into both North and South America, such as the white-tailed deer and the gray hawk, Costa Rica's many physical barriers and microclimates have fostered the development of indigenous plants and animals, such as the mangrove hummingbird and mountain salamander.

What all this biological balderdash means to travelers is that they might spot a North American pale-billed woodpecker and a howler monkey (of South American descent) in the branches of a rain tree, which is native to Central America. And then there are the tourists—migrants, that is—such as the dozens of northern bird species that spend winter holidays in Costa Rica, among them the Tennessee warbler, western tanager, and yellow-bellied sapsucker. In addition to recognizing some of the birds that migrate here, you'll no doubt be at home with some of the plants, like the orchids and impatiens that grow wild in the country but cost a pretty penny in the garden shop back home. But while Costa Rica has plenty of oak trees, squirrels, and sparrows, most of its flora and fauna look decidedly tropical. Not only are such common plants as orchids, palms, and ficuses unmistakably tropical, but many of the resident animals are distinctly neotropical—found only in the American tropics—including sloths, poison dart frogs, toucans, and monkeys with prehensile tails.

The wildlife is spread through an array of ecosystems, which biologists have divided into a dozen "life zones" but which actually consist of a biological continuum almost too multifarious for classification. Though the existence of specific flora and fauna in any given life zone is determined by various physical conditions, the two most important are altitude and rainfall. Average temperatures in the tropics change very little from month to month, but they do change a good bit during the course of the day, especially in the mountains. The Costa Rican highlands are consistently cooler than the lowlands, which means you can spend a morning sweating in a sultry coastal forest, then drive a few hours into the mountains and find yourself needing a warm jacket.

In more temperate parts of the world, cold weather hits the mountaintops a month or two before the lowlands, with Old Man Winter eventually getting his icy grip on everything. In the tropics, only the tops of the highest mountains freeze, so the very highest-altitude flora tends to look completely different from that of even nearby valleys. Altitude also plays a substantial role in regulating humidity, since clouds accumulate around mountains and volcanoes, providing regular precipitation as well as shade, which in turn slows evaporation. These conditions lead to the formation of luxuriant cloud forests on the upper slopes of many mountains. In general, the higher you climb, the more lush the vegetation, except for the peaks of the highest mountains, which often protrude from the cloud cover and are thus fairly arid.

While you may associate the tropics with rain, precipitation in Costa Rica varies considerably depending on where you are and when you're there. This is a result of the mountainous terrain and regional weather patterns. A phenomenon called rain shadow—when one side of a mountain range receives much more rain than the other—plays an important ecological role in Costa Rica. Four mountain ranges combine to create an intercontinental divide that separates the country into Atlantic and Pacific slopes; and thanks to the trade winds, the Atlantic slope receives much more rain than the Pacific. The trade winds steadily pump moisture-laden clouds southwest over the isthmus, where they encounter warm air or mountains, which make them rise. As the clouds rise, they cool, lose their ability to hold moisture, and eventually dump most of their liquid luggage on the Caribbean side.

During the rainy season—mid-May to December—the role of the trade winds is diminished, as regular storms roll off the Pacific Ocean and soak the western side of the isthmus. Though it rains all over Costa Rica during these months, it often rains more on the Pacific side of the mountains than on the Atlantic. Come December, the trade winds take over again, and hardly a drop falls on the western side until May. The dry season is most intense in northwestern Costa Rica (the province of Guanacaste), where most trees drop their foliage and the forests take on a desert visage. That region quickly regains its verdure once the rains return in May, marking the beginning of a springlike season that Costa Ricans nonetheless refer to as winter.

Climate variation within the country results in a mosaic of forests, from those that receive only a few feet of rain each year to those that soak up several yards of precipitation annually. The combination of humidity and temperature helps determine what grows where; but while some species have very restricted ranges, others seem to thrive just about anywhere. Plants such as strangler figs and bromeliads grow all over Costa Rica, and animals such as the collared peccary and coati—a long-nose cousin of the raccoon—can pretty much live wherever human beings let them. Other species have extremely limited ranges, such as the mangrove hummingbird, restricted to the mangrove forests of the Pacific coast, and the volcano junco, a gray sparrow that lives only around the highest peaks of the Cordillera de Talamanca.

It's a Jungle Out There

Costa Rica's incredible natural spectrum is part of what makes it such an invigorating vacation spot, but the landscape that travelers most want to see is the tropical rain forest. The protected areas of the Atlantic and southern Pacific lowlands hold tracts of virgin rain forest where massive tropical trees tower more than 30 m (100 ft) over the forest floor. The thick branches of these jungle giants are covered with an abundance of epiphytes (plants that grow on other plants but are not parasites) such as ferns, orchids, bromeliads, mosses, vines, and aroids; and most of the rain forest's plant and animal species are clustered in the arboreal garden of the canopy.

Although life flourishes in the canopy, the intense sunlight that quickly dries the treetops after downpours results in a recurrent water shortage. Consequently, plants that live up here have developed ways to cope with aridity: many orchids have thick leaves that resist evaporation and spongy roots that can quickly soak up large amounts of water when it rains. Tank bromeliads have a funnel shape that enables them to collect and hold water at the center of their leaves. Acting as miniature oases, these plants attract arboreal animals to drink from, hunt at, or—in the case of certain insect larvae and tree-frog tadpoles—live in their pools. In exchange for vital water, the waste and carcasses of these animals give the plants valuable nutrients, which are also scarce in the canopy.

Many animals spend most or all of their time in the canopy, which can be frustrating for people who come to the jungle in search of wildlife. Peering through binoculars, you might glimpse the still, furry figure of a sloth or the brilliant regalia of a parrot; and it's hard to miss the arboreal acrobatics of monkeys, who leap from tree to tree, hang from branches, throw fruit or sticks, and generally make spectacles of themselves. For a closer look at the canopy, you may want to take a ride on the Rain Forest Aerial Tram, near the Guápiles Highway, or linger on a tree platform at Hacienda Barú in Dominical or the Corcovado Lodge Tent Camp, both in the southern Pacific region.

Because little sunlight reaches the ground, the rain-forest floor is a dim, quiet place, with not nearly as much undergrowth as you saw in those old Tarzan movies. Still, plants from aroids to palm trees have adapted to this shady world. The light level inside a virgin rain forest is comparable to that of the average North American living room or shopping mall, and indeed some of the plant species that grow here have become popular houseplants up north. And the vegetation is not always sparse: whenever an old tree falls, there's a riot of growth as plants fight over the newfound sunlight.

Few travelers are disappointed by the tropical forest, but some are frustrated by the difficulty of spotting animals. Hikers occasionally encounter such earthbound creatures as the coati or the agouti, a terrier-size rodent that resembles a giant guinea pig, and in most areas you're likely to see iridescent blue morpho butterflies, hyperactive hummingbirds, brightly colored poison dart frogs, and tiny lizards standing guard on tree trunks. Most forest critters, however, spend much of their time and energy trying *not* to be seen, and

the thick foliage aids them in that endeavor. An untrained eye can miss the details, which is why a naturalist guide is invaluable here: in addition to spotting and identifying both plants and animals, a good guide can explain some of relationships that weave them together in one of the planet's most complicated ecosystems.

The rain forest is characterized by intense predation. Its inhabitants dedicate most of their resources to the essential tasks of finding their next meal and avoiding *becoming* a meal in the process. Whereas animals must often hide or flee when in danger, plants have developed such survival tactics as thorns, prickly hairs, and toxic substances that make their leaves unappetizing. Because of the relative toxicity of most rain-forest foliage, many insects eat only a small portion of a leaf before moving on to another plant, so as not to ingest a lethal dose of any one poison. You can see the results of this practice by looking up into the canopy—almost every leaf is full of little holes.

Camouflage is another popular animal defense. The tropical rain forest is full of insects that have evolved to resemble the leaves, bark, moss, and leaf litter around them. Some bugs have adopted the colors of certain flowers, or even the mold that grows on plants. They're a chore to spot, but camouflaged critters are incredibly intriguing.

Some creatures go to the opposite extreme and advertise themselves with bright colors. Some hues are meant to help find a mate amid the mesh of green; others serve as a warning to potential predators. Some species of caterpillar, for example, are not only immune to the toxins of the plant on which they live, but they actually sequester that poison within their bodies, making themselves toxic as well. In certain areas you might see brightly colored frogs hopping around the forest floor—their skins are laced with such poisonous secretions that some Indian tribes use them to poison their own darts and arrows. This frog's typical warning pattern mixes bright colors with black, a coloration that conveys a simple message to predators: eat me and die.

Mimicry can scare off predators as well— certain edible caterpillars look like venomous ones, and some harmless serpents have markings similar to those of the deadly coral snake. Such acts of deception often reach amazing levels of intrigue. The cocoons of certain butterflies not only resemble the head of a viper, but if disturbed, they begin to move back and forth just as a snake's head would. One large butterfly has spots on its wings that look like eyes, so that when it opens them it resembles an owl; another butterfly species looks exactly like a wasp.

In addition to avoiding predators, plants and animals must compete with other species that have similar niches—the biological equivalents of jobs. This competition fosters cooperation between noncompetitive organisms. Plants need to get their pollen and seeds distributed as far as possible, and every animal requires a steady food supply, which brings us to everyone's favorite subject: the birds and the bees.

Although butterflies and bees do most of the pollinating up north, tropical plants are pollinated by everything from fruit flies and hummingbirds to beetles and bats. The flowers of such plants are often designed so that their nectar is readily available to pollinators but protected from freeloaders. The beautiful hibiscus flower is designed to dust a hummingbird's forehead with pollen and collect any pollen that's already there while the tiny bird drinks the nectar hidden deep in its base; the flower is too long for a butterfly, and the nectar is held too deep for a bee to reach. No system is perfect, though: you may see a bananaquit—a tiny bird with a short beak—biting holes in the bases of a hibiscus flower in an effort to drink its nectar without getting anywhere near its pollen.

Intense competition for limited resources keeps the rain forest's trees growing taller, roots reaching farther, and everything mobile working on a way to get more for less. The battle for light sends most of the foliage sky high, and the battle for nutrients speeds to a breakneck pace the process of decay and recycling that follows every death in the forest. One result of this high-speed decomposition is that most of the nutrients in a rain forest are present in living things, while the soil beneath them retains few essential elements. Rain-forest soils tend to be nutrient-poor, less than ideal for farming.

A Gorgeous Mosaic

Though the rain forest is most iconic, Costa Rica has other types of forests that are equally rich in life and well worth exploring. The tropical dry forests of the northwestern lowlands are similar to rain forests during the rainy season, but once the daily deluges subside, the dry forest changes profoundly: most trees lose their leaves, and some burst simultaneously into full, colorful flower. The yellow-blossom buttercup tree and the pink tabebuia, among others, brighten up the arid northwestern landscape in the dry season. The dry forest contains many of the plants, animals, and exclusive relationships found in the rain forest, but it's also home to species often associated with the forests and deserts of Mexico and the southwestern United States, such as cacti, coyotes, and diamondback rattlesnakes. Because dry forests are less dense than rain forests, it can be easier to see animals in them; this is especially true in the dry season, when foliage is sparse and animals often congregate around scarce water sources and around trees with fruit or flowers.

The cloud forests on the upper reaches of many Costa Rican mountains and volcanoes are even more luxuriant than rain forests, so deeply lush that it can be hard to find the bark on a cloud-forest tree for all the growth on its trunk and branches. Plants grow on plants that grow on still other plants: vines, orchids, ferns, aroids, and bromeliads are everywhere, and mosses and liverworts cover the vines and leaves of other epiphytes. Because of the steep terrain, a cloud forest's trees grow on slightly different levels, and the canopy is less continuous than that of a lowland rain forest. Because more light reaches the ground, there is plenty of undergrowth, including prehistoric-looking tree ferns, a wealth of flowering plants, and "poor man's umbrellas"—made up of a few giant leaves.

Cloud forests are home to a multitude of animals, ranging from delicate glass frogs, whose undersides are so transparent that you can see many of their internal organs, to the resplendent quetzal, a bird considered sacred by the ancient Maya. The male quetzal has a crimson belly and iridescent green back, wings, and tail feathers, the last of which can grow longer than 2 ft. Those tail feathers float behind the quetzal when it flies, a splendid sight that no doubt inspired its ancient name, "the plumed serpent." Although the tangle of foliage and almost constant mist make it hard to see cloud-forest wildlife, you should still catch glimpses of such colorful birds as the emerald toucanet, collared redstart, and various hummingbirds.

Humidity protects the cloud-forest canopy from the water shortage that often plagues lowland rain forests. In fact, the cloud forest's canopy is usually soaking wet. During most of the year, a moisture-laden mist moves through the cloud forest, depositing condensation on the plants; this condensation causes a sort of secondary precipitation, with droplets forming on the epiphytic foliage and falling regularly from the branches to the forest floor. Cloud forests thus function like giant sponges, soaking up humidity from the clouds and sending it slowly downhill to feed the streams and rivers on which many regions and communities depend for water.

On top of high ridges, and near the summits of volcanoes, the cloud forest is transformed by strong, steady winds that topple tall trees and regularly break off branches. The resulting collection of small, twisted trees and bushes is known as an elfin forest. On the upper slopes of the Cordillera de Talamanca, Costa Rica's highest range, the cloud forest gives way to the *páramo*, a high-altitude ecosystem composed of shrubs, grasses, and hardy herbs. Most of these plants are common in the heights of South America's Andes; the Costa Rican páramo defines their most northerly distribution.

On the other extreme, along both coasts, are river mouths and estuaries with extensive mangrove forests. These primeval-looking, often flooded profusions grow in tidal zones all over the tropics. Many of the trees in mangrove forests grow on "stilt" roots, which prop their leaves up out of the saltwater and help them absorb carbon dioxide when the tide is high. The roots also lend protection to various small fish and crustaceans and are often covered with barnacles, mussels, and other shellfish.

Mangrove forests are fairly homogeneous, with stands of one species of tree stretching off as far as the eye can see. They are also extremely productive ecosystems that play an important role as estuaries: many marine animals, such as shrimp, spend the early stages of their lives in mangrove estuaries, and some species, such as certain kinds of snappers, are born and die there. Vital to the health of the ocean beyond them, mangroves are attractive sites for animals that feed on marine life, especially fish-eating birds like cormorants, herons, pelicans, and ospreys.

The forests that line the Caribbean canals, along Costa Rica's northeastern coast, are dominated by the water-resistant *jolillo* palm. This area is home to many of the same animals found in the rain forest—monkeys, parrots, iguanas—as well as river dwellers, such as turtles, otters, and anhingas. A boat trip up the canals is thus a great opportunity to observe wildlife, as are similar excursions on jungle rivers such as the Río Frío and the Río Sarapiquí. Seasonal swamps like Caño Negro and the *lagunas* of Palo Verde, which disappear during the dry months, are also excellent places to see birds. There's also a vast swamp in the heart of Corcovado National Park, which never dries up but is virtually impenetrable because of the thick, thorny vegetation surrounding it.

In addition to its varied forests, Costa Rica has 1,224 km (760 mi) of coastline, which consists of beaches separated by rocky points. The points are home to a variety of marine life, but even more remarkable, most of the country's beaches are important nesting spots for endangered sea turtles. And submerged in the sea off both coasts are extensive coral reefs, inhabited by hundreds of species of colorful fish, crustaceans, and other invertebrates. With its vertiginous biological variety, the coral reef could well be the marine equivalent of the rain forest.

Where Have All the Jungles Gone?

All this lush forest notwithstanding, you'll soon see that Costa Rica's predominant landscapes are not cloud and rain forests but the coffee and banana plantations that have replaced them. The country's pre-Columbian cultures may have revered the jaguar and the harpy eagle, but today's inhabitants seem to put more stock in less-illustrious beasts: the cow and the chicken. In the last half century, more than two-thirds of Costa Rica's original forests have been destroyed, cut at a rate of between 362 square km (140 square mi) and 765 square km (295 square mi) per year. Forests have traditionally been considered unproductive land, and their destruction was for a long time synonymous with development. In the 1970s and 1980s, international and domestic development policies fueled the destruction of large tracts of wilderness. Fortunately, Costa Rican conservationists grew alarmed by this deforestation, and in the 1970s they began creating what has since grown to become the best national park system in the region.

In addition to protecting vast expanses of wilderness—between 15% and 20% of the national territory—the Costa Rican government has made progress in curbing deforestation outside the national parks. The rate of destruction has dropped significantly, but poaching and illegal logging continue to be serious problems that, if left uncorrected, will eventually wipe out many important species and wild areas.

Deforestation not only spells disaster for the jaguar and the eagle, but it can also have grave consequences for human beings. Forests absorb rain and release water slowly, playing an important role in regulating the flow of rivers—which is why severely deforested regions often suffer floods during the rainy season and drought during the dry months. Tree covers also prevent topsoil erosion, thus keeping the land fertile and productive; in many parts of the country, erosion has left once-productive farmland almost worthless. Finally, hidden within Costa Rica's endless living species are countless unknown or understudied substances that might eventually be extracted to cure diseases. The destruction of this country's forests is a loss for the entire world.

Responsible Travel

With each passing year, more and more Costa Ricans are coming to realize how valuable and imperiled their remaining wilderness is. Costa Ricans visit their national parks in significant numbers, and they consider those protected areas vital to the national economy, both for the natural resources they preserve and for their commercial role as tourist attractions. Local conservationists, however, are still a long way from achieving their goal of involving communities in the protection of the parks around them.

Costa Ricans who cut trees and hunt endangered animals usually do so out of economic necessity, and alas, the people who live near protected areas are often the last to benefit from the tourism that wilderness attracts. When you visit a park or reserve, your entrance fee helps pay for the preservation of Costa Rica's wildlife; but you can also make your visit beneficial to the people living nearby by hiring local guides, horses, or boats; eating in local restaurants; and buying things (other than wild-animal products, of course) in local shops.

You can go a few steps further by making donations to local conservation groups or to such international organizations as Conservation International, the Nature Conservancy, the Rainforest Alliance, and the World Wildlife Fund, all of which support important conservation efforts in Costa Rica. It's also helpful to stray from the beaten path: explore private preserves, and stay at lodges that contribute to environmental efforts and to nearby communities. By planning your visit with an eye toward grassroots conservation efforts, you join the global effort to save the earth's tropical ecosystems and help ensure that the treasures you traveled so far to see remain intact for future generations.

— David Dudenhoefer

WILDLIFE GLOSSARY

AN ASTONISHING ARRAY of creatures has evolved in tiny Costa Rica, sandwiched between the two great American continents. Thanks in part to the protection of the park and refuge system, many are not terribly hard to see. Here is a rundown of some of the most common and attention-grabbing mammals, birds, reptiles, amphibians, and even a few insects that you might encounter. We give the common Costa Rican names, so you can understand the local wildlife lingo, as well as the latest scientific terms.

Agouti (*guatusa*; *Dasyprocta punctata*): A 20-inch tail-less rodent with small ears and a large muzzle, the agouti is reddish-brown on the Pacific side, more of a tawny orange on the Caribbean slope. It sits on its haunches to eat large seeds and fruit.

Anteater (*oso hormiguero*): Three species of anteater inhabit Costa Rica—the giant (*Myrmecophaga tridactyla*), silky (*Cyclopes didactylus*), and collared, or vested (*Tamandua mexicana*). Only the latter is commonly seen, and too often as roadkill. This medium-size anteater, 30 inches long with an 18-inch tail, laps up ants and termites with its long, sticky tongue and has long sharp claws for ripping into insect nests.

Aracaris (*cusingo*): These slender toucans, with their trademark bills, travel in groups of six or more and eat ripe fruit. The collared aracaris (*Pteroglossus torquatus*) on the Caribbean side has a chalky upper mandible; the fiery-billed (*Pteroglossus frantzii*) aracaris on the southern Pacific coast has an orange-red upper mandible.

Armadillo (*cusuco*; *Dasypus novemcinctus*): The species found in the southern United States is widespread in Costa Rica. Mostly nocturnal and solitary, this edentate roots in soil with a long muzzle for varied diet of insects, small animals, and plant material.

Caiman (*cocodrilo*): The spectacled caiman (*Caiman crocodilus*) is a small crocodilian (to 7 ft) inhabiting freshwater, subsisting mainly on fish. Most active at night (it has bright-red eye shine), it basks by day. It is distinguished from the American crocodile by a sloping brow and smooth back scales.

Coati (*pizote*; *Nasua narica*): This is a long-nose relative of the raccoon, its long tail often held straight up. Lone males or groups of females with young are active during the day, on the ground or in trees. Opportunistic and omnivorous, coatis feed on fruit, invertebrates, and small vertebrates.

Cougar (*puma*; *Felis concolor*): Mountain lions are the largest unspotted cats (to 5 ft, with 3½-inch tail) in Costa Rica. Widespread but rare, they live in essentially all-wild habitats and feed on vertebrates ranging from snakes to deer.

Crocodile (*lagarto*; *Crocodylus acutus*): The American crocodile, up to 16 ft in length, is found in most major river systems, particularly the Tempisque and Tárcoles. Despite its size and appearance, it seldom attacks humans, preferring fish and birds. It's distinguished from the caiman by a flat head, narrow snout, and spiky scales.

Ctenosaur (*garrobo*; *Ctenosaura similis*): Also known as the black, or spiny, iguana, this is a large (up to 18 inches long with 18-inch tail), tan lizard with four dark bands on its body and a tail ringed with sharp, curved spines. Terrestrial and arboreal, it sleeps in burrows or tree hollows. Though mostly vegetarian, it consumes small creatures. It lives along the coast in the dry northwest and in wetter areas farther south.

Dolphin (*delfin*): Several species, including bottlenose dolphins (*Tursiops truncatus*), frolic in Costa Rican waters. Frequently observed off Pacific shores are spotted dolphins (*Stenella attenuata*), which are small (up to 6 ft), with pale spots on the posterior half of the body; they often travel in groups of 20 or more and like to play around vessels and in bow wakes.

Frigatebird (*tijereta del mar*; *Fregata magnificens*): A large, black soaring bird with slender wings and forked tail, this is one of the most effortless and agile fliers in the avian world. More common on the Pacific coast, it doesn't dive or swim but swoops to pluck its food.

Frog (*rana*): Some 120 species of frog exist in Costa Rica; most are nocturnal, except for brightly colored poison dart frogs (*Dendrobates* spp.), whose coloration, either red with blue or green hind legs or charcoal black with fluorescent green markings, warns potential predators of their toxicity. Red-eyed leaf frogs (*Agalychnis* spp.) are among the showiest of nocturnal species. Large, brown marine toads (*Bufo marinus*) come out at night.

Howler Monkey (*mono congo; Alouatta palliata*): These dark, chunky-bodied monkeys (to 22 inches long with 24-inch tail) with black faces travel in troops of up to 20. Lethargic mammals, they eat leaves, fruits, and flowers. The males' deep, resounding howls serve as communication among and between troops.

Iguana (*iguana*): Mostly arboreal but a good swimmer, the iguana is Costa Rica's largest lizard: males can grow to 10 ft, including tail. Only young green iguanas (*Iguana iguana*) are bright green; adults are much duller, females dark-grayish, and males olive (with orange-ish heads in breeding season). All have round cheek scales and smooth tails.

Jacana (*gallito de agua; Jacana spinosa*): These birds are sometimes called "lily trotters" because their long toes allow them to walk on floating vegetation. Feeding on aquatic organisms and plants, they're found in almost any body of water. They expose yellow wing feathers in flight. The "liberated" females lay eggs in several nests tended by different males.

Jaguar (*tigre; Panthera onca*): The largest New World feline (to 6 ft, with 2-ft tail), this top-of-the-line predator is exceedingly rare but lives in a wide variety of habitats, from dry forest to cloud forest. It's most common in the vast Amistad Biosphere Reserve.

Jesus Christ Lizard (*gallego*): Flaps of skin on long toes enable this spectacular lizard to run across water. Costa Rica has three species: the lineated basilisk (*Basiliscus basiliscus*) on the Pacific side is brown with pale lateral stripe; the emerald basilisk (*Basiliscus plumifrons*) in the Caribbean lowlands is marked with turquoise and black on a green body; the striped basilisk (*Basiliscus vittatus*), also on the Caribbean side, resembles the lineated basilisk. Adult males grow to 3 ft (mostly tail), with crests on head, back, and base of tail.

Kinkajou (*martilla; Potos flavus*): This nocturnal, arboreal relative of the raccoon (to 20 inches, with 20-inch prehensile tail) has light-brown fur and yellow-green eye shine. It forages actively, often noisily, for fruit, insects, and nectar.

Leaf-Cutter Ant (*zompopas; Atta* spp.): Found in all lowland habitats, these are the most commonly noticed neotropical ants. Columns sometimes extend for several hundred yards from an underground nest to plants being harvested; clipped leaves are fed to the cultivated fungus that the ants eat.

Macaw (*lapas*): Costa Rica's two species are the scarlet macaw (*Ara macao*), on the Pacific side (Osa Peninsula and Carara Biological Reserve), and the great green macaw (*Ara ambigua*), on the Caribbean side, where the population is severely threatened. These are huge, raucous parrots with long tails; their immense bills are used to rip fruit apart to reach the seeds. They nest in hollow trees and are victimized by pet-trade poachers and deforestation.

Magpie Jay (*urraca; Calocitta formosa*): This southern relative of the bluejay, with a long tail and distinctive topknot (crest of forward-curved feathers), is found in the dry northwest, where it's often commensal (omnivorous) with humans. Bold and inquisitive, with amazingly varied vocalizations, these birds travel in noisy groups of four or more.

Margay (*caucel; Felis wiedii*): Fairly small, this spotted nocturnal cat (22 inches long, with 18-inch tail) is similar to the ocelot but has a longer tail and is far more arboreal: mobile ankle joints allow it to climb down trunks headfirst. It eats small vertebrates.

Morpho (*morfo*): Three Costa Rican species of this spectacular large butterfly have a brilliant-blue upper wing surface, one of which (*Morpho peleides*) is common in moister areas; one has an intense ultraviolet upper surface; one is white above and below; and one is brown and white. Adults feed on rotting fallen fruit; they never visit flowers.

Motmot (*pajaro bobo*): Most of these handsome birds of the understory have "racquet-tipped" tails. Nesting in burrows, they sit patiently while scanning for large insect prey or small vertebrates. Costa Rica has six species.

Ocelot (*manigordo*; *Felis pardalis*): Mostly terrestrial, this medium-size spotted cat (33 inches long, with 16-inch tail) has a shorter tail than the margay. Active night and day, it feeds on rodents and other vertebrates. Forepaws are rather large in relation to the body, hence the local name, which means "fat hand."

Oropéndola (*oropendola*; *Psarocolius* spp.): This crow-size bird in the oriole family has a bright-yellow tail and nests in colonies, in pendulous nests (up to 6 ft long) built by females in isolated trees. Males make an unmistakable, loud, gurgling liquid call. The bird is fairly omnivorous, eating much fruit, and far more numerous on the Caribbean side.

Parakeet and Parrot (*pericos,* parakeets; *loros,* parrots): There are 15 species in Costa Rica (plus two macaws), all clad in green, most with a splash of a primary color or two on the head or wings. They travel in boisterous flocks, prey on immature seeds, and nest in cavities.

Peccary: Piglike animals with thin legs and thick necks, peccaries travel in small groups (larger where the population is still numerous); root in soil for fruit, seeds, and small creatures; and have a strong musk odor. Costa Rica has two species: the collared peccary (*saíno, Tayassu tajacu*) and the white-lipped peccary (*chancho de monte, Tayassu pecari*). The latter is now nearly extinct.

Pelican (*pelícano*): Large size, a big bill, and a throat pouch make the brown pelican (*Pelecanus occidentalis*) unmistakable in coastal areas (it's far more abundant on the Pacific side). Pelicans often fly in V formations and dive for fish.

Quetzal: One of the world's most exquisite birds, the resplendent quetzal (*Pharomachrus mocinno*) was revered by the Maya. Glittering green plumage and the male's long tail coverts draw thousands of people to highland cloud forests for sightings from February to April.

Roseate Spoonbill (*garza rosada*; *Ajaia ajaja*): Pink plumage and a spatulate bill set this wader apart from all other wetland birds; it feeds by swishing its bill back and forth in water while using its feet to stir up bottom-dwelling creatures. Spoonbills are most common around Palo Verde and Caño Negro.

Sea Turtle. *See* Close-Up: Tico Turtles, *in* Chapter 8.

Sloth (*perezoso*): Costa Rica is home to the brown-throated, three-toed sloth (*Bradypus variegatus*) and Hoffmann's two-toed sloth (*Choloepus hoffmanni*). Both grow to 2 ft, but two-toed (check forelegs) sloths often look bigger due to longer fur and are the only species in the highlands. Sloths are herbivorous, accustomed to a low-energy diet, and well camouflaged.

Spider Monkey (*mono colorado, mono araña*; *Ateles geoffroyi*): Lanky and long-tailed, these are the largest monkeys in Costa Rica (to 24 inches, with 32-inch tail). Moving in groups of two to four, they eat ripe fruit, leaves, and flowers. Incredible aerialists, they can swing effortlessly through branches using long arms and legs and prehensile tails. Caribbean and southern Pacific populations are dark reddish-brown; northwesterners are blond.

Squirrel Monkey (*mono tití*; *Saimiri oerstedii*): The smallest of four Costa Rican monkeys (11 inches, with 15-inch tail), this one has a distinctive facial pattern (black cap and muzzle, white mask). The species travels in noisy, active groups of 20 or more, feeding on fruit and insects. Found only around Manuel Antonio National Park and parts of the Osa Peninsula, it may have been introduced by humans in pre-Columbian times.

Tapir (*danta*; *Tapirus bairdii*): The largest land mammal in Costa Rica (to 6½ ft), the tapir is something like a small rhinoceros without armor. Adapted to a wide range of habitats, it's nocturnal, seldom seen, but said to defecate and sometimes sleep in water. Tapirs are herbivorous and use their prehensile snouts to harvest vegetation.

Toucan (*tucán, tucancillo*): This bird is familiar to anyone who's seen a box of Froot Loops cereal. The aracaris is one; keel-billed (*Ramphastos sulfuratus*) and chestnut-mandibled toucans (*Ramphastos swainsonii*) are the largest (18 inches and 22 inches), black with bright-yellow "bibs" and multihued bills. The smaller, stouter emerald toucanet (*Aulacorhynchus pras-*

inus) and yellow-eared toucanet (*Selenidera spectabilis*) are aptly named. All eat fruit, with some animal matter, and nest in cavities.

Whales (*ballena*): Humpback whales (*Megaptera novaeanglia*) appear off the Pacific coast between November and February; they migrate from California and as far as Hawaii.

White-Faced Capuchin Monkey (*mono cariblanca*; *Cebus capuchinus*): Medium-size and omnivorous, this monkey (to 18 inches, with 20-inch tail) has black fur and a pink face surrounded by a whitish bib. Extremely active foragers, they move singly or in groups of up to 20, examining the environment closely and even coming to the ground.

WHAT TO READ AND WATCH BEFORE YOU GO

Books

For insight on local culture, pick up *Costa Rica: A Traveler's Literary Companion,* edited by Barbara Ras (Consortium), a collection of translated short stories by the country's best writers. For a factual rundown, consult *Inside Costa Rica,* by Tom Barry and Silvia Lara (Interhemispheric Resource Center). David Rains Wallace's *The Quetzal and the Macaw: The Story of Costa Rica's National Parks* (Sierra Club Books) is an entertaining and informative account of Costa Rica's exemplary conservation efforts. *The Costa Rica Reader* (Grove Weidenfeld), by Marc Edelman and Joanne Kenen, is a critical anthology and comparison of traditional and progressive versions of the country's history.

Some of the most popular books on this country feature its rich natural history. *A Guide to the Birds of Costa Rica,* by F. Gary Stiles and Alexander F. Skutch (Cornell), is a first-rate field guide. Alexander Skutch has also written some entertaining chronicles combining natural history, philosophy, and anecdote, among them *A Naturalist in Costa Rica* (University Press of Florida).

The *Costa Rica: Eco-Traveller's Wildlife Guide,* by Les Beletsky (Academic Press), gives an overview of the most common fauna. For an in-depth look at local ecology, read *A Neotropical Companion,* by John Kricher (Princeton University Press), or *Tropical Nature,* by Adrian Forsyth and Ken Miyata (Macmillan).

Costa Rica has a rich literary tradition, but few of its writers have been translated into English. Those who have can be hard to find in the United States; *Years Like Brief Days* (Dufour Editions) is one of the most popular novels of Fabián Dobles, famous for his humorous depiction of life in rural Costa Rica in the early 20th century. *The Lonely Men's Island* (Editorial Escritores Unidos, Mexico), the first novel of José León Sánchez, recounts the author's years on Isla San Lucas—the Costa Rican version of Alcatraz—where he was sent for stealing a statue of the country's patron saint, La Virgen de los Angeles.

Videos

Jurassic Park (1993) was set on Costa Rica's isolated Cocos Island, but the film was actually shot in Hawaii. Oddly enough, much of the film version of *Congo* (1995), another Michael Crichton novel, was shot in Costa Rica. Most of Ridley Scott's *1492: Conquest of Paradise* (1992) was filmed on Costa Rica's Pacific coast. If you're more interested in the waves that break off that coast, check out the surf classic *The Endless Summer* (1966), both the original and remake of which have Costa Rica footage.

SPANISH VOCABULARY

Words and Phrases

English	Spanish	Pronunciation

Basics

English	Spanish	Pronunciation
Yes/no	Sí/no	see/no
OK	De acuerdo	de a-**kwer**-doe
Please	Por favor	pore fah-**vore**
May I?	¿Me permite?	may pair-**mee**-tay
Thank you (very much)	(Muchas) gracias	(**moo**-chas) **grah**-see-as
You're welcome	Con mucho gusto	con **moo**-cho **goose**-toe
Excuse me	Con permiso	con pair-**mee**-so
Pardon me	¿Perdón?	pair-**dohn**
Could you tell me?	¿Podría decirme?	po-dree-ah deh-**seer**-meh
I'm sorry	Disculpe	Dee-**skool**-peh
Good morning!	¡Buenos días!	**bway**-nohs **dee**-ahs
Good afternoon!	¡Buenas tardes!	**bway**-nahs **tar**-dess
Good evening!	¡Buenas noches!	**bway**-nahs **no**-chess
Goodbye!	¡Adiós!/¡Hasta luego!	ah-dee-**ohss**/**ah**-stah-**lwe**-go
Mr./Mrs.	Señor/Señora	sen-**yor**/sen-**yohr**-ah
Miss	Señorita	sen-yo-**ree**-tah
Pleased to meet you	Mucho gusto	**moo**-cho **goose**-toe
How are you?	¿Cómo está usted?	**ko**-mo es-**tah** oo-**sted**
Very well, thank you.	Muy bien, gracias.	**moo**-ee bee-**en**, **grah**-see-as
And you?	¿Y usted?	ee oos-**ted**
Hello (on the telephone)	Diga	**dee**-gah

Days of the Week

English	Spanish	Pronunciation
Sunday	domingo	doe-**meen**-goh
Monday	lunes	**loo**-ness
Tuesday	martes	**mahr**-tess
Wednesday	miércoles	me-**air**-koh-less
Thursday	jueves	hoo-**ev**-ess
Friday	viernes	vee-**air**-ness
Saturday	sábado	**sah**-bah-doh

Months

English	Spanish	Pronunciation
January	enero	eh-**neh**-roh
February	febrero	feh-**breh**-roh
March	marzo	**mahr**-soh
April	abril	ah-**breel**
May	mayo	**my**-oh

June	junio	**hoo**-nee-oh
July	julio	**hoo**-lee-yoh
August	agosto	ah-**ghost**-toh
September	septiembre	sep-tee-**em**-breh
October	octubre	oak-**too**-breh
November	noviembre	no-vee-**em**-breh
December	diciembre	dee-see-**em**-breh

Useful Phrases

Do you speak English?	¿Habla usted inglés?	**ah**-blah oos-**ted** in-**glehs**
I don't speak Spanish	No hablo español	no **ah**-bloh es-pahn-**yol**
I don't understand (you)	No entiendo	no en-tee-**en**-doh
I understand (you)	Entiendo	en-tee-**en**-doh
I don't know	No sé	no seh
I am American/ British	Soy americano (americana)/ inglés(a)	soy ah-meh-ree-**kah**-no (ah-meh-ree-**kah**-nah)/ in-**glehs** (**ah**)
What's your name?	¿Cómo se llama usted?	koh-mo seh **yah**-mah oos-**ted**
My name is . . .	Me llamo . . .	may **yah**-moh
What time is it?	¿Qué hora es?	keh **o**-rah es
It is one, two, three . . . o'clock.	Es la una. . . . Son las dos, tres	es la **oo**-nah/sohn lahs dohs, tress
How?	¿Cómo?	**koh**-mo
When?	¿Cuándo?	**kwahn**-doh
This/Next week	Esta semana/ la semana que entra	**es**-teh seh-**mah**-nah/lah seh-**mah**-nah keh **en**-trah
This/Next month	Este mes/el próximo mes	**es**-teh mehs/el **proke**-see-mo mehs
This/Next year	Este año/el año que viene	**es**-teh **ahn**-yo/el **ahn**-yo keh vee-**yen**-ay
Yesterday/today/ tomorrow	Ayer/hoy/mañana	ah-**yehr**/oy/mahn-**yah**-nah
This morning/ afternoon	Esta mañana/ tarde	**es**-tah mahn-**yah**-nah/**tar**-deh
Tonight	Esta noche	**es**-tah **no**-cheh
What?	¿Qué?	keh
What is it?	¿Qué es esto?	keh es **es**-toh
Why?	¿Por qué?	pore **keh**
Who?	¿Quién?	kee-**yen**
Where is . . . ?	¿Dónde está . . . ?	**dohn**-deh es-**tah**
the bus stop?	la parada del autobus?	la pah-**rah**-dah del oh-toh-**boos**
the post office?	la oficina de correos?	la oh-fee-**see**-nah deh koh-**reh**-os
the museum?	el museo?	el moo-**seh**-oh

the hospital?	el hospital?	el ohss-pee-**tal**
the bathroom?	el baño?	el **bahn**-yoh
Here/there	Aquí/allá	ah-**key**/ah-**yah**
Open/closed	Abierto/cerrado	ah-bee-**er**-toh/ ser-**ah**-doh
Left/right	Izquierda/derecha	iss-key-**er**-dah/ dare-**eh**-chah
Straight ahead	Derecho	dare-**eh**-choh
Is it near/far?	¿Está cerca/lejos?	es-**tah sehr**-kah/ **leh**-hoss
I'd like . . . a room	Quisiera . . . un cuarto/una habitación	kee-see-ehr-ah oon **kwahr**-toh/ **oo**-nah ah-bee- tah-see-**on**
the key	la llave	lah **yah**-veh
a newspaper	un periódico	oon pehr-ee-**oh**- dee-koh
a stamp	la estampilla	lah es-stahm- **pee**-yah
I'd like to buy . . .	Quisiera comprar . . .	kee-see-**ehr**-ah kohm-**prahr**
cigarettes	cigarrillos	ce-ga-**ree**-yohs
a dictionary	un diccionario	oon deek-see-oh- **nah**-ree-oh
soap	jabón	hah-**bohn**
suntan lotion	loción bronceadora	loh-see-**ohn** brohn- seh-ah-**do**-rah
a map	un mapa	oon **mah**-pah
a magazine	una revista	**oon**-ah reh-**veess**-tah
a postcard	una tarjeta postal	**oon**-ah tar-**het**-ah post-**ahl**
How much is it?	¿Cuánto cuesta?	**kwahn**-toh **kwes**-tah
Telephone	Teléfono	tel-**ef**-oh-no
I am ill	Estoy enfermo(a)	es-**toy** en-**fehr**- moh(mah)
Please call a doctor	Por favor llame a un medico	pohr fah-**vor ya**-meh ah oon **med**-ee-koh
Help!	¡Auxilio! ¡Ayuda! ¡Socorro!	owk-**see**-lee-oh/ ah-**yoo**-dah/ soh-**kohr**-roh
Fire!	¡Incendio!	en-**sen**-dee-oo
Caution!/Look out!	¡Cuidado!	kwee-**dah**-doh

INDEX